Worship in Medieval and Early Modern Europe

Worship in

Medieval and Early Modern Europe

CHANGE AND CONTINUITY IN RELIGIOUS PRACTICE

edited by

KARIN MAAG & JOHN D. WITVLIET

University of Notre Dame Press

Notre Dame, Indiana

Notre Dame, Indiana 46556
www.undpress.nd.edu

Manufactured in the United States of America

Title page art: Rogier van der Weyden, *Altarpiece of the Seven Sacraments.* Courtesy of the Koninklijk Museum, Antwerp.

Library of Congress Cataloging-in-Publication Data
Worship in medieval and early modern Europe : change and continuity in religious practice / edited by Karin Maag and John D. Witvliet.
p. cm.
Includes bibliographical references and index.
ISBN 0-268-03474-5 (alk. paper)
ISBN 0-268-03475-3 (pbk. : alk. paper)
1. Worship—History—16th century. 2. Liturgics—Europe.
3. Reformation. I. Maag, Karin. II. Witvliet, John D.
BV8.W67 2004
264'.0094—dc22

2003025294

∞ *This book is printed on acid-free paper.*

contents

figures

contributors

Kent J. Burreson is Assistant Professor of Systematic Theology at Concordia Seminary, St. Louis, Missouri.

Margot Fassler is the Robert S. Tangeman Professor of Music History, and the Director of the Institute of Sacred Music at Yale University.

Susan M. Felch is Professor of English at Calvin College.

Robert Kingdon is Professor Emeritus of the Department of History and the Institute for Research in the Humanities at the University of Wisconsin-Madison.

Robin A. Leaver is Professor of Sacred Music at the Westminster Choir College of Rider University, Princeton, New Jersey, and Visiting Professor at the Juilliard School, New York City.

Henry Luttikhuizen is Professor of Art at Calvin College.

Karin Maag is Director of the H. Henry Meeter Center for Calvin Studies in Grand Rapids, Michigan. She is also Associate Professor in History at Calvin College.

Bodo Nischan was Professor of History at East Carolina University. He died in October 2001.

Frank C. Senn is Pastor of Immanuel Lutheran Church in Evanston, Illinois.

Bryan D. Spinks is Professor of Liturgical Studies at the Yale Institute of Sacred Music and Yale Divinity School.

Katherine Elliot van Liere is Associate Professor of History at Calvin College.

John D. Witvliet is Director of the Calvin Institute of Christian Worship at Calvin College and Calvin Theological Seminary. He is also Associate Professor in Music and Adjunct Associate Professor in Religion at Calvin College, and currently also serves as Dean of the Chapel.

abbreviations

ARG *Archiv für Reformationsgeschichte.*

EETS Early English Text Society (series).

LU *The Liber Usualis with Introduction and Rubrics in English.* Tournai: Desclée, 1934.

LW Martin Luther, *Works.* Edited by Jaroslav Pelikan and Helmut Lehmann. 55 vols. Saint Louis: Concordia; Philadelphia: Fortress, 1955–86.

RDK *Reallexikon zur deutschen Kunstgeschichte.*

STC *A short-title catalogue of books printed in England, Scotland, & Ireland and of English books printed abroad, 1475–1640.* Edited by Alfred Pollard, G. Redgrave, William Jackson, F. Ferguson, and Katharine Pantzer. 3 vols. London: Bibliographical Society, 1976–1991.

TRE *Theologische Realenzyklopädie.* Edited by Gerhard Müller. 34 vols. Berlin: Walter de Gruyter, 1976–.

WA *D. Martin Luthers Werke; kritische Gesamtausgabe.* 93 vols. Weimar: H. Bohlau, 1883–1990.

acknowledgments

The editors wish to express their thanks to the Governing Board of the Calvin Center for Christian Scholarship for providing the funds for a seed grant in 1999 and a major grant in 2000, to underwrite the costs of a symposium and the expenses of producing this volume. In particular, we wish to thank the Center's directors, Ronald Wells and James Bratt, and the Center's program coordinator, Donna Romanowski, for their unfailing assistance and encouragement. We also thank Dr. Yudha Thianto for his participation in recording the discussions during our symposium, and Milan Norgauer for his work in creating a working bibliography in the early stages of this project. Our thanks also go to Cindy Holtrop, and Emily Cooper, Carrie Titcombe, and Joyce Borger of the Institute of Christian Worship, and the Meeter Center staff members Paul Fields and Susan Schmurr. We wish to acknowledge with thanks the work of the University of Notre Dame Press, its director, Barbara Hanrahan, and the assistant acquisitions editor, Christina Catanzarite. We also deeply appreciate the work of our contributors, both for their active participation at the symposium and for their written contributions. In particular, we wish to honor the memory of Bodo Nischan, whose essay on Lutheran altars and Reformed Communion tables graces this volume. It was with great sadness that we learned of Dr. Nischan's death in October 2001. He epitomized learned and humane scholarship. We wish to dedicate this volume to his memory.

Karin Maag and John D. Witvliet
Grand Rapids, Michigan
May 2003

Introduction

JOHN D. WITVLIET

The transition from the late medieval to the early modern period in Western Europe remains one of the most formative and fascinating periods in the history of Christianity. Even cursory studies of the history of Christianity linger at Luther, Calvin, and Trent. During this period, nearly every traditional dimension of Christian experience—including dominant theological currents, ethical obligations, forms of piety, and structures of churchly political power—was being challenged by some and defended by others. Even the broadest cultural and intellectual histories underline the significance of the multiple religious reformations of this period.[1] The influence of Christianity in this era was so pervasive that no adequate history of the culture, politics, or intellectual developments of the period can ignore it. Even those with little interest in history have a strong sense of the importance of this era. Without interruption, for nearly four hundred years both Protestant and Catholic religious communities have treated this period as a defining era in their own identities.

Some of the most dramatic and revealing developments in the period were liturgical. We cannot fully understand the religious dimensions of this (or any) period without comprehending the varying and changing ways in which the faithful rendered worship to God. Pressing questions of the day included whether worship spaces should be spare or empty, whether the faithful should receive the Eucharist kneeling before an altar rail or seated at a table, whether worship services should focus more on the reception of the Sacrament or the preaching of the Word, and whether music in worship should be sung by professional choirs or untrained worshipers. These questions are actually particular instances of the type of questions that the church has faced in every age: What does true worship look like? What words should be spoken? Who would authorize them? What music would be sung? What should worship spaces look like? What gestures and actions would be central? Who would be the main participants? What would exemplary participation look like?

For this period, as for any other, the answers to these questions provide a reliable barometer of the significant theological and cultural impulses of the time. In every age, worship practices are forged as an alloy of theological self-consciousness and cultural forms of expression. Cultural and theological shifts are frequently accompanied by or arise out of changes in worship, though it is often difficult to tell what comes first. So, for example, metrical psalmody in Geneva is the product of both a liturgical goal (French metrical versions of the Hebrew Psalms written to be sung by common worshipers) and a particular cultural form (the Renaissance rhetorical style of the French court honed by Clément Marot). Shifts in liturgical practice from the medieval to the early modern period reflect both new theological emphases and evolving cultural forms of expression.

Part of the significance of worship also arises out of the complexity and pervasiveness of Christian worship practices. For the purposes of this book, the topic of worship is understood broadly so as to encompass a dizzying array of topics: the sensory framework of worship practices (the visual appearance of worship spaces, the sounds of speech, music, and silence), specific elements of worship services (prayer, preaching, music, sacraments), practices in different settings (home, church, school), as well as different types of services (daily prayer, weekly Eucharist, marriage services, funerals, baptisms). Accordingly, worship practices are of interest to a wide variety of scholarly disciplines: cultural anthropology, visual art and architecture, music, rhetoric, theology, and cultural and social history. The embodied and tangible nature of worship practices makes the study of worship an inherently interdisciplinary task.

Yet for all the rich texture and significance of worship practices, a nuanced understanding of worship practices is hard to come by. Most historical textbooks only touch the surface of the topic. After the basics—the fact that Protestant worship moved from Latin to vernacular and gave more emphasis to preaching—most textbooks and most educated persons in the West (and even a few historians!) have little else to say. What analysis has been done has often focused more on the theological understanding than on the practice of worship. Thousands of pages have been written on how various Reformers conceptualized the presence of Christ in the Lord's Supper. Few have been written on how they actually celebrated the ritual meal.[2]

This book seeks to remedy this lacuna by deepening our understanding about and stimulating new interest in the worship practices of the late medieval and early modern period. It does so by self-consciously going back to the sources, to the documents and images that convey the most accurate possible picture of the actual practices of the period. To whet our appetite for this encounter with historical artifacts, let us examine five examples.

First, consider this prescriptive passage from the pens of a leading ecclesiastical assembly:

> Among the various things that are conducive to the salvation of the Christian people, the nourishment of God's word is recognized to be especially necessary, since just as the body is fed with material food so the soul is fed with spiritual food, according to the words, "man lives not by bread alone but by every word that proceeds from the mouth of God. . . ." We therefore decree by this general constitution that bishops are to appoint suitable men to carry out with profit this duty of sacred preaching, men who are powerful in word and deed and who will visit with care the peoples entrusted to them in the place of bishops, since these by themselves are unable to do it, and will build them up by word and example. . . . If anyone neglects to do this, let him be subject to severe punishment.[3]

At first glance, this stirring call to Gospel-centered preaching sounds like a Protestant manifesto, a counterpoint to the medieval Catholic emphasis on the Mass. But this mandate is from the thirteenth century, a directive of the Fourth Lateran Council. It is but one marker in a complex and impressive history of preaching in the medieval Church.[4] Long before Protestants resuscitated the practice of liturgical preaching, Catholic priests—some itinerant, some monastic, some local parish pastors—devoted their lives to preaching the gospel in the language of common people.

Second, just after the onset of the Reformation in Strasbourg (in modern France), a visitor from Antwerp (in modern Belgium) journeyed to Strasbourg, visited a worship service, and penned this rather rapturous testimony:

> On Sundays . . . we sing a Psalm of David or some other prayer taken from the New Testament. The psalm or prayer is sung by everyone together, men as well as women with beautiful unanimity, which is something beautiful to behold. For you must understand that each one has a musical book in his hand; that is why they cannot lose touch with one another. Never did I think that it could be as pleasing and delightful as it is. For five or six days at first, as I looked upon this little company, exiled from countries everywhere for having upheld the honor of God and His gospel, I would begin to weep, not at all from sadness,

> but from joy at hearing them sing so heartily, and, as they sang, giving thanks to the Lord that He had led them to a place where His name is honored and glorified. No one could believe the joy which one experiences when one is singing the praises and wonders of the Lord in the mother tongue as one sings them here.[5]

This testimony alerts us to tangible changes in worship practices which we might have missed had we read only the theological writings of Luther or Calvin: women joining men in song, everyone holding a hymnal or Psalter. It conveys the striking effect of experiencing these practices for the first time and suggests some of the intensity of the emotional experience of these innovations. This is testimony that helps us imagine what it must have been like to experience the liturgical sea-change of the Protestant Reformation in Strasbourg.

Third, in 1584, an old man in the village of Zwickau (in what is now Germany) paused to reflect on a vivid liturgical experience of his youth, the annual Corpus Christi procession:

> On those feast days, they had a magnificent procession, . . . the images of the saints and the Virgin Mary were borne around the city or churchyard, . . . just as we bear the dead [today] . . . and I helped often and a great deal to carry out this procession . . . The way over which one went around the city was almost entirely strewn with grass. Inside the church the altars were spread with Saint John's Wort, curly mint, and pheasant's eye, which were pleasantly fragrant and lovely to look at. When one came back into the church, all the altars were hung with letters of indulgence. Two offerings were made. . . .[6]

Here is a sentiment that most textbooks leave out, the fond longing of a devout worshiper for the colorful practices of the past, which left lasting impressions on child participants and onlookers. Passages like this help us identify with the objective changes not just in liturgical practices, but also in what it must have been like to experience those changes. We are allowed to enter the emotional world of a sixteenth-century Christian.

Fourth, consider this chart which once hung in the rear of the three parish churches in Geneva, a chart which was titled: "Table pour trouver les pseaumes, selon l'ordre qu'on les chante en l'église de Genève" (A table for selecting Psalms, according to the order that one sings them in the church of Geneva).[7]

	Dimanche au Matin	Dimanche au Soir	Mecredy
1	Ps. 3 et 11	1 et 15	6
2	5	2	9, 1–10
3	7	4 et 137	9, 11–20
4	14	8	38, 1–11
5	25	19	38, 12–22
6	36 et 43	24 et 128	51
7	130 et 138	45	143
8	50	72	18, 1–7
9	115	101	18, 8–15
10	12 et 113	110	22, 1–7
11	91	114 et 23	22, 8–16
12	103, 1–6	103, 7–11	10
13	118, 1–7	118, 8–14	32
14	33, 1–6	33, 7–11	79
15	37, 1–10	37, 11–20	86
16	104, 1–7	104, 8–14	104, 15–18 et 13
17	107, 1–8	107, 9–17	107, 18–23 et 64

Most Genevan musical practices were revolutionized during the Reformation. Polyphonic choral music in Latin was replaced by unison congregational song in the vernacular French. Yet this chart also bears witness to a hidden, unacknowledged continuity with an aspect of medieval practice. It prescribes which Psalms will be sung at each of three weekly worship services over the course of a seventeen-week cycle. The Psalms sung each week were not chosen to fit the theme of the sermon, nor according to any *lectio continua* (an ordering of Scripture readings in canonical sequence), and certainly not according to which ones were congregational favorites. Rather, they were chosen according to a method similar to that of the medieval Breviary's lectionary of Psalms for daily prayer: psalms were assigned to be prayed at specific services, so that all available and published metrical Psalms were sung or read over a certain period of time. In both the medieval office and in Genevan preaching services, the Psalms were a matter of balance and discipline.

Fifth, consider this testimony of Jeremias Drexel, a seventeenth-century Jesuit priest, looking back on a century of liturgical change:

> I think, not without heartfelt sighs, how it was in the world a hundred years ago in Luther's time. Oh unworthy age! Then one could distinguish Catholic from heretic only with difficulty. A person made his confession only once a year and quite reluctantly, without any zeal, or performed such confession only as an outward ceremony and old custom. For commonly, the more seldom we undertake such things, the more negligently and evilly we perform them. Now, however, through the kind watchfulness of God, the times have changed, so that I may truthfully say that whoever in our time makes only one confession in an entire year, gives himself away to everyone and demonstrates to everyone that they should not consider him to be anything other than a completely cold, half-hearted Christian, who, were he not held to it by the commandment [of the Church], would not even once purify his conscience through confession, but would remain jolly with his sins and services.[8]

"Oh unworthy age" sounds like a *Protestant* indictment of common piety in the period of the earliest years of the Reformation. Yet this testimony comes not from a Lutheran or Calvinist but from a Jesuit. Protestant worship was not the only locus of change in the period. Catholic worship underwent its own revival. In his study of confession, W. David Myers chronicles the greater frequency, the greater architectural presence (in the form of the confessional), the more private experience, and the greater sense of "continuous presence" that confession had in Roman Catholic worship at the end of the sixteenth century than at its beginning.[9] Both Roman Catholic and Protestant worship experienced continuity and change during the sixteenth century.

These five vignettes hint at the project of this book: to help us more clearly envision the specific nature of liturgical continuity and change in late medieval and early modern Christian worship practices. They help us picture dimensions of actual liturgical practice. They alert us to aspects of worship that changed, and to those that stayed the same. They even give us a glimpse, however imperfect, of the affective landscape of sixteenth-century Christians. As tangible, historical artifacts of this important era, they bear witness to the faith of these earlier Christians and they lead us to ask more focused questions about specific practices of the period.

The time period in question is itself known for its own return to the sources. Renaissance and Reformation leaders returned with discipline and diligence to rediscovering, retranslating, and rereading ancient sources. It is our intent to treat this period with the same respect. Much modern historical understanding, perhaps especially in religious circles, consists of repeated textbooklike summaries. Even modestly serious students of the history of Christianity (including upper-level undergraduates and seminary students) rarely encounter original sources, and certainly not a wide range of them. In contrast, each essay in this volume begins with (sometimes lengthy) primary sources. As a whole, the volume includes a wide variety of sources, including consistory minutes, school charters, liturgical prayer texts, visual images, and Church order documents. Thus, this book will address the question of change and continuity in worship practices by means of careful study of original source documents.

This task will be carried out in a way that reflects at least three valuable impulses in recent scholarship. The first of these is to widen the timeline in which we consider the changes of the sixteenth century. For too long, historians have looked at a given Reformer's thought and life *in se,* in abstraction from its historical context, particularly from the late medieval period. This tendency is reinforced by the shape of academic institutions. Medieval and early modern historians are often institutionally separated into different departments. They attend different conferences, read different journals, and attend different graduate schools. Even the current widespread emphasis on interdisciplinary studies sometimes fails to break down the boundaries of disciplinary studies and time period for the topic in question. But early modern historians cannot aspire to understand the significance of their chosen period of study without acute awareness of the cultural, social, and intellectual climate of the late medieval period.

One important corrective to this separation has been the concern of the most recent generation of scholars to understand the early modern period much more consciously in light of the late medieval period.[10] Among the most important proponents of this line in the past generation have been Heiko Oberman and Steven Ozment.[11] Fine examples of this work, especially in intellectual history, include that of David Steinmetz.[12] Thus, this collection attempts to follow in the tradition of such well-established collections as *The Pursuit of Holiness in Late Medieval and Renaissance Religion.*[13]

This concern for understanding medieval precedents is reflected in nearly every essay in this volume. Many of the source documents included here are late medieval documents. Several essays dwell on the specific nature of medieval liturgical experience, such as Margot Fassler's analysis of a fifteenth-century devotional anthology.

This wide-angle view of the historical timeline also needs to extend beyond the early part of the sixteenth century into the period of confessionalization. A good deal of lay historical consciousness assumes strong demarcations, not only between Catholics and Protestants, but also among the various factions of Protestantism. Recent work, however, has helpfully reminded us that strong lines of demarcation become fixed much later—in the period of confessionalization in the late sixteenth and early seventeenth century. This concern is reflected in this volume especially by essays that probe late-sixteenth-century topics, such as Henry Luttikhuizen's study of iconoclasm in the 1580s in Haarlem, and Bodo Nischan's treatment of Reformed-Lutheran controversies about altars versus Communion tables.

A second important impulse in recent scholarship which is reflected in this volume is a concern to consider the nature of change in *both* Protestant and Catholic contexts. In his recent survey of Catholic renewal in the early modern period, R. Po-Chia Hsia speaks of the "underlying unity between the histories of the Reformation and Catholicism in early modern Europe."[14] After all, both Catholics and Protestants read Scripture, preached sermons, offered prayers, celebrated baptism and the Lord's Supper, produced liturgies, and developed structures of churchly authority and power. While the particulars of liturgical practice were often different, the broad categories of practices were largely the same.

Thus, the authors of these essays have discovered again how important it is not only to consider both Protestant and Catholic practice, but also to do so collaboratively, with Roman Catholic and Protestant scholars. In his essay in this volume, Robert Kingdon (a Protestant) notes the value of working with Thomas Lambert (a Roman Catholic) in learning about the nature of liturgical participation in medieval Geneva. As these essays remind us, despite our best attempts at objectivity, our own experiences influence how we will interpret and evaluate historical artifacts. Our own participation in Roman Catholic and Protestant communities today still colors our views of this history and alerts us to different dimensions of medieval and early modern experience.

A third impulse reflected in this volume is to employ several complementary methods to study worship practices. For one, it is necessary to attend to both social and intellectual dimensions of historical experience. In recent years, the growth of social history and studies in popular religiosity have given us a far better sense of the texture of sixteenth-century experience.[15] Such studies have highlighted not simply a given Reformer's theology, but the people's experience of Christianity. The mainstay of liturgical scholarship has been the study of the evolution of official liturgical texts, despite the fact that most Christians never read these texts, and often did not even hear or understand them. New attention to the experience of common people is helpful for honest historical inquiry. So Robert Kingdon's work here mines the registers (or minutes) of Genevan consistory meetings to learn about the experience of worship by several Genevans. Karin Maag explores worship practices in schools. And Susan Felch studies the development of English prayer books used by literate laypersons.

This impulse need not (and must not) supplant attention to official liturgical texts, to the intellectual developments of leadership. That work (as evidenced here in the essays of Kent Burreson, Robin Leaver, Bryan Spinks, and Kate van Liere) continues to provide clear and self-conscious examples of the implications of new patterns of thinking. After all, in the increasingly literate culture of the time and in a text-oriented religion such as Christianity, work on liturgical texts cannot be ignored.

Further, it is necessary to work collaboratively from multiple disciplinary perspectives. Christian worship is an especially interdisciplinary topic, involving the study of not only official liturgical texts, but also architecture, vestments, ceremony, music, and iconography. It is composed of a large constellation of liturgical actions: baptism, Eucharist, preaching, prayer, use of Scripture, private devotions, worship in homes and schools, marriages, funerals, and special observances. It is relatively easy for scholars to become experts in one of these practices. But how often are these specific topics understood in larger liturgical, cultural, and intellectual contexts? How often do experts on eucharistic prayers understand the nature of the gestures or movements that accompanied the use of these texts? How many musicologists are aware of how the music they study fits into the overall context of the worship services in which they were sung or played? Conversely, how many cultural historians who cite eucharistic prayers or musical examples are aware of their technical particularities?

For all the impressive work that has flowed from these three important scholarly impulses, a curious student of sixteenth-century worship still needs to work very hard in a research library to uncover work that will provide a basis from which to analyze continuity and change in medieval and early modern worship.

In sum, this book attempts to understand change and continuity in worship practices by describing eleven case studies of liturgical change, accompanied by illustrative source documents. In each case, this will be done with attention to a wide historical timeline, the convergence of Catholic and Protestant concerns, and multiple disciplinary perspectives. Despite recent work in the field, assessing the broad patterns of change and continuity remains an elusive task. The textbook treatments tend to simplify matters too broadly to be of help, typically downplaying the significant continuities of the period. The monographs provide absolutely necessary basic historical research, but often do not set out to assess how their particular topic fits into larger patterns of continuity and change in other geographical regions or with respect to other topics.

Because these essays focus on local practices, this volume does not claim to be comprehensive or exhaustive. The volume includes only eleven topics, each of which is, by definition, idiosyncratic. The essays here are illustrative, not comprehensive. It is the goal of each essay to be local and specific enough (as well as tied to some concrete primary sources) to ground its analysis in the experience of continuity and change as experienced by real, late medieval and early modern European Christians.

This collection of essays covers several traditions (Catholic, Lutheran, Reformed, Anglican), several geographic regions (Sweden, England, Geneva, Low Countries, and the Holy Roman Empire), several liturgical actions (Eucharist, baptism, marriage, daily prayer), several centers of devotional and liturgical action (home, school, church), several dimensions of the context of liturgical action (art, furniture, music), and several levels of meaning and experience (official liturgical texts as well as the experience of worship by lay Christians). Even so, there is no pretense here of being exhaustive. There is nothing here, for example, on the radical Reformation, nothing on Italy or Scotland, nothing on funerals, on preaching, or on the Christian calendar. We eagerly await continued work on all of these topics.

Nevertheless, we believe that this diversity of topics is sufficient to demonstrate the kinds of continuities and discontinuities that a student of medieval and early modern worship must work to understand, especially if we keep our eyes open to the large and growing literature on Christian experience in this period.

Overall, we suspect that the majority of existing work on the period still tends to focus excessively on discontinuity. There are several reasons why various continuities may have gone unacknowledged. Most obviously, the changes of the period were so significant that they have always taken center stage. Further, those changes were often defended with extremely acerbic rhetoric, which would tend to ignore or deliberately conceal continuities in form or practice. In addition, historians within Christian traditions—whether Catholic or Protestant—have had reason to continue emphasizing discontinuity. Gregory Dix and Eamon Duffy have pointed out discontinuity in order to lament it.[16] Protestant historians have pointed it out to celebrate it.[17] Finally, lack of attention to continuity is simply a matter of limited resources. There are only so many pages in historical textbooks to cover the period, and it is discontinuity that stands out as the main story needing to be told.

The book begins with a straightforward description of a fifteenth-century devotional book by Margot Fassler and a description of liturgical change in sixteenth-century Geneva by Robert Kingdon. These two essays provide sympathetic and nuanced treatments of the kinds of liturgical participation widely associated with medieval Catholic and Reformed worship, respectively. Taken together, they demonstrate the significant discontinuities in liturgical practice that are often the staple of most textbook treatments of the period, albeit with uncommon attention to some of the most salient and instructive details in their source documents. This story of discontinuity is surely a main and irreducible theme of this period.

But, as we will demonstrate, this discontinuity is not unqualified. Subsequent essays function, one by one, to complicate this picture with additional types of information and categories of analysis. They raise complications that should be expected—issues of localization, diversity of practice across traditions, variance in the pace and significance of change—as well as some issues that are unexpected, or at least rarely discussed. Each essay, then, both stands on its own as a description and interpretation of a distinct topic, and serves as an illustration of a type of method or analysis that is needed to complete our understanding of worship practices in this period. The editors' introduction to each essay highlights this latter function. The conclusion at the end of the book draws together the series of insights on change and continuity, and makes connections between this work and other recent scholarly work in the field.

Notes

1. Jacques Barzun, for example, identifies the Protestant Reformation as the beginning of the modern era in *From Dawn to Decadence: 1500 to the Present* (New York: Harper Collins Publishers, 2000).

2. For examples of work on the theology of the Lord's Supper, see B.A. Gerrish, *The Eucharistic Theology of John Calvin* (Minneapolis: Fortress Press, 1993), or Ralph W. Quere, *Melanchthon's Christum Cognoscere: Christ's Efficacious Presence in the Eucharistic Theology of Melanchthon* (Nieuwkoop: B. De Graaf, 1977), whose bibliographies include dozens of essays and books on eucharistic theology. The work of Frank C. Senn (*Christian Liturgy: Catholic and Evangelical* [Minneapolis: Fortress, 1997]) and Miri Rubin (*Corpus Christi: The Eucharist in Late Medieval Culture* [Cambridge: Cambridge University Press, 1991]) is remarkable for treating both the practice and understanding of the Lord's Supper. Still, each book cites relatively few sources on actual eucharistic practice.

3. Canon 10, *De predicatoribus instituendis,* Fourth Lateran Council (1215), trans. Norman P. Tanner, S.J., *Decrees of Ecumenical Councils,* vol. 1 (Washington: Georgetown University Press, 1990), 239.

4. This history has been chronicled most recently in H.O. Old, *The Reading and Preaching of the Scriptures in the Worship of the Christian Church,* vol. 3, *The Medieval Church* (Grand Rapids, Mich.: Eerdmans, 1999).

5. See John Witvliet, "Spirituality of the Psalter: Metrical Psalms in Liturgy and Life in Calvin's Geneva," in *Worship Seeking Understanding: Windows into Christian Practice* (Grand Rapids: Baker Academic, 2003): 203–30, for further discussion.

6. Quoted in Susan Karant-Nunn, *Zwickau in Transition, 1500–1547* (Columbus: Ohio State University Press, 1987), 206.

7. The following table is copied from Pierre Pidoux, *Le psautier huguenot du XVIe siècle. Mélodies et documents,* vol. 2 (Basel: Baerenreiter, 1962), 44.

8. Translated in W. David Myers, *"Poor, Sinning Folk": Confession and Conscience in Counter-Reformation Germany* (Ithaca: Cornell University Press, 1996), vi.

9. Ibid.

10. Recent work includes Bruce Gordon, ed., *Protestant History and Identity in Sixteenth-Century Europe,* vol. 1: *The Medieval Inheritance* (Aldershot: Ashgate, 1996).

11. See Steven Ozment, ed., *The Reformation in Medieval Perspective* (Chicago: Quadrangle Books, 1971); Steven Ozment, "Humanism, Scholasticism, and the Intellectual Origins of the Reformation," in F. F. Church and Timothy George, eds., *Continuity and Discontinuity in Church History* (Leiden: Brill, 1979); Heiko Oberman, *The Harvest of Medieval Theology: Gabriel Biel and Late Medieval Nominalism* (Cambridge: Harvard University Press, 1963); Heiko Oberman, ed., *Forerunners of the Reformation* (New York: Holt, Rinehart and Winston, 1966); and John Bossy, *Christianity and the West, 1400–1700* (Oxford: Oxford University Press, 1985). In an earlier era, see the work of Joseph Lortz, *The Reformation in Germany,* trans. Ronald Walls (New York: Herder and Herder, 1968).

12. David Steinmetz, *Calvin in Context* (Oxford: Oxford University Press, 1995), *Luther in Context* (Bloomington: Indiana University Press, 1986).

13. Charles Trinkhaus and Heiko Oberman, eds. (Leiden: Brill, 1974).

14. R. Po-Chia Hsia, *The World of Catholic Renewal, 1540–1770* (Cambridge: Cambridge University Press, 1998), 1.

15. As symbolized by Natalie Davis, "From 'Popular Religion' to Religious Cultures," in S. Ozment, ed., *Reformation Europe: A Guide to Research* (St. Louis: Center for Reformation Research, 1982); and, especially for our purposes, R. W. Scribner, "Ritual and Popular Religion in Catholic Germany at the Time of the Reformation," *Journal of Ecclesiastical History* 35 (1984): 47–77.

16. See Gregory Dix, *The Shape of the Liturgy* (San Francisco: Harper and Row, 1945), and Eamon Duffy, *The Stripping of the Altars: Traditional Religion in England, c. 1400–c. 1580* (New Haven: Yale University Press, 1992).

17. Thus, for example, Bruce Gordon's analysis of many assessments of Zwingli's thought: "The polemic of their age, their own interest in distancing their reforms from the abuses of the late medieval Church, and the confessional nature of subsequent historical scholarship, have served to mask the depth of Zwingli's intellectual, ecclesiastical, and emotional roots in the late medieval world." In "Transcendence and Community in Zwinglian Worship: The Liturgy of 1525 in Zurich," in R. N. Swanson, ed., *Continuity and Change in Christian Worship* (Rochester, N.Y.: Boydell Press, for the Ecclesiastical History Society, 1999), 129.

Starting Points for Assessing Continuity and Change

Psalms and Prayers in Daily Devotion: A Fifteenth-Century Devotional Anthology from the Diocese of Rheims: Beinecke 757

MARGOT FASSLER

Editors' Introduction

Margot Fassler's contribution sets the stage for our discussion of change and continuity in worship in the medieval and early modern period. By analyzing in depth a fifteenth-century devotional anthology in terms of its appearance and usage, she allows readers to gain a sense of what it must have been like to be able to turn to such anthologies for the daily sustenance of one's faith and prayer life.

Worship and prayer life, as presented in this contribution and then compared with later essays in this volume, may seem to have changed significantly in the space of a century. Yet the devotional practices outlined here did not simply disappear. Indeed, their survival is attested to both in the criticisms of the Genevan pastors about muttered prayers, for instance, as indicated in Robert Kingdon's contribution, and in the continued use of works of devotion in the sixteenth century, as attested in the essays by Susan Felch and Katherine Elliot van Liere.

Primary Sources Introduction

The first of the primary sources included with this contribution outlines the "table of contents" of a fifteenth-century prayer book. Notice the wide range of sources for prayers, from texts taken from the Psalms, to prayers of the saints, to prayers specifically devoted to the Virgin Mary. Clearly, works like this offered prayers to suit almost any taste and to fit nearly every circumstance. Devout Christians who owned such books could turn to them and make use of the prayers to hallow every moment of their days. The second primary source provides a translation of a particular prayer, recited before partaking in the sacrament of Communion. Texts such as these offer a glimpse of the rich interior prayer life of late medieval Christians.

A. The contents of a fifteenth-century prayerbook

SECTION I. A Day in the Life

A. Abbreviated Psalter, beginning "Verba mea auribus" [Give ear to my words] (Psalm 5:2–4, 9), and continuing in order through the psalter with selected verses from thirty Psalms, ending with Psalm 142, and the lesser doxology. Two prayers were recited between the selections from individual Psalms, "Adesto deus unus" [Only God, be present] and "Suscipere dignare domine" [Lord, deign to receive].

B. Litany of the Saints.

C. Prayers to take the reader through the stages of the day (liturgical resonances of incipits are provided):

1. For rising from bed
   Surrexit dominus de sepulchro qui pro nobis pependit in ligno [The Lord has risen from the tomb, he who for our sake hung on the cross]
   A classic Easter chant text
2. For washing the hands and eyes
   Domine Deus rex omnipotens qui per prophetam tuum dixisti [Lord God, almighty king, who spoke through your prophet]
   An antiphon for Lent
3. Upon leaving the house
   Vias tuas domine demonstra michi [Lord, show me your ways]

Psalm 24:4, Psalm verse for the Introit and Gradual for the first Sunday of Advent

4. Upon entering the church
   Introibo in domum tuam adorabo ad templum sanctum tuum [I will come into your house, I will worship toward your holy temple] (Psalm 5:8)
5. At the Cross
   Salva sancta crux preciosa [Hail, holy cross, precious . . .]
6. If you wish to make confession
   Per beatorum angelorum archangelorum . . . merita [Through the merits of the blessed angels and archangels]
7. Anyone who wishes to receive communion ought to say . . . [Translated in the second primary source, below]
   Domine quis sum aut qualis [Lord, who am I or what kind of person]
8. When you wish to communicate
   Domine ihesu christe fili dei vivi te supplex queso ut hodie [Lord Jesus Christ, Son of the living God, humbly begging I ask that today]
9. When you are going to communicate
   Domine ihesu christe non sum dignus ut intres [Lord Jesus Christ, I am not worthy that you should enter]

D. Extensive prayers composed by famous saints, sometimes with rubrics explaining a particular quality of the saint, offering exhortations to pray with the saint, or promising Christ's aid from the prayers and nearness to his saints, sometimes with other prayers added. As wear and stains demonstrate, this was the most heavily used section in the book.

1. Augustine: Deus iusticie, Deus mi[sericordi]e, Deus invisibilis [God of justice, God of mercy, God invisible]
2. Another: Domine ihesu Christe universitatis conditor [Lord Jesus Christ, maker of all things]
3. Gregory: Domine sancte pater omnipotens eterne deus qui sedes [Lord, holy Father, almighty eternal God, who are seated]
4. Another: Domine sancte pater omnipotens eterne deus fortitudo mea [Lord, holy Father, almighty eternal God, my strength]

5. Ambrose: Miserator et misericors patiens et multum misericors [Merciful and compassionate, patient and very compassionate]
6. Another: Christe summa dei virtus [Christ, supreme power of God]
7. Jerome: Domine Ihesu Christe qui me dignatus fuisti ad ymaginem tuam creare [Lord Jesus Christ, who deigned to create me in your image]
8. Another: Domini Ihesu Christe da michi compunctionem cordis [Lord Jesus Christ, give me compunction of heart]
9. Another of Augustine: Domine ihesu christe qui in hunc mundum . . . advenisti [Lord Jesus Christ, who came into this world]
10. The prayer Alcuin composed for Charlemagne to say daily: Deus inestimabilis [Incomprehensible God]
11. Another: Dominus Deus omnipotens qui es trinus et unus [Lord, almighty God, you who are three and one]
12. "Whoever has tribulation or impoverishment or infirmity or may be in the anger of God or detained in prison or some other tribulation should say this prayer for 30 days . . . 'O dulcissime Domine Ihesu'" [O most sweet Jesus]
13. Another: Domine exaudi orationem meam [Lord, listen to my prayer]
14. Another: Domine deus omnipotens pius et misericors cui nichil impossible est [Lord, almighty God, holy and compassionate, for whom nothing is impossible]
15. Another: O Bone Ihesu, O piissime Ihesu [O Good Jesus, O most holy Jesus]
16. Another: Domine deus pater omnipotens filius et spiritus sanctus da michi victoriam [Lord God, Father almighty, Son and Holy Spirit, give me victory]
17. A prayer for contemplating Christ: Dulcis Iesu memoria [Sweet Jesus, memory]
18. Another: Confiteor tibi domine deus rex celi [I confess to you, Lord God, King of heaven]
19. Another: Domine ihesu Christe redemptor mundi defende me [Lord Jesus Christ, Redeemer of the world, defend me]
20. Another: Deus propitius esto michi peccatori [God, be well disposed to me, a sinner]

21. Prayer of the Good Angel: O desiderabilis et amabilis creatura angelica [O desirable and lovable angelic creation]
22. Another: Angele Christi qui est deputatus custos vitae meae [Angel of Christ, who have been charged as guardian of my life]
23. Another: Suscipe digneris domine deus omnipotens pater hos psalmos [Deign to accept, Lord God, almighty Father, these psalms]

24–28. Five by St. Isidore, Bishop of Seville:

24. Quo fletu mala mea flete *[sic]* incipiant [With what weeping, weep for my sins, they begin . . .]
25. Succurre michi domine deus meus, antequam mors veniat [Hasten to help me, Lord my God, before death comes]
26. Domine deus meus et salvator meus quare me dereliquisti [Lord, my God and my Saviour, why have you abandoned me]
27. Domine deus meus pone lacrimas meas in conspectu tuo [Lord, my God, place my tears in your sight]
28. Deus glorie qui unus es verus [God of glory, you who alone are true]
29. On the Holy Spirit: Omnipotens sempiterne deus clementiam tuam . . . exoro [Almighty eternal God, I ask for your clemency]
30. On the Angels: O beatissimi angeli in ierarchia [O most blessed angels in the hierarchy]
31. On the Holy Cross: Salva sancta Crux salus et vita mea [Hail, holy cross, my salvation and my life]
32. For the Adoration of the Cross: Domine ihesu Christe fili dei vivi gloriosissime conditor mundi [Lord Jesus Christ, Son of the living God, most glorious maker of the world]
33. Gregory
34. Pope Innocent
35. Prayer of Peter of Luxembourg

E. Prayers to close the day.

1. When going to bed: Gratias ago tibi domine omnipotens deus qui me in hac die . . . dignatus es custodire [I thank you, almighty God, who deigned to guard me this day]
2. When getting into bed: Me mundet et muniat consignet et salvet titulus triumphalis [May your triumphal title (or name?) cleanse and defend, seal and save me]

3. For when suddenly awakened in the night: Gratias ago tibi omnipotens deus, qui me in hac nocte . . . dignatus es custodire [I thank you, almighty God, who deigned to guard me this night]

F. Prayers for the Dead.
   1. By Pope John XII for when passing the cemetery: Avete omnes anime fideles quarum corpora hic & ubique requiescant in pulvere [Hail, all you faithful souls, whose bodies are resting in the dust here and everywhere]
   2. Prayer attributed to St. Bernard: Illumina oculos meos ne unquam obdormiam in morte [Give light to my eyes lest I ever sleep in death]
   3. Hymn to the Holy Spirit: Veni Creator Spiritus [Come, Creator Spirit]
   4. Passions from the Gospels of Matthew and of Mark
   5. Prayers from the Office of the Dead
   6. Passion according to John

G. Readings from the Four Gospels.
   1. John 1:1–14: In principio erat verbum [In the beginning was the Word] (Gospel of Christmas Day)
   2. Luke 1:26–38: Missus est angelus Gabriel [The angel Gabriel was sent] (Gospel of the Annunciation, March 25)
   3. Matthew 2:1–12: Cum natus esset Ihesus in Bethleem [When Jesus was born in Bethlehem] (Gospel of the Feast of the Epiphany)
   4. Mark 16:14–20: Recumbentibus undecim disciplis [At table with the eleven disciples] (Gospel of Ascension)

SECTION II. Devotions to and with Our Blessed Mother

A. Marian Psalter. Petition to Mary to receive prayer, followed by the Marian Psalter, which consists of 150 Ave prayers in trochaic lines. These substitute psalms are divided for the days of the week, from Sunday to Saturday, thus forming a kind of Office.

B. Long prayers to the Virgin, including a prayer to be said before her likeness.

C. The 7 joys of the Virgin.

D. The 5 sorrows of the Virgin.

E. "What follows are holy prayers for holy feasts of our Lady." This vast collection contains texts of hymns and sequences, as well as of prayers. Among them, on pp. 32–36 in modern numbering for the second section, are found the two most famous of all Marian prayers, "O intemerata" [O chaste one] and "Obsecro te domina" [I beseech you, Lady], the most important prayers also in most Marian sections of books of hours.

F. In the midst of this section of prayers is found a miracle story in Middle French, which demonstrates the power of prayer. In the legend a young man has a vision of the Virgin Mary, who shows him written versions of the prayers that follow in the book. She tells him to recite them each day and to encourage others in this practice. People who recite the prayers on Saturday will give her special joy. The first is the joy of the Annunciation, the second of giving birth, the third the sorrow of seeing the Savior of the world die on the Cross, the fourth the joy of the Resurrection, and the fifth the joy of being with her son in heaven as empress of the earth and the sky.

G. Litany of our Lady, one which parallels the litany of the Saints. Like the saints' names, each epithet for Mary is followed by Ora pro nobis [Pray for us].

H. Hours for the Immaculate Conception of the Virgin Mary.

SECTION III. Prayers for Devotion in Church

A. Prayers before the Cross and the Body of Christ
B. Prayers on the Body of Christ
C. Prayer at the Elevation of the Host
D. Prayers of Adoration for the Host
E. Extensive cycle of prayers for feasts of major saints; rubrics in Middle French; prayer texts in Latin

SECTION IV. Versified Miracles of the Virgin in Middle French

B. A prayer to be recited before Communion

"Domine, quis sum aut qualis . . ." A prayer "for anyone who wishes to receive Communion" (source A.C.7, above):

Lord, who am I or what kind of person that I should dare come up to
your table, I who am about to receive your most sacred body?
I know, nevertheless, I know and I truly confess
that you are able to make me worthy, you who alone
can make pure something conceived from impure seed.
I beg you all powerful, all sweet, and all holy one,

that through the merits of the blessed Virgin Mary
and all your elect you may teach me and permit me
with such purity of heart and cleanliness of mind,
with such devotion and reverence, to come up to so
admirable a sacrament, as far as is fitting and expedient.
I implore, that when my heart stirs with the sweetness
of your blessed presence, there may be complete cleansing
of my spiritual languor, there may be washing away of my sins.
May I have constant protection against dangers.
May my heart be enflamed with your love.
Let my soul taste now how sweet you are, Lord,
tasting you so completely that the voluptuousness
of the flesh not deceive it.
O delectable bread!
O sweetest food!
O desirable meal!
O sweet feast restoring all things,
and in you never failing!
May it please you that now,
taking you up faithfully, expediently, and
purely, my soul the sinner may receive
moral virtue from you in this its journey;
and thus it may perfect its journey through you
and to you without the impediment of Satan.
Small is the house of my soul, Lord,
whither you may come, and by
your grace it may grow larger for you.
It is ruined; repair it.
It has done many things that offend you.
But to whom except you will I cry?
Make me pure by my eyes.
Mortify your servants in my members and all lustful actions
so that you, king of virgins and lover of chastity,
may take up peaceful lodging in my tabernacle.
You who, with the Father and the Holy Spirit lives
and reigns, God for ever and ever. Amen.

By means of this short book with a Psalter those may meditate who have care for the world or who suffer under difficulties; who are burdened with business or travels; who journey on the sea or who are about to engage in battle; who may be impelled by the ill will of the devil, or who might be vexed with any other matter; or who made a vow to say the entire Psalter daily and are not able to fulfill the vow either because they fast and are debilitated or because they keep the feasts. Any of the above who wishes a saved soul that he or she might have eternal life, should assiduously recite this Psalter.

Thus the compiler of Beinecke 757—or of an exemplar from which it may have been copied—introduced the Psalter constituting the first section of this fifteenth-century devotional anthology. It is an authoritative opening, of a type common for later medieval prayerbooks.[1] In fact, abridged psalters such as that opening Beinecke 757 were often attributed to the great biblical scholar Jerome, who was, of course, actually responsible for the translation of the Psalter upon which most of these useful compilations were based.[2] But there is much more to Beinecke 757 than its introductory Psalter. The book predates the other primary sources studied in the present collection of essays, and offers insight into a form of piety from the century before the various religious reformations of the sixteenth century had been initiated, forming an introduction to what existed before things either changed, or did not.

Although it is a standard text, the book's preface is pregnant with suggestions about the work of the compiler and his or her intended audience: the book was prepared as a companion for the daily life of people in the world, people who may have business to do, and yet who desire the means to have a prayerful and holy life. The Psalms mentioned in the introduction are offered not only as texts for prayer inside the home or during travels or business. The book also provides for those who diligently observe the major festivals of the Church calendar, and offers a devotional mode not in opposition to ecclesial rhythms of prayer and praise but alongside and in harmony with them. The abbreviated Psalter following the introduction, which contains the most penitential and pleading verses of the Psalms, speaks to the character of the entire collection: the book asks for divine assistance, especially in the most difficult times of life. But it also makes prayer a part of daily routine, so that when hard times come a person might be prepared and trusting that sustenance will be available. The book is a comforter, offering the promise that if a person prays well throughout life, God and the saints will help in direst need.

The contents of Beinecke 757 grow out of the medieval sense of worship: sacramental action produces results; prayer, both corporate and personal, is immediately efficacious. Prayer and private devotion were related in structure and spirit to the Mass liturgy, a ritual that—then as now—offers salvific action to all who partake in it rightly. Reflective of liturgical attitudes growing from the Mass liturgy, public and private prayers were understood as dependable vehicles for the grace of God, and as conduits for the aid and succor of God's saints whose powerful presence was constantly made manifest through several devotional modes. Actions that are not in themselves sacraments, and yet are related to and grow out of the powers of sacramental action, are known as sacramentals. Prayers and personal devotional rituals, the kinds of actions represented in Beinecke 757, belong to this realm.[3] The sacraments of the late medieval Catholic Church and the liturgical and devotional practices surrounding them came under heavy attack by reformers in the sixteenth and seventeenth centuries; the "sacramentals," those lesser manifestations of grace that relate to and grow out of the sacramental sense of worship, were often scorned. But one cannot be readily understood without the other, and therefore Beinecke 757 must be considered within the context of the various types of liturgical action that made its prayers "work" for the people who used them. Central to the entire mode of operation is the personal closeness to the Divine that the sacrament of the Eucharist and veneration of the saints—as reflective of sacramental action—offered to Christians in the later Middle Ages.[4]

My colleagues will explore the ways in which both Catholic and Protestant worship in the sixteenth century both did and did not grow out of earlier phenomena. The purpose of this essay is to offer some background for their analyses. I would suggest at the outset that failures to acknowledge and understand the interdependency of sacraments and sacramentals in the later medieval period has been at the heart of much criticism of fifteenth-century devotional practices, both by reformers of the sixteenth century, and by modern-day reformers.[5] The nature of worship life, taken as a whole, relates profoundly to the nature of personal devotion, especially as encouraged by those responsible for sustaining older traditions or designing new ones. Although this is true in any age, it was especially important in the sixteenth century. When liturgical models were changed or transformed in the course of this period of time, modes of personal devotion and prayer life followed suit. One of the ways in which late medieval worship and early modern worship were alike, then, is that both ritual systems worked—although in different ways—through a powerful interdependency of personal devotion and public rites.[6]

Beinecke 757 suggests the ways in which the public prayer of the Church and the efficacy of sacramental action provided the framework for the devotional lives of nonclerics and nonreligious in the first half of the fifteenth century. These prayers belong to a particular tradition of participation, one that worked alongside the corporate offices of clerics, whose ritual roles were more evident. In a cogent analysis of lay involvement in the Mass liturgy in the later Middle Ages, Virginia Reinburg argues that reformers and moderns have failed to understand the quality of participation because it was so different from the intellectual experiences demanded by the reformers. Reformers were humanists, suspicious of the connection between ecstatic prayer, sacrament, and divine action; they were little able to appreciate the symbolic power of ritual action and its ability to nurture worshipers. In exploring this disconnect, Virginia Reinburg says, "I would argue, that for lay people the ritual itself was a rich layering of associations, of social relationship and rituals expressing those relationships."[7] Beinecke 757 helps us to understand how the associations worked both inside and outside of public, corporate worship.

As Beinecke 757 suggests, it was not that personal devotion, a component of which consisted of praying alongside sacramental action, was disengaged in the late medieval period. It is rather that the quality of lay participation was so different from that which came to be envisaged by the Reformers that they could neither understand nor respect it. Yet one of the ways in which the Middle Ages and the early modern period were contiguous is the extent to which religious reformers defined themselves deliberately in contradistinction to the backdrop of the late medieval period, often becoming negative photographs of the originals they scorned. Thus, just as the Reformers attacked both medieval modes of personal devotion and of public worship, so too they were busy making sure that the prayer lives their own parishioners experienced were intimately related to what happened in the assembly. Helen White has said of the sixteenth century:

> True, a considerable proportion of the religious thinkers of the period were engaged in a return to what they conceived to be the primitive

> state of the Christian community, as regards church government, discipline, and worship. And the prestige of the return to the primitive was enormously reinforced by the scripturalism of the age, which sought in the Word of God the indispensable authority for theory and practice. But not even the most radical primitivist can leap completely out of his time. The most thorough-going rebel is still a child of his day, and the things he most fiercely repudiates yet have power to call the changes of his thoughts. . . . Especially is this true of private devotion. . . .[8]

Let us pick up this leather-bound book, and regard its salient features. The collection is an extensive codex of 150 parchment folios, written in a clear textualis, and by a single well-practiced scribe; the many gatherings are each composed of four sewn leaves.[9] The book is not large, measuring fourteen by twenty centimeters and three centimeters in thickness, a size that would fit comfortably into the lap or on the reading table of a single individual. A *terminus post quem* is provided by a prayer attributed to Peter of Luxemburg, who died in 1387; Beinecke 757 was prepared after this date. The monumental *Manuscrits Datés,* a series of volumes cataloguing examples of precisely datable codices from French libraries, depicts several hands which resemble that of Beinecke 757 in general style and characteristics. The contents and paleographical evidence suggest that the book was copied in the first half of the fifteenth century.[10] The saints mentioned in the litany suggest an origin in the diocese of Rheims. Although it is difficult to be more specific at the present time, closer analysis of the prayer texts found in a forthcoming study will offer more clues as to audience.[11] Most texts are in Latin; but some few are in Middle French. An epilogue containing a collection of devotional mysteries for the Virgin in Middle French is bound at the back; it is contemporary with the main body of the manuscript, and will be treated in a forthcoming study.

The pages of the main body of text are ruled in red ink in double columns of twenty-nine lines. Rubrics introduce sections and individual items throughout the book, and several of these are in Old French. Capitals, used throughout, are painted in blue and red. There is no gold. There are only occasional flourishes, some of which are moderately ornate, and occasionally whimsical, with a face incorporated into the letter stem at one point.[12] There are no illuminations. The hand that copied this book was evidently well practiced in producing liturgical books; the style of the handwriting underscores the quasi-liturgical character of the collection. On a flyleaf bound into the book, one can read the following inscription in a nineteenth-century cursive hand:

> I present this breviary manuscript to the order of venerable knights of the royal order and arch-confraternity of the Holy Sepulchre of Jerusalem. Signed, Jean-Baptist Grossard, native of Montier-en-Der, former Benedictine of the Abbey of Hautviliers, diocese of Reims,—who saved the body of St. Helene from the vandalism of the end of the eighteenth century and gave it to said Order on August 1, 1820, and who in recognition of this act was named an officer of the organization, and who is in his 73rd year.[13]

On the final guard leaf is the following inscription (also in French): "Seen by the first administrator, Lieutenant colonel, Baron Lainé." Baron Lainé added some page numbers to the book, and scrawled his monograph on many of the pages. The book was purchased by the Beinecke Library from Bernard M. Rosenthal, Booksellers. Pasted into the book are notes from an earlier catalogue that describes the library of a nineteenth-century owner, one Canon Girron. The manuscript was volume four in the listing of Girron's books, and the description the catalogue provides is accurate in many of its details. As with so many codices now extant from the late Middle Ages, the survival of Beinecke 757 is a miracle. Even the scant evidence about its history that can be gleaned from later markings and notes demonstrates that it had several owners, at least one of whom was an arch-Catholic who struggled against the antireligious character of the French Revolution. This was not a book that would appeal to humanists of the early modern period; in fact it is precisely the kind of book that new Protestant prayer books, with their commentaries upon the Lord's Prayer, were written to countermand.

There is little bibliography on books such as Beinecke 757, but it is useful to glance though Pierre Salmon's catalogue of Psalters found in the Vatican Library looking for parallel types.[14] A near cousin seems to be Patetta 21, which was made in the late fourteenth or early fifteenth century. It contains the Gospel for the Annunciation, followed by diverse prayers, the prayer that ought to be said before the Psalter, a "consideratio psalmorum in causis diversis," and an abbreviated Psalter that begins with the same verse as that in Beinecke 757 and that occupies the same number of pages. It is clear that several elements of Beinecke 757 were widely known, but that the arrangement of them was local and idiosyncratic.[15] Discussion of the inventory given below will bring forth greater understanding of the contents and their significance.

Beinecke 757 is reflective in its contents of several types of prayer and prayer books, each of which will be mentioned below. At the outset, it is most useful to think of it as belonging to the most important model for lay prayer books throughout the course of the entire Middle Ages, a Psalter with prayers of various cycles added at the end. There are hundreds of examples of this type, from the ninth-century Book of Cerne, to books such as this, which knocks against the door of the late medieval period.[16] In effect Beinecke 757 provides two models for the Psalter with prayers; these constitute the two major sections of the book, yet within these are elements of many other types of books and modes of prayer. In its largest sense, the book falls into two parts, each of which has an introductory Psalter; the first of these is loosely centered around devotion to Our Lord and his saints, and the second around veneration of the Blessed Virgin Mary.

There were numerous ways to consecrate or dedicate one's life to God in the Middle Ages: by becoming a cleric with an affiliation to a secular church; by joining a religious order, either as a full affiliate or as a lay brother; by committing to living as a lay man or woman in a loosely ordered community; or by seeking life as a hermit, with at least an informal association with a religious order or community.[17] Vowing one's life to God was not considered unusual or strange in this deeply religious culture, but rather was expected and accepted, and for people of all states.[18] There were many rules and modes of living for religious by the time Beinecke 757 was penned, but the most all-pervasive of these were the great monastic rules, especially those of Saint Benedict and of Saint Augustine. Whether a person was a Benedictine or an Augustinian, a Dominican or a Franciscan, a Carthusian or a cathedral canon, a nun or a canoness, there was a responsibility to sing a form of the Divine Office.[19] The Office was first standardized in the Latin Middle Ages through adaptation of the Rule of Saint Benedict, a source that originated in Italy in the sixth century but was first widely promulgated throughout much of Europe from the time of the ninth-century monastic reforms spearheaded by Benedict of Aniane.[20] According to the Benedictine Rule, the monastic day was divided by eight set periods (or "hours") of prayer, each of which included a set group of Psalms: Matins (the night office, which lasted two hours); Lauds (at sunrise); the so-called little hours: Prime (at 6:00), Terce (at 9:00), Sext (at 12:00), None (at 3:00); Vespers (at sunset); and Compline (at bedtime).[21] Through the singing of the Office, the entire Book of Psalms would be rendered every week, along with scriptural readings, patristic commentary, saints' lives, hymns, chants of several styles, and many prayers. The Divine Office provided structure and food for prayerful souls, but more than this, it was also the great textbook of the Middle Ages: through singing the Office, clerics, nuns, and monks had much of the Bible by heart, and certainly all the Psalms, as well as a rich tradition of legends, prayers, and hymns. The readings found in the Office, particularly at Matins, provided commentary upon the texts of Scripture; vast quantities of texts were created for the decoration of the psalmody in hymns, antiphons, and responsories, many of which were versified in various ways, and all of which were sung. The later Middle Ages was a time during which the laity envied the stature, learning, and prayer and sacramental lives of the clergy and religious; the Office was, unlike the Mass, something in which all could participate directly.

Although it is not the norm for the laity to pray the Office in the modern age, we would do well to remember that hours of public prayer for the laity began in the first centuries of the common era and continued for centuries thereafter. Throughout the Middle Ages, there were attempts every century to bring the Office, its psalmody, and other spiritual gifts to the public. In the later Middle Ages, it was often the case that a small group of extra devotional services were added to the Office of Matins and other hours too: special hours for the Virgin Mary, for the Cross, for the Trinity, and for the Dead. Some forms of these prayers were added to Psalters owned by laypeople, allowing their prayers and their structures to reflect those of the clergy. Hours of the Virgin, of the Cross, of the Trinity, and of the Dead became the backbone of medieval books of hours; but devotions and prayers to and for these entities continued to be part of other prayer book traditions as well, continuing the early understanding of a Psalter with a group of prayers at the close.

The most popular of all of these special offices of prayer mentioned above was the Little Office of the Blessed Virgin Mary, central to medieval books of hours; this was a truncated version of the Office prepared for the laity, and in many cases for very rich laity.[22] It is possible today through the internet to have access to many attempts at bringing the splendors of these books to larger audiences without destroying them by cutting them apart. [23] A site such as that by Glenn B. Gunhouse, "A Hypertext Book of Hours," for example, offers a fine introduction to an actual Office book.[24] And there are many serious attempts to give web-users access to entire books, and to explain the various uses they reflect, Paris and Rome being the most important.[25] Two books by Roger Wieck include instructive examples of the many types of glorious illuminations found in books of hours; the author has arranged his sumptuous materials in sections that take the reader through the most important parts of the medieval Book of Hours, and many of these texts—in one use or another—are translated in the hypertext books of hours referred to in note 24:[26]

1. The calendar, which provides a table of major feasts throughout the Church year.
2. The Gospel lessons, the four most revered scriptural readings in the medieval canon: John 1:1–14; Luke 1:26–38; Matthew 2:1–12;

Mark 16:14–20. Each of these represents the mystery of the feast for which it served as the Gospel reading at Mass: Christmas, the Annunciation, Epiphany, and the Ascension, respectively.
3. Hours of the Virgin, commonly in two cycles, one to focus on infancy and birth, and the other on the Passion.[27] These are series of Psalms with antiphons, and sometimes with responsories as well.
4. Hours of the Cross. These too are series of Psalms with antiphons.
5. Hours of the Holy Spirit: another series of Psalms with antiphons.
6. Two long prayers to the Virgin, "Obsecro Te" and "O Intemerata."
7. The Seven Penitential Psalms.
8. The Office of the Dead.

Yet another form of prayer that became popular in the fifteenth century was the Marian Psalter, an attempt to keep the steady praying of the 150 Psalms inherited from the monastic office in place, and yet to substitute simple texts that could be recited 150 times by people without the luxury of time for long contemplation. Very different in character from books of hours, or from the Little Office of the Virgin Mary, the Marian Psalter was a set of 150 "hails," and not related specifically to the texts of the Psalms. The steady recitation of Aves in a Marian Psalter was meant to free the mind for prayer and contemplation, just as was the case with the repetition of the Psalter itself by those who knew it by heart.

Several prayer narratives popular in the period—including the mysteries of the Incarnation and Birth of Christ, of the Passion, of the Assumption, meditations upon the holy face, on the holy name of Christ, upon the limbs of Christ, upon the wounds of Christ, upon the various saints and the altars of a church, upon the virtues, and upon one's sins and faults, were encouraged for contemplation during prayer.[28] The Marian Psalter was the perfect background for prayer, keeping the mind focused upon pictures of Christian mysteries and personal acts of contrition. While people prayed the Aves in words, they were contemplating much more than the words themselves indicated. In the second half of the fifteenth century, such prayers and their accompanying mysteries were gathered and standardized by preachers such as Jacob Sprenger, Michael Francisci, and Johannes Erfurt to resemble the mode of prayer that came to be associated with the rosary. There were so many people involved, so many movements and confraternities, that one looks in vain for a linear development of the rosary and the cycles of mysteries to be contemplated in its recital. Anne Winston-Allen says:

> In the end no one person can be credited with the definitive innovation in the growth of the rosary in any of its forms. The link missing in

> [modern scholar Thomas] Esser's chain turns out to be several links, represented by several contributors. The "authors" include redactors and illustrators, but most particularly "users"—the lay public and Observant reformers concerned with the care of souls—who played a role collectively and incrementally, by consensus in selecting the most viable version.[29]

Beinecke 757 is reflective of the Book of Hours, of the ingredients that would make up the rosary, and of the moral literature represented by the various "mirrors of the soul" that were used to examine the conscience and improve character. The elements of the book that I have inventoried above speak to the dynamic state of the various materials contributing to lives of prayer and devotion in the period. The prayers accompany the common actions of each day; they create—or could for those who desired to use it—a measured Office of prayer, but one that takes place at home, on the road, and in church. Many elements present here are borrowed from books of hours, those Office books for the laity or third-order religious described above, including the most important and popular prayers found in them, and an office for the Immaculate Conception of the Virgin. Here are the emphases on the Cross, the Trinity, the dead, and, above all, upon the Virgin; here is the Litany of the Saints. But whereas Beinecke 757 borrows elements from books of hours, it remains primarily a dual Psalter with prayers, one of the Lord and one of the Virgin. In the section for the Virgin, one can see a rosary in the making with the Aves of the Marian Psalter, and the joys and sorrows that underscored the visual accompaniments to this practice of prayer. The anthology is a flexible work, a framework overlaid with numerous traditions, and offering much from which to choose. Its late medieval owners preferred the longer and personal prayers tabulated in the section from pages 29 to 98. One of these prayers is translated in the primary sources accompanying this contribution (pp. 21–22 above).

Beinecke 757 belongs to that diverse category of literature called "devotional," the literature which, alongside the classics that literate people owned and read in the fifteenth and sixteenth centuries, shaped the ways people approached God and thought about God in their daily lives, both in church and at home. The most studied representatives of this literature are the books of hours described above. But scholars know far less about books of the humbler sort, books such as Beinecke 757, than they do about their often lavish first cousins. Because there are so many of them, and so many different kinds of them, fifteenth-century prayer books are difficult to categorize and have failed to attract significant attention from scholars and their audiences. We can ask, what scholarly field owns them, and who would care about the material they contain? In fact there is not even a good inventory of devotional anthologies and manuals of prayer. We simply do not know what quantities survive from the fifteenth century; there is no taxonomy in place for their study.[30] Yet not only does a collection such as Beinecke 757 help us to understand the nature of worship and popular devotion; it also points to the ways in which literary forms, character types, and even narrative sense grew out of and were sustained by the rich devotional life represented here. In her paper "Religious Reading Amongst the Laity in France in the Fifteenth Century," Geneviève Hasenohr describes the contents of a number of representative book collections owned by the laity in the period in which Beinecke 757 was produced, and the taste in reading they reflect. Her conclusions are summarized as follows:

> What can be concluded from this long review? As the clergy hoped, the two poles around which the laity's reading matter was organized were morality, more or less internalized, and devotion. A first group of writings, often with titles such as *Voie, Pélerinage, Miroir,* provides directives towards the Christian life under various literary forms, from the *somme* of the thirteenth century to the short pastoral work of the fifteenth, through the long allegorical poem of the fourteenth. The most down-to-earth were content to exhort obedience to the commandments; others, which fostered a more spiritual outlook on morality, set out to bring about through an alteration of habits a change in the heart, and repeated insistently themes of the contempt of the world and the vileness of the flesh, fitting in with lessons drawn from the lives of the saints. A second group sought to enliven devotion, setting out meditative themes which, alongside the more or less mechanical recitation of the hours (which usually were in Latin), were to encourage the soul to eager prayer of repentance, the action of grace, of love or of compassion. The pivot of this, even more than fear of death, was compassion for the sufferings of the Saviour.[31]

Beinecke 757 represents the second kind of attempt at spiritual formation. Although its contents are complex and varied, the book's patterned rhythms suggest the need people felt for a ritualized devotional life in the first half of the fifteenth century. But the call was not only for a life in which a closeness to the actions of the Mass and Office shaped prayer, but also one in which there was a close and personal sense of affection for Jesus, Mary, and the saints. It is evidence for the sense of character, of suffering, of trust, and of affection that was fostered within prayer lives through a book such as this, a sense that makes a connection between the ritualized life of prayer found here and the development of vernacular literary styles and genres in the first half of the fifteenth century. Beinecke 757 reshapes earlier traditions, it remains consonant with them, and it points to various kinds of devotion that would characterize Catholic devotional life for centuries to come. Central to this devotional sense is a heart that knows the saints and the Lord as human beings who can be experienced. The emotions were not favored by the humanistic reformers of the sixteenth century: heads often won over hearts. But many of the works in this fifteenth-century anthology wear their hearts on their sleeves; the supplicant enters a world peopled by actual humans who could be known, and in the case of Christ, touched, experienced, and joined. The very rich had books of hours with their gold and silver, with ornate and delicately elaborate flowers in the margins, and with human figures depicted in a variety of circumstances. Their less rich brothers and sisters had all these things too, but through prayers and sets of devotions that fired the imagination, and that sustained literary forms of a bewildering variety.

On one side of the literary spectrum is a book such as the *Pety Job*. A book of devotions closely related to the Office of the Dead—the Dirige as found in a book of hours—*Pety Job* is a stunning example of a way in which the character of Job emerged from the pages and illuminations of books of hours to live again within a literary work.[32] In her introduction to the *Pety Job*, found electronically among the many texts of TEAMS (The Consortium for the Teaching of the Middle Ages), Susanna Fein says:

> *Pety Job* must, then, be read in recognition of a culture that fully embraced the Office of the Dead as a ritualized way to enclose and confront death, or at least to accept its mystery through time-honored words of earnest entreaty, rebellion, questioning, and submission. The speeches of the long-suffering Job provided the *Pety Job* poet a lyrical departure point, and the universality of the liturgy offered an emotionally charged context. Repetition of the Latin—whether fully understood or not by auditors—would most likely have been a somber but comforting experience, a memorial to the departed and a prayerful remembrance of one's own fate. Through vernacular translation and gloss the Middle English poet aligns the ancient words of Job to a medieval reader's desire to comprehend his or her own mortal condition, investing words already fraught with the power of long usage with a contemporary fervor and immediacy.[33]

In between the lavishly illumined books of hours and literary works such as the *Pety Job* stood hundreds of fifteenth-century devotional anthologies such as Beinecke 757, books which are for the most part unknown and unstudied. As has been shown here, these books served to keep the psalmody of the medieval Church alive, albeit in varying guises. But they also are a key to the ways in which the piety of the later Middle Ages paved the way for the formation of human character in the arts. This is a highly complex subject, and one upon which many scholars have worked, although it seems without sufficient attention to the subject of prayer.[34] People who offered prayers such as those found in Beinecke 757 in church or at home were drawn into an intricate web of understanding both of the efficacy of prayer and sacraments, and of the immediacy and tender love of God for humankind. Beinecke 757 is a single, humble book, and we cannot expect it to settle by itself the furious arguments that have raged in recent decades over the nature of so-called popular piety, or to tell us who was praying what, and why, and at whose bidding. We cannot say for sure who compiled this book, and whether it was designed by the clergy to promote their political and theological ideals, or for the spiritual needs and desires advanced by the users themselves, or, perhaps, for both sets of reasons.[35] But one thing is clear from this heavily used anthology of prayer: people spoke these texts fervently to a suffering God they could taste and see. The *Pety Job* takes its character from the Office of the Dead and the rich tradition of illuminating it in medieval books of hours. A prayer such as "Quis sum aut qualis" makes the person of Christ present and puts him in dialogue with a striving soul, but within the actuality of the sacrament of the Eucharist. In this prayer, one sees the tradition of human devotion nurtured by the prayer tradition operating within a liturgical framework, and it is this which makes this prayer, and numerous others like it, crucial for understanding late medieval piety and the relationship between clerical and lay traditions of sacramental understanding.[36] The prayer is tender and powerfully dramatic, and is dependent upon eucharistic doctrine as interpreted through the Church for the laity in the later Middle Ages. This window on the eucharistic experience of a late medieval person helps us to understand the unreasoned abuses the Reformers were criticizing. It also is a defense of the passion, joy, and understanding that many experienced who "mumbled" such prayers during Mass. The prayer's spirit points to the many reformers who followed after the work of their sixteenth-century counterparts, men and women who sought to capture a heartfelt sense of prayer and nearness to God and to bring it to their congregants. After changes wrought by Reformers of the sixteenth century, other reformers from later on—the Wesleys or Mother Ann Lee—would create continuity with the traditions the Reformers had left behind. At the moment Beinecke 757 was conceived, there was still a wavering continuity between personal devotion, public worship, sense of character, and meaning in the arts. One, then, could not be known without the other. But the system was too vast to endure, to stretch any further without breaking, and, as we know, it shattered into thousands of traditions in the sixteenth century, some of which attempted to continue this vast "it," others of which defied it. Beinecke 757 offers a look at the part of the fragile whole that is the least understood in our own age, and in some sense, the part most important for answering the kinds of questions scholars presently ask of the fifteenth century and its relationship to the decades that followed.

Notes

An early version of this essay was presented at a conference sponsored by the Beinecke Library, and special thanks are due to Robert Babcock, Curator of Latin Manuscripts at the Beinecke, who brought Beinecke 757 to my attention, and to colleagues in the Program in Medieval Studies for organizing this conference. I am grateful to the staffs of the Beinecke Rare Book and Manuscript Library, of the Sterling Memorial Library, and of Yale Divinity Library for their patience. I wish to thank John Leinenweber for his assistance in preparing this manuscript for publication, Pamela Huckins, who worked with me during the early stages of this investigation, and Gale Pollen, my assistant at the Yale Institute of Sacred Music. I have discussed several of the issues raised in this paper with the team of scholars assembled by John Witvliet and Karin Maag with great profit, and offer thanks to both for their work in organizing the symposium. Susan Felch, Maura Nolan, and Susan Boynton read this paper and offered useful comments.

1. The best discussion of the abbreviated Psalters of the Middle Ages is by Pierre Salmon in *Analecta Liturgica: Extraits des manuscrits liturgiques de la Bibliothèque Vaticane, contribution à l'histoire de la prière chrétienne,* Studi e Testi 273 (Vatican City: Bibliotheca apostolica vaticana, 1974), section III, "Psautiers abrégés du Moyen Âge," 69–119. The earliest examples Salmon knows of the Saint Jerome type appeared in the late tenth century, and for discussion of an early example, see D.H. Turner, "The Prayer-Book of Archbishop Arnulph II of Milan," *Revue Benedictine* 70 (1960): 362–63, a book which the author thinks may be English in origin.

2. The abbreviated Psalter attributed to Saint Jerome existed in many guises. For a plate from the Burnet Psalter at the University of Aberdeen (AUL Ms. 25), a contemporary of Beinecke 757, see www.abdn.ac.uk/diss/heritage/collects/bps/text/280r.htm. The translation of the preface parallels the version prefacing the first section of Beinecke 757, but here the emphasis on Jerome is prominent.

> Jerome arranged his psalter in this way, as he was instructed by an angel through the holy spirit. It is in an abridged form for this purpose, that those who are concerned for the world, those who are sick, those who go on long journeys or sail in danger of shipwreck, those who are about to wage war

> on their enemies or fight against the ill will of devils, those who vow to recite the whole psalter each day and cannot, those who are weakened by fasting, those who keep holy days and cannot recite the full-length psalter then, and those who wish to save their souls according to God's mercy and have eternal life may recite this psalter diligently and they will possess the eternal kingdom.

The introduction to this electronically reproduced masterpiece describes the Burnet Psalter as follows:

> The Burnet Psalter is the second of two medieval illuminated manuscripts to be included in the programme [of electronic reproduction]. It was composed in the first half of the fifteenth century and contains the categories of material common to psalters of the time: a calendar, devotions (prayers and hymns) for personal use, the Psalter itself (the Book of Psalms), and liturgies (forms of worship) for personal use.

3. Augustine is the greatest authority on the differences between sacraments and sacramentals, although his understanding is not as clear-cut as many theologians would like. The literature on his understanding of sign, symbol, and sacramental is vast, but the best work with which to begin is his *On Christian Doctrine*. It is important to note that the major sacraments were numbered as seven only in the later Middle Ages. A major writer on the sacraments in the twelfth century, Hugh of Saint Victor, is flexible in his understanding as to what constitutes a sacrament and how many sacraments there are. See, for example, his *On the Sacraments of the Christian Faith,* trans. Roy Deferrari (Cambridge, Mass.: Medieval Academy of America, 1951), book 2, part 5, sec. 1, p. 279, for an interpretation of the term sacrament based on Augustine.

4. The highly influential Brethren of the Common Life were a lay order that flourished in the late fourteenth and early fifteenth centuries, the period of time in which Beinecke 757 was produced. The Brethren encouraged closeness to God, scriptural study, charitable works, and an organized prayer life. For an introduction and select texts, see John Van Engen, ed. and trans., *Devotio Moderna: Basic Writings* (New York: Paulist Press, 1988). The liturgical practices within the *devotio moderna* as adapted by various monastic traditions were in Latin and emphasized spiritual exercises as well as the Divine Office. For a study of the nuns of Windesheim, with attention to liturgical observances, see Wybren Scheepsma, *Deemoed en devotie. De koorvrouwen van Windesheim en hun geschriften* (Meekness and devotion. The regular canonesses of Windesheim and their writings) (Amsterdam: Prometheus, 1997).

5. A dramatic example of the literature in critique of Catholic sacramentals is Titus Oates (1649–1705), *The witch of Endor: or The witchcrafts of the Roman Jesebel: in which you have an account of the exorcisms or conjurations of the papists, as they be set forth in their amends, benedictionals, manuals, missals, journals, portasses: which they use in their churches* (London: printed for Thomas Parkhurst and Thomas Cockerill, 1679).

6. In her "Hearing Lay People's Prayer," in Barbara Diefendorf and Carla Hesse, eds., *Culture and Identity in Early Modern Europe (1500–1800): Essays in Honor of Natalie Zemon Davis* (Ann Arbor: University of Michigan Press, 1993), 19–39, Virginia Reinburg speaks of the attention both Protestants and reforming Catholics gave to controlling modes of prayer and devotional life, especially through outlawing and changing the kinds of prayer books represented by Beinecke 757 and by books of hours as well. She says:

> Within three years of Luther's ninety-five theses, he, his followers, and his imitators were composing and publishing devotional books explicitly designed as alternatives to the book of hours. All over Western Europe reformed pastors were forming disciplinary institutions aimed at supervising lay devotional life. Christians must pray from the heart, and "the heart requires understanding," Calvin insisted. (32–33)

7. See Virginia Reinburg, "Liturgy and the Laity in Late Medieval and Reformation France," *Sixteenth Century Journal* 23 (1992): 542.

8. See Helen C. White, *The Tudor Books of Private Devotion* (Madison: University of Wisconsin Press, 1951), 11.

9. For a clear introduction to the various terms employed by scholars who work with medieval books, and an explanation of the ways pages were laid out and volumes were constructed, see Barbara Shailor, *The Medieval Book: Catalogue of an Exhibition at the Beinecke Rare Book & Manuscript Library, Yale University* (New Haven, Conn.: Yale University Library, 1988).

10. See, for example, the following plates from Charles Samaran and Robert Marichal, *Catalogue des Manuscrits en Écriture Latine* (Paris: Centre national de la recherche scientifique, 1959–62), I, plate 78, a copy of the dialogues of Gregory from 1410, description, 83; plate 77, a copy of Artistotle's *De regimine principum* from 1407, description, 211; II, plate 89, a Breviary from Bayeux dating from 1425, description, 67.

11. Consultation of Leroquais's catalogues of liturgical manuscripts found in public French libraries is the best way to localize French sources. Of particular importance is his five-volume catalogue of breviaries, manuscripts for the Divine Office. The best on-line site for hagiographical investigation is that sponsored by the Society of the Bollandists, the group of Jesuit scholars that produced the magisterial *Acta Sanctorum* over the centuries, and the many volumes of the *Bibliotheca Hagiographica Latina.* Their website is www.kbr.be/~socboll. ORB, the Online Reference Book of Medieval Studies, contains the useful "An Introductory Guide to Research in Medieval Hagiography" by Thomas Head, orb.rhodes.edu/encyclop/religion/hagiography/guide1.htm.

12. A particularly appealing example of the style is found on page 113. The flourished letter *B* contains a dour face, looking to the left.

13. The original is in French. For a brief introduction to the Equestrian Order of the Holy Sepulchre in Jerusalem, originally founded in 1098, see the organization's homepage, www.d-holliday.com/holysepulchre/hist.htm.

14. *Les manuscrits liturgiques latins de la Bibliothèque Vaticane,* Studi e Testi 251, 253, 262, 267, 270 (Vatican City: Bibliotheca apostolica vaticana, 1968–72).

15. See Salmon, *Analecta Liturgica,* 5: 86.

16. See Michelle P. Brown, *The Book of Cerne: Prayer, Patronage, and Power in Ninth-Century England* (Toronto: University of Toronto Press, 1996). A plate and brief description of the manuscript can be found at www.lib.cam.ac.uk/Exhibitions/Great Collections.

17. Much has been written in recent years about the more excessive strands of female piety in the later Middle Ages, as manifested both in groups and in individuals. Carolyn Walker Bynum's classic study *Holy Feast, Holy Fast* is centered on the intensity of female devotion to the Eucharist and the reasons for it. For study of a Beguine from the period in which Beinecke 757 was written, see Roberta A. McKelvie, *Retrieving a Living Tradition: Angelina of Montegiove, Franciscan, Tertiary, Beguine* (St. Bonaventure, N.Y: Franciscan Institute, 1997). For a study of themes of gender and sexuality within select liturgical repertories, see Bruce Holsinger, *Music, Body and Desire in Medieval Culture: Hildegard of Bingen to Chaucer* (Stanford: Stanford University Press, 2001).

18. For an accessible introduction to monastic culture and its relationship to medieval intellectual and liturgical life, see Jean Leclercq, *The Love of Learning and the Desire for God; A Study of Monastic Culture,* trans. Catharine Misrahi (New York: Fordham University Press, 1961). Case studies of particular interest are found in George Ferzoco and Carolyn Muessig, eds., *Medieval Monastic Education* (London: Leicester University Press, 2001), which includes "Training for the Liturgy as a Form of Monastic Education," by Susan Boynton.

19. For an introduction to the offices of the Eastern Churches in the formative periods of the fourth to ninth centuries, see Robert Taft, *The Liturgy of the Hours in East and West: The Origins of the Divine Office and its Meaning for Today,* 2nd rev. ed. (Collegeville, Minn.: Liturgical Press, 1993). A study of the formative period in the West, with concentration upon one important tradition, is Peter Jeffery, "Eastern and Western Elements in the Irish Monastic Prayer of the Hours," in Margot E. Fassler and Rebecca A. Baltzer, eds., *The Divine Office in the Latin Middle Ages: Methodology and Source Studies, Regional Developments, Hagiography* (Oxford: Oxford University Press, 2000), 99–143.

20. For an introduction to the Rule of Saint Benedict and to the many problems associated with this crucial text and the identity of its author, see Timothy Fry, ed., *RB 1980: The Rule of St. Benedict in Latin and English* (Collegeville, Minn.: Liturgical Press, 1981).

21. The individual parts of the Office and its two most important forms, monastic and cathedral, are outlined in Lila Collamore, "Charting the Divine Office," in Fassler and Baltzer, eds., *The Divine Office,* 3–11.

22. The contribution by Susan Felch deals with the evolution of the prayerbook in sixteenth-century England.

23. Modern-day vandals are kinder only by degree to medieval manuscripts than religious and political reformers of the sixteenth century: the former do not destroy utterly, they rather dismember to sell the leaves individually and thus at greater

profit. More medieval manuscripts were doubtless lost to fire and simple wear and tear than to any other causes, except in England, where the dissolution of the monasteries in the early sixteenth century had a particularly devastating result. Perhaps more than in any other place, the liturgical manuscripts of Sweden were used as binding materials, and this accounts for the large number of fragments surviving from that country. One can estimate that what survives of Continental liturgical manuscripts from the tenth through the late thirteenth century represents around 1 percent of the original number.

24. Glenn Gunhouse's Hypertext Book of Hours is at: gunhouse.tripod.com/hourstxt/home.htm. It is now available as well on ORB: orb.rhodes.edu/encyclop/religion/hagiography/hours/prayers.htm.

25. See especially "Late Medieval and Renaissance Manuscripts on the Web," www.chd.dk/gui/index.html#BrH. From the introduction:

> To search the Web for good illustrations from illuminated manuscripts has been like a walk in the desert for many years. Even the largest and most important collections in the World (no names mentioned . . .) have so far attempted to get around with a few jpegs of the most famous miniatures, not showing the originals, but simple scans from reproductions in popular printed books—already available to everybody in almost every bookshop. Only a few libraries have so far broken the deadlock, and are showing the way to the future:
>
> Aberdeen University Library The most ambitious site concerning a single manuscript: The Aberdeen Bestiary Project has been in preparation for some years; it has recently been accomplished with the addition of a full facsimile of the manuscript to illustrate the transcription and translation of the text (with introductions and comments). A marvellous scholarly achievement.
>
> The Royal Library in Copenhagen offers since 1999 a valuable selection of complete digital facsimiles. An almost inexhaustible source for detailed studies, which, beyond doubt, will revolutionize education all over the World when it has become generally known to students and teachers in art history, codicology and paleography (see below).
>
> The Bodleian Library has also entered the future, and recently transferred its long and proud tradition for a high scholarly standard to the Web, see below: The Bodleian Library Oxford.

26. Each of these sections is discussed at length in Roger Wieck, ed., *Time Sanctified: The Book of Hours in Medieval Art and Life* (New York: George Braziller, 1998).

27. For an English translation of the Little Office of the Blessed Virgin Mary, see www.ewtn.com/library/PRAYER/LITTLE.TXT

28. One of the great models of tenderness in prayer is the *Imitation of Christ*, by Thomas à Kempis, a key text of the Brethren of the Common Life. The text is available electronically at www.ccel.org/k/kempis/imitation/imitation.html

29. Anne Winston-Allen, *Stories of the Rose: The Making of the Rosary in the Middle Ages* (University Park: Pennsylvania State University Press, 1997), 73.

30. Virginia Reinburg has a forthcoming monograph on French prayer in this period, a book that is eagerly awaited. In the meanwhile, the best single-volume introduction to prayer in the Middle Ages is Nicole Bériou, Jacques Berlioz, and Jean Longère, eds., *Prier au Moyen Age: Pratiques et expériences (Ve-Xieme siècles) / textes traduits et commentés* (Turnhout: Brepols, 1991). Contrasting views of the subject can be found in John Bossy, "Christian Life in the Later Middle Ages: Prayer," *Transactions of the Royal Historical Society,* 6th series, 1 (1991): 137–48, and Virginia Reinburg, "Hearing Lay People's Prayer." The eloquent discussions of prayer and devotional literature in sixteenth-century England found in Helen C. White's *The Tudor Books of Private Devotion* have been exceedingly useful in the preparation of this essay. Further bibliography on medieval prayer books can be found in Marianne Briscoe, *Artes praedicandi,* and Barbara Jaye, *Artes orandi.* Typologie des sources du moyen âge occidental. 61 (Turnhout: Brepols, 1992).

31. In Peter Biller and Anne Hudson, eds., *Heresy and Literacy, 1000–1530* (Cambridge: Cambridge University Press, 1994), 205–21, with the passage cited above found on 215.

32. For a splendid rendering of Job on the dungheap from the Office of the Dead in a medieval book of hours, see folio 55r of the manuscript Bodleian Buchanan e3, found at www.bodley.ox.ac.uk/dept/scwmss/wmss/medieval/mss/buchanan/e/003.b.htm

33. See her introduction, the text, and many other related works through www.lib.rochester.edu/camelot/teams/tmsmenu.htm

34. For two recent attempts to study the influence of prayer on vernacular literature, see David Wrisley, "Women's Voices Raised in Prayer: On the 'Epic Credo' in Adenet le Roi's Berte as Grans Pies," in Kathy M. Krause, ed., *Reassessing the Heroine in Medieval French Literature* (Gainesville: University Press of Florida, 2001), and Evelyn Birge Vitz, " 'Bourde jus mise?' Villon, the Liturgy, and Prayer," in Michael Freeman and Jane H. M. Taylor, eds., *Villon at Oxford: The Drama of the Text. Proceedings of the conference held at St. Hilda's College, Oxford, March 1996* (Amsterdam: Rodopi, 1999), 170–94.

35. For reviews of recent scholarship and the sea changes that have taken place in the wake of the provocative work of Thomas Tentler, Natalie Davis, and Steven Ozment, see R. N. Swanson, *Religion and Devotion in Europe, c. 1215–1515* (Cambridge: Cambridge University Press, 1995), which makes good reading alongside John Bossy's *Christianity in the West, 1400–1700* (Oxford: Oxford University Press, 1985).

36. See the text of the prayer in the second of the primary sources accompanying this contribution, pp. 21–22.

Worship in Geneva Before and After the Reformation

ROBERT KINGDON

Editors' Introduction

What was it like to attend worship in medieval Europe? What about in Calvin's Geneva? This essay provides a basic and accessible introduction to the differing experiences of worship in Calvin's Geneva. It includes brief descriptions of liturgical space, vestments, prayers, music, and Communion practices, always highlighting the dramatic discontinuity *of liturgical practice.*

Despite the dramatic differences described here, careful readers, however, may also begin to ask what did not change. What stayed the same—especially those matters that are unspoken and implicit? Note, for example, that while the experience of worship changed, the clergy's desire for frequent gathering for worship did not. While the nature of Church discipline was transformed, the Church's role as a social-religious disciplinarian did not. Even these very broad assertions of continuity begin to help us gain perspective. The development of this book will largely be an attempt to perceive more clearly the underlying continuities that support the obvious discontinuities Kingdon describes.

Primary Source Introduction

In Calvin's Geneva, the Consistory had significant authority and strong control over the life of the Church. In addition to matters of basic governance, the Consistory spent a good deal of time on pastoral and personal discipline cases, meeting with individuals to provide counsel and correction. Detailed notes from these meetings provide significant clues about the experience of worship by Genevan Christians.

Johan Constant from Poitou in France, tailor, about . . .[1]
Answers touching muttering at the sermon that he says the passion, and that he can read and understand it in Latin and that he is more attached than he ever was to the Gospel and that he knows the Pater in Latin and the Ave Maria and his office of Prime, Terce, etc. The Consistory advises, considering his hypocrisy, that he come every Thursday to give an account of his faith and go every Sunday to catechism and that he be admonished more sharply and that he abstain from the sacraments until he is better informed.

Guygnome, wife of Loys Meyniez, from Gex.
Because of frequenting the sermons and living according to religion, and she hides when she goes to the sermon. Answers that she goes willingly to the sermon and does not live in papistry and has small children that she . . . [words omitted] therefore she cannot go every day, but when she can. And does not know the prayer; her husband is teaching it to her. She said it in Latin, and the Ave Maria in Latin, and every day the Pater and Ave Maria. And that she learn it within two weeks and come give an account [of it] and frequent the sermons, and that she not receive Holy Communion unless she knows it by next Saturday.

Jane, widow of Tyvent Mermet,[2] mother-in-law of the secretary Beguin.[3]
On frequenting the sermons and other things. Answers that she serves God as she can and goes to the sermons when she can, and was there last Wednesday and every day. And she does not remember anything he says in his sermons and she does not know whether it is she who mutters in the sermon. And she knows how

to pray to God: said the prayer, and prays God to give her the Holy Spirit; said the confession, and wants to live in the faith of God. [f. 69v] Moreover said that sometimes when children are baptized she goes apart to pray to God that he will always help her, and that she will not abstain for anyone whatever from making the prayers she has been accustomed to on her knees. And says that God is her witness that she did not say on entering here: "What devil wants me here?" And she certainly said it. The Consistory is of the opinion that she be admonished to frequent the sermons and that she be gained if possible by remonstrances and that she cease her muttering and that she be forbidden to mutter any more in the sermon.

Noble Pernete, wife of Bartholomyer Fouson.
On the Word of God, her conscience and frequenting the sermons. Answers yes, when she can, as well as she can, and that she will guard herself from doing wrong and that she prays her Creator to give her the grace to live honestly and to the salvation of her soul. And she has seen and associated with many respectable people, and she was at the sermon yesterday before dinner, and does not remember what the preacher said, and she remembers much of the sermons of former times, and of those here not much, and retains what she can. And there are preachers who are much easier to understand than others. And she prays God to help her and says her prayers and prays for her husband, for her children and not for the dead, and says her *In manus.*[4] And she remembers well the good father who said it was always necessary to have a new heart. And that she always prays in Latin. The Consistory is of the opinion that she be admonished not to mutter any more and to listen to the sermons and to communicate with someone and come here the Thursday before Christmas.[5] And that she be admonished on what she should do and that she should behave herself and pray to God before going to the sermon, and whether she knows how to pray in French, and should follow the catechism that is given on Sundays.

Donne Jane, widow of Philibert de La Ryvaz.[6]
Because of her muttering in the sermon, and whether she has some doubt of the . . . [word omitted]. Answers that she has always lived outside in the village and only recently came [to the city]. And she does not say the Ave Maria, and she sometimes

says some words of the Psalms, and that it would be better for her to stay in her house than go to the sermon, considering that she has children, and she has no scruples about the Word that is presently preached.

Pierre Rouz, haberdasher, native of Pougny near Chancy. Because of the sermons and other things. Answers that at his beginning he asked for alms while saying the Psalms, and since the Gospel he took to the trade of selling haberdashery, and he has a wife and children. And he no longer mutters, and has not asked for charity except from the procurators of the hospital since he was commanded to obey the commandments. And also, meaning no harm, he has taught the feasts to those who asked him. And he has not lent money at interest, and if it is found otherwise he will give it to the Council. He was admonished to refrain and not give a bad example to others and to do better than he has in the past and not to teach the feasts any longer to people who ask.

The widow of Bertheractz,[7] promised wife of Gonrardz de La Palaz.[8]
Because of the rosary. Answers it is not so, because she does not mutter anything, and for this someone sent her here. And she frequents the sermons and prays to God as the Council has commanded her, and she says the Pater with good intentions and goes to the sermons and prays to God as she prayed in former times, with good intentions. And she does not keep feasts because she has no calendar, although sometimes when they are together she talks about feasts with the others. And she does not solemnize them and did not fast this Lent and has no scruples about eating meat and does not scandalize others about religion. Remanded to Monday before the Council. The Consistory is that she be asked whether she wants to marry her husband and what term she plans, before Easter or after, and according to what she answers that she be given a precise term, and admonish her to refrain from scandalizing the church because she constantly stays with her husband at suspect hours, and let them have their wedding promptly. [f. 92v] Answers the questions that she does not know whether their banns have been published or not because *[sic]* Monsieur Glaude Malbuisson,[9] and she means to marry next Monday, and not at a suspect hour, and she left

between eight and nine o'clock, and she will refrain from this if it pleases the Seigneurie. And she goes there by day and not by night, since he is ill and cannot stand, while waiting to be married in the house. Remonstrances.[10]

Noble Bartholemie, widow of Richardet, wife of Achard.
Because of superstitions and rosaries. Answers that she does not know what this is about and she always keeps the feasts because she does nothing, and she does not know what she said, and she has never said the rosary with her fingers, and someone lent it to her. And she has no images either in her house or elsewhere or blessed things, although she has a St. John that was in their chapel.[11] Monday before the Council and the procurator general.[12] The Consistory decided that she be remanded to the Council with her idol and that someone go with her to investigate her idols, and that two be assigned to visit.[13]

Tyvent Chenu's wife.[14]
Because of muttering. Answers that she does not adore images and that she prays to God to give her the Holy Spirit, that he instruct her in His Word, and for all her family. And when she goes late to the sermon she does not understand all that was preached. Said the prayer and the confession. She was admonished.

Notes

1. Material taken from Robert Kingdon, Thomas Lambert, and Isabella Watt, eds., *Registers of the Consistory of Geneva in the Time of Calvin: Volume 1, 1542–1544*, trans. M. Wallace McDonald (Grand Rapids, Mich.: Eerdmans, 2000), 60, 117, 143–45, 166, 179–80, 198–99, 201. Used with kind permission of Wm. B. Eerdmans Publishing.

2. Tyvent Mermet was received into the bourgeoisie on March 29, 1504 (Alfred Covelle, *Le livre des bourgeois de l'ancienne république de Genève* [Geneva: Jullien, 1897], 153).

3. On February 4, 1541, François Beguin was proposed as *secrétaire d'État*, and on February 6 as secretary of the Chambre des Comptes, but both times Claude Roset received more votes. Nevertheless, on June 21, 1541, he appeared before the Council in the character of secretary in connection with a matrimonial case. He was then *secrétaire de la Justice* (there is also a sentence of 1543 against Roud Monet, signed by Beguin). On June 2, 1542, he was also qualified as *secrétaire en Conseil* (R.C. 35, folios 47v, 51, 53, 241v; R.C. 36, f. 29;

P.C. 1e sér., 368 [February 27, 1543]). Beguin, a member of the LX at the time of this consistorial case, also served as *curial* of St. Victor (1536), procurator general (1537–40), councillor and syndic (1547). According to Sordet he was secretary until 1555. Although Galiffe says that Beguin was counted among the Perrinists incorrectly, Sordet says that "regarded as a leader of the party of the Libertins, he was forced to depart in 1556 and renounced his bourgeoisie" (R.C. 35, f. 489 [February 7, 1542]; R.C. 30, f. 62 and f. 175v [September 29, 1536, and February 14, 1537]; Louis Sordet, "Dictionnaire des familles genevoises" [unpublished manuscript, Archives d'état de Genève], 82; J.-B.-G. Galiffe, *Nouvelles pages d'histoire exacte: Procès de Pierre Ameaux* [Geneva: Georg, 1868], 86, n. 1).

4. *In manus:* prayer at Compline drawn from Ps. 30:6 of the Vulgate: *"In manus tuas commendo spiritum meum."* In the liturgy of the diocese of Geneva the *In manus* "was not said except from the first Sunday of Lent until the Sunday of the Passion, and then it was also said at the fêtes; apart from this period there was no respond at Compline" (Pierre-Marie Lafrasse, *Étude sur la liturgie dans l'ancien Diocèse de Genève* [Geneva: Jullien, 1904], 296).

5. In the margin: "Tuesday; Thursday before the next Communion."

6. This is most likely Jeanne Curt, widow of Noble Philippe de La Rive, also reprimanded on November 18, 1557, because of certain images found at her house (Albert Choisy, *Généalogies genevoises: Familles admises à la bourgeoisie avant la Réforme* [Geneva: Kundig, 1947] 42; P.C. 1e sér., 685 [November 18, 1557]).

7. Guillauma, widow of Pierre Bertherat.

8. Conrad Schüffelin, called De La Palle (a direct translation of Schüffelin), from Nuremberg, was admitted to the bourgeoisie in 1519. He possessed various properties in Geneva and was authorized to sell "cannon powder" in 1541 (Jacques Augustin Galiffe, *Notices généalogiques sur les familles genevoises, depuis les premiers temps, jusqu'à nos jours* [Geneva: Barbezat, 1829–95], I:355–56; *R.C.* VIII, p. 288 [February 4, 1519]; R.C. 35, f. 79 [February 18, 1541]).

9. Claude Malbuisson was Conrad de La Palle's son-in-law.

10. The next Monday, March 5, 1543, there was a report in Council about Bertherat and De La Palle, that "she goes to her husband's [fiancé's] house by day and night, although they are not married. Resolved that they should marry this coming Sunday in seven days" (R.C. part. 1, f. 16v.). However, the couple did not contract marriage until July 1, 1543 (Notaires, Claude de Miribello, v. 2, ff. 23–24v).

11. Bartholomie Richardet's brother, Pierre d'Orsières, appeared in Council in connection with a house located in St. Gervais and belonging to the chapel of the D'Orsières. One can therefore suppose that this chapel was at the church of St. Gervase (R.C. 35, f. 499 [February 14, 1542]). Bartholomie Richardet appeared in Council several times because of this house (R.C. 35, folios 82v, 100, and 143v [February 22, March 4, and April 5, 1541]; R.C. 36, f. 77v [July 25, 1542]). However, it appears that the D'Orsières family also had a

chapel at the New Church of Our Lady. Louis Blondel says: "The third chapel (of this church) has on its keystone the arms of the D'Orsières; its altar must have been consecrated to St. Anthony, whose chapel is mentioned in 1436, and again in 1442, as a foundation of the D'Orsières . . . Jean de Crose founded a chaplaincy of the Visitation there in 1502, and in 1454 it is said that it derives from a foundation of the canon Jean Symonet and of Jean d'Orsières" (Louis Blondel, "Le Temple de l'Auditoire, ancienne église de Notre-Dame-La-Neuve," *Genava* new series 5 [1957], 122). This Jean d'Orsières was the grandfather of Bartholomie Richardet (Galiffe, *Notices généalogiques*, I:178–80). Finally, the Richardets also had a chapel at St. Gervase (A.E.G. Finances M 23, f. 81 [not dated, 1535–36]).

12. Pierre Vandel was named procurator general on February 5, 1543, or a little earlier (R.C. 37, f. 4).

13. Bartholomie Richardet was summoned to Council the next day in this connection, and later, on March 5, 1543, the Council reprimanded her "because she took the paintings of St. Barbara from their chapels, which she confessed having taken, and that she did not dare restore them without the heir." She remained in prison for some time (R.C. 37, f. 25v [March 2, 1543]; R.C. part 1, f. 16v [March 5, 1543]; R.C. 37, f. 89v and f. 93v [May 11 and 15, 1543]).

14. Pernette, daughter of the late François de Vaud, called Fornier, wife of Thivent Chenu (Galiffe, II, p. 115). She made her will on February 14, 1535 (Notaires, Jean Duverney, v. 2, pp. 526–30, with a codicil of February 15).

In the city of Geneva, the Reformation led to a revolutionary change in worship, a change that was probably equally revolutionary in a number of other places, particularly those that looked to Geneva for leadership. That is the argument that will be developed in this contribution.[1] The key source upon which this argument is based is the *Registers of the Consistory of Geneva in the Time of Calvin,* and in particular the first volume of those registers, covering the years 1542–44. A striking feature about this volume is the number of passages devoted to persuading people to abandon Catholic practices of worship and adopt Protestant practices. These passages thus provide a detailed record of practice before and after the Reformation, a record that seems to fit ideally into the theme of our project. In fact there are few other historical records from the sixteenth century as full of information on this subject. Later volumes of these registers have much less to say about it. Presumably in later years the people of Geneva had learned how to worship in a Protestant way, and were no longer naive enough to try to worship openly in a Catholic way, running the risks of censure.[2]

The revolutionary change in public worship during the Reformation in Geneva was from a form of worship centered on the *Mass* (*la messe*) to a form of worship centered on the *sermon* (*le sermon*). Those are in fact the two words contemporaries almost invariably use for the two forms of worship, including most emphatically the secretaries who kept the Consistory registers. A Catholic service of worship is always referred to as a *messe;* a Protestant service of worship is always referred to as a *sermon.*[3] Catholic worship was built around the celebration of the sacrament most important to Christians. Protestant worship was built around an exposition of the Word of God cherished by Christians.

This fact then raises the further question about how people behaved during these services. How did pious Catholics behave during a Mass? How did pious Protestants behave during a sermon? What happened when someone who had been Catholic suddenly found himself or herself in a Protestant service? An important answer to this question is provided by a series of cases heard by the Geneva Consistory dealing with accusations of *barbotement,* of praying rather than listening during church services. Attached to this contribution are a number of examples. They provide fresh evidence not previously used to support this argument. These cases reflect a fundamental difference between traditional Catholic and Protestant approaches to worship, and thus merit intensive exploration.

An initial question one must face in examining these cases is what the word *barbotement* means. We have translated it into English with the word *muttering,* but that does not carry its full flavor. *Barbotement* carries a less neutral and more negative connotation than *muttering.* It can frequently be found in the writings of John Calvin, both in his *Institutes* and in his sermons.[4] He uses it in his rather derogatory descriptions of Catholic prayer, both by priests and by the laity. Most of the examples of sixteenth-century French usage of the term in the standard dictionary of that time prepared by Edmond Huguet, in fact, come from the pen of Calvin himself. Most of the others come from the writings of fellow Reformers like Guillaume Farel.[5] Other dictionaries, to be sure, provide examples of other people using the term. But in many circles it had clearly become a standard Protestant epithet. It reflects a settled belief that prayers as they were then offered by Catholics were repetitious and inaudible, carried no real meaning to those who said them, and were repeated in the superstitious hope that God will be pleased simply by hearing a prayer even if it could not be understood by the petitioner.

These cases occur because it had become settled practice for the devout to say prayers during Mass. Celebration of the Mass was very common in Geneva before the Reformation. There were literally hundreds of Masses celebrated every week. Lambert estimates that there were as many as two hundred in the cathedral church of Saint Pierre alone.[6] Most of these Masses, to be sure, were requiem Masses celebrated by chantry priests either by themselves or before small audiences. But in every one of the seven parish churches there was a High Mass on Sundays and on feast days, which every adult in the parish was expected to attend. It is unlikely that everyone took this requirement seriously and actually did attend these Masses on Sundays and feast days, but it is clear that a fairly high percentage of the population took their religious obligations seriously and did attend.[7]

The experience of attending Mass in those days was quite different from attending Mass in a Catholic church nowadays. The Mass then was basically an esthetic experience. Average observers could not even hear much of what the priest said during a Mass, and could not normally have understood it if they did. The altar and the celebrants were separated from the congregation by a screen. The celebrating priest kept his back to the congregation. He spoke in a low voice that could not be heard by most of them. He spoke in Latin, a language most of them did not fully understand. Observers were instructed not even to try to listen but rather to watch and to say prayers during the Mass. We can find this instruction in French manuals for the faithful back in the Middle Ages and continuing down into the eighteenth century. It is this injunction to say prayers that leads to the phenomenon Calvinists called *barbotement*. Most of these prayers one was encouraged to say during Mass were individual, not communal. They most often included the Pater Noster and the Ave Maria. Sometimes they included the Credo. Sometimes they included other formulaic prayers.[8] One example we find in the *barbotement* cases is of a woman who admitted she had prayed the In manus. This is a reference to a prayer for Compline drawn from Psalm 30:6, "In manus tuas commendo spiritum meum," a prayer that had traditionally been used in Geneva as a part of the Office only during Lent and on festivals.[9] Many worshipers carried a rosary, and used its beads as a guide to the prayers that they were saying. The Mass reached a sharply defined climax with the presiding priest's consecration of the elements, announced by a sacring bell, followed immediately by the elevation in which the priest lifted the Host high above his head so that everyone could see. With that consecration, devout Catholics believe, a miracle occurs and the Host in the priest's hands becomes the body of Christ. The Host, in fact, becomes God. Theologians may quibble that there is a difference between the body of Christ and God, but that is a nuance of which most believers in the sixteenth century were unaware. They were convinced that God had entered the church in this form. They knew that they were expected to display due reverence, to adore this God among them.

There was, to be sure, more to a typical High Mass than the simple celebration of the Sacrament. There was a greeting at the beginning and a benediction at the end. There were prayers by the priest. There were prayers by the congregation, often led by a priest, for specific individuals, living or dead, or for specific ends, like a good harvest or a successful pregnancy. There were readings from Scripture, in Latin, usually a selection from an Epistle, and another, this one sung, from a Gospel. There was the kiss of peace, usually administered to a peace board, first kissed and passed among the clergy, then among the entire congregation. There was aspersion with holy water. There was the distribution of Blessed Bread, usually after the Sacrament.[10] Communion for the laity was not a part of the normal Mass. The elements of the Sacrament themselves were on most occasions offered to the clergy alone. Only on Easter was every member of the parish welcomed and expected to receive Communion, following a careful season of preparation, including a full and proper confession and then absolution for each person intending to receive the Sacrament.[11] The only part of the service that resembled a Protestant sermon was the prone, a brief oral presentation in the vernacular rather than in Latin by the parish priest, usually including some announcements and occasionally some catechetical instruction. There was almost never a proper homily or sermon. Most priests did not know how to preach and were not expected to try.[12] The heart of the religious experience for most of the faithful at most services remained observing the Mass and saying prayers by oneself.

This did not mean that medieval Christians did not hear sermons. They just did not hear them within normal church services. Medieval preachers were usually itinerant professionals, normally friars, who came to a city to preach a series of special sermons during special seasons, most commonly Advent or Lent. They usually preached them in a friary or public building, not in a church. In Geneva that meant that sermons were preached either in a large auditorium in the Franciscan house of Rive, near one of the city gates, or in the large courtyard of a Dominican house, located just outside the city walls in a suburb. That Franciscan auditorium, incidentally, is also where the earliest Protestant sermons were delivered by Guillaume Farel and his colleagues.[13]

The Sacrament, however, remained at the very heart of medieval worship. The primary importance of the crucial consecration and elevation of the Host and the miracle of God's arrival was recognized by everyone. People who were pressed for time often came only for this one crucial moment and left soon after. That did not please the clergy, and there were frequent warnings that one's religious obligation to attend Mass weekly meant an entire Mass, not just part of one.[14] The very fact that the warnings were issued, however, reveals that a number of people in fact were not attending entire Masses.

This means that the average medieval Christian received what was most essential for his or her faith primarily through watching a ritual, the Mass, and particularly the elevation of the Host, attentively and in a proper frame of mind, saying prayers, often bolstered by the smell of incense and the touch of rosary beads. He or she did not receive this essential information through listening to a verbal discourse.

All of this changed dramatically with the Reformation. To begin with, the very number and appearance of the churches changed. In Geneva four of the parish churches were closed, and only three remained open. One of the pre-Reformation parish churches became, after some delay, a lecture hall, where Calvin and others spoke. Another was at first turned over to secular purposes but then reopened as a church when the population doubled in size because of religious refugees at the height of Calvin's ministry. Two others were razed to the ground. The Dominican house was also razed, along with all the buildings in the suburbs. The people who had been living there were all resettled within the walls, to facilitate the defense of the city against armed attack. The Franciscan house was turned into a school. A nearby convent of Clare sisters was turned into the General Hospital, an all-purpose welfare institution, primarily for orphans and severely handicapped people.[15]

The interior of the three surviving parish churches also changed. Partitions were removed, particularly the rood screen that had separated the sacred space around the altar from the lay congregation. In subsequent years other partitions that had blocked off parts of the interior into chapels were removed. The altars on which the Sacrament had been celebrated during Mass were all removed, along with the tabernacles containing the blessed Sacrament and the lights signaling its presence. Statues and other traditional visual aids to worship were removed. The walls seem to have been whitewashed, to cover over paintings. The stained glass in the windows was not destroyed, but not maintained either. The cathedral organ was locked up and no longer used. In the resulting large open spaces, Protestants installed pulpits and benches. A high pulpit for the preacher at the best acoustic location in each church was set up, high enough so that all could see him, with a sounding board above his head to make it easier to hear him. There may have been as well a lower pulpit for the cantor, hired to lead the congregation in the singing of psalms. This is the arrangement one finds in the cathedral church of Saint Pierre today, and it may date back to the time of the Reformation. There were certainly cantors active in services in those days. Special seats for dignitaries, including government leaders, arranged in a very precise order of precedence, were set up in front of the pulpit. The rest of the auditors sat on benches, with most of the women and children together near the pulpit and most of the men behind them, all facing the preacher.[16] There were exceptions to this segregation by gender, however, for those who were hard of hearing. The Consistory a number of times ordered, when someone called before them complained that he or she was hard of hearing and thus could not follow sermons, that he or she receive a special place near the pulpit.[17]

These parish churches, furthermore, were staffed with entirely new ministers. Only one of the formerly Catholic clergy, a man named Jacques Bernard, from a local family of some prominence, who had been a member of the local Franciscan community, was given a position as a preacher in the city of Geneva, and he was soon transferred to a pair of the villages dependent on the city. Two other formerly Catholic clergymen were assigned to village churches. The new preachers were almost all immigrants from France. They were highly educated, although not always in theology.[18] Both Calvin and Théodore de Bèze (Beza), for example, had taken university degrees in law and abundant training in what then was called the humanities and what today we would call classical literature and philosophy, but not in theology.

These new ministers were chosen primarily for their skills as preachers, because they were well trained in rhetoric and had experience in public speaking. They also had to have good strong voices. The acoustics in Geneva's churches were not very good for preaching, and modern forms of electronic amplification had not been invented. Each prospective minister had to appear before the Geneva Company of Pastors and deliver a sample sermon. A candidate could be turned back from appointment as a city minister because his voice was too weak. If he were suitable in other respects, he might receive an appointment as a village minister or as a teacher, but he could not preach in the city.[19]

This pool of talent was assembled in order to make possible a service of a very different character. The worship leader looked very different. Instead of a priest in colorful vestments that changed in each liturgical season, he was a preacher dressed for every service in a plain black robe with a starched white collar, the so-called bands of Geneva. To contemporaries he did not look like a clergyman. He looked like a lawyer. The service was built not around a Sacrament but around a sermon. The sermon was in the form of a commentary on Holy Scripture. The preacher would read a few verses from a selected book of the Bible from a copy set before him in the pulpit and then use his allotted time to explain them.[20] There is some reason to believe that Calvin, about whose sermons we are best informed, read from a Hebrew or Greek original, since it is obvious that he did not use the available French translations, but that cannot be demonstrated with certainty.[21] After defining terms, a preacher would then go through the entire passage explaining its sense to contemporary listeners, occasionally adding some rather pointed applications to current events. Now and then these applications made listeners angry. Fairly often the preachers of Geneva were told to stick to the Bible and stop meddling in politics.[22]

This type of service clearly surprised and baffled many people in Geneva. It took some time for many of them to understand that they were supposed to listen in church, not to become preoccupied with private devotions. That explains the cases of *barbotement* that have been highlighted.[23] Most of those facing this accusation were women. Often they were elderly, no doubt sometimes illiterate. When pressed they would say in some distress that they were simply saying their prayers. They were doing in church exactly what they had been taught to do by their parents as children. It had not occurred to them to listen to a sermon. They would ask, is not this what one is supposed to do in church? The Consistory would reply that it certainly was not what people were supposed to do in church, that they should in effect shut up and listen.[24] These same people then would be called back in later sessions to find out what they were learning from sermons. They would be asked: "When did you last attend a service? Who was the preacher? What was the Bible passage upon which he was commenting?" If they had trouble answering these questions they would be told to go to church more often, to listen to even more sermons, to become more fully acquainted with this new way of acquiring religious truth.[25]

Geneva provided plenty of opportunities to hear sermons, and they kept increasing in the early years of the Reformation. On an average Sunday there were eight full services, plus three catechism services. There was an early service at 4:00 or 5:00 in the morning, depending on the season, intended primarily for servants. There was the main service at about 8:00 in the morning. Catechism was always at noon. Then there was a final service at 2:00 or 3:00 in the afternoon, again depending on the season. Two of the parish churches had this full complement of services. One of them had only two of the three services. There were also several services on Wednesday, a day of prayer, when the hours of work in many establishments were curtailed. And there were also single services every other day of the week.[26] By 1549 it was possible to go to church every day, and several times on some days. There was furthermore an obligation laid on everyone in town to attend service at least once a week, ideally on Sunday. While not everyone lived up to this obligation, a good many did. There is plenty of evidence that the churches were usually crowded, sometimes so crowded that there was not room for everyone who tried to get in. Especially toward the end of Calvin's career, when the population of the city literally doubled because of a flood of religious refugees, crowding became a problem. At times special arrangements had to be made to take care of the overflow.[27]

There remains the question of what people actually learned from listening to these sermons. Some complained to the Consistory that they could not understand sermons, that they were hard of hearing, or simply had a "fat head" that kept them from following an oral argument. The Consistory's normal reaction to these reports was that they should try harder, that they should attend more sermons, that they must acquire the habit of finding out about religion in this way.[28] One suspects that for some it became a ritual without much personal meaning, that many people went to sermons for sociability or because it was expected of them. There is strong evidence, however, that many Genevans did learn from these sermons, that they did absorb some theology. A few could even absorb the essence of debate on doctrines as complex and abstruse as predestination.[29]

Just as the Catholic service did not consist solely of the Sacrament, however, the Protestant service did not consist solely of the sermon. It included individual bidding prayers by the minister. Even more important, it included a number of congregational recitations, the most important of which were the Creed and the Our Father, now in French rather than in Latin. Their use took a somewhat different form than in Catholic services. The Our Father, in particular, was no longer repeated in a low voice by individuals as they observed a sacramental celebration. It was now rather repeated in unison by the entire congregation, led by the preacher of the day, usually two times within each service. Calvin resisted suggestions that it be repeated more than twice, on grounds that this would be a step toward superstition. He felt that Catholic practice had turned this prayer and others into mantras or spells with magical properties, not petitions the meaning of which the worshiper really comprehended.[30] This mantralike use of prayer, furthermore, was confirmed for Protestants by its use in Latin, a language most Europeans did not fully understand, although many of them in fact had acquired a limited knowledge of the Latin used in the liturgy.[31] Recitation of the Lord's Prayer, nevertheless, continued to be an essential part of Protestant services. After all, this was the prayer whose use had been recommended according to the text of the Bible by Jesus himself. It remained fundamental to this as to all other kinds of Christian worship.

The Reformed service also included a cappella singing by the entire congregation. Some of this singing was of texts originally written in prose. There was a setting to music of the Ten Commandments, for example, which was widely used in services. Most of the singing, however, was of Psalms taken from the Old Testament. Arrangements were made to translate the entire Old Testament Book of Psalms into French, by translators of considerable eminence, most notably Clément Marot, a poet from the French royal court who had turned Protestant and fled, and Théodore de Bèze, famous as a Latin poet before his conversion to Protestantism, and Calvin's eventual successor as leader of the Genevan Church. These translations were then set to music by composers of some stature. The most gifted of them was Claude Goudimel, who remained in France and eventually died a martyr's death, but the most prolific was Louis Bourgeois who became cantor of the cathedral church of Saint Pierre in Geneva. Some of his tunes, in fact, are surely familiar to many now, particularly Bourgeois's setting for the 134th Psalm, which is still sung in many American churches as the Doxology.[32]

Genevan services were often accompanied by other rituals. Baptisms had to be celebrated in church, before a congregation with an ordained minister presiding, not in private as before the Reformation. They usually took place after the sermon toward the end of a service, most commonly one of the very early or late Sunday services, not the main one. Marriages also were celebrated during a service, usually before the main service began.[33] Another ritual sometimes accompanying a service was a ceremony of reparation, in which people apologized in public, most commonly for having participated in a Catholic service elsewhere. A number of times there was a ceremony of reconciliation, in which people who had been involved in public quarrels formally forgave each other and were welcomed back into the general community.[34]

The sacrament of Communion also became a part of Protestant services. But it was no longer a daily or weekly part of the service. Communion was offered only four times a year. There were elaborate preparations for each Communion service, parts of which are detailed in the Consistory registers. Elders were assigned to each parish church and charged with assisting the ministers in distributing the Communion elements. This was a procedure, incidentally, which Calvin did not recommend in his publications but which he routinely used in practice. There were some interesting debates among the French Reformed in the seventeenth century on the question of whether elders should be entitled to assist in administering Communion. Both sides appealed to the authority of Calvin. Those who wanted the administration of the elements to be limited to ordained ministers, quoted Calvin's writings. Those who wanted the administration of the elements to be shared with elders or deacons, cited Calvin's practice.[35] This is one point among many where it becomes clear that to understand fully the shape and nature of Calvin's influence, we need to consider his ministry as well as his books.

Of special importance in preparing for quarterly Communion was the drawing up of lists of people who should be denied Communion, who were excommunicated. A number of these people were routinely called before the Consistory in the weeks before a Communion service to see if they were now qualified to receive the Sacrament. A good percentage were usually found ready for Communion, having acquired the additional information they needed to be good Christians, or having purged themselves of the misbehavior that had led to their excommunication. A sentence of excommunication, thus, often lasted only until the next Communion service.[36] We know with some precision the results of excommunication for the sample period 1555–56, thanks to a recent Princeton Seminary dissertation by Jung-Sook Lee. She discovered that in those critical years more than half of the excommunicates about whom she uncovered full records were admitted back to Communion at the next time it was served.[37] There were many, however, about whom she did not uncover full records, who may have been denied Communion for longer periods of time. It is clear in any event that there were a number who were judged to be too ignorant or too stubborn, and could thus remain excommunicate for long periods of time, and who in later years might even be banished from the city altogether.

After each Communion service, furthermore, there would be additional discussion of the ritual during meetings of the Consistory. People who had not taken Communion would be called in for questioning and asked to explain their abstention. People who had ignored sentences of excommunication and contrived to receive Communion anyway, would be called in for scolding and punishment.[38]

It is true that Calvin would have preferred Communion more frequently than once every quarter. But the city government made it clear that they did not want more frequent Communion. Calvin bowed to their will on this point. The issue was not that important to him. It was not as important as the maintenance of discipline, an issue on which he was so intransigent that he threatened to leave the city if he did not have his way.[39] Indeed it can be argued that Calvin made a virtue of necessity and made Communion of greater importance than before by demanding that everyone receive it, by insisting that everyone who received it be judged worthy, and by going to considerable lengths to see to it that recipients were in fact worthy.

Even though there was more to a Protestant service than the sermon, however, just as there was more to a Catholic service than the Sacrament, everyone recognized that the sermon was the climax of the normal service. Busy Protestants would now come late to service but in time to hear the sermon, then leave early, after the sermon but before the benediction, just as busy Catholics had come only to witness the consecration and elevation of the Host.[40] And Protestant preachers, just like their Catholic predecessors, would complain and insist that people were obligated to attend an entire service, not just a select part.

Thus the forms of public worship were changed dramatically in Geneva with the Reformation, and they constituted a form of revolution, a religious revolution to accompany the political revolution that had led to the beginning of the Reformation there. People went to worship in buildings that looked radically different. They were led in worship by ministers of a very different character and appearance. Above all they had to deploy a different set of senses. They were expected to absorb what is most essential in religion through hearing a sermon rather than through observing the celebration of a sacrament. This means that if we want to understand fully early Protestant worship in Geneva, we must consider what it replaced, what it was reacting against. It is important to study worship both before and after the Reformation in this case not because of continuities but because of discontinuities.

Notes

1. For other versions of this argument, see my "The Genevan Revolution in Public Worship," delivered as the second of the Stone lectures at the Princeton Theological Seminary, February 16, 1999, and published in the *Princeton Seminary Bulletin* 20/3, new series (1999): 264–80; "The Genevan Revolution in Christian Worship," delivered as a part of a symposium at the Meeter Center in Grand Rapids, Michigan, May 8, 1999; "Worship in Calvin's Geneva," delivered at the Tenth Colloquium on Calvin Studies, at Columbia Seminary in Decatur, Georgia, January 29, 2000.

2. This contribution also makes frequent use of Thomas A. Lambert, "Preaching, Praying and Policing the Reform in Sixteenth-Century Geneva" (Ph.D. diss., University of Wisconsin-Madison, 1998; available from UMI Dissertation Services, no. 9819828).

3. See for instance the case of Jane Pertennaz, on March 30, 1542, in Robert Kingdon, Thomas Lambert, and Isabella Watt, eds., *Registers of the Consistory of Geneva in the Time of Calvin; Volume 1: 1542–1544,* trans. M. Wallace McDonald (Grand Rapids, Mich: Eerdmans, 2000), 28.

4. John Calvin, *L'institution chrétienne* (Geneva: Labor et Fides, 1955–58; rp., Kerygma/Farel, 1978), 3: 352, 361. See also extensive references to Calvin's use of the term in his sermons in Edmond Huguet, *Dictionnaire de la langue française du seizième siècle* (Paris: Edouard Champion, 1925), I: 484.

5. Huguet, *Dictionnaire* I: 484, under *barboterie.*

6. Lambert, "Preaching, Praying," 91.

7. Ibid., 95–96.

8. Ibid., 97–100.

9. Kingdon, Lambert, and Watt, *Registers of the Consistory,* 144, and n. 561.

10. For further information on the medieval ritual of the Mass, see Lambert, "Preaching, Praying," 125–51.

11. Lambert, "Preaching, Praying," 151–53.

12. Louis Binz, *Vie religieuse et réforme ecclésiastique dans le diocèse de Genève pendant le grand schisme et la crise conciliaire (1378–1450)* (Geneva: Jullien, 1973), 390–92.

13. Lambert, "Preaching, Praying," 283–84.

14. Binz, *Vie religieuse,* 390–91; Lambert, "Preaching, Praying," 118–19.

15. Lambert, "Preaching, Praying," 204–6.

16. Ibid., 203–4, 208–11.

17. Kingdon, Lambert, and Watt, *Registers of the Consistory,* 26, 37, 138, 191.

18. On the pastors of Geneva after the Reformation, see W.G. Naphy, *Calvin and the Consolidation of the Genevan Reformation* (Manchester: Manchester University Press, 1994), 53–83.

19. E.g., the brilliant Latinist Claude Baduel. See Robert M. Kingdon and Jean-François Bergier, eds., *Registres de la Compagnie des Pasteurs de Genève au temps de Calvin* (Geneva: Droz, 1962), II: 66–67, re his "too little voice" and assignment to villages; 76, 77, re later village assignments; 92, re his appointment as a teacher.

20. T.H.L. Parker, *Calvin's Preaching* (Louisville, Ky.: Westminster/John Knox Press, 1992), 80–92.

21. Parker, *Calvin's Preaching,* 80–81. See also Max Engammare, "Calvin connaissait-il sa Bible?" *Bulletin de la Société de l'histoire du protestantisme français* 141 (1995): 163–84.

22. See Lambert's references in "Preaching, Praying," 368.

23. For comment on these cases, see Thomas Lambert, "Cette loi ne durera guère: Inertie religieuse et espoirs catholiques à Genève au temps de la Réforme," *Bulletin, Société d'histoire et d'archéologie de Genève* 23–24 (1993–94): 5–24, especially 16–17, and also in his "Preaching, Praying," 352–58.

24. See the case of Jane Mermet in the accompanying primary sources.

25. Jane Mermet, for example, was recalled on November 30, 1542, and reported on the last sermons she had heard. She was "admonished to frequent the sermons." Kingdon, Lambert, and Watt, *Registers of the Consistory,* 151.

26. Lambert, "Preaching, Praying," 285–91.

27. Ibid., 318–19.

28. See the case of Mama Buctin and his wife, who appeared before the Consistory on August 17, 1542: Kingdon, Lambert, and Watt, *Registers of the Consistory,* 111.

29. For further demonstration of this argument, see Robert M. Kingdon, "Popular Reactions to the Debate Between Bolsec and Calvin," in Willem van t'Spijker, ed., *Calvin: Erbe und Auftrag: Festschrift für Wilhelm Neuser zu seinem 65. Geburtstag* (Kampen: Kok Pharos, 1991), 138–45.

30. Archives d'État de Genève, Registres du Conseil, vol. 44, fol. 268c. (October 28, 1549): "Quant au Pater que l'on le dictz deux fois les dimenches deux fois *[sic]* a chascungs sermontz et aussi au cathezimes et que de faire autrement que cella seroit ung enchantement et ung charme comme aultresfois l'on disoyt *In principio erat verbum.*" Quoted in Lambert, "Preaching, Praying," 328, n. 111. Cf. the similar sentiment in the passage quoted in W. Baum, E. Cunitz, and E. Reuss eds., *Joannis Calvini Opera quae supersunt omnia* (Brunschweig: Schwetschke, 1879), vol. 21, col. 457, also dated October 28, 1549.

31. See Calvin's critique of the use of Latin in prayers in his *Institutes of the Christian Religion* (Philadelphia: Westminster Press, 1960), II: chap. 20, sec. 33, 896.

32. For information on the switch, see O. Douen, *Clément Marot et le psautier Huguenot* (Paris: Imprimerie Nationale, 1878–79), II: 611; and for original sources and the actual melody, see Pierre Pidoux, *Le Psautier Huguenot du XVIe siècle: Mélodies et documents* (Basle: Baerenreiter, 1962), I: 120.

33. Lambert, "Preaching, Praying," 291–96.

34. Kingdon, Lambert, and Watt, *Registers of the Consistory,* 270.

35. See Matteo Campagnolo, Micheline Louis-Courvoisier, and Gabriella Cahier, eds., *Registres de la Compagnie des Pasteurs de Genève,* vol. 9 (1604–6) (Geneva: Droz, 1989): 244–49, a brief by Jacques Royer quoting Calvin, and 276–81, a brief by the Geneva Company of Pastors citing Calvin's practice.

36. Lambert, "Preaching, Praying," 248–49.

37. Jung-Sook Lee, "Excommunication and Restoration in Calvin's Geneva, 1555–1556" (Ph.D. diss., Princeton Theological Seminary, 1997; available from UMI Dissertation Services, no. 9730187), 255–62.

38. Claude Curtet, for instance, had abstained from the Lord's Supper at Easter 1542 because of an ongoing quarrel with his brother. Kingdon, Lambert, and Watt, *Registers of the Consistory,* 53. In 1554 the notary André Vulliod was banished from the city after having his tongue pierced with a hot iron because he partook of the Lord's Supper while excommunicated for blasphemy. See Naphy, *Calvin and the Consolidation,* 187, 193.

39. The dispute between the pastors and the Genevan magistrates over the excommunication of Philibert Berthelier is a case in point. Naphy, *Calvin and the Consolidation,* 184–85.

40. Lambert, "Preaching, Praying," 350.

Complexities of Location and Time Period

The Mass in Sweden: From Swedish to Latin?

FRANK C. SENN

Editors' Introduction

The Reformation in Sweden has a reputation for being conservative. As seen in Frank Senn's essay, Lutherans in Sweden seem remarkably Catholic in practice. While the city of Stockholm moved to a liturgy in Swedish by 1530, the enthusiasm for change was not followed in the rest of the country. For a number of years, both the Latin Mass and the vernacular Mass existed side by side. Thus the issues of change and continuity are not clear-cut in the Swedish context, and overall, the religious policy supported by the king was the deciding factor in the rate of any transformation in Swedish worship.

By the 1570s, the liturgy for the Lutheran Swedish Mass was available in a version that included texts in Swedish but also in Latin. Thus the story of Swedish worship rituals in the sixteenth century is a complex one. In contrast to Robert Kingdon's contribution on Geneva, the Swedish model shows how the pattern and relative weight of continuity and change in liturgy could fluctuate in the early modern period.

Primary Source Introduction

City councils in the early modern period could and did enact rules regarding religious practices in their communities. Church orders and liturgies also provide strong sources for information on religious practice. By looking at these different documents, we can see both how important religious questions were to early modern authorities, and how within one Lutheran country it was possible to uphold different languages for use in the worship of God.

A. Resolution passed by the Stockholm City Council in 1530 as recorded in the Book of Resolutions (*Tänkeboken*) of the Stockholm City Council[1]

> Resolved that no Latin Mass should be held here in the city; therefore that priests and monks should be called to the City Hall and thereupon be forbidden to hold Mass in any other language than Swedish.

B. Excerpts from the Swedish Church Order of Archbishop Laurentius Petri, 1571[2]

1. From the Chapter "Concerning the Lord's Supper, Commonly Called the Mass":

> In country places it is well that Mass is always and entirely celebrated in Swedish. But, lest the Latin language seem to be entirely condemned or allowed entirely to disappear, which all clergy should and must understand, some Latin hymns both in the Mass and at other times shall be used, especially in towns where there are schools, on high festivals or Apostles' Days.

2. From the Chapter on "The Order of the Mass":

> When the priest is to celebrate Mass, he vests himself as is customary, and when he comes before the altar, he may kneel down and make his confession to God privately with the Latin *Confiteor.* Yet it is well that thereafter the Swedish words of confession should be read aloud before the people, not mattering whether it occur immediately at the beginning, or afterwards at the end of the sermon. But otherwise in the Mass he is to follow the manner and order as it is set forth in the Swedish Mass Book.
>
> For the so-called *Introitus,* if it is not sung in Latin, these hymns may be sung alternatively: From the depth of my need; Our Father, Thou in heaven above; O our Father, merciful and good; Now to the Holy Spirit let us pray, etc.

The *Kyrie* may be sung three times or nine, as circumstances require; yet on great festivals it must be sung nine times with different tunes, as is customary, in Latin or Swedish.

If the priest desires to use more than one Collect, he may do so, provided that on all occasions that which is *de tempore* or *de festo* is read first.

For the *Graduale,* if it is not sung in Latin, these hymns may be sung alternatively: He who will a Christian be; God be merciful to us; O Lord God of the kingdom of heaven; O Jesu Christ who took on manhood; Blessed are all those who fear the Lord; A mighty fortress is our God, etc.

Thus when a Swedish hymn is sung for the *Graduale,* it may be left at that, and nothing further sung in Latin, unless for various reasons a delay should arise.

The Christian Sequences may also be sung sometimes, especially on these festivals: Christmas, Easter, Holy Thursday, and Whitsunday. Likewise that which by custom has been called the *Tractus* may be sung in Lent. Yet it is sufficient that two or three of them be sung together, so that time is not taken away from the Sermon, concerning which special care should be taken.

On Christmas Day the Sequences *Grates nunc omnes* may be used, with the Swedish hymn of praise, *Praise be thou, Jesu Christ,* between the verses, or *Letabundes,* and between every two verses the hymn, Christ is born of a pure virgin, etc.

At Easter *Victimae paschali* is sung with the Swedish Hymn of Praise, Christ is risen from the dead, between every two verses, except the first, after which the Hymn of Praise is sung immediately.

The *Symbolum* is usually sung in Swedish, yet in order that the *Symbolum Latinum,* which is well known, be not forgotten, it may also in the same way be sung in the towns, especially on all Apostles' Days.

Elevation, Mass vestments, altars, altar cloths, lights, and whatsoever of these ceremonies there are, such as have been adopted here in the kingdom since God's pure word has been preached, we may freely retain as indifferent matters, although such things have been set aside in other countries through the same freedom; yet, if any circumstances arise which require any change in these things, this may be freely done.

Notes

1. *Tänkeboken,* 349. Cited in David Lindquist, *Första-mässa i Stockholm: En liturgihistorisk studie* (Stockholm: Samlingar och studier till svenska kyrkans historia [SSSKH] 12, 1945), 26f. Translated by Frank C. Senn.

2. Cited in Eric E. Yelverton, *An Archbishop of the Reformation, Laurentius Petri Nericius, Archbishop of Uppsala, 1531–73. A Study of His Liturgical Projects* (Minneapolis: Augsburg, 1959), 119–21. Translation revised by Frank C. Senn.

This essay seeks to explore change and continuity in the celebration of the Mass in Sweden from the late medieval Latin Mass to the Reformation Swedish Mass. This change and continuity is bound up with the political course of the Reformation in the Kingdom of Sweden and Finland in the sixteenth century. We will specifically raise the question of why it seems that the Swedish Mass "regressed" (from the Reformation point of view) from an all-vernacular Mass in 1531, through successive revisions, to a bilingual Swedish-Latin rite in 1557 and 1571 (also in 1576). Because this is a complicated story, it may be helpful for the reader to have at the outset a chronology of the Reformation in Sweden and the successive liturgical revisions to which to refer.

1517 Luther's 95 Theses; the Swedes depose Gustav Trolle, the Archbishop of Uppsala, in a typical late medieval church-state conflict.

1520 Stockholm "bloodbath" perpetrated by Danish king Christian II; war of independence waged against Denmark.

1523 Gustav Vasa, hero of the resistance against Denmark, elected king of Sweden; Reformation ideas are promoted in Stockholm.

1526 Publication of *A Useful Teaching* (a catechism) and the Swedish New Testament, both primarily the work of Olavus Petri.

1527 The Estates assemble at Västerås; the Church is placed under the authority of the state, although there is no official break with the papacy.

1528 Translation into Swedish of Luther's German Postil (sermons for the Church year).

1529 Publication of Olavus Petri's vernacular *Manual* (book of occasional services).

1530 Publication of Olavus Petri's Postil.

1530 Stockholm City Council passes a resolution ordering the Mass to be celebrated in Swedish in Stockholm.

1531 Publication of Olavus Petri's *Swedish Mass.*

1531 Laurentius Petri is elected Archbishop of Uppsala by a synod of clergy from throughout the dioceses of the National Church.

1535 First revision of the *Swedish Mass* by Olavus Petri—nucleus of a pericope system restored.

1536 Publication of the Swedish Hymnal.

1536 Church council at Örebrö promotes the use of the *Swedish Mass* and *Manual* throughout the realm, but without royal enforcement.

1537 Second revision of the *Swedish Mass* by Olavus Petri—selection of collects in Swedish expanded; introits and graduals provided to be sung in Swedish or Latin.

1539 King Gustav I appoints the German George Norman to be his Ordinary and Superintendent of the Clergy (a minister of ecclesiastical affairs whose authority transcended that of the bishops). This signaled the creation of a state Church and a break with Rome.

1541 Publication of the full Swedish Bible (the joint work of Olavus and Laurentius Petri).

1541 Third revision of the *Swedish Mass* by Laurentius Petri—further Latin options provided for the priest's Confiteor (Confession of sins), introits and graduals, and Apostles' Creed.

1548 Fourth revision of the *Swedish Mass* by Laurentius Petri—reintroduction of the Nicene Creed and a Latin Communion anthem ("Discubuit Jesus et discipulis" [Jesus and His Disciples Will Take Their Place at This Table]); addition of Swedish hymn "O Pure Lamb of God" after the Agnus Dei; four additional post-Communion collects, three of which were translated from the Latin missals.

1557 Fifth revision of the *Swedish Mass* by Laurentius Petri—an appendix added with a complete cycle of collects for the Church year.

1560 Death of King Gustav I; accession of Erik XIV.

1561 Handwritten Church Order circulated by Archbishop Petri; royal sanction withheld.

1567 Laurentius Petri's treatise *Concerning Church Ordinances and Ceremonies.*

1568 Deposition of King Erik XIV; accession of Johan III.

1571 Promulgation of Laurentius Petri's *The Swedish Church Order* by royal and ecclesiastical authority.

1573 Death of Archbishop Petri.

1574 Ten Articles promulgated at the Church council in Stockholm sketching a plan to return to the spirit of the ancient Church.

1575 *New Church Order (Nova Ordinantia Ecclesiastica)* promulgated by King Johan III.

1576 *Liturgy of the Swedish Church Conforming to the Catholic and Orthodox Tradition (Liturgia svecanae ecclesiae catholicae et orthodoxae conformis)* prepared by King Johan III and promulgated throughout the realm by Archbishop Laurentius Petri Gothus; a liturgical struggle followed.

1583 A *Directory of Public Worship* accepted by the Church which licensed Latin Masses in some circumstances, also noncommunicant masses, and restored medieval musical settings of the Mass.

1592 Death of King Johan III; accession of the Catholic Sigismund III Vasa of Poland.

1593 A national Church council in Uppsala abolishes the Liturgy of King Johan III, restores the 1571 *Church Order* of Laurentius Petri, and adopts the Augsburg Confession.

The late medieval Swedish missal traditions provided texts for the Swedish Mass,[1] but the order of the Reformation Mass in Sweden was influenced by similar reforms of the Mass in Lutheran Germany. It is now well accepted that the order of the Swedish Mass published by Olavus Petri (a.k.a. Olaf Petersson, 1493–1552) in 1531 follows Martin Luther's *Formula Missae et Communionis* (Form of the Mass and Communion) for the Church at Wittenberg (1523), as mediated by the Order of Mass prepared by Andreas Döber for the New Hospital in Nuremberg in 1525. Döber's Order in turn was included in Sluter's *Rostock Hymnal* (1531), which, Conrad Bergendoff suggested, may have been the source used by Olavus Petri.[2] The tell-tale feature that signals the close relationship between Luther's *Formula Missae* and the Swedish Mass is the arrangement of the eucharistic prayer: Preface, leading to the Words of Institution, followed by the Sanctus. No other Reformation Mass-order followed Luther's eucharistic structure. Olavus Petri's eucharistic preface is more expansive than Luther's since it is based, as Yngve Brilioth noted, on the Praefatio Paschalis (Easter Preface).[3] Unlike Luther's *Formula Missae,* Olavus Petri's Swedish Mass is entirely in the vernacular. But Luther had also provided a completely vernacular liturgy in his *Deutsche Messe* (German Mass, 1526). Thus, Olavus Petri took the *order* of Luther's *Formula Missae* as regards the eucharistic prayer, but took the *example* of Luther's *Deutsche Messe* in producing an entirely vernacular liturgy. In this he seems to have been following the ordinance passed by the city council of Stockholm in 1530 that forbade the Mass to be celebrated "in any other language than Swedish." Yet, in the Church Order provided by his brother, Archbishop Laurentius Petri (a.k.a. Lars Petersson, 1499–1573), some forty years later, provision is made for parts of the Mass to be done in Latin. In what would seem to many students of the Reformation as a "backward" move, did the Reformation Mass in Sweden move from being entirely in Swedish to being a bilingual Latin-Swedish liturgy? The purpose of this essay is to explore this question by considering what might have been meant by the Stockholm resolution and by delineating the development that led to the provisions for Latin liturgy in the Swedish Church Order.

It is not surprising that Olavus Petri took cues from Martin Luther in his reform of the Mass in Sweden. Olavus had been a student of Luther's at Wittenberg between 1516 and 1518. There had been no break with the old Church before Olavus returned to Sweden. In fact, he had not experienced any liturgical change while in Germany, and certainly not the iconoclasm that was unleashed on Wittenberg by Andreas Bodenstein von Karlstadt in 1521–22 while Luther was sequestered for safekeeping in the Wartburg. The violence that Luther returned to quell determined his approach to liturgical reform thereafter: it was cautious, if not conservative. Olavus would not have experienced the social upheaval that prompted Luther's reaction to radical reform, but as a man in tune with the generally conservative character of his countrymen, he would also lean toward a conservative liturgical reform.

On the whole the Lutheran reforms of the Mass represent continuity more than discontinuity as far as the order of the Mass is concerned, but also as far as the style of celebration of the Mass is concerned. The liturgy of the Word often remained unchanged in the order of the Lutheran Mass, but the offertory was totally deleted and the Canon of the Mass (eucharistic prayer) was radically revised if not eliminated entirely (except for the words of institution).[4] However, it should be remembered that in the Catholic Mass, the offertory prayers and the Canon of the Mass had been recited silently while the choir sang the Offertorium and Sanctus, respectively. So these texts would not have been missed by ordinary Lutheran worshipers. What would have been missed were the Latin language and the ceremonies of the Mass. But in Lutheran practice Latin could remain either throughout the Mass (as in Luther's *Formula Missae,* which, he said in his introduction to the German Mass, he was not prepared to abandon), or in part (as in the Brandenburg-Nuremberg Church Order of 1533 and Mark Brandenburg Church Order of 1540). Altars, candles, and traditional vestments remained in use. Singing by the congregation (vernacular hymns) and the choir (Latin propers and ordinary) and the use of the organ were actually augmented in Lutheran worship, while liturgical artworks in the places of worship had a somewhat secure position as teaching devices if not as aids in devotion.

Not only was the radical iconoclasm of other Reformations by and large avoided in Lutheranism, but the musical and artistic expressions of liturgy that had developed in the Western Middle Ages were actually augmented. It can no longer be held that vernacular hymn-singing existed only in paraliturgical devotions or as an add-on to the Mass in the Middle Ages. We know that the German carol "Christ ist erstanden" ("Christ is arisen") was sung by the congregation between verses of the Easter sequence "Victimae paschali laudes" ("Praises to the Paschal Victim"), as well as after the Psalms in the Vespers of Easter. Vernacular stanzas sung by the people were interspersed with stanzas of the processional hymns "Gloria, laus, et honor" ("All Glory, Laud and Honor") for Palm Sunday and "Salve festa Dies" ("Hail, Thee, Festival Day") for Easter. As William Anthony Ruff has argued, if the people sang during the Mass, this must be considered a part of the liturgical event and not just peripheral to it.[5] Luther and his musical and poetic collaborators expanded on this tradition of vernacular congregational singing. Moreover, not only did altars, candles, crosses, crucifixes, paintings, and statues remain in churches used for Lutheran worship, but artists like Lucas Cranach the Younger (1515–86) led the way in painting monumental altar panels in Lutheran churches in the mid-sixteenth century. These altar panels depicted allegorically themes in evangelical theology such as law and gospel, Word and Sacrament. Thus, actual practice vindicated Luther's assertion in the *Formula Missae* that "it is not now nor ever has been our intention to abolish the liturgical service of God completely, but rather to purify the one that is now in use from the wretched accretions which corrupt it and to point out an evangelical use."[6]

The resolution of the Stockholm City Council in 1530, abolishing the Latin Mass, was published by civil authority with the sufferance of King Gustav I Vasa, but it applied only to the city of Stockholm.[7] The king was not prepared to extend the abolition of the Latin Mass to the entire nation. Perhaps he was politically sensitive to the presence of a strong German community in Stockholm which was aware of how the Reformation was implemented in the free cities in Germany (within the Holy Roman Empire) through its contacts in the Hanseatic League. In the early years of his reign (1523–60) Gustav Vasa had ample reason to be attuned to German ideas. He had come to power as a hero in Sweden's war of national liberation from Denmark with financial help from the Hanseatic city of Lübeck. He continued to depend on Hanseatic funding to secure Swedish independence. So he was not inclined to alienate the German community in Stockholm.

Moreover, Gustav Vasa was inclined to embrace the Reformation since it gave him license to appropriate church lands and other resources to fill Sweden's empty royal treasury and repay the debt owed to Lübeck. But there had been a revolt in the province of Dalarna in 1527 over high taxes, the preaching of the new Lutheran doctrines, and the king's appropriation of Church treasures. Gustav brought together the Estates to a Riksdag (Parliament) at Västerås in 1527 to work out a compromise between the prerogatives of the Church and the needs of the new state. As a result of this meeting it was decided that all revolts against the king should be put down and punished, and that the king should take the castles and lands of the bishops and provide the bishops with an annual revenue. Furthermore, the nobles were to resume that part of their inheritance that had passed to the Church since 1454, if they could substantiate their claims. At the same time, preachers were to proclaim "the pure word of God . . . according to God's command, but not uncertain miracles, human inventions and fables, as has been much used heretofore."[8] On the other hand, the commoners urged the king to preserve "good old Christian customs," and there was no break with the papacy.[9]

Because of this agreement, Gustav Vasa was not inclined to impose the particular doctrines and practices of the Reformation on the whole nation. He was more than inclined, however, to plunder parish churches of the plate, vessels, vestments, candlesticks, and other valuables with which parishioners had endowed their churches.[10] One of the worst uprisings was the "church bell rebellion" in 1531, occasioned by Gustav's order that each parish church should contribute one church bell to national defense (to be melted down to make armaments).

The decisions at Västerås, however, had a profound bearing on the life of the Church. A Church council was convened in Örebrö in February 1529 to consider especially how to implement the resolution calling for preaching "the pure word of God." There had been many complaints from priests that they were not able to preach the biblical sermons that were now expected. Indeed, the standard education of priests had been only to teach them how to celebrate the Latin Mass. The bishops and other Church leaders at Örebrö agreed to provide daily readings and instruction in the interpretation of the Scriptures in the cathedrals, schools, and monasteries. Model sermons could be provided in church postils; indeed, a translation of a part of Luther's German Postil (1526) had appeared in 1528. Preachers were also to expound on the Lord's Prayer, the Creed, the Ave Maria, and the Ten Commandments one or two times a month "for the good of young and simple folk." Also, "prayer shall precede and follow the sermon." This indicates that the bishops and reformers decided to make use of the late medieval preaching office known as Prone, which included such vernacular elements as hymns, intercessory prayer, and catechetical material. The council also decided to restrict the number of saints' days, make confession and fasting noncompulsory, and provide evangelical interpretations of the old Catholic customs that were still being observed.[11]

As a result of the decisions of Västerås and Örebrö, rebellions broke out in the southern provinces of Västergötland and Småland. The leaders of the uprising gave as reasons for the revolt changes in Church teaching and liturgical practice. Among their charges were that the king had introduced the Lutheran heresy into the realm, despoiled the cloisters and churches, and taken away the tithes and offerings that should go to the churches. According to the rebels, he had also degraded and debased the sacraments, given influential positions in the Church to heretics and renegade monks, taken away confession, confirmation, and unction, and had the Mass celebrated in Swedish.[12] The uprisings were soon put down. The principal leaders, Ture Jönsson and Bishop Magnus of Skara, were given asylum in Denmark over the protests of King Gustav. The king sent out a public letter reminding his subjects that the Recess of the Västerås Riksdag had ordered the preaching of "the pure word of God" and preservation of "good old Christian customs," implying that he was only enforcing what the Estates had ordered.

These experiences also convinced the king that he should exercise caution in promoting the Reformation. It is evident that commitment to the Reformation varied widely in Sweden, and that the provinces were not as convinced of the need for reform as the city of Stockholm. King Gustav, ever the pragmatic politician, allowed the Reformers to preach their doctrines openly and made the printing presses available to them (since he claimed he had no authority over the Word of God), but he allowed no national Church Order to be published. Rather, following the model of Stockholm, he allowed each municipality and parish to make its own decisions regarding liturgical change, whether, for example, the Mass would be held in Latin or Swedish.

This is also why no Church Order was published for the whole realm, such as happened in Denmark in 1537 when the new king Christian III invited Johannes Bugenhagen from Wittenberg to prepare a Church Order for the whole kingdom of Denmark and Norway. The Reformation was implemented in Denmark and Norway in one fell swoop (although King Christian proceeded carefully in Norway, where Reformation ideas were slower to penetrate the populace outside of cities like Bergen and Trondheim). The Swedish Church Order had to await not only the death of King Gustav in 1560, but also the deposition in 1568 of his eldest son and first successor, Erik XIV, who was inclined toward Calvinism and insanity (no intrinsic connection intended). The next king, Johan III, the second son of Gustav Vasa, was sympathetic to the religious confession expressed in the Swedish Church Order (which might justly be termed evangelical catholic). Until 1571, therefore, no liturgical uses were mandated throughout the entire Church of Sweden. Synods of the Church could only make recommendations. A synod convened in Uppsala in 1536 recommended that the Mass be reformed and adopted a resolution approving the use of the Manual and Swedish Mass of Olavus Petri.[13] But the force of this resolution remained ambiguous since royal sanction was withheld.

It is remarkable that there was no published Swedish-language Mass at the time the Stockholm resolution abolishing the Latin Mass was adopted. Olavus Petri, a deacon of the diocese of Strängnäs, was the preacher at the Great Church *(Storkyrkan)* in Stockholm and secretary of the city council. It was typical of the German and Swiss cities that the preacher of the Great Church led the way toward reform in both pulpit and city hall and then published the reformed liturgy. Examples of such preachers include Lazarus Spengler and Andreas Osiander in Nuremberg, Nikolaus Hausmann in Zwickau, Johann Brenz in Schwäbisch-Hall, Huldrych Zwingli in Zurich, Johannes Oecolampadius in Basel, Matthias Zell and Martin Bucer in Strasbourg, and Guillaume Farel and John Calvin in Geneva. Following this pattern, it was only after securing the resolution abolishing the Latin Mass in Stockholm that Olavus Petri published his Swedish Mass in 1531: *Then Swenska messan epter som hon nw j Stockholm holles* (The Swedish Mass as it is now celebrated in Stockholm).[14] The Order of this "Evangelical Mass in Swedish" in its published form is as follows:

Invitation to Confession
Confession of Sins
Prayer for forgiveness said "over the people"
Introit: "some psalm or other song of praise taken out of scripture"
Kyrie eleison (three times)
Gloria in excelsis
Salutation and Collect (the one printed or another for the season)
Epistle (a continuous reading of an epistle by a chapter or a half)
Gradual: "the hymn about God's commandments or some other hymn"
Gospel
Creed: either Apostles' or Nicene (only the Apostles' was printed)
The Preface Dialogue and Paschal Preface leading to the Words of Institution
Elevation of the Host and chalice after the words over each
Sanctus
The Lord's Prayer
The Peace
The Agnus Dei
An Exhortation, if the priest thinks it necessary, and time permits
Administration of the bread and cup to the people
A Swedish hymn or the Nunc Dimittis in Swedish
The post-Communion prayer
The Salutation and Benedicamus
The Aaronic Benediction (but the priest says, "The Lord bless us and keep us," rather than, "The Lord bless you and keep you")

Briefly, we would note that this Order of Mass follows exactly the medieval *Ordo Missae* except that the offertory is omitted and the canon is reworked. The Confession of Sins and Exhortation to the communicants are entirely new texts. Other texts are translations of Latin texts. The provision of whole Psalms to be used as introits, or hymn substitutes, and the Aaronic Benediction reflects Luther's uses. All of the canticles and hymns may be "sung or said." This rubric, along with the omission of a specified place for a sermon within the order of Mass, suggests that what Olavus provided was a low Mass or Communion service. At a High Mass there would have been a place for a sermon but not for general administration of Communion. But following Luther, who argued in his *Formula Missae* that "since the Gospel is the voice crying in the wilderness and calling unbelievers to faith, it seems particularly fitting to preach before mass,"[15] Olavus wrote that "Mass shall not be held unless preaching has preceded."[16]

Olavus's younger brother, Laurentius, having also studied at Wittenberg, was elected archbishop of Uppsala in 1531 by a national convocation of the whole Church in Sweden. Archbishop Petri guided the further development of the Swedish Mass through successive revisions (1535, 1537, 1541) up to the *Messan på swensko* (*Mass in Swedish*) of 1557. The order of the 1557 Mass in Swedish is as follows:[17]

Invitation, Confession of Sins, and Absolution as in the Swedish Mass and/or the Latin Confiteor and Misereatur (the Swedish Confession may also be used after the sermon).

Introit: a Latin psalm, a Swedish hymn of praise, or the Introitus de tempore.

Kyrie eleison (three times).

Gloria in excelsis in Swedish (Ära wari Gudh i högden [All glory be to God on high]).

Salutation and Collect (Laurentius restored the historic cycle of collects in Swedish translation, although they were off by one Sunday after Trinity because he omitted one that seemed too Pelagian).

Epistle: continuous reading or historic pericope selection.

Gradual: the traditional Latin Gradual or a Swedish hymn.

Gospel.

Sermon (also provided for in this location in the 1541 revision of the Swedish Mass). If the sermon was within the Office of Prone, the general intercessions would occur after the sermon and the office might conclude with the Confession of Sins, as noted above.

The Apostles' or Nicene Creed said or sung in either Swedish or Latin.

Eucharistic preface leading to the Words of Institution as in 1531 (with a musical setting).

Sanctus.
The Lord's Prayer.
The Peace.
The Agnus Dei in Swedish (O Gudz Lamb) followed by the Swedish hymn "O Rene Gudz Lamb" ("O Pure Lamb of God").
Optional Exhortation.
The Administration of the bread and cup.
A post-Communion prayer (from a selection of five).
The Salutation and Benedicamus.
The Aaronic Benediction.

It is clear from the ample directions for singing the Psalms, canticles, hymns, Creed, eucharistic preface, and words of institution, as well as the inclusion of a sermon, that this is a High Mass, but with general administration of Communion. It has been fully provisioned with additional texts of collects and the possibility of using the traditional lectionary. The common preface may be used instead of the expanded paschal preface, which provides the option of a briefer prayer of consecration (perhaps for a weekday celebration). No directions are given regarding the preparation of the elements on the altar. We may assume that this was done either before the Mass or during the singing of the Creed. A small woodcut in the printed Mass pamphlet above the common preface shows a priest wearing a chasuble giving the Sacrament to a communicant who is kneeling at the altar.

Three years after the publication of the 1557 Mass in Swedish, King Gustav died and was succeeded by his eldest son, Eric XIV. In 1561 Archbishop Petri prepared a handwritten manuscript of a Church Order which included this Order of Mass. The new king had Calvinist leanings and was not prepared to sanction this Church Order. He was playing up his Calvinist leanings because he was also competing in a pool of eligible royal bachelors for the hand of Queen Elizabeth I of England in marriage. Ten years later, after the accession of Johan III, who had Catholic leanings because of his marriage to the sister of King Sigismund II of Poland, the old archbishop was finally able to get his Church Order authorized and promulgated. In this official Swedish Church Order *(Den svenska kyrkoordningen)* which applied to the entire National Church (including Stockholm), we find the following paragraph at the end of the chapter "On the Lord's Supper, Commonly Called the Mass": "In country places it is well that the Mass be always and entirely celebrated in Swedish. But, lest the Latin language, which all clerks should and must understand, seem to be entirely condemned or allowed entirely to disappear, some Latin hymns both in the Mass and at other times shall be used, especially in towns where there are schools, on high festivals or Apostles' Days."

The chapter "The Order of the Mass," which follows, specifies which parts of the Mass could remain (or be reinstated) in Latin: the priest's silent confession (Confiteor), in addition to the Swedish prayer of confession read aloud before the people; the Introitus or a vernacular hymn; the nine-fold Kyrie; and the Graduale or a vernacular hymn. Other sections that could be in Latin included the "Christian Sequences" for Christmas Day ("Grates nunc omnes," interspersed with the Swedish hymn "Praised Be Thou, Jesu Christ") and Easter Day ("Victimae paschali," interspersed with the Swedish hymn "Christ Is Risen from the Dead"); sequences for Holy Thursday and Pentecost (sequences not specified); the Tractus during Lent; and the *Symbolum Latinum* (the Nicene Creed), especially on all Apostles' Days, could also use Latin. Since the Church Order goes no further in outlining the Order of the Mass, which otherwise follows and now makes definitive the form of the Swedish Mass published in 1557, it would seem that the main purpose of the chapter "The Order of the Mass" is really to indicate which parts of the Mass could be sung in Latin.

Does the 1571 Church Order reflect a reversion to pre-Reformation ways in the second generation of the Reformation in Sweden? Or were other dynamics at work—both liturgically and politically? Moreover, what did the Stockholm City Council understand by "the Mass in Swedish" when no published *ordo missae suecana* existed? What liturgical experiments had been taking place in Stockholm before 1530? How did these changes play with the temper of the Swedes when they were transported to the country as a whole?

We have referred to the revolt in Dalarna in 1527 and the further unrest in Småland and Västergötland in 1529 caused by the plundering of parish churches and liturgical changes. Specifically what these changes were is difficult to ascertain. But the accusation that "the Mass had been changed so as to be held in Swedish" suggests that there could have been early experimentations in vernacular liturgy, due in part to geographical proximity to Denmark. For instance, Hans Tausen, a priest in Malmö at the southern tip of the Scandinavian peninsula across the strait from Copenhagen (Skåne was Danish territory in the sixteenth century), had published a Danish hymnal and Order of Mass based on Luther's *Formula Missae* and *Deutsche Messe* in 1528.[18] Certainly there were at least discussions about vernacular liturgy and other reforms in the Stockholm City Council in 1529–30 leading up to the resolution.

Olavus Petri's Swedish Mass was subtitled "as it is now celebrated in Stockholm." This implies that the Mass was being celebrated in Swedish; certainly the 1530 city council resolution assumed that a form of Swedish Mass was available when it mandated holding the Mass in Swedish in all parishes of the city. What was this form and how early was it in use?

A verse-chronicle of Stockholm published by Messenius in 1629 says:

On Master Olof's wedding day
Our Lutherdom had made such sway
That mass in Swedish first was sung
So all men followed their own tongue.
For so had Master Olof seen
How things at Wittenberg had been
There first at Carlstadt's wedding-feast
Was German mass said by a priest.[19]

There are several problems with this chronology. Karlstadt was married on January 19, 1522, after his famous Christmas Day Mass in Wittenberg in which the words of institution were said in German and Communion was administered in both kinds. Olavus Petri's wedding day was February 11, 1525. But this was before his reformatory writings began to appear in 1526, including the New Testament in Swedish and the first little Swedish hymnal. It seems that 1525 would have been too early for a Swedish Mass.

However, what Karlstadt actually did in Wittenberg on Christmas Day suggests what the first steps toward vernacular liturgy in Swedish might have been. As Christer Pahlmblad has recently suggested, during the Middle Ages and into the sixteenth century the word *Mass* sometimes referred only to the act of consecration.[20] Thus, as with Karlstadt's so-called German Mass in 1521, it may have been deemed sufficient simply to recite the Words of Institution in Swedish to have a Swedish Mass. Furthermore, Olavus Petri's translation of the New Testament into Swedish in 1526 would have provided for the Epistle and Gospel readings in the vernacular. His Postil of 1530 *(En liten postilla),* published in response to the Örebrö Council in 1529, also provided translations of catechetical material that was probably used in the late medieval pulpit office known as Prone. The catechectical texts were used either before the Mass (if it was a Low Mass or communion service) or within the Mass after the Gospel reading (if it was a Latin High Mass). Zwingli had already made use of this pulpit office as his liturgy of the Word for Zurich in 1525. It comprised the Bidding Prayer (intercessions), Our Father, Hail Mary, sermon, announcements of deaths, and Confession of Sins.[21] The material provided in Olavus Petri's Postil included vernacular forms of the introductory and concluding prayers of the pulpit office, the Our Father, Hail Mary, Apostles' Creed, and Ten Commandments, as well as an admonition before Mass began and an exhortation to communicants.[22] Thus, already by 1530 it would have been possible to celebrate a Mass in which the Epistle and Gospel readings, the sermon, intercessory prayers, Our Father, Hail Mary, Apostles' Creed, Ten Commandments, possibly the Confession of Sins, the exhortation to the communicants, and the Words of Institution were in Swedish.

In addition, we must remember that the Reformation inherited from the Middle Ages two styles of celebration: the Low Mass (at which people might receive Communion) and the High Mass (at which they usually did not receive Communion). We may thus conclude that what Olavus Petri provided was a Low Mass and that the Latin High Mass continued to be celebrated, albeit with a vernacular pulpit office and consecration of the Sacrament using the form in the Swedish Mass. In the understanding of the time, it could still be claimed that in all the parishes in Stockholm the Mass was not being celebrated "in any other language than Swedish."

We have seen that the Synod of Uppsala in 1536 approved the use of the Swedish Mass for the entire realm. But this use remained voluntary and had to be decided by each municipality and parish. Pahlmblad has searched parish records to find evidence of the introduction of the Swedish Mass. Two such instances are telling: the Mass was celebrated in Swedish for the first time in Skellefteå (a town on the coast some 300 kilometers north of Stockholm) on Christmas Day in 1536, "but it was not much welcomed." And in the parish church of Umeå (in the same vicinity) the Mass was celebrated in Swedish for the first time on Candlemas in 1537. In both parishes the Latin Mass continued along with the Swedish Mass until the 1540s.[23] These examples illustrate that change was slow in coming, especially away from Stockholm.

The resolution of the Uppsala synod of 1536, approving the use of the Swedish Mass of Olavus Petri, was not carried out uniformly in all dioceses. When Bishop Johannes Magni of Linköping, a learned and well-traveled man, returned from the meeting in Uppsala, he sent out with his cathedral chapter an encyclical to his clergy in which he discussed the resolutions of the synod. Enclosed in this encyclical was a Latin Mass, which, according to the letter, could be celebrated in the vernacular if the congregation and its pastor so desired (although no translation was provided). In a detailed study of this "Missa Lincopensis," Kjöllerström demonstrated that it was a revision of the Order of Mass in the *Breviarium Lincopense* based on the weekday votive Masses; hence the omission of the Gloria and Credo, in which the texts were revised to infuse an evangelical spirit into the old rite. The model for the liturgical revisions might have been Johannes Oecolampadius's *Das Testament Jesu Christi* (1528). All references to the Mother of God and the saints in the prayers were eliminated, and in their place, as in the Confiteor, were *"omnes sancti christifideles."*[24]

It is interesting that in his 1537 revision of the Swedish Mass, Olavus Petri also made provision for an evangelical Latin Confiteor that could be said by the priest. He also made provision for the use of the Introit and

Gradual in Latin (though not without calling attention to the fact that a Swedish Psalter now existed!).[25] This allowance may have been designed to gain greater acceptance of the Swedish Mass outside of Stockholm. Provisions for chants, however, indicate that the Swedish Low Mass was being gradually transformed into a Swedish High Mass.

Provisions for a sung Swedish Mass were furthered by Archbishop Laurentius Petri. In 1540 the first rudiments of a Church Order appeared under the authority of the king's ordinarius for ecclesiastical affairs, his German counselor George Norman. Article IV of these *Articuli Ordinantiae,* in Latin and Swedish, direct that the *Summa Missa* (i.e., the Latin High Mass) should continue to be celebrated daily. Considering the more ruthless approach to implementing aspects of the Reformation being pursued at the time by Norman, the hand of the archbishop must have been in these articles. Norman ceased being the King's ordinarius in 1545, and thereafter liturgical reform was guided entirely by Archbishop Petri. The 1548 revision of the Swedish Mass for the first time included the Nicene Creed printed in Swedish (hitherto it had only been referred to in its Latin text) and Olavus Petri's lovely Swedish hymn "Pure Lamb of God" was added after the Agnus Dei. In the Vadstena Articles in 1552 a distinction was made for the first time between the "said" and the "sung" Mass, the former being entirely in Swedish and the latter being in Swedish and Latin. The archbishop's last revision of the Swedish Mass in 1557 was, as we have seen, a blending of the Swedish and Latin along the lines later specified in the 1571 Church Order.

In 1568 Laurentius Petri prepared in manuscript form the treatise *De Officijs Ecclesiasticis* (Concerning the Ecclesiastical Offices), instructing students in the cathedrals to sing daily in Latin the seven canonical prayer offices and the Latin propers of the High Mass.[26] This was the year of King Johan III's accession to the throne. Johan III was completely in sympathy with the archbishop's "evangelical catholicism" and was prepared to carry it even further after Laurentius Petri's death in 1573.[27] The whole system of Latin canonical hours and Latin propers in the cathedrals was not abolished until 1614. Even so, books of Latin chants were published in Sweden as late as 1620.[28] The use of Latin undoubtedly continued in the schools and universities.

Messenius's verse-chronicle, published during the reign of Sweden's first "authentically Lutheran" king, Gustav II Adolf, who took his army to Germany during the Thirty Years' War to rescue Lutheranism from the forces of Catholicism, expresses the view of the age of Lutheran orthodoxy that Lutheran ideas and practices had been immediately implemented upon their arrival in Sweden and that they were welcomed by the people. After the old medieval liturgical books—the Breviary with the Antiphonary and the Missal with the Graduale—were replaced with vernacular hymnals during the course of the seventeenth century, a more characteristically Lutheran liturgical ethos developed in the Church of Sweden. Thereafter the very gradual transformation of the Mass in Sweden from Swedish Low Mass/Latin High Mass to Swedish High Mass/Latin Propers would not have been so obvious to liturgical historians who might also be imbued with the romanticism of later times.

Liturgical history cannot be studied solely from the point of view of published liturgical orders. In the case of Sweden we have seen that the Reformation developed for two generations before there was an authorized Church Order to regulate practice throughout the whole national Church. During the years between 1530 and 1571 local parishes were free to determine the speed with which they would embrace liturgical change, or whether they would embrace it at all. Unfortunately for the study of actual liturgical change, sources documenting medieval Swedish customs and practices are sparse and those describing the implementation of the Reformation in the parishes are spare. But the few that exist challenge assumptions that the Reformation Swedish Mass was swiftly implemented or enthusiastically received. As Wilhelm Moberg has written, "A great deal of time was to pass before people were transformed spiritually from Catholics to Protestants. Here was no case of a spontaneous conversion." He adds that "it is quite possible that, but for Gustav Vasa's monetary straits, the Swedes would have remained Catholics to this day."[29] It is difficult to assess Moberg's "what if" contention. We must recognize that Sweden's leading reformers seemed to understand the conservative temper of their fellow countrymen, and to some extent shared it. Unlike the situation in Reformation England,[30] "the stripping of the altars" (or, in the case of Sweden, the plundering of church vessels) was not for theological purposes but to fill the empty coffers of the new state.

After the period under study in this essay, King Johan III (1568–92) led the Church of Sweden to embrace or reclaim even more of the Catholic tradition in his humanistically inspired return to the *consensus quinquasaecularis*. He strove to enrich the churches stripped bare by his father. He moved in a more "high church" direction than the Church Order of 1571 with his *New Church Ordinance (Nova ordinantia ecclesiastica)* of 1575 and his Swedish-Latin *Liturgy of the Swedish Church Conforming to the Catholic and Orthodox Tradition* (*Liturgia svecanae ecclesiae catholicae et orthodoxae conformis,* popularly known as the Red Book because of the color of its binding) of 1576. While the gnesio-Lutheran theologians at Uppsala took exception to Johan's Church policy, there was no popular uprising against it in either Sweden or Finland (where Johan had been duke). The 1571 Church Order was restored after Johan's death by the Uppsala synod of 1593, which also adopted the Augsburg Confession, in worried anticipation of the accession of the Catholic King Sigismund III Vasa of Poland and the threat of the Counter-Reformation that he might bring to Sweden. But that is another story.

In the period under study the Church of Sweden moved liturgically from the options of a Swedish Low Mass and a Latin High Mass to a bilingual Swedish-Latin High Mass. This change emerged gradually during the sixteenth century from a blending of texts of the medieval Latin Mass with Swedish texts which were largely a reworking of this material. There was no introduction of something entirely new in the parishes. In some places, such as Stockholm, the change from Latin to Swedish was more immediate and more complete. In other parts of the country the people would have noticed little change in the outward celebration of the Mass, except that as time went on there was less Latin and more readings in Swedish and congregational singing of vernacular hymns. Even the elevation of the Host and chalice, which had been the most conspicuous moment in the medieval Mass, was not abolished until 1595. Nor were the outward accouterments of liturgical celebration—vestments, altar, lights, candles, and so forth—abolished. One must therefore be impressed more by the degree of continuity than of discontinuity between the late Middle Ages and the Reformation period in the celebration of the Mass in sixteenth-century Sweden.

Notes

1. See Eric E. Yelverton, *The Mass in Sweden,* Henry Bradshaw Society vol. 59 (London: Harrison and Sons, 1920), 2–47.

2. Conrad Bergendoff, *Olavus Petri and the Ecclesiastical Transformation in Sweden 1521–1552* (Philadelphia: Fortress Press, 1965), 151ff.

3. Yngve Brilioth, *Nattvarden i evangeliskt gudstjänstliv* (Stockholm: Svenska kyrkans diakonistyrelses bokförlag, 1926; rpt., 1951), 340.

4. See Frank C. Senn, *Christian Liturgy—Catholic and Evangelical* (Minneapolis: Fortress Press, 1997), 332ff.

5. William Anthony Ruff, *Integration and Inconsistencies: The Thesaurus Musicae Sacrae in the Reformed Roman Eucharistic Liturgy* (Ph.D. diss., Karl-Franzois-Universität, Graz, Austria, 1998), 493ff.

6. Martin Luther, "An Order of Mass and Communion for the Church at Wittenberg," *Luther's Works,* vol. 53, ed. and trans. Ulrich S. Leupold (Philadelphia: Fortress Press, 1965), 20.

7. On the relationship between civil and ecclesiastical authority in Stockholm during the Middle Ages and the Reformation, see Robert Murray, *Stockholms kyrkotyrelse intill 1630—Talets mitt* (Stockholm: SSSKH 20, 1949).

8. John Wordsworth, *The National Church of Sweden* (London: A. R. Mowbray, 1911), 199.

9. See Michael Roberts, *The Early Vasas. A History of Sweden, 1523–1611* (Cambridge: Cambridge University Press, 1968), 83ff.

10. See Wilhelm Moberg, *A History of the Swedish People: From Renaissance to Revolution,* trans. Paul Britten Austin (New York: Pantheon Books, 1973), 164–70.

11. See Bergendoff, *Olavus Petri,* 45–47.

12. Ibid., 48–49.

13. See Sven Kjöllerström, *Missa Lincopense. En liturgi-historisk studie* (Stockholm: SSSKH 4, 1941), 53ff.

14. Yelverton, *The Mass in Sweden,* 25ff.

15. *Luther's Works,* 53:25.

16. *Samlade skrifter* 2 (Uppsala: Almqvist och Wiksells Boktrycheri, 1914–17), 403.

17. *Messan på swensko 1557,* facsimile ed. with introd. by Siggtrygg Serenius (Uppsala: Tord Wetterqvist AB, 1969).

18. See Senn, *Christian Liturgy,* 395–96.

19. Wordsworth, *The National Church,* 213.

20. Christer Pahlmblad, *Mässa på svenska. Den reformatoriska mässan I Sverige mot den senmedeltida bakgrunden* (Lund: Arcus Förlag, 1998), 25ff.

21. See Bard Thompson, *Liturgies of the Western Church* (Cleveland: World Publishing Co., 1961), 147–48.

22. See Olavus Petri, "Een lijten postilla," *Samlade skrifter* 3: 1–470.

23. Pahlmblad, *Mässa på svenska,* 46–47.

24. Kjöllerström, *Missa Lincopense,* 66.

25. See Bergendoff, *Olavus Petri,* 158.

26. See Pahlmblad, *Mässa på svenska,* 47–48; Eric E. Yelverton, *An Archbishop of the Reformation, Laurentius Petri Nericius, Archbishop of Uppsala, 1531–73. A Study of His Liturgical Projects* (Minneaoplis: Augsburg, 1959), 109–11.

27. See Senn, *Christian Liturgy,* 418ff., for a discussion of the liturgical program of King Johan III.

28. *Liber Cantus Upsalensis,* ed. and intro. by Pehr Edwall (Lund: C. W. K. Gleerup, 1943).

29. Moberg, *A History of the Swedish People,* 169.

30. See Eamon Duffy, *The Stripping of the Altars: Traditional Religion in England 1400–1580* (New Haven: Yale University Press, 1992).

four

Becoming Protestants: Lutheran Altars or Reformed Communion Tables?

BODO NISCHAN

Editors' Introduction

It is widely known that not all sixteenth-century Reformations were the same in scope, force, and motivation. The degree of discontinuity with medieval Catholic practice ranged from the relatively conservative reforms of Lutherans and Anglicans to the radical reforms of the Anabaptists.

Often, the changes we associate with these traditions did not crystallize until decades after the initial wave of reform. The phase of consolidation of confessional identity among Protestants in the later sixteenth and early seventeenth centuries thus not only established the parameters of belief and practice for each group, but also carefully distinguished each confession from the others, based on specific doctrinal and liturgical differences.

Some Protestant leaders, especially Lutherans and Anglicans, expended just as much energy over what they wanted to retain as they did over what they wanted to change. Bodo Nischan's contribution helpfully lays out the controversy between Lutherans and the Reformed over one particular aspect of worship, namely the use of altars versus Communion tables. By studying both artwork and textual sources presented in this essay, we can come to realize that the configuration of space in church and the use of liturgical furniture were not minor issues but reflected deep theological divisions between confessional groups. The relative amount of change and continuity as compared with medieval practices was thus carried out with one eye on the pre-Reformation situation and another on the liturgical choices made by rival Protestant groups.

Primary Sources Introduction:

Both Lutherans and the Reformed wrote extensively, and at times quite stridently, about their understanding of the appropriate forms of worship, and how these differed from the choices made by other Protestants. As the pioneer of the German Reformation, Luther laid out his perspective on matters such as the use of altars in church, only to be later opposed by the Reformed, who argued on theological and scriptural grounds that the Lutherans were mistaken.

A. The German Mass and Order of Service (1526): Martin Luther's Preface[1]

In the first place, I would kindly and for God's sake request all those who see this order of service or desire to follow it: do not make it a rigid law to bind or entangle anyone's conscience, but use it in Christian liberty as long, when, where, and how you find it to be practical and useful. For this is being published not as though we meant to lord it over anyone else, or to legislate for him, but because of the widespread demand for German masses and services and the general dissatisfaction and offense that has been caused by the great variety of new masses, for everyone makes his own order of service. Some have the best intentions, but others have no more than an itch to produce something novel so that they might shine before men as leading lights, rather than being ordinary teachers—as is always the case with Christian liberty: very few use it for the glory of God and the good of the neighbor; most use it for their own advantage and pleasure. But while the exercise of this freedom is up to everyone's conscience and must not be cramped or forbidden, nevertheless, we must make sure that freedom shall be and remain a servant of love and of our fellow-man.

Where the people are perplexed and offended by these differences in liturgical usage, however, we are certainly bound to forego our freedom and seek, if possible, to better rather than to offend them by what we do or leave undone. Seeing then that this external order, while it cannot affect the conscience before God, may yet serve the neighbor, we should seek to be of one mind in Christian love, as St. Paul teaches (Rom. 15:5–6; I Cor. 1:10; Phil. 2:2). As far as possible we should observe the same rites and ceremonies, just as all Christians have the same baptism and the same sacrament of the altar and no one has received a special one of his own from God. . . .

Concerning the Service

Since the preaching and teaching of God's Word is the most important part of divine service, we have arranged for sermons and lessons as follows: for the holy day or Sunday we retain the customary Epistles and Gospels and have three sermons. At five or six o'clock in the morning a few Psalms are chanted for Matins. A sermon follows on the Epistle of the day, chiefly for the sake of the servants so that they too may be cared for and hear God's Word, since they cannot be present at other sermons. After this an antiphon and the *Te Deum* or the Benedictus, alternately, with an Our Father, collects, and *Benedicamus Domino*. At the mass, at eight or nine o'clock, the sermon is on the Gospel for the day. At Vespers in the afternoon the sermon before the Magnificat takes up the Old Testament chapter by chapter. For the Epistles and Gospels we have retained the customary division according to the church year, because we do not find anything especially reprehensible in this use. And the present situation in Wittenberg is such that many are here who must learn to preach in places where this division is still being observed and may continue in force. Since in this matter we can be of service to others without loss to ourselves, we leave it, but have no objection to others who take up the complete books of the evangelists. This we think provides sufficient preaching and teaching for the lay people. He who desires more will find enough on other days.

Namely, on Monday and Tuesday mornings we have a German lesson on the Ten Commandments, the Creed, Lord's Prayer, baptism, and sacrament, so that these two days preserve and deepen the understanding of the catechism. On Wednesday morning again a German lesson, for which the evangelist Matthew has been appointed so that the day shall be his very own, seeing that he is an excellent evangelist for the instruction of the congregation, records the fine sermon of Christ on the Mount, and strongly urges the exercise of love and good works. But the evangelist John, who so mightily teaches faith, has his own day too, on Saturday afternoon at Vespers, so that two of the evangelists have their own days when they are being read. Thursday and Friday mornings have the weekday lessons from the Epistles of the apostles and the rest of the New Testament assigned to them. Thus enough lessons and sermons have been appointed to give the Word of God free course among us, not to mention the university lectures for scholars.

This is what we do to train the schoolboys in the Bible. Every day of the week they chant a few Psalms in Latin before the lesson, as has been customary at Matins hitherto. For as we stated above, we want to keep the youth well versed in the Latin Bible. After the Psalms, two or three boys in turn read a chapter from the Latin New Testament, depending on the length. Another boy then reads the same chapter in German to familiarize them with it and for the benefit of any layman who might be present and listening. Thereupon they proceed with an antiphon to the German lesson mentioned above. After the lesson the whole congregation sings a German hymn, the Lord's Prayer is said silently, and the pastor or chaplain reads a collect and closes with the *Benedicamus Domino* as usual.

Likewise at Vespers they sing a few of the Vesper Psalms in Latin with an antiphon, as heretofore, followed by a hymn if one is available. Again two or three boys in turn then read a chapter from the Latin Old Testament or half a one, depending on length. Another boy reads the same chapter in German. The Magnificat follows in Latin with an antiphon or hymn, the Lord's Prayer said silently, and the collects with the *Benedicamus*. This is the daily service throughout the week in cities where there are schools.

On Sunday for the Laity

Here we retain the vestments, altar, and candles until they are used up or we are pleased to make a change. But we do not oppose anyone who would do otherwise. In the true mass, however, of real Christians, the altar should not remain where it is, and the priest should always face the people as Christ doubtlessly did in the Last Supper. But let that await its own time.

B. From Johannes Bergius, *The Pearle of Peace & Concord. Or a Treatise of Pacification Betwixt the Dissenting Churches of Christ*[2]

IV. Of Ceremonies

Q. 86. About what Ceremonies is the Difference [between Lutherans and Reformed]?

A. Chiefly about these five Ceremonies:

1. About Baptisme in case of necessity.
2. About Exorcisme, or the Adjuration of the Devil in Baptisme.
3. About the breaking of bread and the Oblate or *Hostie* in the Supper of the Lord.
4. About private Confession and Absolution.
5. About Images.

Q. 89. Wherefore do you reject Exorcism in Baptisme? which consisteth in these words, Come out thou uncleane Spirit, and give way to the holy Spirit.

A. Because the cleare words doe import,

1. That children are possessed of the Devil, if not corporally, yet spiritually.
2. That the Devil must come out of them upon the Ministers Adjuration.
3. That such Adjuring is done in the name, that is, by the command and by the vertue of the Father, Son, and holy Ghost. All which is false and erroneous, and therefore a manifest abuse of the name of God, and nullifying of holy baptisme.

Q. 92. Why do you reject the Hostes or Oblates, or round little Wafer-Cakes in the Lords Supper?

A. First, because they had their rise and original in the depth of Popery, together with the Idolatrous Masse; and then because they can hardly be used for bread to be eaten, which yet the Lord hath ordained for the holy Supper. Yet will we not condemn those that esteem it and use it for right bread.

Q. 93. Why do you use the breaking of bread instead of it?

A. First, because of the example of Christ and the Apostles, who used it in the first Institution, and have recorded it among those things which they received of the Lord.

Secondly, because of Christs command to do the same, which he and the Apostles did at that time. For though the same reach not to the circumstance of time and place, yet it extends itselfe to the whole service and sacred ceremony which they then used.

Thirdly, for a remembrance that his body was broken for us, and bruised upon the crosse, and that we many shall be but one *Bread,* or *one Body,* as we are made partakers of one bread.

Fourthly, because of the Doctrine of the Apostle, *That the bread which we break, and the Cup which we bless,* is the communion of the Body and Blood of Christ. Now as we may not omit the blessing of the Cup, so we may not omit the breaking of the Bread.

Fifthly, because in the first Apostolical Church from this holy Ceremony the whole supper of the Lord was called the breaking of bread, *Act. 2. 42,46.*

Sixthly, because it was used in the Primitive Christian Church for a thousand years together.

Q. 97. Wherein lyeth the controversie about Images?

A. First in that they do altogether omit this Commandement of God about Images in their Catechismes. And then again in that they use such Images as are prohibited.

Q. 98. They say it is but an Appendix or Explication of the first Commandement, therefore they may omit it for childrens easier learning?

A. We answer, first, that it is a distinct Commandement. Again, if it were but an Appendix or Explication, yet is it much more necessary than the Explication of Luther or of any other man, because God himself hath spoken it from Heaven, and that to the whole people of Israel young and old, and hath written it himself into tables of stone; which also belongeth not to the Ceremonial and Judaical Law, but to the Moral Law that concerneth all men; yea is most of all necessary for simple Laymen and children, as being naturally most inclined to love Images and Idols.

Q. 99. But why do you count it a distinct Commandement?

A. First because it hath a distinct and different meaning, that we shall not onely have no other Gods, but also that we shal not worship and serve the true God in a false and forbidden manner, not by images, or other humane fictions and inventions, but onely according to his word. And then againe, because else the tenth Commandement is torne and broken into two, whereas it forbiddeth but one sort of sin, namely, all evil lusting and concupiscence, and is alledged in Scripture but as one Commandement, *Rom. 7.7.* & *13.9.*

Q. 100. But why do you reject all Images, whereas God hath onely prohibited them so far as that we shall not worship them?

A. We do not reject all Images, but onely the idolatrous, superstitious or offensive Images; as first the pictures of God because he hath clearely forbidden to be resembled by any image; and then the pictures of Christ and of the Saints and Angels, or of other Creatures which in Popery are adored, because God hath also forbidden us to have or keep any such Idols or Images, *Exod.20.23. & 34.13; Lev.26.1. Deut.4.12, 15, 16, 17, 18 & 7.5, 25, 26. & 12.3.*

Q. 101. But they plead that they keep them not for Adoration, but onely for a Memorial and Instruction of the Laity and for an Ornament of their Churches?

A. We answer, 1. That God hath commanded us to teach his people not by dumb Images but by his word; and hath also ordained not painted or carved Crucifixes, but the Sacrament of the Lords Supper for a memorial of Christs death.

2. That this excuse cannot serve for idolatrous images, but onely for historical.

3. Though they themselves do not worship or adore these images, yet they become occasions of Idolatry unto others who doe adore and worship them; as sad experience does evidently testifie in these times in many Protestant places where Popery is brought in againe; as also in those places where Papists and Protestants live together.

Q. 103. But why do you reject Altars, Surplises and the like?

A. We turn Alters into Tables, because we hold no sacrifice of the Masse, but the Lords Supper upon them. But whether they be Tables of stone or wood, this we take for a thing indifferent.

Burning Candles we account a token of darknesse, therefore we use them not at noon day; for where no darknesse is there is no need of a Candle, especially in the worship of God.

Surplices we use none, because it is the peculiar ornament of Masse-Priests at their idolatrous Sacrifice of the Masse: yet do we not therefore condemn those who retain them and use them in their Churches. . . .

Latin Songs or Prayers we use none in the Church, that not only the learned but the whole congregation may sing together and pray together, and understand what they sing, and what they pray, and say *Amen* unto it, according too the Apostolic doctrine, 1 Cor. 14, 15, 16, 17.

Notes

1. Martin Luther, *Luther's Works* (St. Louis and Philadelphia: Fortress Press, 1955–86), vol. 53: 61 and 68f.

2. Johannes Bergius, *The Pearle of Peace & Concord. Or a Treatise of Pacification Betwixt the Dissenting Churches of Christ* (London: John Rothwell, 1655), 146–159; originally published as *Unterscheidt und Vergleichung der Evangelischen/In Lehr und Ceremonien* (Berlin: Georg Rungen, 1635). Bergius (1587–1658) served as the Hohenzollerns' Reformed court preacher in Berlin.

"Is it prohibited in the New Testament to use an altar that has been cleansed of all impurity. . . . for the celebration of the Lord's Supper?"[1] This, according to Lazarus Theodorus, author of *Synopsis . . . and Summary of the Controversies That Today's So-called Lutherans and Calvinists Engage in Much to the Confusion of the Common People,* published in 1615, was one of the principal issues over which Germany's Protestants were arguing. As Abraham Taurer put it, "Can the church of the Reformation in good conscience keep the altars that were built under the papacy and use them . . . for the celebration of the sacrament?"[2] Taurer, a Lutheran from Magdeburg, thought that they could; Zwinglians and Calvinists, called the Reformed in Germany, adamantly disagreed, insisting that these "instruments of papal blasphemy" had to be replaced by Communion tables. This controversy, which originated in the 1520s, gained new momentum in the late sixteenth century as the heirs of the Wittenberg and Helvetic reformations sought to consolidate their positions by demarcating themselves clearly from each other and from their common Catholic foe. The debate over altars and Communion tables was important because it went to the very core of just what it meant to be a Protestant, in faith and in practice, and also because it hinted at emerging denominational differences.

To understand the issues involved, a brief look at how altars evolved in the pre-Reformation Church is in order.[3] Of all the spaces in a medieval church none was more sacred than the altar. It was here that the bread and wine were transformed into the body and blood of Christ to be offered in the bloodless sacrifice of the Mass; here also the relics of the saints and martyrs were venerated. Because of its holiness and centrality in worship and piety, great care was taken to adorn the altar and its surrounding structure. Its form and use had evolved gradually over a fifteen-hundred-year period. The earliest altars undoubtedly were simple wooden tables in private homes where people gathered for the celebration of the agape or Eucharist. When religious services were transferred from private homes to special buildings, Communion tables continued to be used.[4] During the persecutions of the second and third centuries, Christians frequently held their eucharistic meals in catacombs at the graves of martyrs, where they would place a stone plate over the tomb to create a table altar. Later, especially after the legalization of Christianity by Emperor Constantine in 313, more permanent structures were erected. These table altars, now occasionally also made of stone, consisted of a top, or *mensa,* with attached legs, *stipes,* that might number from one to five or more.

The growing cult of martyrs from the fourth century onward led to churches' being built as close as possible to their graves, with altars frequently located directly over the martyrs' remains, or, if that proved impractical, with their relics being transferred from their original resting places to the new churches where they were placed into receptacles directly beneath or within the altar. The space between the table's legs often was walled in, giving the altar a box- or chestlike form. To allow worshipers to see or touch its holy contents an opening, called a *fenestrella,* covered with a lattice or door, often was left in front of the altar.

By the sixth century wooden altars generally had been replaced by stone; also in the Western Church it became customary for a church to have several side altars in addition to the main or high altar. This was associated partly with the continued and growing veneration of saints and their relics and partly with the introduction of private Masses. While the earlier altars had been free-standing, allowing the celebrant to walk around them and preside over the Communion service while facing the people, the new side altars were placed against the wall so that the officiant no longer faced the people but instead turned toward the altar, with his back to the congregation. These architectural and liturgical changes, art historians such as Alexander Nagel have argued, presaged a "significant development not only in the history of the altar, but also in the nature and function of the Christian image"[5] which took place at the dawn of Christianity's second millennium: the introduction on the rear edge of the altar of a panel decorated with sacred pictures or figurines—the altarpiece *(retabulum).*

As long as the celebrant had stood on the far side of the altar, altarpieces would have constituted an impermissible obstruction. The new *retabula* that started to appear in increasing numbers from the eleventh century onward forced him to officiate in front of the altar, with his back to the people. The altarpieces, made out of stone or wood, provided ample new iconographic opportunities, as is evidenced by their increasing complexity and magnificence, especially in Germany and the Netherlands. (See Figure 4.1.) This development reached its apogee in the early fourteenth century with the

4.1. Rogier van der Weyden, *Altarpiece of the Seven Sacraments*. Courtesy of the Koninklijk Museum, Antwerp.

so-called *Flügelaltar*, whose movable wings made it possible to vary the altarpiece imagery in accordance with the changing requirements of the liturgical year.[6] One of the most spectacular and best known of these is Matthias Grünewald's *Isenheim Altarpiece* of 1515 which, in its varying positions, shows the Annunciation, nativity, crucifixion, entombment, and resurrection of Christ, with side panels portraying scenes from the lives of Saints Sebastian and Anthony, and, in its fully opened position, revealing a carved centerpiece (by Nicolas Haguenau) depicting a seated Saint Anthony, with Saint Jerome standing on his left and Saint Augustine on his right.[7] *Retabula*, both of the winged variety or with a single panel, proliferated in the fifteenth century, largely as a result of the growing sponsorship of nonecclesiastical and nonaristocratic patrons.

There were other important liturgical developments in the late Middle Ages. The celebrant's new position between altar and congregation provided visual reinforcement for the view that he functioned as a mediator between God and man, a distinction that was further augmented by the fencing off of altars through rails and other architectural devices. From the thirteenth century onward crosses, crucifixes, and candles, which had previously been positioned above or to the side of the altar, began to appear on it. Also, the increasing veneration of relics led them to be displayed on top of altars, not in or beneath them as had previously been the practice. Concurrently, the principal liturgical act for which altars had been constructed in the first place, the celebration of the Lord's Supper, the Mass, increasingly was being transformed into a visual act where looking at the transubstantiated bread and wine, visual Communion, became a substitute for receiving the Eucharist itself. By the end of the fifteenth century, the clergy, while encouraging the adoration of the host, were complaining bitterly that people were coming to church solely to gaze at the elevated Host and rarely, if ever, stayed long enough to commune and witness the completion of the Mass. Not Holy Communion but the elevation marked the climax of the late medieval Mass,[8] restructuring the Sacrament of the altar into what Charles Zika has called a "visual theophany."[9]

Altars on the eve of the Reformation thus were tightly linked to the very core of late medieval theology and piety, both of which were challenged by the Protestant Reformers. Not surprisingly, how they viewed and treated altars was inextricably coupled with other theological issues, specifically their understanding of the Eucharist and their appreciation, or lack of it, for the art and liturgy of the old Church. While the Swiss and Wittenberg Reformers agreed on what they did not want, the sacrificial Mass, they arrived at dramatically different conclusions about the role of externals in worship and piety. Martin Luther and his followers were willing to allow some material props and much traditional ritual, provided these were not explicitly prohibited by Scripture or imposed as a legalistic requirement.[10] By contrast, Ulrich Zwingli and John Calvin, convinced that true worship and piety could only be spiritual, took an exceedingly dim view of religious externals, especially of ceremonies not specifically mandated by Scripture, particularly those that hinted at old "papal superstitions," and above all, that *idolum Romanum*—the veneration and adoration of the consecrated Host.[11] Accordingly, the Helvetic Reformers undertook to remove most accessories of medieval worship, including altars, which they replaced with simple movable wooden Communion tables. In Calvinist Geneva, where the Lord's

Supper was celebrated three or four times a year, "two tables were set up in church" whence the bread and wine were distributed during Communion.[12]

The Lutherans, aiming mainly to do away with what was unscriptural, opposed only the notion of a sacrificial altar but kept the main or high altar, without its late medieval relic cases and monstrances, for the celebration of the Eucharist. They often left the relics beneath the altars because they were difficult to remove but covered them if visible; also the side altars, while no longer in use, were not always removed. Crucifixes, paintings, and other altar decorations were kept.[13] As Luther explained in his German Mass order of 1526: "We retain the vestments, altar, and candles until they are used up or we are pleased to make a change. But we do not oppose anyone who would do otherwise. In the true Mass, however, of real Christians, the altar should not remain where it is, and the priest should always face the people as Christ doubtlessly did in the Last Supper."[14]

Luther's preference for a free-standing altar from behind which the minister would officiate while facing the congregation was put into practice only in Württemberg and parts of Thuringia. It was also realized in the one church that Luther personally dedicated in 1544, the Torgau castle church, but there only until the end of the century when the erection of an altarpiece —the former retable of Dresden's Schloßkapelle—forced ministers to revert to officiating before the altar with their backs to the people.

Luther himself indirectly encouraged this practice by favoring the continued use of altarpieces, thereby actually negating his 1526 proposal. He thought that they were helpful as a "layman's bible" for people who could not read or write, "especially for . . . children and simple people who are more apt to retain the divine stories when taught by picture and parable than merely by words or instruction."[15] In 1530 he went so far as to connect altar panels to the sacramental realities: "Whoever is inclined to put pictures on the altar ought to have the Lord's Supper of Christ painted . . . Since the altar is designated for the administration of the Sacrament, one could not find a better painting for it."[16]

This, of course, was precisely what the Reformed found so objectionable. "Altarpieces, by their very location and presentation, are devotional images *par excellence,* and raise questions about the legitimacy of images in Christian worship in the clearest manner," Martin Kemp has noted.[17] Zwingli denied that church images and altars belonged in the realm of religious liberty, thus rejecting the Lutheran claim that Christians were free to use or not use them.[18] For the Zurich Reformer all images in churches inevitably ended up becoming idols.[19] Calvin sharpened the biblical ban on idolatry even further by giving the Old Testament image prohibition the status of an independent commandment, the second within the Decalogue. For him there was no such thing as an innocent religious image; its very use already was an act of idolatry.[20] Cultic objects like altars and paintings, he insisted, represent a false religion, an improper mixing of the spiritual and the material in worship, a denial of God's transcendence and an attempt to bring him down to human level through visible means. For Calvin the only true form of worship was "spiritual worship" devoid of all material props and humanly devised ceremonies. Above all, it was worship that had been commanded by God.[21] "External symbols" were acceptable to Calvin only if they aided the worshipers' "rise to God by offering spiritual worship [and] elevating their mind to God."[22]

The late medieval altars and panels that Lutherans had kept and new altarpieces which they introduced from the late 1530s onward could not "serve as *ladders* by which the faithful might *ascend* . . . to heaven."[23] They therefore were bound to be a thorn in the side of the Reformed and create new friction among Protestants, especially as the two Reformation Churches sought to consolidate their positions in the late sixteenth century. Not surprisingly, therefore, Lutherans and Reformed alike used the altar-image question for both polemical and pedagogical purposes: to communicate their key doctrines and to help create a new Protestant Church, or, better, Churches, with a clear sense of identity and mission.

On the Lutheran side these efforts became particularly evident in the many splendid new altarpieces that were produced by the Cranach workshop in the mid-1500s.[24] While these altarpieces resembled their late medieval forerunners in structure and appearance, they emphasized different iconographical themes: Mariological and saintly motifs generally were abandoned and replaced by evangelical ones such as the law-gospel theme; the life, death, and resurrection of Christ; or the Last Supper. "The first image to employ unequivocal Lutheran iconography" was the largely unknown *Schneeberg Altarpiece* (1539), a monumental eleven-panel polyptych on the law-gospel theme, by Lucas Cranach the Elder.[25] Far better known is the altarpiece that Cranach completed for Wittenberg's Stadtkirche in 1547,[26] a year after Luther's death. Its panels and predella portray the church, very much in line with the definition found in the Augsburg Confession, as the place where the Word is preached and the sacraments are rightly administered. Another interesting example, this one by Lucas Cranach the Younger, is the 1565 panel for the castle church in Dessau which portrays the Lord's Supper but, in true evangelical fashion, has transformed the apostles into the various Lutheran leaders whom the donor, Joachim of Anhalt, clearly supports.

In the second half of the century these winged altarpieces increasingly had to compete with fixed altars, which gained in monumentality and popularity.

But it was not until the end of the century that we reach what Helmuth Eggert has called "the golden age of the Protestant altarpiece. The size of the altars increases; in height and width they compete with the gigantic late Gothic shrines."[27] These altars were found especially in central and northern Germany, mostly in Saxony, Hamburg, Schleswig-Holstein, and Prussia.

One of the most magnificent of these late Renaissance altars was constructed in Danzig's Saint John's Church.[28] (See Figure 4.2.) The altarpiece by Abraham von dem Blocke, with panels portraying the life of John the Baptist, was completed in 1612 but, in a city sharply divided between Lutherans and Reformed,[29] had already become an issue much earlier. Jakob Adam, a Reformed sympathizer and pastor of Danzig's Elisabeth Church, himself the center of much controversy because he had reintroduced the *fractio panis* as part of the Communion rite,[30] condemned the altar's construction as pure idolatry and a distortion of the Gospel's "unadorned truth." Saint John's Lutheran dean, Johann Walther, defended it, charging that Adam was preaching a "patched, gruesome, unpleasant, immoral and impure untruth."[31] The new altar, Walther insisted, hardly violated the commandment against idolatry as Adam alleged. Not the altar but how Calvinists treated images, specifically how they had redivided the commandments and interpreted the Decalogue, was the problem.[32]

Altars, it is clear from this exchange, had become a divisive topic between Lutherans and Reformed which touched on a number of issues that went far beyond the question of whether they had to be replaced by Communion tables. For Lutherans their retention clearly had become a confessional marker, just as their replacement with Communion tables had become a confessional issue for the Reformed.[33] As Andreas Veringer, the Lutheran pastor of Freudenstadt (near Stuttgart), observed in his dedicatory sermon for a new house of worship in 1608: "We have a beautiful altar . . . in our newly built church to testify that we have nothing in common with Zwinglians and Calvinists who destroy altars."[34] Johann Valentin Andreae made the same point as he described the church, "a building of royal magnificence," which he envisioned for the center of Christianopolis, his Lutheran utopia: "Truly I cannot admire more the art and beauty of this structure, especially when I think of those people who under the pretext of religious enthusiasm plunder our churches and declare that barren houses of worship are sufficient, yet in no way shun domestic luxury."[35] Significantly, this inner-Protestant debate peaked at the turn of the century, just when the Lutheran altar building boom was reaching its apogee.

In remonstrating against altars, the Reformed principally used two arguments, both of which had earlier been cited by Zwingli and Calvin: first, that altars are unscriptural, and second, that they are idolatrous. Calvinists pointed

4.2. Altarpiece by Abraham von dem Blocke, Danzig. Courtesy of the Herder-Institut, Marburg.

out that the stone altars still found in many Lutheran churches had first been used by Jews to prepare burned offering to Yahweh. "They do not belong in the service of the New Testament because Christ's death on the cross has completely satisfied and canceled [the need for further] sacrifices."[36] The Lord's Supper therefore must not be called the "sacrament of the altar" but the "table of the Lord," as Paul had done in his letter to the Corinthians (I Cor. 10:21), insisted the anonymous author of *Christiana Concordia,* a lengthy treatise that detailed the liturgical changes the Reformed were advocating.[37] Bartholomäus Pitiscus of the Palatinate noted that "when Christ instituted the sacrament he was using a table, not an altar,"[38] to demonstrate, Jacob Fabricius, rector of Danzig's Reformed gymnasium, explained, "that he was serving not a sacrificial but a heavenly meal to quench our thirsty souls with grace."[39]

Up to the time of Constantine, the early Church had never used any altars, insisted Christoph Pezel of Bremen. That changed, however, once Christianity was legalized and became the established religion of the Roman Empire, particularly from the fifth century onward when the popes increasingly filled the political power vacuum left by the collapsing empire. As "papists" began to restore altars, they also brought back the Levitic priesthood while they transformed the Lord's Supper into the sacrificial Mass.[40] Other idolatries quickly followed: at first relics were "secretly hidden" in altars, then publicly displayed on them;[41] "picture panels, explicitly prohibited by scripture, were erected and had to be consecrated to this or that saint."[42] The new altarpieces forced priests to officiate with their backs toward the congregation, thereby enhancing the "papal mass magic"; candles—the Reformed called them "lights of anti-Christ" or "dark mass lamps"—of the sort normally found in dance halls and houses of ill repute, were placed on altars.[43] Bells ordinarily used to call cattle to their feeding troughs were introduced as sacramental bells "to confirm the sacrificial mass and bread's transubstantiation";[44] side altars were added so that more masses could be celebrated; and finally, the ultimate blasphemy: the Lord's Supper became a sacrifice that man was offering to God.

The Lutherans could claim that they had eliminated past abuses and therefore were free to keep the old altars for Communion. The Reformed categorically rejected this argument: by definition all altars were sacrificial altars and therefore idolatrous; their continued use not only violated the words of Scripture but, worse, incited people to new idolatry. Just because the general public insisted that altars were necessary for proper worship was hardly a good argument for tolerating them, noted the defenders of Anhalt's second reformation.[45] Such popular demands merely confirmed the dangers that altars posed, a problem compounded by the fact that many still contained the relics that had never been removed during the earlier Lutheran reform; also, as long as these papal altars persisted, Jesuits would try to use them to reintroduce the old Catholic idolatry.[46]

By constructing more altars with panels, crucifixes, and other artworks, the Lutherans only were adding to these heathenish practices. In the view of the Reformed, the Lutherans claimed that pictures are the layman's Bible; however, Scripture nowhere justifies such a claim. "For God has directed that his people gathered in worship be instructed by the words of a properly appointed preacher, not through pictures. And nowhere did he promise that his Holy Spirit who works through the writings of prophets and apostles will also reveal himself through pictures."[47] The altarpieces and panels still found in many churches violate the second commandment, can only lead to idolatry, and therefore provoke God's wrath, the Reformed insisted. Our Lord wants us to honor him by worshiping his Son, not by portraying Christ as a "public bath attendant"[48] hanging from a cross. And the New Testament instructs us to use a Communion table for the celebration of the Lord's Supper, "not a mass altar that is decorated like a doll's house with puppets and pictures."[49] The many "idol altars" *(Götzenaltare)*[50] still found in Lutheran houses of worship therefore had to go. In regions where the Reformed came to power and carried out another reformation in the late sixteenth and early seventeenth centuries—notably in the Palatinate, Nassau-Dillingen, Bremen, Anhalt, and Hesse-Kassel—the altars that had survived the earlier Lutheran reform were indeed replaced by simple wooden Communion tables.[51]

How, then, did the Lutherans respond? In their answers, they stressed two points that more or less corresponded to the Calvinists' main arguments: first, altars are not prohibited by Scripture, and second, they are not idolatrous because past abuses have been eliminated. "The apostles preached fervently against idolatry . . . but none of them ever stormed an altar or directed others to attack and destroy one," observed Simon Gedicke of Magdeburg in a lengthy treatise *On Pictures and Altars,* which he published largely to counter the recent Reformed iconoclasm in nearby Anhalt.[52] Aegidius Hunnius's *Thorough Report about Altars,* also written to counter the Calvinists' second reformation, similarly noted that when the apostle Paul came to Athens, where he found an altar dedicated to an unknown God (Acts 17, 16–31), "he used the occasion to preach Christ to them [the Athenians] and condemn their idolatry. But not once in his entire sermon did he encourage them with a single word to destroy and break the altar."[53]

Nowhere in the entire New Testament are altars prohibited for the celebration of the Lord's Supper, insisted Gedicke.[54] The Mosaic commandment against idolatry that Calvinists invoke was aimed against the pagan altars of the Canaanites which were dedicated to heathen gods.[55] By contrast, Lutheran altars—even those that had previously been abused by the papal Church—are used for the celebration of the Lord's Supper, not for idolatrous heathen worship. By insisting on Communion tables, while eliminating altars and other so-called popish ceremonial, the Reformed claim to restore the pristine practices of the apostolic church and observe the Lord's Supper exactly as Christ had done. Only there are certain inconsistencies in this argument, the Lutherans contended. "Christ did not use a wooden table when he instituted the holy evening meal; we therefore do not require such a table either in our churches for that would violate Christ's institution," maintained Taurer of Magdeburg.[56] Also, if the Reformed really intended to recreate the precise "circumstances" of that first Communion service, as they claim, then they should celebrate the Lord's Supper only at night, around 8:00 P.M., in a tavern, and only after eating a hefty meal and drinking heavily, with some people undoubtedly in a drunken stupor and lying on the floor.[57] Aside from insisting on their "wooden Zwinglian haberdasher tables"—Lutherans also called them "carousing tables"[58]—the Reformed themselves could not agree on just how to observe the Lord's Supper: in some churches they sit at a table, in others in pews. "In the electoral Palatinate and other Calvinist places communicants still do not sit down but walk around the [Communion] table even though many of them view this as a papist or ubiquistic practice."[59] In Basle the sick still receive private Communion even though Zwingli and Calvin opposed this; in England they commune while sitting at long banquet tables. "Since the Zwinglians and Calvinists themselves cannot achieve any uniformity in their own churches how, then, do they dare to prescribe a specific form to us," wondered Gedicke.[60] How precisely the Sacrament was celebrated, and whether or not an altar was used, was ultimately a matter of Christian freedom. What truly mattered in Communion was the Sacrament's essence—Christ's true presence—not the "circumstances" under which our Lord instituted the Sacrament which Calvinists were trying to recreate.[61]

Equally inconsistent to Lutherans was the Reformed argument that altars needed to be torn down because they had been misused for the sacrificial Mass. Such logic would also require the destruction of all pulpits whence friars once proclaimed their blasphemies, the elimination of all "church bells . . . which had summoned people to the idolatrous mass," and even the tearing down of church buildings because they had been the sites of such horrendous impieties.[62] If everything that had ever been misused for idolatry were eliminated, then "what happens to Holy Scripture, the sun, moon, planets and God's other creations. Heretics have misused the bible to varnish their errors; pagans have prayed to the sun and the stars; and the Epicureans and the godless still abuse God's gifts," observed Philipp Arnoldi, the superintendent of Tilsit in Prussia.[63] "Why," wondered Gedicke, "is it not possible to reform the altar just like the church when, instead of the [sacrificial] mass, the blessed Lord's Supper is consecrated on it and distributed according to Christ's order?"[64] Like other Lutherans, he insisted that the same rule that applies to the church in general also holds true for altars: "*Tollatur abusus et maneat usus* . . . eliminate the abuse and keep the proper use."[65] As Arnoldi summarized, "Even though temples and altars have been misused by papists and others, evangelical freedom allows us to keep both in our church."[66]

Lutherans dismissed the Calvinist charges of "idolatry" as "useless babble and gibberish designed to confuse the common man."[67] "Idols exist in a person's heart, not in wood and stone; and where the heart is pure and has been reconciled with God, no altar panel or picture can be regarded as an idol," Gedicke insisted.[68] Arnoldi thought that "papist and Lutheran altars" differ like "light and darkness" or "Baal and Christ," for Lutherans celebrate the Lord's Supper on altars, according to Christ's institution, with communion in both kinds for clergy and laity alike, no papal transubstantiation, and certainly without that "horrible mass sacrifice in which God's eternal son again and again is crucified."[69] Since these superstitions have been eliminated, the Church of the Augsburg Confession can hardly be charged with idolatry, especially since it treats altars as indifferent objects which Christians are free to use or not use, observed Hunnius.[70]

What is true for altars applies equally to altarpieces and panels. Not the pictures themselves are idols: "They have no mouths that talk, or eyes that see . . . or hands that reach"; what matters is how people treat them.[71] The new iconoclasm that accompanied the introduction of Calvinism in some German territories therefore could not be justified, thought Crato of Magdeburg: "Nobody here offers any sacrifices or prayers to these pictures or uses them for any other idolatry."[72] Polycarp Leyser, the Dresden court preacher and church councilor, complained that "wherever these Calvinists gain the upper hand, they remove all pictures, paintings, crucifixes from churches and altars . . . as has already happened in France, the Low Countries, and other places where churches now look like horse stables."[73] Others like Vincenz Schmuck, who fled the Hessian Reformed "emendation" in 1608, agreed and likened the appearance of Reformed churches to "Turkish mosques."[74]

Lutherans denied the Calvinist claim that Scripture prohibits altarpieces and other paintings in churches: "Pictures in the New Testament . . . fall under Christian freedom and therefore can be considered as indifferent matters or adiaphora."[75] They also noted what they perceived as inconsistencies in the Reformed argument. Calvinists claimed that panels and altars had to go because they were misused for papal idolatries. But "what about the crucifixes and panels . . . which Lucas Cranach and other [evangelical] Christians have painted?"[76] And if, for argument's sake, all pictures in churches really were idolatrous because they are specifically prohibited in the Decalogue, what about the embroidered and woven "eagles, lions, griffins, unicorns, doves, sheep, dogs, etc.—or roses, lilies, foliage and flower bouquets—[on clothing] that young princely ladies and matrons wear to church?"[77] Or what about the images on jewelry and coins that people brought to church? "If our Calvinist friends really are such pure Christians with such tender consciences that they cannot tolerate any pictures in church, why do they not object to the images that are imprinted on the red gulden or silver thalers which they carry in their pockets? I have never seen them throw any of these away," noted Leyser.[78] After all, according to Calvinist logic, "a picture is a picture, regardless of whether it is carved, painted, cast, minted, or embroidered . . . and therefore an idol," thought Crato.[79] To claim that their second commandment against "graven images" applied only to church paintings is "like saying that blaspheming, cursing, whoring, adultery, gluttony, boozing, and stealing are prohibited in church but not at home," reasoned Arnoldi. "See what nonsense you end up with if you argue that pictures may be kept at home but not in church?"[80]

"To summarize, no valid argument can be cited against altars and crucifixes, which stand at the very center of this debate," Johann Arndt, pastor of Quedlinburg, concluded.[81] He thought that the current controversy and new reforms not only were unnecessary but worse, ended up confusing many. "I really would like to know how we help people by celebrating the Lord's Supper on a wooden table? Or why it has to happen and would be an improvement? The main reason, I suspect, is that they view the Lord's Supper as a mere symbol."[82]

Arndt was of course partly correct, for a principal issue dividing Lutherans and Reformed in this age of confessionalism was Communion, specifically the mode of Christ's presence. An equally important issue, at least for the Reformed, was the role of worship in general. The Lutherans' retention of altars, panels, and other liturgical paraphernalia simply constituted for the Reformed an unacceptable mixing of the material and the spiritual which, augmented by the hated Lutheran doctrine of "ubiquity," could only help reinforce the very papal idolatry that the Protestant Reformers had sought to destroy.

In a most stimulating essay on the "Reformation as Re-Christianization" Scott Hendrix has recently argued that the sixteenth-century Protestants aimed at "rerooting the faith in Europe" but disagreed on how this rerooting could best be accomplished.[83] Having rejected the sacrifice of the Mass as idolatrous, the Wittenberg and Helvetic "reformers were trying to position Christ, in a nonidolatrous way, at the center of eucharistic piety."[84] The issues that divided them, Hendrix insists, must be understood as differences in strategy in the restructuring of the Western Church. In its confessionalized form, the Reformation gave rise to early modern Protestant denominations whose worship practices variously reflect both change and continuity with the late medieval Church.

Continuity between the old and the new was very evident in the Lutherans' retention of altars and other liturgical paraphernalia in the celebration of the Lord's Supper, and in their belief that the Sacrament mediated forgiveness by bringing the individual communicant into direct confrontation with the living Christ. At the height of the inner-Protestant Communion controversy, Polycarp Leyser, the outspoken Dresden court chaplain, could therefore claim, with some justification, that "Lutherans have far more in common with Romanists than with Calvinists."[85] His "better Papist than Calvinist" adage, of course, confirmed the worst suspicions of the Reformed and helped bolster their call for a "second reformation" to eliminate remaining vestiges of late medieval piety that blurred Protestant-Catholic distinctions.

Change from the old to the new Churches, on the other hand, was best exemplified by the unadorned Communion tables on which Calvinist pastors placed the bread and wine that enabled the individual believer to commune spiritually with the risen Christ. From the Reformed perspective, compromise with the Lutherans simply was impossible: the altars had to be replaced by Communion tables to safeguard the evangelical heritage that they saw threatened in the late sixteenth century by a resurgent Catholic Church and their unwitting "ubiquitist" collaborators.

Regardless of whether they favored altars or Communion tables, early modern Protestants were united in a common belief in the absolute sovereignty of Christ's saving act; however, they strongly disagreed over how this was to be communicated to the individual believer. The liturgical practices and artifacts over which they argued—altars or communion tables?—hint at these disagreements and point to differences between the emerging Lutheran and Reformed Churches.

Notes

1. Lazarus Theodorus, *Synopsis doctrinae Lutheranae & Calvinianae. Das ist/ Summarischer Auszug und Bericht Von den Streidthändeln/so heutigs tages zwischen den also genanten Lutheranern und Calvinisten mit grosser verwirrung der einfeltigen Leute vorgehen* . . . (Frankfurt am Oder: Hartmann, 1615), 195.

2. Abraham Taurer, *Hochnothwendiger Bericht/Wider den newen Bildstürmerischen Carlstadtischen Geist/im Fürstenthumb Anhald* ([Eisleben: Graubisch,] 1597), Riii[a].

3. The definitive work on the altar's history remains Joseph Braun, *Der Christliche Altar in seiner Geschichtlichen Entwicklung,* 2 vols. (Munich: Koch, 1924). See also Edmund Bishop, *On the History of the Christian Altar* (London: J. H. Day, 1905);

Karl Heimann, *Der christliche Altar: Übersicht über seinen Werdegang im Laufe der Zeiten* (Abensberg/NDB: Aventinus, 1954); Cyril E. Pocknee, *The Christian Altar in History and Today* (London: Mowry, 1963); and "Altar," in *TRE* 2: 305–27.

4. Early Christian writers referred to them by the Latin terms *mensa, altare,* or *altarium,* but avoided *ara,* which they associated with pagan sacrificial altars.

5. Alexander Nagel, "Altarpiece," in Jane Turner, ed., *The Dictionary of Art,* 34 vols. (New York: Grove, 1996), 1: 708; see also *TRE* 2: 320.

6. For details, see Max Hasse, *Der Flügelaltar* (Dresden: Dittert, 1941); Walter Grundmann, *Die Sprache des Altars. Zur Glaubensaussage im deutschen Flügel- und Schreinaltar* (Berlin: Evangelische Verlagsanstalt, 1966); Barbara G. Lane, *The Altar and the Altarpiece: Sacramental Themes in Early Netherlandish Painting* (New York: Harper & Row, 1984); Peter Humfrey and Martin Kemp, eds., *The Altarpiece in the Renaissance* (New York: Cambridge University Press, 1990); Jeremy Dupertuis Bangs, *Church Art and Architecture in the Low Countries before 1566,* Sixteenth Century Essays and Studies, vol. 37 (Kirksville, Mo.: SCJ Publishers, 1997), 95–124; and Nagel, "Altarpiece" in *Grove Dictionary of Art,* 1: 707–13.

7. For an excellent recent description and analysis, see John Dillenberger, *Images and Relics. Theological Perceptions and Visual Images in Sixteenth-Century Europe* (New York: Oxford University Press, 1999), 25–52. Reproductions of the altarpiece are found in Georg Scheja and Bert Koch, *The Isenheim Altarpiece* (New York: Harry Abrams, 1969); and Ruth Mellinkoff, *The Devil at Isenheim: Reflections of Popular Belief in Grünewald's Altarpiece* (Berkeley: University of Calfornia Press, 1988).

8. Significantly, the "elevation" became a confessional issue in the Reformed-Lutheran Communion controversies of the late sixteenth century; see Bodo Nischan, "The Elevation of the Host in the Age of Confessionalism: Adiaphoron or Ritual Demarcation?" in *Lutherans and Calvinists in the Age of Confessionalism,* variorum CS (Aldershot: Ashgate, 1999), essay 5.

9. Charles Zika, "Hosts, Processions and Pilgrimages: Controlling the Sacred in Fifteenth-Century Germany," *Past and Present* 118 (February 1988): 31.

10. See Leonhardt Fendt, *Der lutherische Gottesdienst des 16. Jahrhunderts* (Munich: Reinhard, 1923); Ernst Strasser, "Der lutherische Abendmahlsgottesdienst im 16. und 17. Jahrhundert," in Hermann Sasse, ed., *Vom Sakrament des Altars* (Leipzig: Dörffling & Franke, 1941), 194–233; and Friedrich Kalb, *Theology of Worship in Seventeenth-Century Lutheranism* (St. Louis: Concordia, 1965).

11. For details, see Ernst Saxer, *Aberglaube, Heuchelei und Frömmigkeit. Eine Untersuchung zu Calvins reformatorischer Eigenart* (Zurich: Zwingli, 1970); and Carlos M. N. Eire, *War Against the Idols: The Reformation of Worship from Erasmus to Calvin* (New York: Cambridge University Press, 1986).

12. Antoine Cathelan, *Passevent Parisien Respondant à Pasquin Romain: De la vie de ceux qui sont allez demourer à Genève, et se disent vivre selon la réformation de l'Évangile: Faict en forme de Dialogue* (Paris, 1556; rpt., Paris: Liseux, 1875), 74.

13. On the Lutheran attitude toward works of art in church, see Hans Carl von Haebler, *Das Bild in der evangelischen Kirche* (Berlin: Evangelische Verlagsanstalt, 1957), 9–44; Margarete Stirm, *Die Bilderfrage in der Reformation* (Gütersloh: Gerd Mohn, 1977); Carl C. Christensen, *Art and the Reformation in Germany* (Athens:

University of Ohio Press, 1979), and *Princes and Propaganda: Electoral Saxon Art of the Reformation,* Sixteenth Century Essays and Studies, vol. 20 (Kirksville, Mo.: SCJ Publishers, 1992); Sergiusz Michalski, *The Reformation and the Visual Arts: The Protestant Image Question in Western and Eastern Europe* (London and New York: Routledge, 1993), 1–42; Peter Poscharsky, ed., *Die Bilder in den Lutherischen Kirchen: Ikonographische Studien* (Munich: Scaneg, 1998), esp. 5–40; and Dillenberger, *Images and Relics,* 78–113.

14. WA 19, 80, 26–30; translation from LW 53: 69.

15. "Passional" in the 1529 Wittenberg edition (WA 10^{II}, 359, Z); translation from LW 43: 43.

16. WA 31^{I}, 415, 23–31; translation from LW 13: 375.

17. Humphrey and Kemp, eds., *Altarpiece,* 6.

18. Bernard J. Verkamp, "The Zwinglians and Adiaphorism," *Church History* 42 (1973): 486–504.

19. On Zwingli's position, see Charles Garside, *Zwingli and the Arts* (New Haven: Yale University Press, 1966); Eire, *War Against the Idols,* 73–86; Hans-Dietrich Altendorf, "Zwinglis Stellung zum Bild und die Tradition christlicher Bildfeindschaft," in H. D. Altendorf and Peter Jezler, eds., Bilderstreit: *Kulturwandel in Zwinglis Reformation* (Zurich: Theologischer Verlag, 1984), 11–18; Lee Palmer Wandel, "The Reform of the Images: New Visualizations of the Christian Community at Zürich," *ARG* 80 (1988): 105–24, and *Voracious Idols and Violent Hands: Iconoclasm in Reformation Zurich, Strasbourg, and Basel* (New York: Cambridge University Press, 1995), 1–101.

20. For a summary of Calvin's views, see *Institutes* I, xi, 12. See also Eire, *War Against the Idols,* 195–233; Michalsky, *Reformation and the Visual Arts,* 59–74; and Daniel W. Hardy, "Calvinism and the Visual Arts: A Theological Introduction," and Philip Benedict, "Calvinism as a Culture? Preliminary Remarks on Calvinism and the Visual Arts," in Paul Corbey Finney, ed., *Seeing Beyond the Word: Visual Arts and the Calvinist Tradition* (Grand Rapids, Mich.: Eerdmans, 1999), 1–45.

21. He details how the Sacrament is to be celebrated in *Institutes* IV, xvii, 43.

22. John D. Witvliet, "Images and Themes in Calvin's Theology of Liturgy: One Dimension of Calvin's Liturgical Legacy," in David Foxgrover, ed., *The Legacy of John Calvin* (Grand Rapids, Mich.: CRC Product Services, 2000), 139.

23. Ibid.

24. For details, see Oskar Thulin, *Cranach-Altäre der Reformation* (Berlin: Evangelische Verlagsanstalt, 1955); Hartmut Mai, "Kirchliche Bildkunst im sächsisch-thüringischen Raum als Ausdruck der lutherischen Reformation," *Sächsische Heimatblätter* 26 (1983): 244–50; Heinrich Magirius, "Die Werke der Freiberger Bildhauerfamilie Ditterich und die lutherische Altarkunst in Obersachsen zwischen 1550 und 1650," in Hans-Herbert Möller, ed., *Die Hauptkirche Beatae Mariae Virginis in Wolfenbüttel* (Hameln: Niemeyer, 1987), 169–78; Jan Harasimowicz, *Kunst als Glaubensbekenntnis* (Baden-Baden: Koerner, 1996), 25–39; and Helmuth Eggert, "Altaretabel (prot.)," in *Reallexikon zur deutschen Kunstgeschichte* (Stuttgart: Metzlersche Verlagsbuchhandlung, 1937– ; hereafter cited as RDK), 1: 565–602. Note also the excellent recent study by Freya Strecker, *Augsburger Altäre zwischen Reformation*

(1537) und 1635: Bildkritik, Repräsentation und Konfessionalisierung (Münster: LIT, 1998): "Im Südwesten dringt das Altarbild oder Retabel—wenn auch mit einiger Verzögerung—mit dem strengen Luthertum vor" (40).

25. I am indebted to Professor Bonnie J. Noble from the University of North Carolina at Charlotte for introducing me to this altarpiece and for this citation from her paper "The *Schneeberg Altarpiece* and the Emergence of Monumental Lutheran Painting," presented at the annual meeting of the Sixteenth Century Studies Conference (Cleveland, Ohio, November 3, 2000).

26. Illustrations in Thulin, *Cranach-Altäre,* 9–32; and Dillenberger, *Images and Relics,* 104.

27. *RDK* 1: 571.

28. See Alfred Muttray, "Der Hochaltar in der Sankt-Johanniskirche zu Danzig," *Zeitschrift des Westpreußischen Geschichtsvereins* 62 (1922): 57–82; Willi Drost, *Kunstdenkmäler der Stadt Danzig,* 5 vols. (Stuttgart: Kohlhammer, 1957–72) 1: 33–47; and Katarzyna Cieslack, "Die 'Zweite Reformation' in Danzig und die Kirchenkunst," *Zeitschrift für Historische Forschung,* Beiheft 12 (Berlin, 1991): 165–73.

29. These controversies are detailed in Reinhold Curicke, *Der Stadt Dantzig Historische Beschreibung,* but only in the 1686 edition (available at the Biblioteka Gdanska), 301–82. Because of continuing Lutheran-Reformed controversies, the Danzig City Council ordered the deletion of these pages in the more readily available 1687 edition, published by Johann and Gillis Janssons at Amsterdam and Danzig. For a distinctly Reformed interpretation of the Danzig controversy, see Christoph Hartknoch, *Preussische Kirchen-Historia* (Frankfurt am Main and Leipzig: Simon Beckenstein, 1686), 653–862.

30. Hartknoch, *Kirchen-Historia,* 777. On the *fractio panis* as a confessional issue, see Bodo Nischan, "The 'Fractio Panis': A Reformed Communion Practice in Late Reformation Germany," *Church History* 53 (1984): 17–29, reprinted in *Lutherans and Calvinists,* essay 4.

31. Johann Walther, *Widerlegung Des newlich publicirten und außgesprengten Famoßlibells Iacobi Adami, Calvinischer Prediger in S. Elisabeth Kirchen/darinn Er alle reine/Evangelische/Lutherische Prediger zu Dantzig/mit ungrund und unwarheit ansticht* . . . [Leipzig: Tobias Beyer, 1613], 133. See also Hartknoch, *Kirchen-Historia,* 778f.

32. Walther, *Widerlegung,* 136–58.

33. The implications for church architecture were first discussed by Josef Fürttenbach, master-builder for the city of Ulm, in *Kirchen Gebäw. Der Erste Theil. In was Form vnd Gestalt/nach gerecht: . . . Item wo/vnd an welchen Orthen der Tauffstein vnd Altar . . . Ihren gebührenden Stand haben sollen* . . . (Augsburg: Johann Schultes, 1649), Bii[b]–Cii[b]. In addition, see Nicolaus Müller, *Über das deutsch-evangelische Kirchengebäude im Jahrhundert der Reformation* (Leipzig: A. Deichert'sche Verlagsbuch., 1895); Georg Germann, *Der protestantische Kirchenbau in der Schweiz. Von der Reformation bis zur Romantik* (Zurich: Orell Füssli, 1963), 11–24; Dieter Großmann, *Protestantischer Kirchenbau,* Beiträge zur Hessischen Geschichte, 11 (Marburg a. d. Lahn: Trautvetter & Fischer, 1996), 7–25; Hélène Guicharnard, "An Introduction to the Architecture of Protestant Temples Constructed in France before the Revocation of

the Edict of Nantes," in Finney, ed., *Seeing Beyond the Word,* 133–55; and the excellent collection of essays in Klaus Raschzok and Reiner Sörries, eds., *Geschichte des Protestantischen Kirchenbaues. Festschrift für Peter Poscharsky zum 60. Geburtstag* (Erlangen: Junge, 1994). For a discussion of the evolution of the Reformed Communion table, with ample illustrations, see "Les tables de communion," in Marcel Grandjean, *Les Temples Vaudois: L'architecture réformée dans le pays de Vaud (1536–1798)* (Lausanne: Bibliothèque Historique Vaudoise, 1988), 480–89.

34. Andreas Veringer, *Ein Christliche Predigt/Von der newerbawten Kirchen zur Frewden Statt . . . Anno 1608 den 1. Maij* (Stuttgart: Gebhard Grieben, 1608), 12[b]. "Der große steinernde Altartisch ist noch frühgotisch, aber mit Masken und Apostelfiguren aus farbigem Stuck im Renaissancestil überklebt," notes Eduard Paulus, *Die Kunst- und Altertums-Denkmale im Königreich Württemberg. Inventar: Schwarzwaldkreis* (Stuttgart: Paul Neff, 1897), 92. The centrality of the altar in Lutheran worship was emphasized in other dedicatory sermons of the period: e.g., Paulus Jenisch, *Der Lehr vnd Trostreiche LXXXVII. Psalm . . . Kurtzer vnd Summarischer weiß/bey einweihung der newerbaweten Kirchen zu Görlitz/im Ampt Thieben . . . erkleret* (Leipzig: Johan Börners, 1604), 16, 94f; Peter Streuber, *Einweyhung. Der Newerbaweten Schloßkirchen zu Sora* (Sora/Niederlausitz, 1613), Aiv[b], Di[a]f; and Paul Röber, *Außerlesene Zeit-Predigten Auff Etliche hohe Fest- Son- vnd Land-Tage* (Frankfurt am Main: Balthasar C. Wulf, 1658), 570–626, sermon 24, "Vindicae Altarium."

35. Johann Valentin Andreae, *Christianopolis: Utopie eines Christliches Staates aus dem Jahre 1619* (Leipzig: Koehler & Amelang, 1977), 124–25.

36. *Bericht und lehre Göttliches Worts/Was von den Ceremonien unnd eusserlichen Kirchenbreuchen . . . zu halten sey* (Herborn: C. Rabe, 1592), 133; reprinted in Zerbst/Anhalt in 1596.

37. *Christiana Concordia. Das ist/Christliches wiederholtes einmütiges Gespräch/von allen streittigen Religionspuncten/beydes der Lehr und Kirchen Ceremonien belangendt* (Newstadt a. d. Hardt: M. Harnisch, 1591), 236.

38. Bartholomäus Pitiscus, *Außführlicher bericht/Was die Reformirten Kirchen in Teutschland glauben oder nicht glauben: Item/was sie für Ceremonien gebrauchen oder nicht gebrauchen . . . In der Churfürstlichen Pfaltz zu Heydelberg* (Amberg: Michael Forster, 1608), 404.

39. [Jacob Fabricius], *Kurtzer Bericht Was in etlichen benachbarten der Reformirten Religion verwandten/Kirchen der Lande Preussen/von den fürnembsten Puncten Christlicher Religion bishero gelehret worden . . .* (Hanau: Wilhelm Antonius, 1603), 186f.

40. Christoph Pezel, *Auffrichtige Rechenschafft Von Lehr vn Ceremonien, So inn den Evangelischen Reformirten Kirchen/nach der Richtschnur Göttliches Worts angestellet* [Bremen: Bernhard Peters, 1592], 72f.

41. *Endliche Ablehnung Der Theologischen Facultet zu Wittenberg Einrede/wider die Fürstliche Anhältische Christliche Kirchen Reformation. Gestellet durch die Prediger im Fürstenthumb Anhalt.* (Zerbst: B. Schmidts Erben, 1598), Kiv[b].

42. Pitiscus, *Außführlicher Bericht,* 425–29.

43. *Christiana Concordia,* 244.

44. Ibid., 255.

45. *Bericht und Lehre,* 115.

46. *Christiana Concordia,* 240f.

47. Theodorus, *Synopsis doctrinae Lutheranae et Calvinianae,* 223.

48. Johannes Olearius, ed., *Stattliches/außführliches und gar bewegliches Schreiben Der löblichen Ritterschafft im Fürstenthumb Anhalt/so mit der Calvinischen Reformation nicht zu frieden* (Halle: Paul Greber, 1598), 15[a].

49. *Christiana Concordia,* 239.

50. [Jacob Fabricius], *Der Ander Theil/Der Verantwortung D. Jacobi Frabricii . . . Wider Die Probation und Läster Schrifft Michaelis Coleti . . .* (Oppenheim: Hieronymus Galler, 1615), 428.

51. In Mecklenburg-Güstrow, where the Reformed temporarily gained power in 1618, altars immediately were replaced by "Calvinist wooden tables"; see G.C. Friederich Lisch, "Ueber des Herzogs Johann Albrecht II. von Güstrow calvinistische Bilderstürmerei und die Altäre in den Klosterkirchen zu Dargun und Doberan und der Schloßkirche zu Güstrow," *Jahrbücher des Vereins für mecklenburgische Geschichte und Alterthumskunde* 16 (1851): 199–202.

52. Simon Gedicke, *Von Bildern und Altarn/In den Evangelischen Kirchen Augspurgischer Confession . . .* (Magdeburg: Johan Francken, 1597), Diii[b].

53. Aegidius Hunnius, *Gründlicher Bericht Von den Altaren/ob dieselben heutigs tags in den Evangelischen Kirchen sollen abgeschafft werden . . .* (n.p., 1618), Bv[b]; this work was first published at Ursel in 1584.

54. Simon Gedicke, *Calviniana Religio/Oder Calvinisterey/So fälschlich die Reformirte Religion genannet wird/Kurtzer Außzug und Bericht/nach den fürnembsten Hauptpuncten Christlicher Lehre und Ceremonien* (Leipzig: Abraham Lamberg, 1615), 467–79.

55. Hunnius, *Von den Altaren,* Aviii[b].

56. Taurer, *Hochnothwendiger Bericht,* Si[a].

57. Ibid., Tiii[a]; Olearius, ed., *Bewegliches Schreiben,* 24[b].

58. Gedicke, *Calviniana Religio,* 476, 469.

59. Gedicke, *Von Bildern und Altarn,* Ciii[a].

60. Ibid., Cii[a–b].

61. Taurer, *Hochnothwendiger Bericht,* Siii[b]-Tiii[b].

62. Gedicke, *Von Bildern und Altarn,* Tiv[b]; Hunnius, *Von den Altaren,* Aix[b].

63. Philipp Arnoldi, *Caeremoniae Lutheranae. Das ist/Ein Christlicher/Gündlicher Unterricht von allen fürnembsten Caeremonien, so in den Lutherischen Preussischen Kirchen/in verrichtung des Gottesdienstes/adhibirt werde . . . Den Calvinischen Caeremonienstürmern entgegen gesetzt* (Königsberg: Johann Schmidt, 1616), 101.

64. Gedicke, *Von Bildern und Altarn,* Vi[a].

65. Ibid.; see also Hunnius, *Von den Altaren,* Aix[b].

66. Arnoldi, *Caeremoniae Lutheranae,* 100f.

67. Ibid., 99.

68. Gedicke, *Calviniana Religio,* 478.

69. Arnoldi, *Caeremoniae Lutheranae,* 89f.

70. ". . . weil wir denselbigen [Altar] auß keiner Superstition und aberglauben/ sondern als ein frey Mittelding/auß Evangelischer Freyheit gebrauchen/welcher

eusserlicher umbstandt sonst der Substantz und wesen des Abendmahls nichts gibt oder nimpt" (Hunnius, *Von den Altaren,* Biv[b]). The same point was made by [Theolog. Facultet zu Wittenberg], *Notwendige Antwort/Auff die im Fürstenthumb Anhalt Ohn langsten ausgesprengte hefftige Schrifft/Darinnen . . . die jetzige unnötige Newrung/ mit Abwerffung der Bilder/Altäre/auch anderer Ceremonien, vergeblich beschönet . . .* (Wittenberg: Zacharias Lehmann, 1597), 4[b]–5[a].

71. Gedicke, *Von Bildern und Altarn,* Bii[a].

72. Adam Crato, *EXAMEN Der Anhaltischen genanten/und von Doctor Andreas Carlstat entlehneter Schlußsprüche/von abtilgung der Altarn und Bilder . . .* (Magdeburg: Paul Donat, 1597), Civ[b].

73. Polycarp Leyser d. Ä., *Calvinismus, Das ist: Ein Erclerung des Christlichen Catechismi Herrn Doctoris Martini Lutheri/In acht Predigten . . .* (Leipzig: Johann Beyer, 1596), 16[a].

74. Vincenz Schmuck, *Assertio. Wiederholtes Bedencken Uber dem newen Hessischen Catechismo, Confession, und genannten Verbesserungs Puncten* (Leipzig: Michael Lautzenberger, 1611), Hi[a].

75. Theodorus, *Synopsis doctrinae Lutheranae et Calvianae,* 213.

76. Crato, *Examen,* Gi[a].

77. Ibid., Fiii[b].

78. Polycarp Leyser d. Ä., *Christianismus, Papismus & Calvinismus* (Dresden: Matthes Stöckel, 1602), 22.

79. Crato, *Examen,* Fiv[a].

80. Arnoldi, *Caeremoniae Lutheranae,* 138.

81. Johann Arndt, *IKONOGRAPHIA. Gründtlicher vnd Christlicher Bericht/Von Bildern/jhrem uhrsprung/rechtem gebrauch und mißbrauch . . .* (Halberstadt: Georg Koten, [1597?]), 48[a].

82. Ibid., 10[a]. The same point was made by other Lutheran writers, e.g., Hunnius, *Von den Altaren,* Aii[a]–Aiii[a].

83. Scott Hendrix, "Rerooting the Faith: The Reformation as Re-Christianization," *Church History* 69 (2000): 568.

84. Ibid., 569.

85. Polycarp Leyser d. Ä., *Eine wichtige/vnd in diesen gefährlichen Zeiten sehr nützliche Frag: Ob/wie/vnd warumb man lieber mit den Papisten gemeinschafft haben/ vnd gleichsam mehr vertrawen zu Jhnen tragen solle/denn mit/vnd zu den Calvinisten* (1602; rpt., Leipzig: Abraham Lamberg, 1620), 2.

Worship Outside of "Church"

five

Change and Continuity in Medieval and Early Modern Worship: The Practice of Worship in the Schools

KARIN MAAG

Editors' Introduction

A full view of worship cannot be limited to what happens on Sunday, or whenever a congregation's primary worship services are scheduled. Worship practices in nearly every time and place spill over into other facets of community life. In sixteenth-century Geneva, liturgical change at the time of the Reformation not only reordered church practices, but also changed practices in the homes and schools. This essay extends the argument of Robert Kingdon's overview to probe specifically these school-based worship practices.

This essay also begins to make more explicit the idea that while the content and particular practices of worship did change, much also remained the same. Although medieval and Reformation leaders in Geneva may have disagreed on the form of worship that boys were to learn in school, they did agree that learning prayers and incorporating religious ritual in the daily schedule of classes was fundamental in ensuring that these pupils would later become good Christian citizens of Geneva.

Primary Sources Introduction

The following paragraphs are taken from what may seem like an unlikely source for information about worship practices: the charters or statutes of schools. Apart from laying out the structure of the curriculum, these documents focused their attention on making sure that the boys' spiritual education was nurtured, as well as their intellectual training. Note that the first document has a more personal intent, as it reflected the intentions of the man who funded the first Genevan public school.

A. Pre-Reformation

I. From the charter of foundation for the College de Versonnex, Geneva, 1429[1]

On 30 January 1429, in the presence of the notary and the witnesses listed below, honorable and prudent François Versonay, citizen of Geneva, appeared. For the good and salvation of his soul and those of his relatives and benefactors, he wishes to put to pious and salutary use some of the goods which God has entrusted to him. He added that in his opinion, education is a good work, because it banishes ignorance, leads to wisdom, shapes morals, teaches virtues, and because of all this, it facilitates and encourages the smooth and effective running of public affairs. . . .

All schoolchildren who come to the school will have to recite daily a Paternoster and an Ave Maria on their knees in front of the altar to be built in the school. This is to be done for the soul of the said François and of his relatives and benefactors, and so that during the entire day that follows, the souls and minds of the students will be directed to the knowledge of their Creator, and so that their piety may increase. Failure to do this will lead to being punished with a ruler for the boys and young men, and to a whipping for the small children. . . .

The said François Versonay, impelled by his piety, will also establish and fund a chantry in the said school, centered on the altar to be built there. The chantry will be to the praise and honor of the Almighty, the holy Virgin Mary his mother and all the heavenly host, especially Saint Nicholas and Saint Catherine the virgin. . . . The rector and his successors in this chapel of Saint Nicholas and Saint Catherine will be required to celebrate or have an appropriate chantry priest celebrate a Mass every

Monday morning in perpetuity for the healing and salvation of the above-mentioned benefactors. All the schoolboys at the school, together with their masters, must attend this Mass, under pains of punishment with the ruler for the boys at every level.

II. From the "Statutes and ordinances of the school, which must be observed both by the rector and regents as by the pupils. Done on 8 April 1502."[2]

Firstly, the rector of the schools of this city must diligently and conscientiously see that his pupils are taught good morals, virtues, and knowledge. Also, on feast days the said rector must read a lesson from the gospels, epistles, and life of the saints, and the schoolboys must be there to hear him according to their capacity. Furthermore, the said rector must lead his pupils to the noon church service on Sundays. Also, all instructors citywide must bring and accompany their pupils to the rector of the schools so that these pupils too can attend the church service in the order prescribed by the rector, and listen to the readings on the gospels or the epistles on feast days.

B. Post-Reformation

From "L'ordre estably en l'escole de Geneve par noz magnifficques et tres honnorez seigneurs syndiques et conseil de ceste cité de Geneve . . . 1559."[3]

On the schoolchildren

The principal and regents must divide all the pupils into four groups, not according to their classes, but according to their neighborhoods, and must make a list of each group, giving one list to each regent. Thus the pupils must come to church in their own group, and be seated in a specific place in each church, assigned to them by the magistrates. No one else should be allowed to sit there.

All the pupils must come to church in good time, to the Wednesday morning service and to the two Sunday services, one in the morning and one in the afternoon, and to the catechism service. They are to sit in their seats and listen to the sermon attentively and with reverence.

In each church, one of the regents should be there in good time, so as to oversee his group. If necessary, after the sermon he should read out the list of pupils and take note of those who were absent or failed to listen attentively to the Word of God. These pupils, if found to be at fault, will be punished publicly the next day in school according to the seriousness of their offense. . . .

The pupils should begin each day in their classrooms with the prayer specially written for them in the catechism. Each one should in turn recite it devoutly. . . . After the morning classes, each one in turn should recite in each class the Lord's Prayer and a brief prayer of thanksgiving. . . . The pupils should return to the college both in winter and summer at 11 o'clock and then should practice singing the Psalms until noon. From noon to one they should be taught for an hour, and then should have a snack, followed by prayers, followed by writing exercises or homework. Then they should have two more hours of class, and then gather at the sound of the bell in the assembly room. . . . Finally, three pupils each day in class order should recite in French the Lord's Prayer, the Creed, and the Ten Commandments. After this, the principal should dismiss them, blessing them in God's name.

On Wednesdays, as stated above, they are to attend the morning sermon. . . . On Saturdays . . . from three to four . . . they should recite the passages that will be dealt with on the following day in the Catechism session, and the regents should explain the meaning to them in a clear and understandable way, according to their level. . . .

On Sundays, they should listen to the sermons, meditate on them, and take notes on them. During the week before the celebration of the Lord's Supper, one of the ministers of the Word of God should give a short talk about the Lord's Supper in the assembly room, exhorting his hearers to fear God and maintain peace among themselves.

Notes

1. Original in Latin, translated into French by J.A. Galiffe in *Matériaux pour l'histoire de Genève* (Geneva: J. Barbezat, 1829), 1: 139–48. English translation by K. Maag.

2. In Jules Vuy, "Notes historiques sur le Collège de Versonnex et documents inédits relatifs à l'instruction publique, à Genève, avant 1535," *Mémoires (Institut Genevois)* 12 (1867): 39–40. Translated from the Latin by K. Maag.

3. Original in French, published in Sven and Suzanne Stelling Michaud, eds., *Le Livre du Recteur de l'académie de Genève* (Geneva: Droz, 1959–80), 1: 68–69. Translated from the French by K. Maag.

In 1538, in an anonymous text designed to recruit pupils for Geneva's Latin school, the writer laid out the entire curriculum to be followed in the classes. He detailed the textbooks and topics of study at length and then continued, "Because we cannot expect that our labor and study will bear fruit unless the Lord helps us and enlightens us with his Holy Spirit, we always begin and end our classes with prayer."[1] This brief statement encapsulates much of what was done in Geneva and other educational centers around Europe in linking together academic study and the worship of God. Prayer and study, devotion and intellectual work were activities that took place in school, and the scholarly ethos developed by the authorities stressed worship as a key component of the educational experience.

In the context of change and continuity in medieval and early modern worship, this contribution seeks to understand worship as it took place in schools both prior to the Reformation and afterward. The forms of worship inculcated in children in school play an important role in the larger story of worship in the medieval and early modern period. Indeed, the centrality of worship in school reflects the civic and religious leaders' hopes that as children learned the rituals, these would become increasingly established in common practice. Although only a small proportion of the total population had the opportunity to receive formal education, those who did attend school, particularly beyond the basic vernacular level, were destined for significant careers and leadership positions in their society.[2] Thus the worship practices that the pupils absorbed through daily repetition during their school days shaped not only the immediate recipients but also the wider society, as the pupils took what they had learned and continued their practices in adulthood. For instance, a particularly telling example of the impact of education on worship practices and even confessional allegiance in the wider community comes from the work of the Jesuits in establishing schools to bring the elite youth of Eastern Europe back from Protestantism to Catholicism in the seventeenth century.[3]

The main sources for such a study include charters and statutes, but also other documents outlining how the learning communities worshiped and what the purpose of this worship was. Although these charters and statutes are not perfect sources, given that prescriptive statements do not always accurately depict actual practice, they do reflect the intent of the educational authorities.[4] In addition to the main themes of change and continuity, this contribution also seeks to examine the following questions: Why were the authorities both before and after the Reformation so keen to see worship as a key component of education? Should we distinguish between worship and religious instruction, and if so, how? And finally, how did worship in the schools influence worship in the cities at large?

To analyze these matters effectively, I will focus on one city, namely Geneva, and examine worship in its Latin schools both prior to the Reformation of 1536 and after it, within the broad temporal framework of 1400–1600. Geneva provides an excellent case study, not least because of the generally good survival of its primary sources. The change from Catholicism to Protestantism in the city also enables us to assess whether and in what ways worship in the schools actually changed. Information from other centers of education across Europe will also be included when relevant, for purposes of comparison.

At first, it may seem odd to consider worship practices in schools. Most would agree that while schools are for learning, churches are for worship. Yet in medieval and early modern times, as in some parochial settings today, practices of learning and worship were interrelated. In other words, when analyzing worship in schools, one must be aware of the intimate connection between devotional and instructional activities.[5] The children in Geneva's schools, whether Catholic or Protestant, did not simply pray or follow a style of worship of their own choosing. Instead, they were formally taught to pray, and they learned specific statements of faith, in specific languages. Thus it is at times difficult to categorize the nature of activities described in statutes and charters. For instance, in the post-Reformation Latin school, the Genevan pupils not only attended the catechism service on Sunday afternoon in church as a group, but they also studied on Saturday in class the material to be covered in the Sunday catechism service.[6] The Genevan statutes indicate that the schoolboys were to recite the relevant sections of the catechism and listen to the explanations provided by their regents. Opinions may differ as to whether the recitation and subsequent explanations of the catechism constitute a devotional or worship activity or not. On the one hand, some may consider it more doctrinal or instructional, as catechetical study was intended primarily to teach correct doctrine; but on the other hand, the aim was to prepare the boys better for the catechism service in church on Sunday, to deepen their knowledge and understanding of the faith. This hybrid character of many worship-related activities detailed in the Genevan curriculum does, however, illustrate how effectively education could be used to shape the faith of those who attended school. Thus, worship in schools should be understood in broad terms, covering not only liturgical and church-based activities but also instruction in the fundamentals of the faith, as this instruction served as the bedrock for later faith practices.

In the late medieval and early modern period, education was available for boys and young men at three different levels. The first, vernacular schools (sometimes also open to girls) provided access to basic reading, writing, and counting skills in the language of the area. The focus here was to give the children access to basic literacy, but also to train them in the fundamentals of their faith. Thus the textbooks used were primers, which contained the alphabet but also the basic prayers that the children were meant to learn. In the medieval period in England, for instance, these prayers and devotional texts included the Lord's Prayer, the Hail Mary, the Creed, and the hours of the Virgin, often in English and Latin side by side.[7] Through these primers, children at this level simultaneously learned to read and absorbed the key prayers that they would use in worship both at church and at home throughout their lives.

The second level, Latin schools, was for a more restricted group (boys only), as these provided liberal arts instruction in Latin, focusing on the classics and at times also offering teaching in Greek and the beginnings of Hebrew. The teachers, known as regents in France and Geneva, generally had some university-level education, thus equipping them to provide instruction in the ancient languages and classical texts.[8] This level was of interest only for those who intended to follow careers where such training would be useful, as in the liberal professions, or for sons of well-off families, whose parents could afford both the costs of study and the loss of a wage-earner during these years. Basic literacy was generally a precondition for entry, though many Latin schools did allow boys who could not yet read into the first class.[9] Such pupils, like the children in the vernacular schools, concentrated on acquiring the ability to read through the use of primers, sometimes in the vernacular, and sometimes in bilingual vernacular-Latin versions.[10] The age range of boys in the Latin schools was between approximately seven and sixteen years of age. The final level was that of the university, attended by those who wished to teach in Latin schools or university, or to enter careers in law, theology, or medicine. It should be noted at this stage that many boys and young men attended the various levels of schooling only long enough to acquire the basic skills they were looking for, and did not necessarily ever complete the entire curriculum.[11] In this contribution, I will focus on the

Latin school level, as it included a wider group of people than the universities, but was less ephemeral than the largely unregulated vernacular schools, for which few sources survive. Studying worship in the Latin schools also offers a distinct advantage in that the fifteenth and sixteenth centuries saw a rise both in the number of such schools and in the level of interest of citizens and city councils in what they perceived to be *their* school. Thus the city authorities were willing to invest significant sums of money to provide suitable buildings and high-caliber regents for their sons' education.[12] In other words, the schools were not tangential to the late medieval and early modern urban experience, and hence a study of worship in these schools will be intimately linked to worship in these cities as a whole.

The Genevan Reformation of 1536, led by Guillaume Farel, Antoine Froment, Pierre Viret, and latterly John Calvin, made significant changes to both the doctrines and the practice of worship in the city and surrounding countryside. Many of these changes that took place citywide were clearly apparent in the schools as well, if one compares the two primary sources from 1429 and 1559 that accompany this contribution. The first is the foundation charter of 1429 which established a Latin school in Geneva, through the generosity of the donor, François de Versonnex. De Versonnex, a citizen of Geneva by birth, was known for his charitable gifts, as he also provided funds for two local hospitals to house the poor and sick.[13] In the foundation charter for the Latin school, de Versonnex insisted that many aspects of current Catholic devotional practice take place in the establishment he was funding. For instance, students were to recite the two most common Latin prayers, the Paternoster and the Ave Maria, on a daily basis. De Versonnex also planned that an altar dedicated especially to Saint Nicholas and Saint Catherine the virgin would be placed in the school, and provided funding for a chantry priest, so that there would be a weekly Mass in the school, which all pupils were to attend. His rationale for these practices was consistent with contemporary Catholic beliefs: the prayers of the faithful in this world would aid the souls of the deceased in achieving their salvation, as would the celebration of memorial Masses. Indeed, his entire charter reflects his aim, as it begins "for the good and salvation of his soul and those of his relatives and benefactors." Providing funding for Geneva's Latin school was a meritorious work in de Versonnex's eyes, one that would help to ensure that God would have mercy on him and his extended family. The students and regents in the school did not remain passive recipients of de Versonnex's gift, but were co-actors with him, helping to perpetuate the effect of his good work through their prayers and attendance at the weekly school Mass. Thus the worship taking place in the collège de Versonnex was not intended only for the benefit of the students and their masters. The benefactors of other educational foundations across Europe prior to the Reformation insisted on similar prayers and religious services in return for their donation. In 1482 in Stratford-on-Avon, for instance, a priest named Thomas Jolyffe granted lands and tenements to the guild of Holy Cross of Stratford, to fund a Latin grammar school. In the act of endowment, Jolyffe noted that "the aforesaid grammar priest and his scholars shall twice a week, viz. on Wednesday and Friday, sing an anthem of St. Mary and after the said anthem say devoutly for the aforesaid souls of Master Thomas Jolyffe, John and Jane his parents, and for the souls of all the faithful departed 'Out of the deep.'"[14]

In Geneva, Catholic religious practices persisted beyond de Versonnex's day, as the 1502 statutes, written well after de Versonnex's death but still over thirty years before the Reformation, also provides insight into the importance of traditional worship practices in the school. The mention of feast days and special activities planned for these days sets the document firmly in its Catholic context, as do the instructions to have the rector read to the children from the life of the saints.

When one turns to the 1559 statutes of the *schola privata,* or Latin school, both the form and the intended result of worship in school were different. By 1559 Geneva had been Protestant for over twenty years, but a perennial lack of funds and sufficient teaching personnel had made it impossible to do more than offer intermittent instruction until then. In 1559 Geneva inaugurated its academy, which brought together a Latin school and a center of higher studies, known as the *schola publica.* The statutes of the academy dealt both with the more advanced level and with the Latin school classes. Gone were the altar, the references to the saints, the Masses, and the Latin prayers. There was no weekly worship in the school itself, nor was there a chantry priest. Instead, pupils now recited prayers in French, including the Lord's Prayer, and practiced singing psalms daily for an hour at a time. Apart from the change of language and the disappearance of prayers to Mary, the frequency of prayer in the 1559 statutes is striking. Prayers are mandated at four specific times during the day: before the start of classes, at the end of the morning, prior to recess, and at the end of the school day.[15] Thus in the 1559 regulations prayer was to be the framework or undergirding of the educational process.

As the Latin school was now funded by the city, rather than through the donation of a private individual, it is not surprising that all mention of prayer for the souls of deceased benefactors is omitted in the 1559 text. Indeed, because it is a different kind of document, focusing above all on procedures, the statutes of 1559 give very little inkling as to the purpose of worship in the post-Reformation Genevan Latin school. Genevans could and did still leave money to the city school in their wills, but now such gifts no longer had any impact on the giver's salvation.[16] Yet some school ordinances following the Reformation did retain a focus on the value of the schoolboys' prayers for the donor and family. The ordinances of the Latin school of Sandwich in England, dated 1580, specified, "And on every Saturday in the afternoon, before their going to church, the master and usher or one of them with all the scholars devoutly on their knees, the scholars aloud to say one prescribed form of prayer, wherein shall be made mention of the church, the realm, the prince, the estate of the town and the founder and his posterity."[17] The fact that the school in Sandwich was the result of private philanthropy left more room for personal specifications regarding the worship to be carried out by the pupils than in the schools run and funded by the civic and ecclesiastical authorities. The hybrid theological and liturgical character of the Anglican settlement in England may also help to explain why prayers for benefactors and their families were retained in English schools after the Reformation, while such prayers were no longer acceptable in Calvinist areas.

Another clear change that can be noted between the pre- and post-Reformation Genevan documents is the frequency of church attendance. Although in both cases there is evidence that the schoolboys were to attend church as a group (an issue to which we will return), the 1559 statutes vastly increase the number of parish church services attended by the pupils. Whereas the statutes of 1502 mandate going once a week as a group, namely Sundays at noon, the 1559 statutes have the boys in church in their reserved seating area four times a week: once on Wednesday, and three times on Sunday, including one catechism service. Not only were the schoolchildren to attend these services, but the 1559 text also lays out in detail the preparations that were there to ensure that the pupils received the maximum benefit from going. Thus, in the week prior to the celebration of the Lord's Supper, for instance, one of the ministers was to lead a session in the school, instructing the boys and making them aware of the importance of the upcoming celebration of the Sacrament. On Saturdays, the day before the catechism service, the pupils were to go over the material that would be covered the next day, once again ensuring that they would be active rather than passive participants in the service.[18] Finally, the 1559 document even gives instructions for Sundays, when the boys were not officially in school. They were to listen to the sermons, meditate on them, and write them down. All of these provisions help to point to one main difference between the earlier documents and the post-Reformation ones, namely that church attendance ceased to be a meritorious act in and of itself. By the Reformation period, the faithful, including schoolboys, were to do more than simply be physically present. Instead, they had to try to engage their minds in the worship process, to understand and comprehend the doctrinal significance of what they were doing in church. Part of the reason for the difference in what was required of the pupils was certainly due to the increasing emphasis on preaching as the key feature of worship in post-Reformation churches. The same contrast can be seen in England, if one compares, for instance, the act of foundation of a free grammar school in London in 1503 with the statutes of Westminster school in 1560. While the London grammar school acts called for the teacher (a priest) and pupils to attend Matins, Mass, and Evensong "without jangling or talking or other idell *[sic]* occupacion," the Westminster statutes stated that on saints' days, the students were not only to attend church but also to provide a summary of the sermon, either in English or in Latin, depending on the student's level.[19] Thus as the focus of worship changed, the sought-after response among pupils changed as well: although they were still meant to be obedient and attentive, they were also to understand and explicitly reflect on the central part of everyday worship in Protestant areas, namely the sermon.

And yet, making hard and fast distinctions between worship as it took place in the medieval and in the early modern period in the schools is perhaps less than helpful, as such distinctions focus primarily on the most immediately perceivable differences, ones that have divided and still to an extent divide Protestants and Catholics today. The banning of the Mass and devotion to the saints affected worship in early modern Reformation schools just as in the city as a whole. The strong emphasis on catechetical instruction and receiving the Word of God as preached in the sermon was a characteristic of Reformed Protestantism that was clear to all. Thus in a sense because the elements of change between the medieval and early modern Genevan school documents are most readily apparent, observers could conclude that in fact there was little continuity in terms of worship in the schools before and after the Reformation. However, our project asks us to look more closely at these documents and search out their similarities as well as their very obvious differences.

My central argument is that while there were significant differences of form in the worship done in the schools, the aim of worship practices remained essentially the same both before and after the Reformation. Thus, continuity of purpose undergirded the authorities' perception of the role of worship in school in both the medieval and early modern periods. In other words, those who wrote the charters and statutes for the Genevan schools had the same aims in mind when it came to worship: its central purpose was to teach the children about God and enable them to grow in faith.[20] For instance, de Versonnex's charter explains that one of the purposes of daily prayer in the school is "so that during the entire day that follows, the souls and minds of the students will be directed to the knowledge of their Creator, and so that their piety may increase."[21] Such a statement would not be out of place in a Calvinist document. This intentional use of liturgical practices to build and reinforce faith also emerges in post-Reformation documents: the reason for catechetical training, church attendance, and the pastors' visits prior to celebrations of the Lord's Supper was to teach the boys about the faith and inculcate religious practice in their daily lives. The Bernese school ordinances of 1616 echo this approach: "The purpose and goal of the school should be to train youth properly and well, first of all in the fear of God, pure religion, and Christian faith . . ."[22]

Another striking similarity between pre- and post-Reformation worship practice was the insistence that pupils attend church as a group, even on days that were not schooldays. This system was not unique to Geneva; the school ordinances of Zwinglian Zurich in 1532 state, "As soon as the bells stop ringing, they [the pupils] should then be led to church in an orderly fashion, and stand in one place together. A *Burgermeister* should be requested to leave a place for them in the chancel, alongside older people who are hard of hearing and those who may want to make sketches or take notes during the sermon."[23] There are several possible reasons why the authorities in these cities insisted on pupils' attending church services as a group, both before and after the Reformation. First, such a system ensured that the boys would generally attend, since the regents kept a list of those who were absent, and punishments were forthcoming for those without valid excuses.[24] Leaving church attendance of schoolboys up to the authority of the family was not necessarily a successful strategy, as not all families were likely to perceive that such frequent attendance was necessary for anyone, let alone youngsters.[25] Second, having the boys sit together, generally somewhere in the front, and therefore under the eye of the congregation, could help to ensure more attentiveness among the boys than if they were scattered around the building and able to sneak out more easily. Finally, by including regulations on church attendance in the school ordinances, the authorities were seeking to ensure that the school's worship activities and those of the city as a whole were not separate. Because the boys and their teachers were also part of the community of the faithful, they were to worship with their community on a regular basis.

This practice of joining townsfolk for worship contrasts interestingly with the situation in the German territories, especially in Hesse, as reported by William Wright. He argues that "daily matins and vespers became almost exclusively school worship services in the schools of the Protestant territories in the sixteenth century." His description of the daily worship in Melsungen in 1557 includes the singing of hymns and psalms (at times in Latin), Latin readings from the Old and New Testaments, and a sermon three days a week.[26] Thus this worship was different from the Genevan and Swiss practice not only in terms of its attendance, but also in terms of language, as Latin disappeared from church services in Reformed areas.

The other common factor linking the documents from Catholic and Calvinist Geneva is the realism of the authorities when it comes to the natural propensity for worship among the pupils. Both de Versonnex's charter and the 1559 statutes lay out clearly the penalties for not attending the Mass or the sermon, or not saying the correct prayers at the correct time. The authorities seem to have had little confidence that the boys would freely follow the worship pattern laid out in these texts, or that their behavior in church, for instance, would be consistently good. Hence regents had to accompany their charges and sit with them in church, to watch over their conduct. Thus the similar intention to use worship in schools to promote the piety and faith of the children was mirrored by a level-headed perception that these forms of worship and devotional practices had to be taught, and did not come naturally to the pupils. In both Catholic and Protestant educational contexts, worship was a learned activity, not an innate one.[27]

Hence in the broader context, religious practice in the schools was vital for both Catholic and Protestant authorities as much because it showed children, and by extension the community at large, the right way to worship, as because of its intrinsic religious value. By the time they left the most advanced class, the boys who attended Geneva's Latin school would have absorbed the liturgical practices of their day, and would, the authorities hoped, continue in these practices throughout their adult life. In particular, the students were to play a significant role in teaching older members of the community the correct way to worship. This is especially true for Geneva in the years immediately following the Reformation, when the children were to provide assistance for the implementation of specific liturgical changes. One of the most important was the singing of psalms. It should be noted that the use of schoolchildren to help in the musical leadership in worship predated the Reformation. In England, for instance, special institutions known as song schools were created specifically to provide for the training of boy choristers to provide music for worship services. Those attending the song schools could learn reading, and perhaps some writing, as well as focusing on learning both the techniques of singing and the music for worship.[28] The role played by these schoolboys in church is illustrated in an extract from the statutes of the grammar, song, and writing schools at Rotherham in England in 1483: "The master instructor of singing for the time being and the said boys shall every Friday for ever devoutly chant at the Jesus altar in the parish church, at the Jesus mass and at vespers on the same days there for ever, . . . and on every eve of a feast of the Blessed Mary at vespers, an anthem of Our Lady at her altar in the chapel on Rotherham bridge; and every Saturday throughout the year at vespers, when it is not an eve of the Blessed Mary, an anthem of the Blessed Mary at her altar in the same church."[29] In such cases, though the boys studied more than simply music in school, the chief purpose for their instruction was to prepare them to participate in worship.

The Reformation authorities retained the focus on using schoolboys as leaders of music for services in church, though in most cases music was now a part of the curriculum rather than the main reason for the school's existence. In Lutheran areas, schoolboys attending the Latin schools were taught the chorales that the congregations sang in church. In his work, Gerald Strauss notes that if the visitation committee found that the congregational singing was rather tentative and lacking in confidence, the amount of time spent in singing practice in the local school would be increased.[30] In Lutheran Augsburg, the *Kirchenordnung* of 1537 stated that children attending the German schools should be taught the hymns so that they could help with the singing during worship services in their parishes.[31] In the case of Geneva, we have already seen how the 1559 statutes set forth an hour of psalm singing in school per day. At a time when the Genevan congregations were still getting used to this facet of church worship, the children were being trained to help the congregations learn the melodies and the words. Thus both Lutheran and Calvinist authorities preserved an element of continuity in worship from Catholic schooling by retaining the focus on having the schoolboys help sustain the musical elements of the church services. Once again, though the form of singing changed, the leadership role played by the boys in worship continued to be fostered through practice in class and performance in church.

The role of the schoolboys in leading the singing in Geneva was so important that in April 1543, the Genevan Small Council (the ruling body of magistrates in the city) discussed the appointment of a cantor. His tasks included teaching the children to sing for an hour a day and having them lead the congregation in the singing of the Psalms. Indeed, the significance of this task was such that the council agreed to pay Guillaume Franc, the first cantor, the sum of one hundred florins a year.[32] Yet even offering the inducement of a salary and having the children practice daily did not always guarantee results. Indeed, one of Franc's successors, Guillaume Fabri, got into trouble with the magistrates in August 1545 after an evening service at the church of Saint Gervais, where the singing was a disaster because the children performed so badly.[33] The fact that the authorities were so concerned about this problem that they considered terminating Fabri's contract indicates how important the children were as leaders of the psalm singing. Thus the schoolboys' daily hour of psalms in school not only served to build up their own knowledge of God and practice of the faith, but also made a significant contribution to worship in Geneva as a whole.

The schoolboys also served as instructors in another area of religious practice in the city, namely in prayer. The 1559 ordinances list three specific texts that the pupils were to recite daily in turn, namely the Lord's Prayer, the Ten Commandments, and the Creed, all in French. These were the core documents of belief in Calvinist Geneva, and were also the texts that everyone had to be able to recite from memory before being allowed to partake in the Lord's Supper. As the Latin school pupils recited these prayers in school on a daily basis, they were among the most proficient, and indeed their expertise was called upon by those who had more difficulty learning these key statements. For instance, on March 23, 1542, Jaques Emyn, a pack-saddler, appeared before the Genevan Consistory to be questioned about his faith. He managed to recite the Lord's Prayer fairly well, but seemingly could not handle the Apostles' Creed or the Ten Commandments. Significantly, the records state, "Also the said Jaques offered that if someone sent him a young child or any other that would teach him to say his faith and creed, that he would be pleased, and would spare no effort with him."[34] Although Emyn did not specifically request a schoolboy, the most likely children able to teach someone else these texts were those who had benefited from the regular instruction in the Latin school.

Thus the children who attended Geneva's Latin school, especially after the Reformation, could find their newly acquired knowledge of Reformed liturgy put to use, not only in school but also outside it, to help guide the Genevan community as a whole to forms of worship that were distinctive both in language and in form. As worship shaped the communal identity of the city, the participation of the pupils in these rituals both underlined their belonging to this community and their exemplary status within it.[35]

In sum, while there was a considerable amount of change in the forms of worship in schools following the Reformation, the aims remained the same as they had been in Catholic times. Like the rest of the Genevan inhabitants, those attending the Latin school shifted from traditional Catholic devotional practices such as reciting Latin prayers, invoking the Virgin Mary and the saints, and attending Mass, to Reformed practices, including singing psalms, reciting vernacular prayers, and listening to sermons. However, the divergence of forms was counterbalanced by a similarity of intent: the aim of worship in the Latin school was to imbue the pupils with habits of worship that would then continue throughout their lifetime and have a ripple effect on their surroundings. By molding the worship practices and devotion of one of the most malleable sectors of the population, the authorities, both Catholic and Protestant, hoped to shape the faith not only of the schoolboys, but also of the wider community of which they remained a part.

Notes

1. *L'ordre et maniere d'enseigner en la ville de Geneue au College. Description de la ville de Geneue* (Geneva: Jean Girard, 1538), [A3v].

2. Karin Maag, "Education and Literacy," in Andrew Pettegree, ed., *The Reformation World* (London: Routledge, 2000), 535–44.

3. See Rona Johnston Gordon, "Patronage and Parish: The Nobility and the Recatholicization of Lower Austria," in Karin Maag, ed., *The Reformation in Eastern and Central Europe* (Aldershot: Ashgate, 1997), 226–27.

4. See in this context Susan Karant-Nunn's critique of surveys of Luther's impact on German education in "The Reality of Early Lutheran Education: The Electoral District of Saxony—A Case Study," *Lutherjahrbuch* 57 (1990): 128–29.

5. For an interesting light on this question, albeit from a slightly later period, see C. John Somerville, "The Distinction Between Indoctrination and Education in England, 1549–1719," *Journal of the History of Ideas* 44 (1983): 387–406.

6. See the Genevan school statutes of 1559 as presented in primary source 2.

7. See Nicholas Orme, *English Schools in the Middle Ages* (London: Methuen, 1973), 62–63.

8. George Huppert, *Public Schools in Renaissance France* (Urbana: University of Illinois Press, 1984), 51–52. A similar level of training for Latin school teachers was expected in England: see Orme, *English Schools,* 150–51.

9. Huppert, *Public Schools,* 41–42.

10. For information on the books used by pupils in the entry-level class in Geneva, see Henri Delarue, "Les premiers manuels en usage au collège de Genève," in *Le Collège de Genève 1559–1959: Mélanges historiques et littéraires* (Geneva: Alexandre Jullien, 1959), 57–75, esp. 59–61.

11. Huppert, *Public Schools,* 44.

12. See Huppert, *Public Schools,* esp. chap. 3, 29–46.

13. J. B. Galiffe, *Genève historique & archéologique* (Geneva: Georg, 1869), 304.

14. "The Grammar School Endowed by Master Thomas Jolyffe, Gild Priest, 1482," in Arthur Leach, ed., *Educational Charters and Documents 598–1909* (Cambridge: Cambridge University Press, 1911), 385.

15. Genevan statutes of 1559, primary source 2.

16. For a partial list of gifts given to the Genevan Academy, see Charles Borgeaud, *Histoire de l'université de Genève: L'académie de Calvin 1559–1798* (Geneva: Georg, 1900), 35–36.

17. "Sandwich School, 1580: Religious Observances," in David Cressy, ed., *Education in Tudor and Stuart England* (New York: St. Martin's Press, 1975), 89.

18. Similar regulations appeared in the statutes of other Reformed Latin schools, as in Montauban, for instance. See Elizabeth Hudson, "The Protestant Struggle for Survival in Early Bourbon France: The Case of the Huguenot Schools," *Archiv für Reformationsgeschichte* 76 (1985): 282.

19. "Foundation of Free Grammar School by Ex-Lord Mayor, 25 Jan. 1503," and "Statutes of Westminster School. 1560," in Leach, ed., *Educational Charters,* 436–39, 519.

20. Hudson finds similar religious purposes in French Calvinist and Jesuit Latin schools: "The notable fact is that both the Huguenot and Jesuit collèges assumed full responsibility for producing devout Christians as well as well-lettered citizens." Hudson, "The Protestant Struggle," 282.

21. See primary source 1.

22. See Karin Maag, "The Spectre of Ignorance: The Provision of Education in the Swiss Cities," in W. Naphy and P. Roberts, eds., *Fear in Early Modern Society* (Manchester: Manchester University Press, 1997), 140.

23. Ibid., 144.

24. The regents of the school in Sandwich, mentioned above, also had to note for subsequent punishment the names of the students who "absent themselves from such coming to the church, or from being at the church, or came tardy to it, or otherwise use not themselves reverently there in prayer." "Sandwich School," in Cressy, ed., *Education,* 89.

25. Indeed, one of the problems facing Reformation clergy was that families often failed to live up to the high hopes of their pastors that parents would play a leading role in inculcating religious faith and practice into their youngsters. Gerald Strauss, *Luther's House of Learning* (Baltimore: Johns Hopkins University Press, 1978), 130–31.

26. William J. Wright, "The Impact of the Reformation on Hessian Education," *Church History* 44 (1975): 195.

27. For other examples of the emphasis in schools on learning faith and worship practices following the Reformation, see Anthony Fletcher, "Prescription and Practice: Protestantism and the Upbringing of Children 1560–1700," in Diana Wood, ed., *The Church and Childhood* (Oxford: Blackwell, 1994), 335–36. "The school day included prayers and attendance of the scholars at the local church on Sundays was normal." See also Somerville, "Indoctrination and Education," 388.

28. On song schools, see Orme, *English Schools,* 62–68.

29. "Foundation of Jesus College, Rotherham, with Three Schools of Grammar, Song and Writing, 1 Feb. 1483," in Leach, ed., *Educational Charters,* 433.

30. Strauss, *Luther's House of Learning,* 232–33. See also primary source A in Bodo Nischan's contribution to this volume.

31. Philip Broadhead, "'One Heart and One Soul': The Changing Nature of Public Worship in Augsburg, 1521–1548," in R.N. Swanson, ed., *Continuity and Change in Christian Worship* (Woodbridge: Boydell Press, 1999), 124.

32. Registres du Conseil de Genève 37, fols. 61, 68, 70, 85, cited in Pierre Pidoux, *Le Psautier Huguenot du XVIe siècle: Mélodies et documents,* 2 vols. (Basle: Baerenreiter, 1962), II, 19.

33. Registres du Conseil 40, fol. 202v, in Pidoux, *Le Psautier Huguenot,* II, 28.

34. Robert M. Kingdon, et al., eds., *Registers of the Consistory of Geneva in the Time of Calvin. Volume 1: 1542–1544* (Grand Rapids, Mich.: Eerdmans, 2000), 22.

35. On the importance of worship in early modern cities as an expression and reflection of communal patterns, see Broadhead, "Public Worship," 116–27, and Bruce Gordon, "Transcendence and Community in Zwinglian Worship: The Liturgy of 1525 in Zurich," in Swanson, ed., *Continuity and Change,* 131.

The Development of the English Prayer Book

SUSAN M. FELCH

Editors' Introduction

The sensibilities of Reformation revision resulted not only in altered public worship patterns, but also in changing practices of private devotion. Many of the prayer books that form the sources for this contribution were intended for laypeople, especially laywomen. Hence extending the parameters of worship beyond what went on in church services to include worship in schools and at home allows us to encounter the experience of a broader range of people within medieval and early modern society.

In this essay, Susan Felch describes the development of the books used to guide personal and family worship in England. Along the way, she highlights several points of discontinuity, from the obvious, such as the rise of the vernacular, to the more subtle, including a change from memorization to reading prayers. She also highlights several key areas of continuity, namely the continued use of books, the need to balance discipline and flexibility, and the use of texts that embody a communal, rather than individual, view of the Church.

Primary Sources Introduction

The prefaces of prayer books and primers often provide insights both into the purpose of those who had the books printed and into the ways in which the prayer books were meant to be used. The writers of the prefaces clearly felt that their readers needed more than simply the texts of the prayers. So, they provided a framework of devotion, which readers could then use as a means of integrating the sacred into their daily lives in a variety of ways.

A. *Thys Prymer in Englyshe and in Laten*[1]

[B6v] The Preface and Manner to Live Well, Devoutly, and Salutarily Every Day for all Persons of Mean Estate.
Compiled by Master John Quentin, Doctor in Divinity at Mary's.[2]
Translated out of French in the English by Robert Copland, printer at London.

For to begin the manner of salutary or healthful living. And to come to perfection (how well I have more need to be instruct[ed] than for to teach other[s]) yet keep these small[3] doctrines here following to your powers. First, rise up at six of the clock in the morning in all seasons and in your rising do as followeth: Thank our Lord of the rest that he gave you that night. Commend you to God, to our blessed lady, Saint Mary, and to that saint which is feasted that day, and to all the saints of heaven. Secondly, beseech God that he preserve thee that day from deadly sin and at all other times. And pray him that all the works that other doeth for you may be accept[able] to the laud of his name, of his glorious mother, and of all the company of heaven.

When you have arrayed you, say in your chamber or lodging Matins, Prime, and hours if ye may. Than go to the church [bef]ore ye do any worldly works if ye have no needful business, and abide in the church the space of a low mass [mean]while, where ye shall think and thank God of his benefits.

Think a while on the goodness of God, on his [B7r] divine might and virtue. Think what gift he hath given to you to create you so nobly as to his image and likeness. Think also what grace he hath done to you in the sacrament of baptism, cleansing your soul from sin. Think how many times ye have offended him since ye were christened. Think how meekly he hath abided your returning from sin. Think from how many dangers he hath preserved your body and soul. Think how ill ye have bestowed the time that he hath given you to do penance. Think how many times he hath forgiven you in shrift and how many times ye have fallen [in]to sin again. Think in what pain ye had been now and ever if God had taken you out of this world when ye were in deadly sin.

Then know how dearly he bought you from the danger of the devil, suffering continual pains in this world about the space of thirty-two years, going barefoot in cold and heat, suffering hunger and thirst and many shameful injuries, and how dearly he redeemed you, giving his precious body, his blood, and his soul. And at this point consider all the pains of his woeful passion as God will give you grace. Think also what pain his dear and glorious mother suffered all that while.

Consider his sharp judgement at the hour of death. And touching this death, think often thereon and that ye cannot escape it, nor knoweth when nor how, in what estate, nor what place nor time, day [B7v] nor hour. Think then what shall become of the worldly goods that ye have gathered and spared[4] with great labor and how loath ye shall be to leave them and all your friends and kinsfolk. And that more is when your soul in great pain shall leave your body to rot in the earth. Consider then what shall become of your strength, beauty, youth, health, and other wealth of the body.

Think what the poor soul shall do when it goeth alone without company where it was never. Think what it shall do when it seeth the horrible enemies that would draw it to perdition if ye die in deadly sin. Think how woeful a journey it shall be when ye must yield a general reckoning of all your works, words, and thoughts without exception of any thing. Think how God shall give you grace. Think on the horrible pains of hell and on the cruel company of devils, where without end ye shall never have release if ye die in deadly sin. And think on the inestimable joy of the saints in heaven, the which our Lord hath promised you if ye live out of deadly sin and love him above all thing[s]. And have ye a perfect hope if ye live well, ye shall come to that glory. Amen.

And these be the thoughts that I will that ye have in the church. And if by any other reasonable business ye may not be so long in the church, as is it said here afore, yield thanks to God of his goodness. And think [B8r] on the residue in your house once in the day or in the night if ye may.

When ye are come from the church, take heed to your household or occupation [un]til dinner time. And in so doing, think some time that the pain that ye suffer in this world is nothing to the regard of the infinite glory that ye shall have if ye take it meekly.

Then take your refection[5] or meal reasonably without excess or overmuch forbearing of your meat, for there is as much danger in too little as in too much. If ye fast once in a week it is enough beside vigils and umber days out of Lent. And if ye think the fasting be not good nor profitable, do by counsel.[6] Rest you after dinner an hour or half an hour as ye think best, praying God that in that rest he will accept your health, to the end that after it ye may serve him the more devoutly.

The residue of the day bestow in your business to the pleasure of God. As touching your service, say unto Terce afore dinner. And make an end of all before supper. And when ye may, say Dirge. And Commendations for all Christian souls at the least way on the holy days and, if ye have leisure, say them on other days at the least with three lessons.

Shrive you every week to your curate except ye have great let,[7] and beware ye pass not a fortnight except very great let. If ye be of power, refuse not your alms to the first poor body that asketh it of you that day, if ye [B8v] think it needful. Take pain to hear and keep the Word of God. Confess you every day to God without fail of such sins as ye know that ye have done that day. Consider often either by day or night when ye do awake what our Lord did at that hour the day of his blessed passion and where he was at that hour.

Seek a good and faithful friend of good conversation[8] to whom ye may discover[9] your mind['s] secrets. Inquire and prove him well [bef]ore ye trust in him. And when ye have well proved him, do all by his counsel. Daily tell and follow virtuous company. Eschew the fellowship of them that ye would not be like. After all work, praise and thank God. Love him above all things and serve him and his glorious mother diligently. Do to none other but that ye would were done to you. Love the wealth of another as your own. And in going to your bed, have some good thought either of the passion of our Lord, or of your sins, or of the pains that souls have in purgatory, or some other good spiritual thoughts. And then I hope your living shall be acceptable and pleasing to God.

B. Thomas Bentley, *The Monument of Matrones*[10]

[B1r] To the Christian Reader, Grace and Truth in Christ

Having myself taken no small comfort (good Christian reader) by the reading and perusing of divers very godly, learned, and divine treatises, of meditations and prayer, made by sundry right famous Queens, noble Ladies, virtuous Virgins, and godly Gentlewomen of all ages (who to show themselves worthy patterns of all piety, godliness, and religion to their sex, and for the common benefit of their country, have not ceased, and that with all careful industry and earnest endeavor, most painfully[11] and diligently in great fervency of the spirit, and zeal of the truth, even from their tender and maidenly years, to spend their time, their wits, their substance, and also their bodies, in the studies of noble and approved sciences, and in compiling and translating of sundry most Christian and godly books) [. . .]

And thereupon considering with myself what great profit and singular pleasure might thereby come also to other of like mind to myself, if the same their excellent and rare works (dispersed into several pamphlets and in part something obscured and worn clean out of print, and so out of practice) were by some painful[12] hand collected together and revived, or brought again to their former good and godly use in the church, me thought I could not better spend my time, nor employ my talent, either for the renown of such heroical authors and worthy women, or for the universal commodity of all good Christians than, in and by some apt treatise or collection, to reduce these their manifold works into one entire volume, and by that means, for to register their so rare and excellent monuments, of good record, as perfect precedents of true piety and godliness in womankind to all posterity.

Whereupon, God working in me both the will and consent, I undertook the same in his fear, which when after a sort I had done and perceived that there wanted yet many things to make the same an absolute and perfect book for the simpler sort of women, according to my mind, to satisfy myself further in this my purposed collection, I fell to the perusing of the Holy Bible, and many other good books as well of prayer as of other divine matter such as from time to time have been penned by divers godly learned men, out of the which (that I might now particularly apply that unto them, women I mean, which generally heretofore was written of them, or by some other for them, as also to the intent that all godly and devout women readers might have in some, measure, wherewith to exercise their faith, to stir up their devotion and to satisfy their godly desires and also very readily and without tediousness or distraction of the mind virtuously inclined, [B1v] whatsoever they would either by prayer ask, by meditation ponder, by precepts learn, or by examples imitate, or avoid to their comfort and edification) I endeavored for their sakes, by all possible diligence, to cull and bring out of the rich store and treasury of the approved works of many learned men, things both old and new concerning the same, both for private and public use, adding thereunto such plenty of heavenly and spiritual helps, both for profit and pleasure, as the diversities of so divine matter and verity of so honorable inventions would afford.

Besides, to avoid confusion and disorder (a thing very prejudicial to so holy an exercise) I have carefully digested the same into such a plain, easy, familiar, and certain method, order, and direction, both for matter and manner, as I could possibly devise or was requisite for such a work, to make it profitable to the simple and unlearned reader.

Lastly, because the diversity of matter forced a distinction of the treatises, I fitly, as I could, have divided and contrived the whole book into seven several parts or Lamps, all which for divers good and approved considerations I term or entitle by this general name, *The Monument of Matrons.*

And now make bold, yet under the deliberate view and careful correction of many very grave, wise, learned, and godly Divines, thereunto appointed by authority, as also with the approbation and allowance of the right reverend father in God, my Lord the bishop of London, to publish the same abroad in print, as a book, in the judgement of them that are learned, not unprofitable to the church but very necessary, and in some respect more proper and peculiar for the private use of women than heretofore hath been set out by any. Which I have done, not for that there lacked prayerbooks sufficient for women to read, but only to increase the plenty of heavenly comforts, wherewith this our church and realm of England (thanks be to God) floweth: as also to make this treatise heretofore (in part) private to myself and a few of my friends, now public and common also to you good Christian readers.

For behold (I protest) I have not labored for myself, but for you and all them that seek knowledge, fear God, be devout, and would (not by fits and starts, as those that can find scarce any leisure to attend upon the Lord and his service as they ought, but) day and night continually and incessantly, either silently in heart with Hannah, or openly in mouth with Mary, as they are bound, spend their whole life, and make it their whole work to pray, meditate, and read God's word with other such good books, or at the least to allow to themselves some little portion or part of the day and night, to prostrate themselves apart from all company in prayer and meditation, before the Lord of heaven and earth their creator, redeemer, and savior, and that in all Christian perfection and humble obedience to his word and commandments. So have you, good reader, by the goodness of God, who worketh all our works for us, here now at the length in this Monument or collection contained (if you list[13] so for distinction or names sake to call or entitle them) not only a burning Lamp for virgins, but also a crystal Mirror for Matrons, as also a delectable Dial for to direct you to true devotion, with a perfect Precedent or register of holy prayer for all women generally to have recourse unto, as to their homely or domestical library [. . .]

[B3r] So now least you should gather by any method, order, division, title, direction, or application that you shall find in this book, or any part thereof, that I go about nicely,[14] curiously,[15] or strictly to enjoin you to observe hours, days, feasts, times, or seasons, or to bind you unlawfully to an impossibility, as of necessity, to use all or every of these prayers and meditations, in place, manner, and form as they are set down (although it is to be wished that for the most part they might, if it were possible or the necessities of this turbulent life would permit) that you should not mistake me, I say, and judge that my purpose is in any respect to hinder common prayer, or interrupt the ministration of the word and sacraments in the church, where and at what time I know we ought all to glorify God together with one heart, spirit, and mouth, and to be no otherwise occupied, either in reading or in praying, than the public minister is, unless we would be deemed mere superstitious and under the pretense of several[16] devotion to commit manifest ungodliness, I think it very necessary for me to let you understand (gentle reader) that my meaning hereby was and is simply first to play the part of a faithful collector, by following my copies truly and placing their works and prayers together as I found them referred[17] by the authors for private or public use.

Secondly, for order and memory sake, after the good example of the learned fathers of our time, to entitle, reduce, and apply those other godly meditations and prayers, which for the matter I found worthy the more often use in the church or elsewhere unto some more special place, apt time, and peculiar purpose, than heretofore (to my knowledge) by any others have been entitled, referred, or applied.

But thirdly, and principally by the means of some plain form and easy method of prayer and meditation, to prepare for the unlearned at all times and in all places such and so many sorts as to avoid ignorance and tediousness[18] might conveniently serve to further their godly desires, to the glory of God, the confusion of Satan, and their own eternal comfort in Christ Jesus: referring them notwithstanding, which you shall find proper for the church to be used there only at convenient times by the ordinances of the church lawfully permitted, the rest which are more private to be used elsewhere at your discretions, when and so often as opportunity shall serve, and God's spirit by his heavenly motion give you any occasion.

For as I would not have you think hereby that I myself do in all respects observe this order here prescribed (although I assure you I strive to do it either within book or without and repent from the bottom of my heart the often omission of it in times past) so I with you, good readers, which Christianly have consecrated and vowed to give yourselves to this holy exercise (as the Lord, I say, in mercy shall give you grace, leisure, time, and occasion, and not suffer you to be tired with any worldly necessity) in the name and fear of God, to observe this or that order, method, form, or direction, which he in his word doth allow of, or you know best will keep you in the continual faith, fear, and favor of God [. . .]

[B4r] But now if in wading so far in this argument of prayer, and in making this volume so big, any shall think or say, that I, by mine idleness and time thus spent am very chargeable[19] unto them, and considering the plenty of prayerbooks more portable already extant, shall judge me to have taken a very needless or bootless travail, or to have labored in vain and spent my strength for nothing, as he that would add stars to the sky, or light a lamp at noon day and [B4v] therefore shall deem me worthy in their opinions to lose both *oleum et operam.*[20] Oh forgive me this wrong I pray you and considering that I could not otherwise either satisfy myself to go forward in my determined purpose, according to the prescript order of this collection, or pleasure the simple reader with such plenty and variety of profitable matter, especially in so good paper and fair usual letter, a thing to the aged and feeble sighted reader very grateful and much desired. Let me entreat you whosoever you be, to measure the same rather by the goodness of the contents, of the which the godly can never have enough than by the bigness or dearness of the volume, which to the willing and desirous mind are ever best cheap. So no doubt shall the pleasure and profit of the one at the least countervail, if not far surmount, the pain and charges of the other [. . .]

Therefore leaving to all and every of the worthy works of other godly men or women howsoever here or elsewhere extant, their particular use in the church of God as they were published and to the honorable authors themselves their due deserved praise and perpetual commendation to all posterity, with exhortation to all godly

Christians reverently, willingly, and thankfully to read, receive, and embrace the same, as wherein to the better fulfilling of so heavenly an exercise of our faith most agreeable to God's good will and word is perfectly supplied and accomplished, by the rare gifts, ornaments, and graces of the Holy Ghost in the compilers, whatsoever otherwise through ignorance, wanteth both in me and perhaps in you also (good readers) if you be unlearned. (Give them, therefore, O give them, I say, and that worthily of the fruit of their own hands, and let their own works praise them in all the world.) I, to conclude, humbly submit myself unto the grave judgements of the godly learned, and mine heroical authors living, of whom I meekly crave pardon for this my bold enterprise attempted both with bashfulness, doubtfulness, and fear to become a writer in this so learned an age or to trouble your studies with my rude labors. And here lastly I offer these my labors such as they are unto the good liking and favorable correction as well in matter as in manner of you my right Christian learned readers, of whom in full recompense and satisfaction of any fruit, that either you or the simpler sort shall hereby reap, I only now make this request, as dutifully to reverence the divine works of so noble and learned authors, by whose holy travails you perceive yourselves to enjoy most inestimable benefits, so friendly to take in good part those first fruits of my poor studies, proceeding from a well meaning [B4v] mind and built upon so good foundations as from him that did that he could, though not that he ought to benefit all and to hurt or offend none. That they being now as lamps well esteemed of in the opinion of the rich in virtue and knowledge and gratefully accepted and approved of the learneder sort, as the monuments of so famous matrons, may yet at the least for their sakes become welcome and approved of all other simple Christians and I, by that means, greatly encouraged to go forward in virtuous studies for the benefit of my country with hearty thanksgiving unto God both for his mercy and your great courtesy and goodness towards me in whom I bid you farewell and unto whose heavenly defense, almighty protection, divine favor, and continual blessing, I finally commend and betake both these my labors, myself, and you dear and well beloved readers, beseeching you to love me, as I love you unfainedly,[21] to speak of me and my work, no worse than I do of you and yours Christianly, and that for his sake alone that loved us all most dearly and in that love for us all endured all manner of reproach and slanders that might be most patiently, even to the effusion of his most precious blood often and sundry times truly, as well in fervent prayer as in sweat and otherwise on the cross for our eternal glory to whom therefore and for all the inestimable benefits of his bloody prayers, driry[22] death, and bitter passion be evermore rendered and given as of writers and readers, so of angels, men, and all creatures in heaven, in earth, or in the deep, all possible praise and perpetual glory that heart can think, hand can work, or tongue can speak, Amen.

Yours as his own in him that is all in all and our own forever.

Thomas Bentley

Notes

1. (Rouen, 1538; STC 16008.5).
2. Quentin received his Doctor of Theology at Paris in 1473; Mary C. Erler, "*The Maner to Lyue Well* and the Coming of English in François Regnault's Primers of the 1520s and 1530s," *The Library*, 6th series, 6(1984): 229–43.
3. Few.
4. Saved.
5. Refreshment or meal; often a small meal.
6. Seek the counsel of others.
7. Encounter a major hindrance.
8. Habit of life.
9. Reveal.
10. (London, 1582; STC 1892).
11. With great care and effort.
12. Careful.
13. Desire.
14. Foolishly.
15. Elaborately.
16. Individual.
17. Assigned.
18. Weariness.
19. Burdensome.
20. *Oleum et operam perdere:* to lose time and trouble.
21. Sincerely.
22. Dreary.

First, rise up at six of the clock in the morning in all seasons and in your rising do as followeth: Thank our Lord of the rest that he gave you that night. Commend you to God, to our blessed lady, Saint Mary, and to that saint which is feasted that day, and to all the saints of heaven. Secondly, beseech God that he preserve thee that day from deadly sin and at all other times. And pray him that all the works that other doeth for you may be accept[able] to the laud of his name, of his glorious mother, and of all the company of heaven.

When you have arrayed you, say in your chamber or lodging Matins, Prime, and hours if ye may. Than go to the church [bef]ore ye do any worldly works if ye have no needful business, and abide in the church the space of a low mass [mean]while, where ye shall think and thank God of his benefits.[1]

So now least you should gather by any method, order, division, title, direction, or application that you shall find in this book, or any part thereof, that I go about nicely, curiously, or strictly to enjoin you to observe hours, days, feasts, times, or seasons, or to bind you unlawfully to an impossibility, as of necessity, to use all or every of these prayers and meditations, in place, manner, and form as they are set down (although it is to be wished that for the most part they might, if it were possible or the necessities of this turbulent life would permit) that you should not mistake me, I say, and judge that my purpose is in any respect to hinder common prayer, or interrupt the ministration of the word and sacraments in the church, where and at what time I know we ought all to glorify God together with one heart, spirit, and mouth, and to be no otherwise occupied, either in reading or in praying, than the public minister is, unless we would be deemed mere superstitious and under the pretense of several devotion to commit manifest ungod-

> liness, I think it very necessary for me to let you understand (gentle reader) that my meaning hereby was and is simply first to play the part of a faithful collector, by following my copies truly and placing their works and prayers together as I found them referred by the authors for private or public use.

These two devotional instructions, penned nearly a century apart, trace the trajectory of the English prayer book through the sixteenth century. The first, in straightforward prose, recommends a daily routine: get up at six o'clock; thank God for the night's rest and commit your day into his care; recite a set of fixed prayers; continue your devotions by going to church. The second, in a winding sentence that soon loses its grammatical sense of direction, warns against a settled routine of formulaic prayers and carefully segregates individual devotions at home from the ministry of the Word and the sacraments at church. The first we recognize as Catholic and medieval, the second as Protestant and early modern. The differences could not be more clear, or so it seems.

In fact, juxtaposing these two works, both of which are prefaces to collections of written prayers, reveals a more complex relationship between medieval and early modern modes of piety than the excerpts—and our own prejudices—might suggest.

The first selection, written by the French cleric Jean Quentin in the fifteenth century, is entitled "The Preface and Manner to Live Well, Devoutly, and Salutarily Every Day for all Persons of Mean Estate" and appears to be influenced by the *devotio moderna,* a late medieval movement that emphasized spiritual development and meditation as epitomized in Thomas à Kempis's *Imitation of Christ.*[2] The preface was initially printed around 1500 as "La manière de bien vivre dévotement par chascun jour" and was later translated into English by Robert Copland, a member of Wynkyn de Worde's printshop and a poet, translator, and printer in his own right. The first English version was attached to a 1529 Latin primer published by François Regnault for sale in England.[3]

The Latin primers were printed versions of the wildly popular manuscript Book of Hours, a late medieval best-seller that provided a compact version of the eight canonical monastic hours—Matins, Lauds, Prime, Terce, Sext, Nones, Vespers, and Compline—for use by the layperson.[4] The canonical hours, also known as the Divine Office, were composed of prayers and hymns taken largely from the Psalms and other scriptural passages and appeared in many different forms, each focusing on a religious theme, saint, or season. There were, for instance, Hours of the Cross; Hours of the Holy Spirit; Hours of the Compassion of Our Lady—each with its own designated prayers and hymns. These various services were collected in a liturgical book known as the Breviary. The centerpiece of the Book of Hours, however, was a single set of canonical hours, the Little Office of the Blessed Virgin Mary. The Little Office had developed as early as the eighth century but began to appear in Breviary manuscripts only in the eleventh century. During the following two centuries it became attached to the Psalter, the original lay prayer book, and by the late thirteenth century was appearing on its own as a supplement to, or even replacement for, the Book of Psalms.

In the monastic houses, the recitation of the hours was a time-consuming obligation that required the services of trained liturgists to guide worshipers through the complicated Breviary, with its varying sets of offices. The thirteenth-century Book of Hours simplified daily devotions for the layperson by installing the Little Office of the Blessed Virgin Mary as the single service to be recited each day. The Little Office, however, was soon augmented by other liturgical elements such as the Gospel lessons; prayers to the Virgin; the seven penitential Psalms; Psalms of the Passion; the Litany and Dirge; the Commendation of Souls (a recitation of Psalms 119 and 139 particularly popular in England); other topical hours, such as the Hours of the Cross; and a variety of occasional prayers. In addition, books of hours usually opened with a calendar, often illustrated with the traditional labors of the months, or, by the fifteenth century, the ages of man. But the particular use of these additional elements was not prescribed, their employment being left to the discretion of the individual worshiper.

The encyclopedic nature of the Book of Hours meant that manuscripts varied considerably from one another, so that it is more accurate to speak of books of hours rather than the Book of Hours, if the latter term implies a fixed format and set of prayers. Any specific Book of Hours, for instance, would certainly feature the Little Office of the Blessed Virgin Mary, but might or might not include, for instance, the Hours of the Cross; the Oes of Saint Bridget, a popular set of fifteen short prayers each beginning "O Jesu" or "O blessed Jesu"; the Jerome Psalter, a compilation of biblical texts; or any number of occasional prayers. Indeed, books of hours show astonishing flexibility in terms of both structure and content. Personalized prayers might be added, as in the "Prayer for Myself" written for Blanche of Burgundy and included in the Savoy Hours.[5] As Virginia Reinburg notes, "Devout medieval people collected prayers the way twentieth-century cooks collect recipes. The variety of texts and images found in these manuscripts is staggering."[6]

As books of hours made the transition from manuscript to print culture, and thus became even more widely available, it is not difficult to see why Quentin's preface was selected to introduce many primer editions.[7] Not only did it provide an overall guide for the devotional life of the ordinary layperson—those of "mean estate" addressed in the title—but it also offered a simplified timetable for reciting the hours. Although in a monastic setting Matins would be said around midnight, Lauds at 3:00 A.M., Prime at 6:00 A.M., with Terce, Sext, Nones, Vespers, and Compline following at regular three-hour intervals,[8] Quentin recommends condensing the prayers into fewer time slots more easily fitted into a working person's schedule. Matins (with Lauds collapsed into it) and Prime can be said at home after one has arisen from bed and dressed. These first three offices, presumably of the Blessed Virgin Mary, may be augmented with additional hours, for instance, the Hours of the Cross, if time permits ("say . . . hours if ye may," lines 21–22). Terce should be said before the noontime meal of dinner, with the remaining four hours recited between dinner and supper. Quentin leaves the exact timing as well as the particular grouping of Sext, Nones, Vespers, and Compline to the discretion of the lay Christian. He also recommends the recitation of the Dirge and the Commendations for Souls at least on feast days and, when time permits, on other days as well.

The schedule Quentin suggests takes into account that busy laypeople cannot follow the strict regime of the monastic houses and strikes a balance between organizing daily life around prayer and attending to other responsibilities. His short preface defers repeatedly to the discretion of individual believers. They should observe his pattern as best they can ("following to your powers," lines 11–12), and such phrases as "if ye may" (line 22), "as ye think best" (line 81), "if ye have leisure" (line 88), "if ye be of power" (lines 91–92), or "if ye think it needful" (line 93), which pepper his account, further soften the requirements. He recommends daily attendance at church "if ye have no needful business" (line 23) and suggests that devout believers stay throughout a low Mass, but recognizes that "reasonable business" (line 68) may curtail the time actually spent in church. Indeed, it is possible to complete at home the meditation one begins during Mass ("And think on the residue in your house once in the day or in the night," lines 70–71).

To live "well, devoutly, and salutarily every day," requires, therefore, a good deal of conscious thought and deliberate choice on the part of the believer. The recitation throughout the day of the Little Office of the Blessed Virgin Mary, with its set prayers, is only one aspect of the devotional life. The prayers to be said immediately upon arising from bed, for instance, are not specified. Quentin merely outlines their general content: thanksgiving; recognition of God, Mary, and the saints; and prayer for the coming day (lines 13–20). Such prayers might have been spontaneous, although books of hours often included written prayers to be said "when you rise up," frequently offering several from which to choose. For instance, the morning prayer in one

Quentin-prefaced primer begins, "Holy Trinity, be helping unto me. O God, in thy name I shall lift up mine hands," and concludes with the following petition: "I beseech thy mercy, father most merciful, that thou wilt grant me to spend the day that is to come in thy holy service with all humility, discretion, devotion, and charitable love, that I may be able to do my service due and pleasant unto thee in all my works."[9]

In addition to prayer, Quentin urges other pious practices. The devout Christian should eat moderately and fast prudently, confess sins daily to God and weekly to the curate, give alms, choose a spiritual mentor, and spend time with virtuous friends—all actions that require initiative on the part of the individual believer.

The emphasis of the preface, however, falls not so much on these outward activities as on the inward life of the Christian, particularly on developing the capacity to think about spiritual matters while engaged in everyday responsibilities. This inner life of spiritual meditation is renewed each morning during Mass—not by following the liturgy from a missal or by receiving the Eucharist, but by using the time in church to meditate privately, or, as Quentin puts it, to "think and thank God of his benefits" (line 25). Again, as with the prayers to be said upon arising from bed, Quentin outlines a set of topics for contemplation rather than specifying particular prayers or readings. This section, more than a third of the entire preface, recommends meditating upon God's goodness; one's creation in the image of God; one's re-creation in the sacrament of baptism; one's many sins and God's grace; the sufferings of Christ and Mary; one's death and loss of worldly goods; the horror of dying in deadly sin; the pains of hell; and the glories of heaven (lines 26–65). A devout believer might follow Quentin's advice to meditate during Mass simply by standing quietly and contemplating the topics as outlined. Or, an open book of hours in hand, she might follow the visual choreography performed by the officiating priest while reading—or reciting—composed prayers, for many books of hours included a set of prayers to be said at various points throughout the Mass.[10]

The conscientious layperson who followed Quentin's spiritual advice would develop a rhythm of daily life that integrated contemplation into the active life, a life directed by love of God and love of neighbor. Although he recommends contemplation throughout the day—while engaged in necessary work one should "think" on spiritual matters—Quentin in no way suggests that the active life is itself unholy. To the contrary, he states that the ordinary business of the day should be done "to the pleasure of God" (lines 84–85). Such a life, moreover, should be lived in conscious awareness of belonging to the community of saints. The first prayers of the morning invoked the saints in heaven, while the recitation of Matins and Prime in the bedchamber or the house probably incorporated family and servants, who formed the immediate earthly community. The individual meditation during low Mass was performed in a communal setting, accompanied by visual participation in a communal rite. And the prayers within the books of hours, while admitting of variety, provided a common core to household devotions throughout the West, recited in a common language, Latin. To put it another way, Quentin's preface and the books of hours supplied set common prayers to be recited at home and varied private prayers to be contemplated at church, thus interleaving both domestic and public spheres, as well as communal and individual prayers.

Quentin's advice was apparently well received in England: it was reprinted in thirty-six editions of the primer between 1529 and 1556. While it is difficult to know how many people actually incorporated his rubric into the fabric of their everyday lives, the continued popularity of the treatise suggests that it presented an attractive devotional ideal for the ordinary layperson and marked a strong sense of continuity between late medieval and early modern expressions of piety.[11]

But even within the devotional orbit of the books of hours and printed primers, there were signs of significant changes, not least of which was the linguistic movement from Latin to English. Despite the early-fifteenth-century injunction against the translation of the Bible into English, manuscript primers written entirely in English appeared throughout that century.[12] More conservative books, whether manuscript or printed, retained Latin for Scripture passages and prayers, but began to include rubrics, or explanatory headings, in English. So the owner of a 1498 printed primer could read the words "These prayers following ought to be said [bef]ore thou depart out of thy chamber at thine uprising" before reciting the actual prayers in Latin.[13] English, not always very idiomatic, soon began showing up not only in the headnotes, but in doggerel verse beneath the woodcuts, as in this quatrain accompanying the opening of Lauds:

> How Mary, the mother and virgin,
> Visited Elizabeth, wife of Zachary,
> Which said, Blessed be thou cousin
> And blessed be the fruit of thy body.[14]

and in the translation of indulgences:

> To all them that be in the state of grace that daily say devoutly this prayer before our blessed lady of pity, she will show them her blessed visage and warn them the day and the hour of death, and in their last

> end the angels of God shall yield their souls to heaven, and he shall obtain five hundred years and so many lents of pardon[15] granted by five holy fathers, popes of Rome.[16]

and in versions of popular liturgical and nonliturgical elements such as the fifteen Oes of Saint Bridget.

The lessons from Job in the Dirge were rendered in somewhat awkward rime royal, the choice of much of Chaucer's verse, although not written with his genius, as in these opening lines:

> Save me (Oh Lord) my days be brief and short.
> For what is the man who thou dost magnify?
> Or why from him thine heart dost thou transport,
> Comforting him in the morning, and suddenly
> Thou tempest him again with adversity?
> Why dost thou not so much as suffer me a little
> As for to tarry the swallowing of my spittle[17]

The steady movement toward the vernacular culminated in October 1538 when François Regnault produced a bilingual primer. "This primer in English and in Latin," as it was called, prominently displayed the English text in the center of each two-page opening with the Latin relegated in smaller print to the outer margin (see figures 6.1 and 6.2).[18] Less than ten years later, Thomas Cranmer would state the case for the use of English succinctly in his preface to the Litany: "And to the intent, therefore, [that] your hearts and lips may go together in prayer, it is very convenient and much acceptable to God, that you should use your private prayer in your mother tongue that you, understanding what you ask of God, may more earnestly and fervently desire the same, your hearts and minds agreeing to your mouth and words."[19] By 1538, however, the bilingual primers already provided an implicit imprimatur for the use of the vernacular only two years after William Tyndale had been burned at the stake for translating the Bible into English.

The English-Latin primers also introduced into the daily recitation of prayers the habit of reading. It is not by accident that Quentin, in his preface, recommends that one "say" the Hours of the Blessed Virgin Mary (lines 21 and 85). But by the late 1530s, English men and women who desired to live "well, devoutly, and salutarily every day," might recite the hours in Latin, as they had been taught from their youth, or read them in English. Certainly the arts of memory soon would have begun to be transferred to the English devotional material, as well. It is quite possible that the rhymed version of

Matyns.

Here Gabriell maketh Annunciacyon

Of Chrystes Incarnacyon.

Domine labia
mea aperies.

Et os meū annūcia
bit laudem tuam.

Deus in adiutorium
meum intende.

O Lorde open
thou my lyppes.
And then ſhall
my mouth ſhewe
forthe thy prayſe
O god bēde thy
ſelfe ī to my help

6.1. STC 16008.5, *This prymer in Englyshe and in Laten,* D7 verso. By permission of the Folger Shakespeare Library

Matutine. Fo.xxxij

Lorde haste the to helpe me.
Glory be to the father, to ye sonne and to the holy ghoste.
As it was in the begynnynge: as it is nowe/and euer shalbe. Amen.
Prayse ye the lorde. ¶ Betwene Septuagesima (which begynneth the .iiij. saterday before clene lente) and Easter/for Prayse ye the lorde ye muste say. Laude be to the kyng of eternall glorye. ¶ The Inuitatorye. Hayle marye full of grace/ the lorde is with the. Hayle marye.

¶ The .xciiij. psalme.

Come & let vs ioyfully gyue thankes vnto the lorde: let vs reioyse in god our sauyoure/let vs approche in to his presēs with prayse and thankes geuynge/and synge we vnto hym in Psalmes. Hayle marye full of grace, the lord is with the.
For god is a greate lorde, and a great kyng ouer al goddes, which shall nat forsake his people/in whose power are all the costes of the erthe/and he beholdeth: the toppes of mountaynes. The lorde is with the.

The

Domine ad adiuuandum me festina.
Gloria patri & filio & spiritui sancto.
Sicut erat ī principio et nunc et semper & in secula seculorū amen. Alleluya.
¶ Tempore quadragesimali. Laus tibi domine rex eterne glorie.

Inuitatoriū. Aue maria gratia plena dominus tecum. Aue maria gratia plena dominus tecum.

¶ Psalmus .xciiij.

Venite exultemus dño iubilemus deo salutari nostro preoccupemus faciem eius in cōfessione & in psalmis iubilemus ei. Aue maria gratia.

Quoniam deus magnus dominus et rex magnus super omnes deos: quoniam non repellet dominus plebē suā quia in manu eius sūt omnes fines terre: et altitudines mōtium ipse conspicit. Dominus tecum.

6.2. STC 16008.5, *This prymer in Englyshe and in Laten,* D8 recto. By permission of the Folger Shakespeare Library the Dirge, for instance, was created specifically as a mnemonic device. But, at least initially, devout Christians who had learned their prayers in Latin would not readily have found the English versions on their tongues or in their hearts, but only in their books.

A third significant change, in addition to the movements from Latin to English and from recitation to reading, was the gradual shifting of the prayer book from sacred object to changeable text. As Eamon Duffy has argued, the illuminations (or woodcuts), rubric print, and signs of the cross that filled both manuscript books of hours and early printed primers made these prayer books "more than texts."[20] As sacred objects, the primers provided not simply a set of formulaic prayers to be enunciated day after day, but also a consecrated space for worship and contemplation. Moreover, this space was consonant with that of public and communal worship, for not only the prayers but the very appearance of the books invoked the iconography of the parish church and the liturgy.

Throughout the 1530s, however, transitional primers began to appear that cautiously modified tradition in light of the new doctrinal sensibilities.[21] Although the Little Office of the Blessed Virgin Mary remained intact, as did most of the other liturgical elements, legendary material in the head-notes was eliminated; indulgences, the saints' list, and Marian prayers were pruned; and Gospel accounts from Tyndale's 1534 New Testament were added. The last Regnault primer was even bound with an English translation of the exposition of Psalm 51 by Girolamo Savonarola, an Italian cleric greatly admired by the Reformers.

More directly confrontational were the reformist primers that followed the lead of Luther's 1522 German primer, the *Betbüchlein,* whose preface William Marshall first translated into English in 1534. The preface complained of the "pestilent infections of books and learnings with which the Christian [has] been piteously seduced and deceived," particularly singling out those "garnished with glorious titles and with red letters" such as "the garden of the soul" or "the paradise of the soul."[22]

George Joye's 1530 *Ortulus Anime,* the first English reformist primer and also the earliest primer printed entirely in English, presented itself, however, as just such "a garden of the soul."[23] In light of the Lutheran animus against the *Hortulus,* the title itself may have been a deliberate attempt to insinuate Protestant teaching under the guise of a traditional primer, but the movement from sacred object to doctrinal text was hard to miss. Woodcuts and other visual elements were eliminated, a catechetical dialogue for children, which appeared on lists of prohibited books, was included, as was a plea for the English translation of the Psalms. The calendar was shortened, the fifteen Gradual Psalms, the Litany, and the Dirge with Commendations were all omitted, and the text of the Penitential Psalms, now renamed the Seven Psalms, followed Joye's 1530 English translation of Bucer's Latin Psalter, rather than the traditional Vulgate.

Other reformist prayer books soon appeared, along with scriptural primers, compilations of prayers found in the Bible which entirely discarded the format of the canonical hours.[24]

The proliferation of traditional, transitional, reformed, and scriptural primers during the reign of Henry VIII—the sixteenth-century equivalent of our contemporary worship wars—was sufficiently troubling to generate the first authorized primer in 1545 whose preface called for "the avoiding of the diversity of prayer books that are now abroad, whereof are almost innumerable sorts which minister occasion of contentions and vain disputations, rather than to edify."[25] The authorized primer looks quite traditional in many ways: Joye's catechectical dialogue, Savonarola's exposition, and Tyndale's Epistles and Gospels are evicted; the complete set of eight canonical hours, the Litany and Dirge, and the Psalms of the Passion are reinstated, although some elements are reduced in size. But there are no promises of indulgences, and prayers to the saints and Mary are trimmed, while not being entirely eliminated.

Four years later, with Henry dead and a young Edward on the throne, Cranmer's 1549 *Book of Common Prayer* regularized not only the eucharistic worship service of the English Church, but the daily prayers as well.[26] It collapsed elements of Matins, Lauds, and Prime into the single service of Morning Prayer, and combined Vespers and Compline to form Evening Prayer, omitting Terce, Sext, and Nones. Edward's authorized primer of 1553, printed by William Seres, incorporated these revised morning and evening prayers and also included other reformed elements from the *Book of Common Prayer* such as the revised 1544 Litany without the Dirge and Commendations as well as a variety of prayers. The Marian primers, commencing in 1555 and printed largely in bilingual editions, returned to the format and content of the earlier French-printed primers, with some additional English prayers retained from Henry's 1545 primer and others drawn from the services of English monastic houses. Elizabeth's English Primer of 1559, however, reinstated her father's 1545 primer, including the eight canonical hours, the Dirge, and the Commendations, although she also allowed at least six editions of the Edwardian Seres primer, with its simplified morning and evening prayers, to be printed during her reign, thus permitting the side-by-side production of two quite distinct books.

By 1560, then, there were at least four "authorized," but distinct, primers in circulation: the original 1545 authorized primer; the 1553 Edwardian primer; the 1555 Marian primer, resembling the French-printed primers from the

1530s; the 1559 Elizabethan primer, reinstating Henry's 1545 primer; and reprints of the 1553 reformed Edwardian primer.

These competing, but authorized Tudor prayer books illustrate both the difficulty of regulating private devotions and the increasing diversity—and interchangeability—of the available prayer books. Although Henry could hope that his authorized primer would bring an end to "the diversity of prayer books that are now abroad," it did no such thing. Indeed, in addition to the traditional, transitional, reformed, scriptural, and authorized prayer books of the first part of the century, Elizabeth's reign saw the proliferation of books of private prayer. These idiosyncratic collections of prayers, psalms, hymns, and meditations were used by individuals, but might also find their way to a relatively large public, as exemplified by the many reprints, enlargements, and generally public-domain use of a book like Edward Dering's *Godly Private Prayers for Householders.*[27] But whether used by individuals, family groups, or semipublic gatherings of the godly, these prayer books were now interchangeable texts rather than sacred objects, and their departures from both the books of hours and the *Book of Common Prayer* precluded their use in common, public worship.

Such prayerbooks might be very short. The *Two Fruitful and Godly Prayers* printed by Richard Lante and Richard Banks in 1545 is only six pages long. The first prayer to the Trinity, written in traditional rime royal, begins

O Holy God of dreadful majesty
Verily one, three, and three in one
Whom angels serve, whose works all creatures be
Which heaven and earth directest all alone;
We thee beseech, good Lord, with woeful moan
Spare us wretches and wash away our guilt
That we be not by thy just anger spilt.[28]

James Cancellar's *Alphabet of Prayers,* dedicated to Robert Dudley, the earl of Leicester, on the other hand, was an extensive reworking of morning and evening prayers, complete with psalms, collects, anthems, versicles, and responses.[29] It was reprinted in at least seven subsequent editions.

Another compilation, "A form of prayer to be used in private houses every Morning and Evening," achieved semiauthorized status by virtue of being included at the end of the ubiquitous Sternhold and Hopkins metrical psalter. Consisting of a single long prayer for the morning and another for the evening, accompanied by fewer than a dozen other prayers for various occasions (such as mealtimes), the Sternhold and Hopkins "form of prayer" provided a simple, stripped-down devotional format of unimpeachable Protestant character.

Many Elizabethan Bibles were bound with a *Book of Common Prayer* at the front and a Sternhold and Hopkins at the back, thus presenting their owners with a choice between an authorized public and a semiauthorized private form of morning and evening prayers.

By the end of the century, Andrew Maunsell's catalogue of theological books included nearly one hundred separate titles under the heading of "Prayer," and most of these were prayer books intended for private—that is, family or individual—use.[30]

The movement from the traditional primers through the transitional, reformist, scriptural, and authorized prayer books to the proliferation of private devotional books brings us to our second selection, taken from the preface to Thomas Bentley's seven-part *The Monument of Matrons,* published in 1582.[31] By the 1580s the changes already apparent in the 1538 Regnault bilingual primer were firmly entrenched. With the exception of recusants, English men and women now regularly used the vernacular rather than Latin for their daily devotions. And private prayer books—printed in many editions, with widely varied content and formats, and without an integrated visual apparatus—had ceased to be sacred objects, intimately joined to the parish church and a common liturgy. While both the *Book of Common Prayer* and the private prayer books had their roots in the missals, breviaries, and books of hours of the late medieval Church, by the end of the sixteenth century public prayer and private prayer inhabited separate spheres.

Bentley, indeed, is at pains to distinguish his encyclopedic compilation of prayers both from a set pattern of recitations, as in the traditional saying of the hours, and from official Church services. Whatever "method, order, division, title, direction, or application" readers may find in his book, they are not to imagine that these constitute an officially sanctioned regimen of daily piety. Nor are the private prayers intended as a substitute for, or even corollary to, public worship. Bentley does not conceive of the individual Christian taking *The Monument* to church in order privately to "think and thank God of his benefits" during the performance of the Mass. The purpose of public worship is corporate participation in which believers listen to the sermon, join in the sacraments, and "glorify God together with one heart, spirit, and mouth" (lines 110–11). It would be, says Bentley, mere superstition and even an act of impiety to read or pray privately during a public worship service.[32] The *Monument,* which does not refer explicitly to the *Book of Common Prayer,* in fact contributes to the growing division in England, as in other Protestant countries, between public and private prayer, a division formalized in the 1647 Westminster Confession's distinctions among private, secret, and public prayer: "God is to be worshiped everywhere in spirit and truth; as, in private families daily, and in secret, each one by himself; so, more solemnly in the public assemblies" (21.6).[33]

Bentley's purpose in compiling his prayer book, then, is to provide a "treasury" or "domestical library" from which his readers may make their own selection of devotional materials for their own private use, and he is keenly aware that there is now an abundance of works from which to choose. He frequently refers to "divers . . . treatises" (lines 5–6), "manifold works" (line 27), "the rich store and treasury" (line 49), or "the plenty of prayerbooks" (line 152) and sees his own role as that of "a faithful collector" (line 117). Indeed, the landscape of prayer books and other devotional materials looked quite different from the way it had appeared earlier in the century. Although books of hours and primers were not uniform in either their content or their formats, they did share a core of common elements: the Little Office of the Blessed Virgin Mary, the Litany and Dirge, and a finite set of other liturgical and extraliturgical texts. The works collected by Bentley, however, have little in common with each other apart from their devotional orientation. Queen Elizabeth's translation of Margaret of Navarre's "Godly Meditation of the Inward Love of the Soul Towards Christ Our Lord" does not resemble, in form or content, Elizabeth Tyrwhit's set of morning and evening prayers, Dorcas Martin's mother/daughter catechism, or even the acrostic poems on the queen's own name.

The Monument of Matrons is itself a large book, over 1500 pages in length, divided into seven sections or lamps, and published by two different printers, Henry Denham and Thomas Dawson. Several considerations seem to have motivated Bentley, who was probably the churchwarden at Saint Andrew Holborn, to produce this anthology.[34] One, undoubtedly, was his desire for royal patronage.[35] The *Monument* is dedicated to Queen Elizabeth, and the third lamp in particular is devoted to psalms, meditations, and prayers suitable for use on her Accession Day, November 17. But Bentley's desire to encourage private devotions seems equally genuine. Furthermore, he appears to have had an antiquarian's interest in preserving and protecting devotional materials that were in danger of being "worn clean out of print" (lines 20–21). He defends the bulkiness of his compilation by arguing that its clear print and large size makes it accessible to the "aged and feeble sighted reader" who will be "very grateful" (line 162) and adds that devout believers will not demur at the size or cost of a volume that offers so much "goodness" (lines 163–66).

The sheer amount and variety of that "goodness," however, necessitated that Bentley's audience would be composed not of "sayers" but of readers. While the weekly or perhaps daily recitation of the *Book of Common Prayer* may well have inscribed those public prayers in the memories and on the tongues of worshipers by 1582, the prayers in *The Monument of Matrons* were meant to be read. Not only does Bentley address his readers as such (lines 4, 78, 91, 115, 142, 180, 190, and 209), but his whole project is directed toward the preservation of a library of devotional material to which pious worshipers can resort at will. The *Monument*'s cornucopia allows, and even encourages, its users to select their own devotional materials, to browse freely through the library for those selections most suitable to their own needs, desires, and situation in life.

The particular readers Bentley has in mind are women, although he acknowledges that these devotional materials are "for the universal commodity of all good Christians" (lines 25–26). Originally, he intended to publish only women authors, but subsequently added material "penned by divers godly learned men" (line 38) though addressed to women. Although the primary audience is female, Bentley makes clear that women's writing is good for men, as is men's for women. The title page of the first lamp explains that the *Monument* contains "the worthy works partly of men, partly of women, compiled for the necessary use of both sexes," while in the preface Bentley notes that he himself, along with his friends (whose sex is not differentiated) has so profited from reading women's devotional writing that he now desires "to make this treatise heretofore (in part) private to myself and a few of my friends, now public and common also to you good Christian readers" (lines 76–78).

Bentley's desire to encourage daily worship, to make prayer books "public and common" returns us to the concerns of Quentin at the beginning of the century. Although by the 1580s the landscape of devotional life had been altered—with the movement from Latin to English, from integrated public and private prayer to separated spheres, and from recitation to reading—it had not been destroyed. For all the discontinuities, significant strands of continuity remained.

First, both Quentin and Bentley wanted to promote the development of a vital devotional life on the part of individual believers, and they recognized that such a life requires discipline and flexibility. Quentin recommended a daily schedule based on monastic contemplation but adjusted to fit the demands of an active life. Bentley denied that he was articulating a specified regimen, but then outlined a ten-step plan of devotional meditation, from recitation of the commandments through petitionary prayer, which, he acknowledged, he strove to follow consistently with or without his book in hand (line 140). Both saw the value of a daily life guided by worship and prayer. For Quentin, the recitation of the monastic hours provided a ready-made template; for Bentley, however, as for other Protestants both before and after him, the demise of this traditional structure did not lead to amorphous spontaneity but to the creation of a new "method, order, and direction" (line 56).

In fact, attempts to impose "method, order, and direction" were rife in the sixteenth century. The 1549 *Book of Common Prayer,* returning to themes sounded in Henry's 1545 authorized primer, noted that "where heretofore, there hath been great diversity in saying and singing in churches within this realm: some following Salisbury use, some Hereford use, some the use of Bangor, some of York, and some of Lincoln: Now from henceforth, all the whole realm shall have but one use."[36] The same preface, however, acknowledged that "when men say Matins and Evensong privately, they may say the same in any language that they themselves do understand."[37] This concession to differences (here limited to the choice between Latin and English) simply recognized the impossibility of demanding uniform practice in matters of prayer and piety, a fact acknowledged, as well, by the medieval Church. As Brightman notes with regard to the medieval liturgical uses, "Uniformity was neither known, nor aimed at or desired; a broad Gregorian basis was common, but the rest varied indefinitely in detail, theoretically from province to province, in practice rather from diocese to diocese, and among the greater foundations from church to church."[38] Both the proliferation of devotional forms in the sixteenth century, and the attempts to impose some degree of order on them, simply continued the practices of the medieval Church.

Second, both Quentin and Bentley understood the importance of a written collection of prayers to serve as a resource for the individual believer and as a concrete reminder of her inclusion in the larger corporate Body of Christ. The books of hours and primers may have tended to emphasize the universal communion of the saints with their verbal and visual reminders of corporate worship, but the variety of illuminations and extraliturgical prayers also provided a rich treasury for individual contemplation and choice. The *Monument,* on the other hand, persistently reminded its readers that it was a variegated compilation, to be used by private individuals in private devotions; yet, with equal persistence, it insisted on being set within the context of the universal Church. Bentley, worried that his encyclopedia, along with other recently printed prayer books, might displace corporate attendance at morning and evening prayers in church (lines 107–13), sought to mitigate the danger by warning against the substitution of private prayer for public prayer and by positioning the *Monument* under the protection of the bishop of London as a book "not unprofitable to the church" (line 70).

Moreover, although readers might use the prayers privately, prostrating "themselves apart from all company in prayer and meditation" (line 88), they did so as part of the universal Church. Indeed, one of the main virtues of the *Monument* was that it provided devout women with "perfect precedents of true piety" (line 29), both by reprinting female authors and by displaying examples of godly women drawn from the Bible and Church history. Although the sense of joining in prayer with the saints in heaven, so evocative of the books of hours, may have disappeared, it was replaced with an equally strong sense of participation in the heroical line of righteous women from Eve through the queen herself. And, in addition to subtly realigning the individual's relation to the Church universal, Bentley also encouraged a sense of corporate national identity, not only dedicating the *Monument* to the queen, but reminding readers that particular works, as well as the entire *Monument* itself, were composed "for the common benefit of my country" (lines 9–10, 204). Furthermore, although many of the prayers in the *Monument* were newly composed, many others were traditional in both form and matter. Even the Hours of the Cross, a favorite optional office from the books of hours and primers, made a modified reappearance under a new title, "The Hymn of the Passion of Christ," and in a new translation as part of Tyrwhit's *Morning and Evening Prayers* in Lamp Two.[39] Such continuity with older forms of piety reinforced the sense of participation in the universal Church.

Third, both Quentin and Bentley recognized that while prayer fosters an intimate union between God and the believer, this union is expressed in the active as well as the contemplative life. It has become commonplace to note that the books of hours and primers brought ordinary laypeople into the sacred space reserved for those in the monastic life, that the recitation of the hours served to sanctify secular time. Yet, when Reinburg notes the "stillness, attentiveness, and peace" we see in the books of hours illuminations that show medieval people at prayer, she, and we, may be reading too much into a particular artistic style.[40] While it is true that Quentin stressed the need to stay intimately aware of God throughout the day, by meditating on Christ's passion and thus lessening the danger of dying in a state of deadly sin, it is also true that such awareness was intended to motivate the believer to activity in the world: caring for the poor, choosing good friends, doing one's business "to the pleasure of God" (lines 84–85). And while "typical" Protestant piety might seem to focus on living out one's faith in action, Bentley's preface, in fact, encouraged his readers to pray "day and night continually and incessantly, either silently in heart with Hannah, or openly in mouth with Mary," and to "spend their whole life, and make it their whole work to pray, meditate, and read God's word" (lines 82–86). Indeed, Bentley's final remembrance of Christ's "bloody prayers, dreary death, and bitter passion" (lines 217–18) is not too far distant from Quentin's recommendation to meditate on "how dearly [Christ] redeemed you, giving his precious body, his blood, and his soul" (lines 41–42). For both authors, the active life of prayer encompasses the entire person, requiring conscious decisions and vigilant care. There is no thought in either preface of mechanically performed prayer or superstitious routine. Both rely on the initiative and discretion of the individual believer to live a life of piety and worship.

In sum, despite the doctrinal upheavals of the sixteenth century and the shifts in prayer books from Latin to English, from recitation to reading, and from sacred object to changeable texts, pious Christians continued to buy and use books that helped them shape their individual practices of prayer. United with believers from earlier ages, they sought the common goal of living lives "acceptable and pleasing to God" (Quentin, line 109).

Notes

1. For all the sixteenth-century texts, I have modernized archaic forms as well as the spelling, punctuation, capitalization, and paragraphing and have corrected obvious printing errors. Additions to the text are placed in square brackets; signature indications are also given in the text between square brackets. I have not followed prose lineation and have omitted hyphens where they serve only to divide a word at the end of a line. When a word is broken across a page, I have ignored the hyphen and placed the complete word after the signature mark.

2. For discussions of "The Manner to Live Well," see Helen C. White, *The Tudor Books of Private Devotion* (Madison: University of Wisconsin Press, 1951), 150–53; W.A. Pantin, "Instructions for a Devout and Literate Layman," in J.J.G. Alexander and M.T. Gibson, eds., *Medieval Learning and Literature: Essays Presented to Richard William Hunt* (Oxford: Oxford University Press, 1976), 411–12; and Mary C. Erler, "*The Maner to Lyue Well* and the Coming of English in François Regnault's Primers of the 1520s and 1530s," *The Library,* 6th series, 6 (1984): 229–43.

3. *This prymer of Salysbury use is set out a long without ony serchyng* (Paris, 1529; STC 15961.3). Erler provides a chart of the thirty-six editions of the *Manner* published between 1529 and 1556; Erler, *"The Maner to Lyue,"* 234–37.

4. Useful introductions to the books of hours may be found in Roger S. Wieck, ed., *Time Sanctified: The Book of Hours in Medieval Art and Life* (New York: George Braziller, 1988), and Janet Backhouse, *Books of Hours* (London: The British Library, 1985). For the history of the primer, see Edmund Bishop, "On the Origin of the Prymer," in Henry Littlehales, ed., *The Prymer; or, Lay folks' Prayer Book* (EETS, 1895–97), xi–xxxviii; and E. Hoskins, *Horae Beatae Mariae Virginis, or, Sarum and York Primers with Kindred Books and Primers of the Reformed Roman Use* (London: Longmans, Green, 1901).

5. Yale, Beinecke 390, fol. 25. Wieck, ed., *Time Sanctified,* 39.

6. Virginia Reinburg, "Prayer and the Book of Hours," in Wieck, ed., *Time Sanctified,* 39–44.

7. The earliest extant prayer book printed in England dates from 1477–78 and came from the press of William Caxton (STC 15867). At least twenty-nine editions

intended for an English readership were produced before 1500 by printshops in England, France, and Antwerp.

8. Actual hours of recitation depended upon the seasons and local regulations.

9. *Thys prymer in Englyshe and in Laten* (Rouen, 1538; STC 16008.5), D6v–D7r.

10. For comparisons with Genevan practices, see Robert Kingdon's essay in this volume.

11. Erler argues, however, that the preface served more commercial functions, advertising the presence of English-language material or assuring the censors of doctrinal orthodoxy; Erler, "*The Maner to Lyue*," 229–30.

12. For a description of the English manuscript primers and transcriptions of two primers, see Henry Littlehales, *The Prymer or Prayer-Book of the Lay People in the Middle Ages* (London: Longmans, Green, 1892); and Henry Littlehales, *The Prymer; or, Lay folks' Prayer Book.*

13. *Hore beate marie virginis secundum usum Sarum* (Paris, 1498; STC 15888), R4r.

14. *Hore beatissime virginis Marie ad legitmum Sarisburiensis ecclesie ritum* (Paris, 1527; STC 15954), C3r.

15. A lent of pardon is an indulgence of forty days.

16. *Hore beatissime virginis,* G4v.

17. *Thys prymer in Englyshe and in Laten,* Q6r–Q6v.

18. *Thys prymer in Englyshe and in Laten.*

19. *An exhortacion unto prayer, thought mete by the kynges majesty, and his clergy to be reade to the people in every churche afore processions* (London, 1544; STC 10620), A7r–A7v.

20. Eamon Duffy, *The Stripping of the Altars: Traditional Religion in England c. 1400–c. 1580* (New Haven: Yale University Press, 1992), 211–32.

21. On sixteenth-century printed prayer books, see William Maskell, *Monumenta Ritualia Ecclesiae Anglicanae,* vol. 2 (London: William Pickering, 1846); White, *The Tudor Books of Private Devotion;* and Charles C. Butterworth, *The English Primers (1529–1545): Their Publication and Connection with the English Bible and the Reformation in England* (Philadelphia: University of Pennsylvania Press, 1953); Ian Green, *Print and Protestantism in Early Modern England* (Oxford: Oxford University Press, 2000), chap. 5. A monograph by Faye L. Kelly examines prayers, but not prayer books, for their insights into popular culture: Faye L. Kelly, *Prayer in Sixteenth-Century England* (Gainesville: University of Florida Press, 1966).

22. *Certeine prayers and godly meditacyons very nedefull for every Christen* (London, 1538; STC 20193), B1r–B1v.

23. *Ortulus anime. The garden of the soule: or the englisshe primers newe corrected and augmented* (Argentine [i.e., Antwerp], 1530; STC 13828.4).

24. Most of these early English scriptural primers rely on Otto Brunsfelsius's *Precationes Biblicae* printed in Antwerp in the 1520s.

25. *The primer, set foorth by the kynges majestie and his clergie* (London, 1545; STC 16034), ***1v.

26. Cranmer's revision of the Sarum liturgy was influenced by such humanist documents as Cardinal Quiñones's *Breviarium Romanum nuper reformatum* (1535; 1536, 2nd rev. ed.) and the Lutheran *Simplex ac pia deliberatio* (1543, German ed.; 1545, Latin ed.; 1547 English ed.). See Edgar C.S. Gloucester, introd. to *The First*

and Second Prayerbooks of King Edward the Sixth (London: J. M. Dent and Sons, 1910), vii–viii; F. E. Brightman, *The English Rite: Being a Synopsis of the Sources and Revisions of the Book of Common Prayer,* 2nd rev. ed., 2 vols. (London: Rivingtons, 1921), 1: xxvi–xxviii; and John E. Booty, ed., *The Book of Common Prayer 1559: The Elizabethan Prayer Book* (Charlottesville: University Press of Virginia, 1976), 341, 352.

27. Edward Dering, *Godlye private praiers for housholders in their families* (London, 1574; STC 6684.5). *Godlye praiers* went through at least fourteen additional issues or editions by 1627.

28. *Here after foloweth twoo fruitfull and godly praiers* (London, 1545; STC 20197.3), no signature.

29. James Cancellar, *The Alphabet of Prayers, verye fruitefull to be exercised and used of every Christian Man* (London, 1564; STC 4558).

30. Andrew Maunsell, *The first part of the catalogue of English printed books* (London, 1595; STC 17669).

31. For discussions on *The Monument of Matrons,* see Colin B. Atkinson and William P. Stoneman, " 'These griping greefes and pinching pangs': Attitudes to Childbirth in Thomas Bentley's *The Monument of Matrones* (1582)," *Sixteenth Century Journal* 21 (1990): 193–203; Colin Atkinson and Jo B. Atkinson, "Subordinating Women: Thomas Bentley's Use of Biblical Women in *The Monument of Matrones* (1582)," *Church History* 60 (1991): 289–300; Colin B. Atkinson and Jo B. Atkinson, "Thomas Bentley's *The Monument of Matrones* (1582): The First Anglican Prayer Book for Women," *Anglican Theological Review* 74 (1992): 277–88; Micheline White, "A Biographical Sketch of Dorcas Martin: Elizabethan Translator, Stationer, and Godly Matron," *Sixteenth Century Journal* 30 (1999): 775–92; and Colin B. Atkinson and Jo B. Atkinson, "The Identity and Life of Thomas Bentley, Compiler of *The Monument of Matrones* (1582)," *Sixteenth Century Journal* 31 (2000): 323–48. Bentley undoubtedly anticipated that *The Monument of Matrones* would enjoy a long life as the encyclopedia of devotion for female readers. Only such optimism would account for his investing so much time and money in the project. This optimism, however, was misplaced, for only one edition, and probably only one printing, was published.

32. See Kingdon's analysis of the same issue.

33. For a discussion of seventeenth-century attitudes toward private and secret prayer, see Bryan D. Spinks, "What Was Wrong with Mr. Cosin's Couzening Devotions? Deconstructing an Episode in Seventeenth-Century Anglican 'Liturgical Hagiography,' " *Worship* 74 (2000): 308–28.

34. See Atkinson and Atkinson, "The Identity and Life of Thomas Bentley."

35. See, for instance, John King, *Tudor Royal Iconography,* 244, although this claim is disputed by Atkinson and Atkinson, "The Identity and Life of Thomas Bentley," 323–48.

36. *First and Second Prayerbooks,* 4

37. *First and Second Prayerbooks,* 5.

38. Brightman, *The English Rite,* 1: xiii.

39. Thomas Bentley, *The Monument of Matrones* (London, 1582; STC 1892), 2: N2r–N2v.

40. Reinburg, "Prayer and the Book of Hours," 44.

seven

Catholic Reform of the Divine Office in the Sixteenth Century: The Breviary of Cardinal Francisco de Quiñones

KATHERINE ELLIOT VAN LIERE

Editors' Introduction

To return to a purer, earlier form of liturgical practice, to the centrality of Scripture, was a constant aim among reforming groups, both within the Catholic Church in the medieval period, and among the Protestant Reformers of the sixteenth century. This essay describes the reform of the daily patterns of prayer in the sixteenth-century Catholic Church as set out in the Breviary, the Catholic clergy's prayer book. Like the contributions on schools and on prayer books for laypeople, this essay expands the domain of worship once again, this time to include the corporate prayer life of the clergy.

For the first time in this collection of essays, both the medieval and the early modern examples of worship in this contribution are Catholic, yet issues of change versus continuity remain as crucial as ever. Any simplistic model assuming continuity for Catholic worship and change among Protestants collapses when faced with the reality of shifting forces within the Catholic Church. The revision of the Breviary undertaken by Cardinal Francisco de Quiñones was intended to restore the prayers of the Daily Offices of the Church to their original purity, yet the alterations made by Quiñones and his assistants upset those among the clergy who wished to see the medieval accretions retained. Thus the balance between continuity and change in the revisions of the Breviary in the sixteenth century depended very much on the perspective of the critic—whether he was comparing the texts, their layout, and their usage to the more recent or to the more distant past.

Primary Sources Introduction:

The primary sources accompanying this contribution are texts taken from the Roman Breviary, first from a Roman Breviary of 1481 and then from Quiñones's 1535 version. Both texts indicate the prayers and readings to be used during Matins, the first and longest prayer service of the days on the first Sunday of Advent. By comparing these two approaches, we can see how Quiñones and his assistants radically shortened the medieval liturgy (for example by reducing nine lessons to three, eliminating all nonbiblical lessons, and reducing the choral elements) while still retaining the most crucial features of the medieval Divine Office.

A. Roman Breviary (1481): Matins for the First Sunday of Advent[1]

FIRST SUNDAY IN ADVENT at Matins.
Invitatory: The Lord, the King who is to come, Come let us adore.
Psalm. O Come [let us sing unto the Lord . . . Psalm 94 (95)]

Hymn:[2]

O Word that goest forth on high,
From God's own depths eternally,
And in those latter days wast born
For succor to a world forlorn;

Pour light upon us from above,
And fire our hearts with ardent love,
That, as we hear thy truth today,
All wrong desires may burn away.

And when, as judge, thou drawest nigh,
The secrets of our hearts to try,
To recompense each hidden sin
And bid the saints their reign begin;

O let us not, weak sinful men,
Be driven from thy presence then,
But with thy saints forever stand
In perfect love at thy right hand.

To God the Father, God the Son,
And God the Spirit, ever one,
Praise, honor, might, and glory be
From age to age eternally.

Seek the antiphons in the psalter in the appropriate places, and likewise the versicles.

Our Father *said quietly.*[3]
Verse: And lead us not [into temptation]
Response: But deliver us [from evil].

Absolution: Hear, O Lord Jesus Christ, the prayers of your servants, and have mercy on us, as you live and reign with the Father and the Holy Spirit forever and ever.
Response: Amen.

Verse: Your blessing, please, Lord.
Blessing: May the Eternal Father bestow on us an everlasting blessing.
Response: Amen.

On this night the Book of the Prophet Isaiah is put out, which is read until Christmas both on Sundays and on ferias, if any occur.

Lesson I. *Here begins the Book of the Prophet Isaiah . . .* [Isaiah 1:1–4]

Note that after the lesson, the lector always says: Now on us, O Lord, have mercy. (*Except in the three days before Easter and in the Office of the Dead.*)

R: Long, long had I been watching. Behold, now do I see God coming in power, as in a cloud of light that covers the entire land. Rush out to meet him. Ask: "Tell us, are you the One who shall rule the people, Israel?"
V: All you sons of earth and sons of men, rich and poor together, rush out to meet him and say:

R: Rush out . . . *repeat the words [above] until* Tell us.
V: O ruler of Israel, listen, you who lead Joseph like a sheep.
R: Tell us . . . *repeat the words [above] until* O ruler.
V: Lift up your heads, you gates, lift yourselves up, you everlasting doors, that the King of Glory may come in.[4]
R: Who [shall rule over the people of Israel.]
V: Glory [be to the Father and to the Son and to the Holy Ghost]
R: Long, long had I been watching . . .
And the whole [above sequence] is repeated.

V: Your blessing, please, Lord.
Blessing: May the only-begotten son of God see fit to bless us and help us.
R: Amen.

Lesson II. [Isaiah 1:5–9]

R: I saw in the night visions, and behold with the clouds of heaven there came one like a son of man, and to him kingship and honors. And all peoples, nations, and languages shall serve Him.
V: His dominion is an everlasting dominion, which shall not pass away, and his kingdom one that shall not be destroyed.[5]

V: Your blessing, please, Lord.
Blessing: May the grace of the Holy Spirit illuminate our minds and hearts.
R: Amen.

Lesson III. [Isaiah 1:10–15]

R: The Angel Gabriel was sent to the Virgin Mary, espoused to Joseph, announcing the word to her; and the Virgin trembled at the light. Do not fear, Mary, for you have found favor with the Lord. Behold, you will conceive and give birth, and He shall be called the Son of the Most High.
V: The Lord God will give to him the throne of His father David, and he will reign over the house of Jacob forever. Behold.[6]

Absolution: May His pity and mercy help us; who lives and reigns with the Father and the Holy Spirit, forever and ever.
R: Amen.
V: [Your] blessing, [please, Lord.]

Blessing: Lord God almighty, be near to us and merciful.
R: Amen.

Lesson IV. Sermon of Pope Saint Leo: Dear brothers, we must undertake the celebration of this holy, good, glorious and singular feast, the birth of our Lord and Savior, with the most faithful devotion. We must prepare for it as much with our own strength as with his help, and diligently examine all the secret hiding places in our hearts, lest there be in us some hidden sin that confounds and consumes our conscience, and offends the eyes of the divine majesty. For though Christ our Lord rose again and ascended into Heaven after his passion, we believe that he now is considering and observing attentively how each one of his servants works to prepare and arrange for the celebration of his feast, without avarice, anger, pride, or lust. And thus he will dispense the grace of his mercy to each and every one whom he sees adorned with good manners.

R: Hail Mary, full of grace, the Lord is with you. The Holy Spirit will come upon you, and the power of the Most High will overshadow you. The child to be born from you shall be holy, and he shall be called the Son of God.

V: How shall this be, since I know no man? And the Angel replied, "the [Holy] Spirit [. . .]"[7]

V: Your blessing, please, Lord.
Blessing: May Christ give us the joys of eternal life.
R: Amen.

Lesson V. If Christ beholds someone clothed in the light of love, adorned with the pearls of justice or mercy, chaste, humble, compassionate, benign, and sober; if he finds or recognizes such a one, to him he will dispense his body and blood through the priesthood of his ministers, not as a judgment but as a remedy. Yet if he finds another adulterous, drunken, greedy, and proud, the same thing will be said to him which the Lord himself said in the Gospel: "Friend, how did you come in here without a wedding garment?" And may the Lord spare him from the fate which is described next: "Bind his hands and his feet and cast him into the darkness outside, where there will be weeping and gnashing of teeth."[8]

R: I await Lord Jesus Christ the Savior, who shall reform
our humbly fashioned bodies with the splendor of his own.[9]
V: Let us live soberly and uprightly, in hopeful expectation
of blessedness and of the coming in glory of our great Lord.[10]
Who shall reform [. . .]

V: Your blessing, please, Lord.
Blessing: May God kindle the fire of his love in our hearts.
R: Amen.

Lesson VI. Behold what a sentence on the Day of Judgment awaits him who approaches the feast of our Lord without the remedy of penitence and defiled by the squalor of his sins. For in his birth, dearest brothers, Christ is joined like a husband to his Church as in a spiritual wedding. Then truth springs forth from the earth. Then justice looks down from the Heavens. Then the bridegroom goes forth from the bridal bed; that is, the Word from the Virgin's womb. For he goes forth with the Church his bride; that is, he takes on human flesh. As we are invited, therefore, to these most holy nuptials, and as we prepare to enter into the banquet of the Father and the son and the Holy bridegroom, let us see with what sort of garments we should be attired. Let us therefore, with God's help, cleanse as thoroughly as we can both our hearts and our bodies; so that our divine host shall detect nothing in us that is fetid, sordid, dark, or unworthy in his sight.

R: I beseech you, Lord, do send the one you are to send.[11] Behold the affliction of your people. As you have promised, come, and deliver us.
V: O ruler of Israel, listen, you who lead Joseph like a flock. You who sit enthroned above the Cherubim.[12] As [it was in the beginning, is now, and ever shall be, world without end. Amen.]

Absolution: May the omnipotent and merciful Lord release us from the shackles of our sins.
R: Amen.
V: Your blessing, please, Lord.
Blessing: May the reading of the Gospel be a salve and protection to us.
R: Amen.

Alternative blessing if two Gospels are read: By these Gospels may our offenses be washed away.
Alternative blessing if three Gospels are read: May Christ the Son of God teach us the words of the Holy Gospel.
Alternative blessing when no Gospel is read: May He bless us who lives and reigns without end.

The three absolutions given above are said in this order before "Lord, your blessing, please," whenever nine lessons are read, except in the three days before Easter and in the Office of the Dead, in which cases neither absolutions nor "Your blessing please, Lord," nor "But you, Lord [have mercy]," are said. At other times, however, the reader begins with the verse, "Your blessing please, Lord." But on weekdays when three lessons are said, "Hear [the prayers of your servants . . .]" is said at the first lesson on Monday and Thursday; "[May] the loving-kindness [and mercy of him . . .]" is said at the second lesson on Thursday and Friday; and "From the shackles [of our sins . . .]" is said at the third lesson on Wednesday and Saturday. And this is observed for the whole year.

Lesson VII. From the Gospel of Luke: In those days Jesus said to his disciples, "There will be signs in the sun and the moon and the stars, and upon the earth distress of nations, *etc.*[13]

Homily of Pope Saint Gregory: A little before the Holy Gospel reading which you have just heard, the Lord had said these words: "Nation will rise against nation, and kingdom against kingdom, and there will be great earthquakes in various places, and pestilences and famines."[14] And after saying certain other things, he added what you have just now heard: "And there will be signs in the sun and the moon and the stars, and upon the earth distress of nations bewildered by the roaring of sea and waves." Surely in all of this we recognize things that have already come to pass, and other things which we fear will come to pass soon. For the rising of nation against nation and the distress of nations on earth are events that we see even more often now in our own time than we read about in books.

R: Behold, a virgin shall conceive and bear a son, says the Lord. And his name shall be called Wonderful, God, the Mighty One.
V: He shall sit upon David's throne and reign over his kingdom forever.[15]

V: Your blessing, please, Lord.
Blessing: May the Lord's help always remain with us.
R: Amen.

Alternative blessing when it is the Office of a feast day: May he or she or they whose feast we celebrate intercede with the Lord for us.
R: Amen.

Lesson VIII. You know how often we hear about an earthquake demolishing innumerable cities, even in other parts of the world. We suffer pestilence without end. It is true that nowadays we do not see many overt signs in the sun and the moon and the stars, but we deduce from the present movement of the air that these things, too, are not far off. Before Italy was given up to be destroyed by the pagans, bright flames appeared in the sky, presaging the human blood that would later be shed. Great distress of sea and waves has not occurred recently, but since many things already foretold have now come to pass, there is no doubt that the few things remaining will also follow. For when events occur just as they were predicted, this provides certainty that future events will do the same.

R: Nations, hear the word of the Lord, and announce it to the ends of the earth. And in the islands which are near, say,[16] "Our Savior is coming."
V: Announce it and make it heard; speak and cry out. *Etc.*

V: Your blessing please, Lord.
Blessing: King of angels, lead us to the [society of eternal citizens.]
R: Amen.

Lesson IX. Therefore, dearest brothers, we say this: let your minds remain alert and cautious, and not languish in ignorance or false security; let them be ever aroused by fear and by zeal for good works; and let them be ever mindful of these further words of our redeemer: "men fainting for fear and in expectation of the things that are coming on the world; for the powers of Heaven will be shaken."[17] For what does the Lord call "powers of Heaven" but angels, archangels, thrones, dominations, principalities and powers?[18] At the coming of the harsh judge these powers will appear clearly before our eyes to make the same demands, but ever so much more harshly, than our invisible creator is making of us now in his gentle way.

R: Behold, the days are coming, says the Lord, when I shall make a righteous branch spring from David's line, a king who will rule wisely, maintaining justice and right in the land. And this will be the name given to him: the Lord our Righteousness.
V: In those days Judah will be kept safe, and Israel will live undisturbed. And this [is the name they give him: "The Lord our justice."][19]

From this Sunday until Christmas and from Septuagesima Sunday until Christmas a ninth response is sung, for the Te Deum is not said, unless in a feast of nine lessons.

B. Quiñones Breviary (1535): Matins for the First Sunday of Advent[20]

FIRST SUNDAY OF ADVENT at Matins.
Sunday prayer: Our Father [Who art in Heaven . . .]
This is said at the beginning of each hour throughout the year.

Confession: I confess to Almighty God, to the blessed Mary, ever Virgin, to the blessed Archangel Michael, to blessed John the Baptist, to the Holy Apostles Peter and Paul, to all the saints, and to you, Father: that I have sinned exceedingly in thought, word, and deed. Through my fault, through my fault, through my most grievous fault. Therefore I beseech blessed Mary ever Virgin, blessed Michael the Archangel, blessed John the Baptist, the Holy Apostles Peter and Paul, all the saints, and you, Father, to pray to the Lord our God for me.

Absolution: May Almighty God have mercy upon you, and forgiving your sins bring you into life eternal.
Response: Amen.

Verse: May the almighty and merciful Lord grant us forgiveness, absolution, and remission of our sins.
Response: Amen.

The above confession with absolution is said in the above manner at Matins every day of the year. Then, the verse:
O Lord, open my lips.
Response: And my mouth shall proclaim your praise.
And he who says this makes the sign of the cross over himself, and

does the same at all other hours, while he says Oh, Lord, make speed to save, *etc. and* Make us turn, *etc.*

Verse: O God, make speed to save me.
Response: O Lord, made haste to help me. Glory be to the Father, and to the Son, and to the Holy Spirit. As it was in the beginning, is now, and ever shall be, world without end, Amen. Hallelujah. Hallelujah *is said this way at all hours throughout the year, except from Septuagesima Sunday until Easter. At that time, until the Thursday of the Lord's Supper, in its place is said:* Glory to you, Lord, King of eternal glory.

Invitatory: O Lord, we await your coming. Come quickly, and remove the yoke of our captivity.
This is said until but not including Christmas Eve, both on Sundays and ferias,[21] *unless it is a saint's feast. And it is repeated again at the end of the following psalm.*

Psalm: O Come let us sing unto the Lord . . . [Psalm 94 (95)]

Then O Lord, we await . . . *as above.*
The above psalm is said in the above way throughout the year with the [appropriate] seasonal invitatory, except in the three days before Easter.

Hymn:[22]

Hark! a thrilling voice is sounding;
"Christ is nigh," it seems to say,
"Cast away the works of darkness,
O ye children of the day."

Wakened by the solemn warning
Let the earthbound soul arise;
Christ, her Sun, all ill dispelling,
Shines upon the morning skies.

Lo, the Lamb, so long expected,
Comes with pardon down from heaven;
Let us haste, with tears of sorrow,
One and all to be forgiven.

So when next He comes in glory,
And the world is wrapped in fear,
With His mercy He may shield us,
And with words of love draw near.

Honor, glory, might, and blessing
Be to God: the Father, Son
And the everlasting Spirit,
While eternal ages run.

The above hymn is said at Matins until and including Christmas Eve, both on Sundays and ferias, unless it is a saint's feast. Immediately after the hymn three psalms are said, as arranged in the Psalter. [The Psalms given in Quiñones's Psalter for Sunday Matins are 1, 9a (9), and 17a (18).]

When these are finished, Our Father *is said.*
Verse: And lead us not [into temptation].
Response: But deliver us [from evil].

Then three lessons are said, and before each one:
Verse: Lord, your blessing, please.
And before the first [lesson], which is always from the Old Testament, is said the Benediction: May God the Father Almighty be nearer to us and merciful.

Here begins the prophecy of Isaiah. **Lesson I.** [Isaiah 1:1–15]
[Verse:] Now on us, O Lord, have mercy.
Response: Thanks be to God.
All lessons throughout the year are ended this way, except in the three days before Easter.

Verse: Your blessing, please, Lord.
Blessing: May the only-begotten son of God see fit to bless us and help us.
Response: Amen.
This blessing is said in similar fashion throughout the year before the second lesson, which is always from the New Testament.

Here begins the Gospel according to Luke. **Lesson II.**
[Luke 1:1–25]

[Response:] Now on us, Lord *as above.*
Verse: Your blessing, please, Lord.

Before the third lesson, unless it is a saint's feast, is said:
Blessing: May the grace of the Holy Spirit enlighten our minds and our hearts.
Response: Amen.
But if it is the feast of any saint or saints, this Blessing is said: May he (or she or they) whose feast we celebrate intercede for us with the Lord.
Response: Amen.
On Saturdays when the Blessed Virgin is commemorated, this Blessing is said: May the Lord grant us strength and peace through the Virgin Mother.
Reponse: Amen.

Note, however, that the third lesson, for the three days before Easter and for moveable feasts of the Lord, is assigned in the appropriate places in the Dominicale [i.e., this section of the breviary]. And what is said on Saturdays for the Blessed Virgin will be found in the same Office assigned for Saturdays; but for the rest of the year it is always found in the Calendar.[23]

When the three lessons are finished, throughout the year, both on Sundays and ferias, the psalm Miserere [50 (51)] is said. If, however, it is a feast, the hymn Te Deum is said.

Notes

1. Source: *Breviarium Secundum Romanae Curiae . . .* (Venice, 1481). Vatican Microfilms list 47.14 (unpaginated: pp. [13]–[18]). This text is from the first five pages of the *Dominicale* (also called the *Temporale*), the section of the breviary that contains the readings for non–saints' days throughout the year. (In this Breviary it immediately follows the *Calendar.*) Because the first Sunday in Advent is the first day represented in the *Dominicale,* these pages also include some general instructions concerning the rest of year which are not repeated later in the Breviary. Italics are used here to distinguish instructions, explanatory comments, and names of the constituent parts of the liturgy, from the words meant to be said or sung. There are no italics in the original text. When only the beginning of a familiar text is given in the Breviary, additional words are supplied here in square brackets. In lessons I–II, the full biblical

text is given in the Breviary but is condensed here to verse and chapter numbers. Psalms in both breviaries were identified not by numbers but by the initial words *(incipit)*. The numbers used here follow the Vulgate numeration, with the Hebrew number in parentheses.

2. This anonymous translation of the Latin hymn *Verbum superbum prodiens* is taken from the *Hymnal of the Protestant Episcopal Church in the U.S.A. (1940)*.

3. The instruction "said quietly" *(secreto)* means that the words are to be whispered privately, while others are beginning the subsequent text.

4. Psalm 24 (23):7.

5. Daniel 7:13–14.

6. Luke 1:26–31.

7. Luke 1:34–35.

8. Matthew 22:12–14.

9. Philippians 3:21.

10. Titus 2:13.

11. Exodus 4:13.

12. Psalm 79 (80):1.

13. Luke 21:25.

14. Luke 21:10–11.

15. Isaiah 7:14, 9:6–7.

16. Jeremiah 31:10.

17. Luke 21:26.

18. Colossians 1:16.

19. Jeremiah 23:5–6, 33:14–16.

20. Source: J. W. Legg, ed., *Breviarium Romanum a Fr. Card. Quignonio editum et recognitum, juxta editionem Venetiis A.D. 1535 impressam* (Cambridge: Cambridge University Press, 1888), 19–22. This excerpt represents the first four pages of the *Dominicale,* which in this Breviary immediately follows the Calendar and the Psalter. As in the 1481 Breviary, these pages include some general instructions concerning the rest of year which are not repeated later. Italics are used (both here and in the original text) to indicate instructions and names of the constituent parts of the Office, as opposed to the words to be spoken.

21. *Ferias* are days that are neither Sundays nor feasts. See also p. 179.

22. This translation of the Latin hymn *Vox clara ecce intonat* is by Edward Caswall (1849).

23. Of the possible dates for the first Sunday of Advent (November 27 through December 3), three are saint's days, having their own proper reading assigned in the Calendar; the readings for the other four days are all from 2 Corinthians.

For at least 1500 years, the Divine Office, or the liturgy of the hours, has been a locus of continuity within the Christian Church. The earliest Christians gathered for communal prayer at sunrise and sunset, and third-century sources testify to the custom of further daily prayers at the third, sixth, and ninth hours (i.e., about 9:00 A.M., noon, and 3:00 P.M.). In Western Christendom, these prayer rituals gradually ceased to be a public affair for the whole Christian community, and became more and more the special preserve of the clergy, particularly the growing monastic movement. By the time Benedict composed his famous Rule for monks in the mid–sixth century, the Divine Office was part of the basic architecture of monastic life, with a clearly established pattern of eight prayer hours a day: Matins, Lauds, Prime, Terce, Sext, None, Vespers, and Compline (Matins and Lauds, both said in the middle of the night, could also be counted together as one hour, yielding a total of seven hours).[1] Monks might spend eight or more hours a day in choir praying and singing these canonical hours. The Divine Office also loomed large in the life of many secular clergy. For those who lived as canons and were responsible for performing daily cathedral services, the Office was as inescapable as it was for monks. By the eighth century all the clergy in many dioceses were formally required to pray the hours together daily, in imitation of the monastic practice.[2] Pious laymen too could participate by attending daily prayers in a nearby monastery or cathedral. The later medieval proliferation of books of hours, a simplified liturgy of the hours which could be used by the laity, testifies to a vigorous lay interest in the daily prayer of the Church as an essential part of Christian life.[3]

Within this basic framework, the forms of daily prayer both evolved over time and varied at any given time, like so many aspects of Christian worship, by locality and by religious order. Despite the efforts of papal reformers to standardize liturgy, many dioceses and parishes maintained their own usages, as did most religious orders. The calendar of saints, which imposed special commemorative Offices for saints' feast days, varied even more dramatically from place to place.[4] But such diversity did not diminish the essential unity of this universally recognized liturgical form. From the early through the late Middle Ages, from Portugal to Poland, a pilgrim traveling through Christian Europe would have had little trouble finding a house of worship in which the eight hours of the Divine Office were sung daily. This universality, like that of the Mass, provided continuity throughout Christendom from the reign of Charlemagne to that of the Emperor Charles V seven centuries later. After the Protestant Reformation of the sixteenth century, the Roman Catholic tradition of the Divine Office took a further step toward unity and away from diversity, when the Council of Trent (1545–63), which forcefully regularized so many aspects of Catholic doctrine and liturgy, ordered the adoption of one standard form of the Office throughout the Catholic world. The resulting Tridentine *Breviarium Romanum,* issued by Pope Pius V in 1568, was a largely traditional version of the Divine Office imposed as a uniform standard on all the faithful. It became the canonical form of daily prayer for the majority of Catholics, and remained so until Vatican II in the twentieth century.[5] Twentieth-century reforms have shortened the daily cycle of prayers and replaced Latin with the vernacular, but even today modern Catholics (both lay and religious) who say or sing the liturgy of the hours in their own language may with some justice claim to be standing in a continuous tradition that reaches back to late antiquity.

For all this continuity, the Divine Office has also been a locus of great changes in the history of Christian liturgy, and the period on which this book focuses witnessed some of the most profound changes of all. Most dramatic, of course, was the large-scale abandonment of the liturgy of the hours by most Protestant Reformers, a logical consequence of suppressing the monastic orders. This did not signify a rejection of the idea of daily common prayer; on the contrary, the Reformers saw the late medieval monastic Office as a perversion of an earlier ideal of public communal worship for the whole Christian community, laity included. Thus in Protestant and Reformed Europe, while the Office vanished in its familiar monastic setting, crucial vestiges of it were often preserved within a newly revitalized tradition of lay worship. Perhaps the most famous example is Thomas Cranmer's heavy borrowing from the Divine Office to produce his Anglican *Book of Common Prayer*, which reduced the eight prayer hours to Morning and Evening Prayer.[6] In a similar spirit, Luther and some of his followers saw fit to preserve Matins and Vespers and restore their communal character by substituting them for daily Masses in churches and schools.[7] In a sense, too, Calvin's use of the Psalms in Geneva constituted a Reformed adaptation of the Divine Office. Here the Psalms were wrested from their medieval context, translated into new vernacular metrical verses, and sung to new tunes by a lay congregation, but they were the same Psalms that had for centuries formed the core of the Catholic Divine Office.[8] In a still broader sense, the evolution in this period of personal prayer aids like books of hours, such as Susan Felch describes in her contribution to this volume, should also be understood as part of the story of the early modern evolution of the Divine Office, since these genres also sprang initially from the liturgy of the hours.

The same late medieval/early modern period saw changes *within* the Roman Catholic tradition of the Divine Office as well. While Cranmer and then Calvin refashioned the liturgy of the hours to their Reformed purposes, Catholic reformers were seeking to revise the Office in gentler ways, although these attempts have generally received less attention than the bolder reforms of their Protestant counterparts. The best known Catholic revision of the Divine Office is, of course, the Tridentine *Breviarium Romanum* already mentioned, which remained the Roman Catholic standard for almost four centuries. But to see the Tridentine Breviary of 1568 as the only Catholic reform of the Divine Office in this period is to overlook the diversity and complexity of early modern Catholic reform. The Tridentine Breviary represented the culmination, and in part the rejection, of decades of papal attempts to reform the Divine Office, beginning in the early sixteenth century. Many of these attempts were stillborn (for reasons not always clear), but one did bear fruit in the mid-1530s, a decade before the Council of Trent opened. Around 1530 Pope Clement VII commissioned the Spanish cardinal Francisco de Quiñones (c. 1482–1540) to revise the Roman Breviary. Together with several assistants, Quiñones fulfilled this charge with a new *Breviarium Romanum* first published in 1535. A second, substantially revised version followed in 1536. The two versions together were issued in at least 110 editions.[9] While it never supplanted the older *Breviarium Romanum,* Quiñones's work coexisted with the older Breviary and was widely used throughout Europe for the next three decades. But its reception was strangely mixed. Despite its broad popularity—indeed, in large part because of it—the work was severely attacked by the theologians of the Sorbonne and other Catholic critics.[10] In 1558 Pope Paul IV (who had worked on an abortive Breviary reform of his own in the 1520s)[11] banned Quiñones's Breviary altogether. This ban was ineffective, but when the new Tridentine Breviary appeared a decade later, it was accompanied by a papal bull definitively prohibiting the use of all earlier forms, including that of Quiñones.[12] Thus as a book, the Quiñones Breviary forms a sort of cul-de-sac in liturgical history.[13] But its dramatic rise and fall, and the reasons for its contested reception, afford an opportunity to investigate the world of Roman Catholic prayer—both the practice of the Divine Office and the theoretical disputes about the nature of prayer—in this highly formative period.

This investigation must begin with a brief foray into the medieval background of the Breviary. The Roman Breviary, which Clement VII commissioned Quiñones to reform, contained the form of the Divine Office used by both the papal curia and the Franciscan Order. It had not been substantially reformed since the thirteenth century.[14] The so-called Roman Office (or Roman Rite) was the most widespread form of the Divine Office in the medieval Western Church. Evolved from liturgies used in the earliest churches of Rome, this rite had gradually been extended in the early Middle Ages (especially by the reforming pope Gregory VII, r. 1073–85) to more and more dioceses of Christendom. In the thirteenth century Innocent III (r. 1198–1216) had undertaken to simplify and shorten this Roman Office for use in the papal curia by the pope's own chaplains—busy men who could seldom spare eight or more hours a day to pray the Office. Soon afterward this newly simplified Roman Rite was also adopted by the Franciscan Order, whose members appreciated its leaner form for similar reasons. The influence of these energetic mendicants, who left few parts of Europe untouched in this era, proved decisive; in the later thirteenth century several other religious orders and some dioceses adopted the revised Roman Office, and even some orders that did not adopt it in its entirety, such as the Dominicans, nonetheless drew on it in their own subsequent liturgical reforms.[15] From then on the revised Roman Office continued steadily to supplant other versions of the Divine Office throughout Western Christendom, although its formal supremacy was not declared until the issue of the Tridentine *Breviarium Romanum* in 1568.

In the same formative period of the High Middle Ages, volumes called Breviaries, which contained the rules, chants, and texts needed to pray the Office, were becoming increasingly common. Originally the Divine Office was performed using a bulky collection of psalters, antiphonaries, homiliaries, legendaries, and other anthologies, reflecting the eclectic nature of the Office itself and the sedentary life of the monks who mostly prayed it. The Breviary (which in Latin, *breviarium,* simply denotes a "brief" compendium) became particularly popular among the mendicants (Dominicans and Franciscans), whose peripatetic way of life made such a portable compendium essential.[16] Thus from the thirteenth century onward historians often speak of "the Breviary" as a synonym for the Divine Office, and "the Roman Breviary" as the most widely used form thereof.

If this shortened Roman Rite appeared compact compared with its earlier medieval antecedents, it still remained a complex liturgy governed by a complex set of rules. At the core of the Divine Office, in theory, was the Holy Scripture, with a special place given to the Psalter. For many Christians, the ideal was to read the whole Bible within the Office each year, and recite all

150 Psalms each week.[17] But to say that biblical texts were the main ingredient of the Divine Office is akin to saying that a cathedral consists mainly of stone blocks; it is true, but the arrangement of the blocks leaves a good deal to human creativity, and there are other elements which, if structurally less crucial, still appear indispensable to many admirers. Each of the eight daily prayer hours comprised a core of Psalms, sandwiched between sequences of other texts, some Biblical and some not. Antiphons and short antiphonal prayers called versicles-and-responses, which appeared at most hours of the day, were largely extracted from Scripture. The longer prayer hours also included short Scripture readings called *capitula;* short verses called responds recited in response to these; canticles (biblical songs) and hymns (nonbiblical songs). The longest hour, Matins (also called Vigils), could include as many as eighteen Psalms, and between three and nine longer readings ("lessons") drawn from scriptural, patristic, or other sources, often accompanied by homilies and more responds. The hours of Lauds and Vespers normally included five Psalms each; Compline and the "lesser hours" of Prime, Terce, Sext, and None usually had three Psalms each.

The shorter prayer hours were often the same day after day, but the content of the longer hours, especially Matins, varied from day to day according to three different overlapping cycles: the seven-day week; the annual liturgical calendar (known as the Temporale); and the annual cycle of feast days (known as the Sanctorale).[18] The annual liturgical calendar commemorated the major events in the life of Christ and the story of salvation, from Advent through Corpus Christi.[19] During a season such as Advent or Lent, many of the prayers and readings of the Divine Office were chosen for their seasonal relevance. These seasons took up roughly half the year. The other half—that is, the short period from Epiphany until nine weeks before Easter, and the much longer period from Corpus Christi to Advent—were nonseasonal, or "ordinary time." In ordinary time, the daily liturgy was governed simply by the weekly cycle; Sunday was a feast day and had a longer Office than the other days of the week, which were called "ferias." Both the weekly cycle and the annual seasonal cycle of the Temporale were interrupted by the Sanctorale, the annual cycle of saints' feast days. Each saint's day had its own set of "proper" prayers and readings which displaced most of the ordinary ("ferial") Office for that day. Matters became exceedingly complex in the parts of the year where the feasts of the Temporale were moveable, and thus overlapped with the feasts of the Sanctorale differently every year. (There were thirty-five possible patterns of overlap, given the span of thirty-five dates for Easter.) Certain Temporale feasts were too important to be displaced by certain feasts from the Sanctorale, so a hierarchy had been devised to rank feasts (as "single," "double," "semidouble," etc.) and dictate priority when two coincided. If the saint's feast ranked as less solemn than the Temporale feast with which it competed, it was often moved to a different day.

By the sixteenth century these complexities had resulted in a number of unfortunate consequences for the Divine Office. The number of canonical saints' days had grown dramatically since the early Middle Ages, both from the addition of new saints to the calendar (some two hundred were added between 1100 and 1558)[20] and from the growing practice of celebrating the "octave" (the eighth day or, in some cases, the entire week after a feast) as a feast unto itself. In the Roman Missal of 1474, only six days in the year were entirely feast-free.[21] Since the liturgy for a saint's feast displaced much of the ferial liturgy with its cycle of readings from Scripture and the Psalter, the swelling saints' calendar brought the result that the complete ferial Office was said on very few days of the year, and the ideal of reading the whole Bible in a year and the whole Psalter in a week was accordingly frustrated.

This expansion of the Sanctorale was not entirely unwelcome to the clergy who were obliged to pray the Divine Office every day, for a concurrent medieval development had lengthened the ferial Office to the point where many found it unduly burdensome. By the thirteenth century, a series of *additional* daily Offices had been added to the clergy's daily prayer obligations on almost all non–feast days of the year; these accretions included the Office of the Dead, the "Little Office" of the Virgin Mary, the seven penitential psalms, and the fifteen gradual psalms.[22] Beloved as these additional Offices were, they added to an already substantial daily prayer obligation. On a feast day, they could be omitted, which created an extra incentive to add feasts to the calendar.[23]

The erosion of the ferial Office, and with it the Scripture and the Psalms within the Divine Office, was one of many abuses that thoughtful Catholics by the fifteenth century lamented. This is not to say that there was a groundswell of support for reforming the Breviary in this period; on the contrary, even the most critical observers were far readier to reprimand the clergy for failing to perform the Divine Office properly than to suggest that the Office itself might benefit from revision. But by the early 1500s an important current of reformist sentiment was making itself felt in Rome: the humanist movement, with its concern for historical scholarship and literary eloquence. Humanist scholars had a new set of motives for looking critically at the Breviary. They were interested in the literary and historiographical merit of its rich store of hymns, prayers, and lessons—especially the numerous saints' lives, which they saw as fair game for critical scholarship. The two Medici popes in this period—Leo X (r. 1513–21) and Clement VII (r. 1523–34)—were energetic patrons of the humanist movement in its many facets, including humanist-inspired projects to revise the Breviary. Leo X lent his support to a project by the Neapolitan bishop Zacharias Ferreri to devise "an ecclesiastical breviary rendered much shorter and easier, and purged of all errors." Ferreri produced no results in Leo's lifetime, but his main objective, to judge from a new hymnal he published in 1525, was to render prayer in metrical Latin poetry in a humanist style, purged of all medieval grammatical and stylistic "barbarities."[24] If anything concrete came of Ferreri's efforts on the breviary, it probably vanished in the destructive sack of Rome in 1527. But a few years later Clement VII evidently encouraged a more distinguished ecclesiastic to reform the Breviary: Gian Pietro Caraffa, founder of the new Theatine Order (and later Pope Paul IV).[25] No version of this liturgical reform survives either, whether in manuscript or printed form. From the circumstantial evidence that does survive, it seems Caraffa's aims were essentially humanist and conservative at the same time; he wished to rid the existing text of barbarous medieval style (replacing, for example, "uncouth hymns") and cut out certain readings of dubious historical accuracy, but not to revise the basic structure of any of the Offices.[26] Whatever became of Caraffa's work, it seems that by 1530 Clement had lost hope in it, for it was around this time that he commissioned Cardinal Quiñones to undertake his own Breviary reform project.

Thus the humanist movement forms part of the historical backdrop to Quiñones's reformed Breviary, which can in some ways be described as a humanist work. But this characterization is only partly accurate. Humanism actually ranked rather low on Francisco de Quiñones's list of qualifications as a liturgical reformer. His chief qualification was his membership in the Franciscan Order, the religious order that claimed the longest and closest historical link with the Roman breviary. Indeed from 1523 to 1528 Quiñones had served as its minister general.[27] Like his more famous Franciscan patron, Cardinal Francisco Jiménez de Cisneros (1436–1517), Quiñones was an outspoken critic of laxity, ignorance, and decadence within his own order and a keen sponsor of monastic reform. As a youth he had been a page in Cisneros's household, and he later studied at Cisneros's newly founded University of Alcalá, among other places. In 1523 he had approved the separation of certain Observant Franciscans who sought a more austere and solitary life, and later came to be called Recollects.[28] He also oversaw the formation of the separate Capuchin Order. For the Franciscan Order as a whole in Spain, he had composed a set of reform guidelines in 1523 which painted a damning picture of "monstrous" ignorance, indiscipline, and spiritual indifference.[29] Along with many other recommendations, these guidelines urged that the order cease to admit unlettered *idioti,* and require new novices to be well versed in Latin (a requirement already stipulated in early statutes, though routinely ignored) and able to say the Divine Office "clearly and fluently."[30]

Quiñones had also explicitly recommended an extra hour a day of private prayer for all members of the order.[31] More than anything, Quiñones's spiritual and liturgical ideals were shaped by this reformed Franciscan milieu.

This is not to say that Quiñones was actively involved in monastic or liturgical reform when Clement VII summoned him to work on the Breviary, for it was his diplomatic career that brought him to the pope's attention. As a scion of one of Spain's most aristocratic families, and a cousin of Charles V, Holy Roman Emperor and king of Spain, Quiñones found his way into Habsburg political circles (in this respect too his career seems to echo that of the friar-cardinal-archbishop Cisneros, who had ended his career serving as regent of Castile).[32] When his ecclesiastical duties took him to Rome in 1525, Quiñones earned the trust of Pope Clement VII and was soon serving as a diplomatic intermediary between emperor and pope. In 1528 Clement rewarded him with the dignity of Cardinal of the Holy Cross in Jerusalem. In the same year he was allowed to resign the Franciscan generalship.[33] By 1532 he had been named both governor in the papal states and bishop of Coria and Spain. Both charges added to the already considerable moral awkwardness of being a mendicant friar while holding multiple benefices and secular responsibilities.[34] Although his diplomatic activity seems to have slowed down after 1535, one may still wonder how Quiñones found time for scholarship in such a busy life. Nor is there much evidence that he had a real scholarly bent. He would thus seem in some ways an unlikely choice to revise the Roman Breviary. But Quiñones did not work alone. If not a great scholar himself, he was—again like Cardinal Cisneros—a great patron of scholars. He was assisted on the Breviary by three Spanish scholars who resided in his household: Diego Neyla, Gaspar de Castro, and Juan Ginés de Sepúlveda.[35] The last-named, one of the leading Spanish humanists of that era, regarded Quiñones as an important patron.[36] The cardinal may very well have delegated nearly all of the work to these assistants.

Their joint effort appeared in 1535, shortly after the death of its sponsor, Clement VII. It was accompanied by a letter of approval from his successor, Paul III (r. 1534–49). Whether Quiñones was its main editor or merely an editorial supervisor, the new Breviary clearly reflected his own conflicting preoccupations as a friar deeply immersed in the affairs of the secular world. It was intended to be particularly useful for overtaxed clergymen who did not have time for many hours of daily communal prayer. This and other editorial principles were laid out for the user in a substantial preface under Quiñones's name. This preface described the new Breviary as "extremely convenient to use thanks to the great simplicity and considerable brevity of its layout."[37] To that end it was far more concise than its predecessors. Most strikingly, it eliminated the parts of the Office that were intended for choir recitation: most of the antiphons, *capitula,* and responds, and numerous hymns. It further omitted the additional daily Offices that had crept into the Breviary in the later Middle Ages—that is, the Office of the Dead, the "Little Office" of the Blessed Virgin Mary, the seven penitential psalms, and the fifteen gradual psalms.

By thus shortening the Divine Office, Quiñones produced the first Breviary in history to acknowledge openly a practice that had been common for centuries: reciting the daily Office in private. Private recitation had taken place since the early Middle Ages, but canon law still acknowledged it only as an exception to the general rule of communal prayer in a monastery or cathedral choir, even though for secular parish clergy the latter was often a practical impossibility.[38] The papal letter of authorization that introduced Quiñones's new Breviary made clear that it was intended particularly (although not necessarily exclusively) for the secular clergy.[39] Monks who chanted the Divine Office together in choir were not expected to find this book useful. Regular clergy, such as Franciscans, would have to seek the special permission of their superiors if they wanted to use it.

The new book was also, in modern parlance, much more user-friendly than its predecessors. Older Breviaries seemed to assume that the user was thoroughly familiar with the structure of the Office and the rules by which it varied from day to day; thus they can leave an uninitiated modern reader thoroughly baffled. According to Quiñones, many sixteenth-century clerics felt baffled too. There was, he claimed in the preface, "great confusion because of the complexity and multitude of rules."[40] Even if one could eventually sort them all out, "many times there was more business to find out what should be read, than to read it when it was found out."[41] The new Breviary therefore aimed at as few and as simple rules as possible. It is laid out in the traditional order, with a Calendar of saints followed by the Temporale and the Sanctorale. But it also includes some novel explanatory material that actually enables a patient beginner to understand how to use it. The Calendar is preceded by five introductory pages of "general rules" (expanded to nine in the second recension) which are much more detailed than those in any earlier Breviary.[42] Indices of saints' feasts and Old and New Testament books acknowledge the user who does not have the Calendar memorized, or who wants to know where a particular Bible chapter appears in the lectionary. (Like earlier Breviaries, this one does not provide the full biblical texts for each lesson; this would almost double its size. One still requires an accessory Bible or lectionary.)

Ease of use was just one of the "three great advantages" advertised in Quiñones's lengthy justificatory preface to the new Breviary. The primary advantage Quiñones promised was that the book would nurture "expertise in both the Old and New Testaments."[43] He sought to make the Daily Office once again a source of spiritual nourishment to the individual cleric. There were, he argued, three reasons for the origin of the clergy's daily Office obligation: to offer prayers to God on behalf of the general population; to render themselves more virtuous by contemplating divine things; and most importantly, to educate themselves, as teachers of religion, by the daily reading of Holy Scripture and sacred history.[44] But over the centuries, Quiñones suggested, "through human negligence," this third objective had slipped from sight. The scriptural content of the Office had diminished, so that instead of the Bible being read through each year, as originally intended, many books were now "more tasted than really read," and the Psalter, originally meant to be read through each week, was similarly slighted; some Psalms were repeated again and again, while others were omitted altogether.[45] The new Breviary sought to restore the Scriptures to their rightful place. Most of the Old Testament and all of the New Testament except for parts of the Apocalypse were to be read over the course of the year. The Scripture readings were thus much longer on average than before. But they were also fewer, for Quiñones radically simplified the structure of Matins (the long night Office that contained all the substantial lessons). Traditionally, Matins on feast days could include as many as nine lessons. In the new Breviary, Matins was no longer divided into nocturns, and it always contained just three lessons. The first was always from the Old Testament; the second from the New Testament; and the third from the New Testament, a patristic source, or a saint's life, depending on the day.

Even more drastic was Quiñones's revision of the Psalter. In the old Roman Breviary, each hour of the Office included some Psalms, but these varied in number by hour and by day. "Proper" Psalms for special seasons and saints' days frequently displaced the ferial Psalms. In the new Breviary, each hour of each day had three Psalms (except Lauds, where a canticle took the place of a third Psalm).[46] This scheme accommodated all 150 Psalms each week. To ensure that this distribution was never interrupted, Quiñones's rule was simple and severe: no proper Psalms ever. The same Psalms would be read without exception every Friday of the year (for example), whether it was Advent, Christmas Day, Lent, Good Friday, or a saint's feast.[47]

Modern scholars, relying too much on Quiñones's preface and too little on the contents of the Breviary itself, have often exaggerated Quiñones's innovations. In one such misleading description, "to all intents and purposes Quiñones had reduced the Office to the recitation of the Psalter and the reading of Holy Scripture."[48] From such comments, one would never guess that the Quiñones Breviary retained more than a hundred saints' lives and dozens of patristic homilies (by authors such as Jerome, Gregory, and Augustine) from the old Breviary. Quiñones did not expel the saints or the Church Fathers from the Divine Office. He did, however, ensure that celebration of saints' feasts would not unduly disrupt the weekly and seasonal cycles of the ferial Office. He significantly reduced the number of saints' days to be commemorated, heavily favoring early saints (thirty-one were popes, most from the first three centuries) and eliminating many medieval ones; Bernard, Bonaventure, Clare, Dominic, Francis, Thomas Aquinas, and Thomas of Canterbury were the only medieval saints who survived.[49] He also curtailed the celebration of octaves, restricting them to a few high feasts such as Christmas and Easter. Still, with all these revisions, the new Breviary included well over a hundred saints' days, each with its own "proper" lesson recounting the saint's life and miracles. These proper lessons, read during the morning hour of Matins, disrupted the ferial Office less than in the old Breviary, for they intervened only as the third lesson of the morning; the first two lessons, from the Old and New Testament, followed a yearly calendar that was not interrupted by feasts. All of these revisions undeniably reduced the role of the saints in the Daily Office, but there was much more in Quiñones's Breviary than Scripture and Psalms. Scarcely a week went by without the commemoration of a Christian martyr.

It is tempting to suppose that Quiñones's elimination of so many saints reflected a humanist skepticism about the authenticity of some of their stories. Certainly in his reworking of the saints' lives that he retained, humanist principles were employed. The third "great advantage" advertised in the preface was that "the stories of saints contain nothing to offend serious and learned ears, as they did before."[50] To accomplish this Quiñones and his collaborators made both stylistic and historiographical changes. (Given what we know about Quiñones's credentials, this may well be the part of the project where his assistants, particularly the humanist Sepúlveda, had the freest hand.) They eliminated a number of lessons that seemed be of dubious historical accuracy, and revised others, making use of two late-fifteenth-century humanist sources: Platina's *Liber de Vita Christi ac Omnium Pontificum* (1479) and Mombritius's *Sanctuarium* (c. 1480).[51] In a few instances, this led to rather bold critical assertions. The revised reading for the feast of Mary Magdalene (July 22), for example, began with the admission that "there is still no little controversy about her among learned and serious men. According to some, the various histories that are mentioned in the Gospel refer to one woman; according to others, they refer to many."[52] But such emendations were rare. There remained a great deal of legendary and apocryphal material.[53] On the whole, Quiñones and his assistants wielded their critical scalpels cautiously. They did nothing so bold as to rewrite the metrical hymns in the Breviary, as their predecessor Ferreri had set out to do; they retained most of these exactly as they stood, even though the unclassical style of these early medieval compositions made many humanists cringe. On the whole, their emendations to the saints' lives seem to have been guided as much by the overarching goal of shortening and simplifying the whole Office as by any strong and consistent humanist principles.

In short, the new Breviary was presented to the world under somewhat contradictory auspices. It claimed to remedy profound defects in the traditional Roman Breviary, yet it came with the disclaimer that it was intended only for a restricted audience. It should not have been too surprising, then, that in practice these intended restrictions were all but ignored. The new Breviary proved astonishingly popular with a wide clerical audience across Europe. Between February 1535 and July 1536 it went through eleven printings (at Rome, Paris, Venice, Lyons, Antwerp, and Cologne). A revised second edition, issued between July 1536 and 1567, went through over one hundred. These considerably outnumbered editions of the older Breviary published in the same period.[54] The Quiñones Breviary never received formal approbation from the pope like its predecessor; clerics who wished to use the new Breviary had to apply individually to the Holy See for individual permission. Yet this proved no great obstacle. As a matter of papal policy such permission was granted automatically and free of charge to all secular clergy, and in practice it was also widely granted to regular clergy.[55] The Society of Jesus, founded in 1540, the year of Quiñones's death, soon began to use it widely.[56] (One of the features that distinguished the Jesuits from older religious orders was the refusal of their founder, Ignatius Loyola, to oblige them to pray the Divine Office daily in choir; thus private recitation was the Jesuit norm, and Quiñones found an obvious market there.)[57] As Quiñones had hoped, its brevity and ease of use evidently enticed clerics who had given up the Daily Office altogether to resume the practice.[58] It is difficult to say what these receptive clerics across Europe most appreciated about the book: the convenience of the shorter Daily Office, the simplified calendar, the greater abundance of Scripture reading, or some combination thereof.

The work's critics were more vocal about what they disliked. In July 1535, just five months after the Breviary's initial publication, the theology faculty of the Sorbonne issued a detailed condemnation. Before all else they decried the omission of antiphons, responds, *capitula,* and homilies, and the Office of the Blessed Virgin.[59] Quiñones had anticipated many of these complaints. He knew that those short elements that had recurred at almost every hour of the traditional Office, as well as the daily Offices for the Virgin Mary and for the Dead, would be missed for precisely the same reasons he had chosen to omit them: they were so familiar and so often repeated in the old Breviary that many had committed them to memory. To those who might be tempted to complain, Quiñones had offered one of his boldest pieces of advice: they should try to think differently about the nature of prayer. Too many old and familiar words can actually prevent one from concentrating on the meaning of what one was praying. Reading Scripture, especially when much of it is new and unfamiliar, both enlightens the reader more and pleases God more, when one concentrates on the meaning of the words:

> Some may find it laborious in this breviary to have to read so many things out of the book, while in the old book many things were repeated so often that they were memorized and thus could simply be said by heart; but this will be compensated for by the knowledge of Holy Scripture, which will increase daily, and by the mental exertion, which God requires from us above all else when we pray (and which is demanded more by reading than by reciting from memory). In this way the extra work will prove both profitable and salutary.[60]

In a way such advice sounds odd coming from a staunch defender of weekly Psalm recitation; the Psalms were prayed from memory too, and this obviously did not require the kind of "mental exertion" Quiñones was commending here. But his reverence for the Psalter did not blind Quiñones to the spiritual danger of mindless recitation. He made this point still clearer in the second recension, which was issued one year after, and probably in response to, the Sorbonne's attack. Its amplified preface responded explicitly to the Paris doctors and other critics. In it Quiñones repeated verbatim the above argument about the importance of self-conscious prayer, and then underscored it with a bit of creative exegesis of Paul's first Letter to the Corinthians: "For as Paul says, we should pray both with the spirit and with the mind. For the mind of one who prays merely with the tongue (that is, inattentively and as if busy with something else) is unfruitful. This is a real danger for those who run through the psalms by heart."[61]

The second recension as a whole was consistent with the tone Quiñones took in the revised preface. It made some aesthetic alterations to satisfy its critics, but did not retreat from the fundamental principle that the core of the Divine Office was Holy Scripture, and that its purpose was at least in part didactic. To appease the conservatives who missed the traditional antiphons, versicles, and responds, the second recension restored many of these, making the daily Office somewhat longer than in the first. It also restored some saints to the calendar (the second recension had 150 feast days as opposed to 143 in the first), and the celebration of octaves and vigils for some major feasts. But the general scheme of Psalms and Scripture readings, and the shortening and critical editing of the saints' lives, which the

Sorbonne doctors had also criticized, stood essentially unaltered.[62] Thus overall the second recension retains the characteristic features of the first.

These changes were apparently sufficient to placate the doctors of the Sorbonne, who let the second recension stand without further condemnation.[63] No other written critiques survive from before Quiñones's death in 1540. But as the Breviary outlived Quiñones and became more widely used, its very popularity created new critics. That most of the surviving debate emanates from Spain may be a historical accident, but it probably suggests that the Quiñones Breviary found its widest audience there. In part the Breviary's later Spanish critics challenged Quiñones for the same reasons that the Paris doctors had done: the new arrangement of the Psalms was a departure from tradition; the omission of the Office of the Blessed Virgin was an offense to the Mother of God; the suggestion that Mary Magdalene might have been several women was scandalous; in these dangerously heretical times, all unnecessary change should be avoided; and so on. But the Breviary's great popularity in Spain also led these Spanish critics to address the more fundamental question of the nature and purpose of the Divine Office. The Dominican Domingo de Soto, for example (a distinguished natural law theologian from the University of Salamanca), protested that "the purpose of prayer is not to learn the psalms, or to study the Holy Scriptures, as [the Quiñones Breviary] maintains, but to utter praise and pour out supplications to God."[64] Soto was not necessarily averse to the notion of private recitation for certain qualified, studious clergyman; but he was distressed that in Spain the Breviary had found its way into choirs, where lazy canons used it (without proper authorization, but nonetheless) to dispense with their choral obligation; they would say the hours at home using Quiñones and then "sit mute in the choir."[65] For canons, Soto insisted, performance of the Divine Office was an obligation tied to their benefice, not an opportunity for self-improvement. "Especially in these times, when the heretics are trying to drive out the sacred institution of prayer from the church altogether," a Breviary that opened the door to such abuses was a grave danger.[66]

The most vitriolic attack on the Quiñones Breviary was submitted to the Council of Trent in 1551 by Spanish theologian Juan de Arze, a canon of Palencia. A much lesser figure than Soto, Arze is not known to posterity for much apart from his objections to the Breviary, but these he made abundantly clear in a diatribe that fills nearly one hundred printed pages.[67] He too decried the way the popular Breviary was corrupting the choral Office, and cited several dioceses where the Quiñones Breviary had been imported into the cathedral choir Office, causing great public scandal and corroding the canons' knowledge of the traditional Office.[68] But Arze was upset not only by these unauthorized uses; he also disputed Quiñones's claim that individual secular clergy needed a shorter Office. In his view, this was merely self-serving and slothful. No one should be absolved of his daily obligation by praying for just "one puny hour a day, even in Lent."[69]

Arze was also suspicious of the quantity of Scripture reading in the Breviary. To the "idiot cleric," unadorned Scripture posed a great danger.[70] "There is a great difference between praying, and reading the Holy Scripture; their ends are very different."[71] Likewise, "reading is far different from the interpretation of doctrine." The Church assigns the latter to "more qualified ministers *(potioribus ministris),*" and the task of prayer and Psalm-singing to the "ruder clergy *(rudioribus clericis).*"[72] The Breviary of Quiñones dangerously confuses these roles by assigning "nude and rude reading of Holy Scripture" to the "vulgar clergy." Such unfiltered exposure to the Word of God has led to the dreadful heresies of the Waldensians, Wycliffites, Albigensians, Lutherans, Adamites, Bohemians, Taborites, Anabaptists, and Zwinglians.[73] The pope must protect his flock against such errors by banning this Breviary, urged Arze.

Not all orthodox Catholic Spaniards agreed about the evils of private recitation and of so much Scripture reading. Martín de Azpilcueta, one of the most distinguished canonists of the sixteenth century and a doctor from the University of Salamanca like Soto, continued to defend the Quiñones Breviary robustly even *after* Pius V had authorized the Tridentine Breviary of 1568 and banned that of Quiñones. In Azpilcueta's view, since the decrees of the Council of Trent were not yet approved in many nations, the Breviary question remained open, and the Quiñones Breviary still had much to recommend it, in particular the central role it gave to Scripture. Defending the merit of praying by reading Scripture instead of reciting familiar verses, Azpilcueta echoed Quiñones's own conception of prayer:

> Despite its faults, [the Quiñones Breviary] has always seemed commendable to me. Firstly, because almost all of Holy Scripture is read once in each year, and a good part of it is read twice, and the Psalter is read once each week. And because it removes many trivial stories written by unlearned men, and many lessons (both from the [saints'] histories and from the expository homilies) that were so short as to be ridiculous—they scarcely contained a whole sentence. And because it removes the confusion created by anticipating and postponing feast days. And because it removes the need to determine which, and how, and how many commemorations should be said, and to seek out chapters, responds, versicles, psalms, and even lessons—all of which can distract one's attention from God. Although all these complexities can be stimulating to those who are diligent and well versed in the art of

prayer, their sheer excess can be downright harmful to others. And because everything that is recited in this breviary is either Holy Scripture, or history or serious exposition written by learned men. And because it is helpful and consoling to students and scholars since they learn in the process of reciting, and they may have more free time left for their studies; and since as Lactantius says, learning and religion should be joined together, and one cannot last long without the other.[74] And because it gives relief to no small number of preachers, confessors, and others busy with and committed to other kinds of virtuous action. And because it cannot be denied that it increases the attention of the devout somewhat (albeit not enough) through its renewed variety day in and day out; and for other reasons which I omit for the sake of brevity.[75]

Despite such robust support, ultimately the Breviary's critics won out over its defenders. Evidently Arze's arguments carried great weight at Trent, and may have contributed to the pope's final decision to ban the Quiñones Breviary definitively.[76] Another factor was the hostility of Paul IV (r. 1555–59), who had liturgical reform plans of his own; he ceased granting licenses to use Quiñones in 1555 and prohibited its use altogether in a (rather ineffective) decree of 1558.[77] The making of the Tridentine Breviary, which eventually supplanted that of Quiñones altogether, is beyond the scope of this study, but it should be noted that Quiñones's Breviary influenced that of 1568 in two profound albeit contradictory ways. First and most conspicuously, the Tridentine commission reacted decisively against some of Quiñones's stated principles and against the concept of "novelty" in general. The 1568 Breviary restored the Office of the Virgin, the Office of the Dead, and the penitential and gradual Psalms. The older pattern of Matins with nine lessons, which many of Quiñones's critics had insisted was mandated by canon law, was restored. Quiñones's revision of the Psalm arrangement, which had come in for some of the fiercest criticism of all, was completely abolished in the Tridentine Breviary, which restored the custom of varying the Psalms according to season and to feast. Perhaps the most significant difference between Quiñones's Breviary and that of 1568 was in their respective attitudes toward private reading. In general the reformers at Trent were adamant about restoring the primacy of corporate worship. The final decrees of the Council refer only to the public recitation of the Office without even mentioning the possibility of private recitation.[78] The Tridentine Breviary was emphatically a Breviary for common recitation. Never again would a distinct form of the Divine Office for private use be sanctioned by the Church.

At the same time, however, despite the weight of opinion against Quiñones and against liturgical innovation in general, the Tridentine commission could not avoid adopting a number of Quiñones's innovations. The deliberations during the Council of Trent touched on many of the same "abuses" that Quiñones had addressed, such as the erosion of the ferial Office and the need to prune the Sanctorale, albeit without explicitly acknowledging his work. The Tridentine Breviary pruned the calendar quite dramatically, eliminating many octaves and some feasts, leaving more than half the year free for the saying of the ferial Office, in a fashion quite similar to Quiñones. Another similarity between the two Breviaries was the user-friendly layout; although it did not reproduce all of Quiñones's convenient cross-references, it offered a relatively clear and comprehensive set of rubrics compared with older Breviaries. It seems that once Quiñones had revealed the emperor's nakedness by publicizing the inability of many clerics to use the old Breviary, the Tridentine reformers had to acknowledge the wisdom of making the Breviary more accessible to the inexpert.

What is the place of this popular but short-lived and controversial Breviary within the broader history of Christian worship in the early modern era? If we accept the testimony of Quiñones himself, the strongest impulse behind his liturgical revisions (whether the first or the second recension) was to restore the Divine Office from its "corrupted state" to an earlier, purer model followed by the early Church. Like most premodern reformers, Quiñones walked a fine line between promoting his revisions as a change for the better and insisting that he had really changed nothing at all. In both versions of his preface, after enumerating the failings of the older Breviary and the distinct improvements made in this new one, he tried to erase the impression of substantial change: "If one ponders diligently and considers carefully the advice of the ancient fathers, he will understand clearly that this is not so much a newly invented breviary, as it is a restoration of the ancient breviary in a more satisfactory and refined form."[79]

In a broad sense, this desire to improve by restoring an ancient model may be called a humanist impulse, although Quiñones and his collaborators did not rigorously employ humanist scholarly methods. But if the goal of restoring a pristine, ancient model resonates with humanist scholarly principles, Quiñones himself was less forthcoming than most humanists about what his prototype was.[80] The most likely inspiration for Quiñones's guiding principles—reading through the Psalms weekly and the Bible annually—was early monastic practice, hardly a favored model among Christian humanists. Thus sixteenth-century humanism is not really an adequate explanation for what motivated Quiñones. A restorative impulse was common to a broad spectrum of reformers in this era, including Catholics and Protestants, humanists and their critics. The Christian concept of *reformatio* predated the Protestant Reformation by many centuries.[81] But in trying to restore, all reformers necessarily innovate, and Quiñones was no exception. There was no clear blueprint for the pristine, original Divine Office in which all of Scripture was read every year and the entire Psalter every week. Scripture itself, the favored authority of all Christian reformers, offered only the most meager guidelines. Thus Quiñones's revised order of the Psalms and of the Scripture readings, and his revised calendar of saints, were inevitably somewhat original, despite his protests that they were not.

For his critics, this was precisely the problem. Quiñones's innovations created an aesthetic discontinuity in the Divine Office which, for them, overshadowed any theoretical continuity with the designs of "the ancient fathers." They missed beloved antiphons, hymns, proper Psalms, feast days, and Offices for the Virgin. It is easy to dismiss this attitude as reflexive conservatism that values the merely aesthetic aspects of the Office over its intrinsic meaning. But there was a deeper side to this conservative critique. These critics correctly perceived that the Quiñones Breviary, with its scarce choral elements and its abundant long Scripture readings, validated a powerful (and to them disturbing) trend away from corporate prayer and toward a notion of prayer as a private, individual act. Even Quiñones himself did not presume to offer the new Breviary as an exclusive new form of the Office for the whole Church, but merely as an alternative for some of its members. For Quiñones and his defenders, accepting the realities of a busy and largely secularized clergy, it made sense to uphold two different forms of the Office: one for the monastic clergy, who still had time to pray for many hours a day, and another for those who did not, because of studies, administrative duties, or other responsibilities. For his critics, however, this two-tiered system was a grave threat to the unity of the Church. They worried not only about only the diachronic continuity of the Office through the centuries, but about synchronic continuity of practice across Christendom. If *any* cleric who felt himself too busy to pray the Office in choir could easily get a license to use the Quiñones Breviary, where would it stop? Knowing the weakness of the human will, how would the choral Office then survive outside monasteries?

The Tridentine Breviary, which superseded that of Quiñones, sought a compromise between these two notions of continuity. The reformers at Trent agreed with Quiñones about many of the faults of the old Breviary, and so like Quiñones, they tried to keep Psalms and Scripture more prominent. But they were also eager to re-emphasize the worth of corporate prayer, and not to allow individual deviation from this ideal. Thus they insisted on returning to an Office that could be sung in choir, which necessarily reduced the amount of Scripture reading. In the long run the Tridentine effort to end private recitation by failing to acknowledge it, proved a failure. Ironically, Quiñones's most enduring legacy may have been that Thomas Cranmer drew heavily from the Quiñones Breviary in composing the Anglican *Book of Common Prayer,* which proved, over the subsequent centuries, a more genuinely communal form of the Divine Office in practice than the Roman Breviary.[82]

This legacy, however, would undoubtedly not have pleased Quiñones very much, for his vision of the Divine Office remained strictly clerical, as the Catholic tradition required. In this sense, there is profound continuity among all the Roman Breviaries discussed here so far. For if we compare any one of them with the reforms and reworkings of the Divine Office taking place in Protestant Europe in roughly the same era, the change wrought by the Protestant Reformation is dramatic. While Quiñones and his critics differed about whether the Office was essentially a communal or a private exercise, all still took for granted the notion of the Divine Office as an essentially clerical exercise. Catholics like Arze and the other reformers of Trent, who were eager to preserve the tradition of the choral Office, might put more emphasis on the communal nature of prayer, but the community they envisioned was one of monks or canons; if it included the laity at all, it assigned them the role of spectators. Likewise, Quiñones's Scripture-heavy Divine Office—even if it provoked predictably dire warnings from his critics about the slippery slope toward Lutheranism—was still intended as a part of a program of personal spiritual development for the clergy, not a broader movement to improve the biblical education of the whole Christian flock. In this it embodies a fundamental difference that endured between the Protestant and Catholic traditions throughout the early modern period.

Notes

1. For the best general introduction to the early history of the Divine Office, see Robert Taft, *The Liturgy of the Hours in East and West* (Collegeville, Minn.: Liturgical Press, 1986). On the Office in Benedict's Rule, see Taft, 130–40. I am grateful to Margot Fassler for directing me to this and other essential bibliography at an early stage of this project.

2. Taft, *The Liturgy*, 299. For discussions of the general obligation on all clergy and how it was understood, see Stephen Van Dijk and Joan Hazelden Walker, *The Origins of the Modern Roman Liturgy: The Liturgy of the Papal Court and the Franciscan Order in the Thirteenth Century* (Westminster, Md.: Newman Press, 1960), 37–40; Pierre Salmon, *The Breviary Through the Centuries,* trans. (Sister) David Mary (Collegeville, Minn.: Liturgical Press, 1962), 1–20.

3. On the monastic origin of the Book of Hours as an offshoot of the Divine Office, see Edmund Bishop, "On the Origins of the Prymer," in *Liturgica Historica* (Oxford: Clarendon Press, 1918), 211–37.

4. For a selection of recent scholarship highlighting the diversity of the medieval Office, see Margot E. Fassler and Rebecca A. Baltzer, eds., *The Divine Office in the Latin Middle Ages: Methodology and Source Studies, Regional Developments, Hagiography* (Oxford: Oxford University Press, 2000).

5. The thorough reform of the Divine Office by the Second Vatican Council, issued in 1971, was preceded by six minor reforms, the most substantial of which was that of Pius X in 1911. For these reforms between Trent and Vatican II, see J.A. Goenaga, "Le diverse riforme dell'Ufficio dal secolo XVI al Vaticano II," in D. Borbio, ed., *La celebrazione nella Chiesa*, vol. 3: *Ritmi e tempi della celebrazione* (Torino: Elle Di Ci, 1994): 368–90.

6. See Francis Aidan Gasquet and Edmund Bishop, *Edward VI and the Book of Common Prayer*, 2nd ed. (London: J. Hodges, 1890); G.J. Cuming, *The Godly Order: Texts and Studies Relating to the Book of Common Prayer* (London: Alcuin Club, 1983), 1–25.

7. Frank C. Senn, *Christian Liturgy, Catholic and Evangelical* (Minneapolis: Fortress Press, 1997), 338–42. See also J.N. Alexander, "Luther's Reform of the Daily Office," *Worship* 57 (1983), 348–60. For Luther's own pronouncements about the Divine Office, see the 1523 pamphlet "Concerning the Order of Public Worship," in *LW*, 53: 38–39.

8. The practice in Geneva was influenced by Calvin's experience in Strasbourg. For a lucid discussion of the latter, see Hughes Oliphant Old, "Daily Prayer in the Reformed Church of Strasbourg, 1525–1530," *Worship* 52 (1978): 121–38.

9. Scholars now refer to these two versions as the first and second recensions. The English scholar J.W. Legg produced critical editions of both recensions: the first (based on a Venice 1535 edition) published in Cambridge in 1888; the second (based on an Antwerp 1537 edition) was published in London, 1908–12 (in two volumes). These will be cited hereafter as Legg 1535 and Legg 1537.

10. For the most thorough discussion of Quiñones's project, the publishing history of the Breviary, and its reception, see the introductory material to both editions of Legg.

11. Before becoming Paul IV, he was Gian Pietro Caraffa, founder of the Theatines. On his liturgical reform, see below, note 25.

12. The bull mandating the adoption of the 1568 Breviary, *Quod a nobis*, provided exemptions only for communities that could show that their own Office tradition dated back more than two centuries. This bull appeared in subsequent editions of the Roman Breviary until 1911. See, for example, Manlio Sodi and Achille Maria Triacca, eds., *Breviarium Romanum, Editio Princeps (1568)* (Vatican City: Libreria Editrice Vaticana, 1999), 3–6.

13. I borrow this apt metaphor from Simon Ditchfield, *Liturgy, Sanctity, and History in Tridentine Italy* (Cambridge: Cambridge University Press, 1995). However, he ultimately rejects the metaphor, arguing persuasively that because of its lasting influence on the *Breviarium Romanum* of 1568, the Quiñones Breviary was "not a liturgical cul-de-sac" (25).

14. For what follows, see Van Dijk and Walker, *The Origins;* Taft, *The Liturgy*, 307ff. The former is a meticulous monograph on these liturgical developments and the historiographical complexities associated with them; the latter offers a succinct summary.

15. On the adoption of the revised Roman Office outside the Franciscan Order, see Van Dijk and Walker, *The Origins*, 398ff.

16. It is sometimes claimed that the mendicants invented the Breviary, but Van Dijk and Walker refute this myth definitively, showing that the first breviaries were for choir use, and date to the eleventh century or earlier (*The Origins,* 26ff.).

17. Benedict was one of many early authorities who upheld the ideal of reading the entire Psalter in a week, although this ideal was far from universally upheld in medieval liturgies. See Saint Benedict, *The Rule of Saint Benedict in Latin and English with Notes* (Collegeville, Minn.: Liturgical Press, 1981), rule 18. Sources from the seventh and eighth centuries suggest that in several Roman monasteries the monks were accustomed to reading the entire Bible in the course of a year within the Divine Office; Salmon, *The Breviary,* 63–64. Both Gelasius and Gregory the Great also commended this ideal; Suitbert Bäumer, O.S.B., *Geschichte des Breviers* (Freiburg im Breisgau: Herder, 1895) [French ed., rev. and trans. by R. Biron: *Histoire du bréviaire* (Paris: Letouzey et Ané, 1905; reprint, Paris: Cerf, 1967), 394.]

18. For a thorough introduction to the medieval liturgical calendar, see John Harper, *The Forms and Orders of Western Liturgy from the Tenth to the Eighteenth Century,* (Oxford: Clarendon Press, 1991), chap. 3 and appendix I.

19. The main seasons were Advent, Christmas, Epiphany, Lent, Holy Week, and Easter. The feast of Corpus Christi was added to the calendar in 1264, and fell in May or June (two months after Easter).

20. Ditchfield, *Liturgy, Sanctity, and History,* 31.

21. Harper, *Forms and Orders,* 53. In theory, the missal shared a common calendar with the Breviary, but it must be remembered that before 1568 this was not strictly prescribed. Therefore the missal calendar can only be taken as an approximation of the calendar used by contemporaneous Breviaries.

22. The origin of the obligation is somewhat murky, but Bishop, "On the Origins of the Prymer," undertakes to reconstruct it, attributing it to the zeal of certain early medieval monks. While many clergy objected to the excessive length of the Office with these accretions, the accretions themselves were quite popular. See, for example, the comment of Martin of Senging to the Council of Basle in 1435: "The Divine Office is recited in disorderly fashion, in haste, without devotion, and with a perverse intention, viz. an itching desire to get to the end of it: the clergy come to prefer to the canonical Office the superficial additions which are tacked on to it." Quoted in Pierre Battifol, *History of the Roman Breviary,* trans. Atwell Y. Baylay (London: Longmans, Green, 1898), 226.

23. Ditchfield, *Liturgy, Sanctity, and History,* 32–33; Battifol, *History,* 224–25. Quiñones himself alleged this motive among the clergy; Legg 1537, I, xxvi.

24. *Hymni novi Ecclesiastici* (Rome, 1525). A description, with excerpts, is given in Legg 1537, II, 7–12. The description of Ferreri's projected new Breviary comes from the title page of the hymnal; Legg 1537, II, 11.

25. On Caraffa's reform, see Bäumer, *Histoire du bréviaire,* 410–16; Battifol, *History,* 248–52; Legg 1537, II, 12–14; Ditchfield, *Liturgy, Sanctity, and History,* 27–30. The first mention of Caraffa's project appears in a papal brief of 1524 authorizing the Theatines to develop their own Breviary. In another papal brief five years later, Clement expressed approval with Caraffa's progress so far (see text in Legg 1537, II, 12–13).

26. Ditchfield, *Liturgy, Sanctity, and History,* 28.

27. The most thorough account of Quiñones's career remains the introductory chapter in Legg 1537, II, 87–103. More recent but much briefer are two encylopedia entries: I. García, "Francisco de los Angeles de Quiñones," *Diccionario de historia eclesiástica de España* (Madrid: Instituto Enrique Flórez, Consejo Superior de Investigaciones Científicas, 1973), III, 2037–38; and Juan Messeguer Fernández, O. F. M, "Francisco de Quiñones," *New Catholic Encyclopedia* (New York: McGraw Hill, 1967), vol. 12, 30–31. Messeguer has researched Quiñones's life in more detail than any modern scholar, but unfortunately never produced his intended full-length biography. His researches are available only in three disparate journal articles listed in the bibliography of his article in the *New Catholic Encyclopedia.* Many of the relevant Franciscan sources on Quiñones's career are printed in Luke Wadding, ed., *Annales Minorum,* 32 vols., 3rd ed. (Rome, 1736; reprint, Florence: Quaracchi, 1933), vol. 16, which covers the years 1516–40.

28. See Juan Messeguer Fernández, O. F. M, "Programa de gobierno del P. Francisco de Quiñones, Ministro General O. F. M. (1523–1528)," *Archivo Ibero Americano* 81 (1961): 18–23.

29. "Admoniciones o Avisos del Padre Francisco de los Angeles de Quiñones a las provincias españoles," Valladolid, August 28, 1523 (Roma, Archive of St Isidore, 1/9, 153–68); printed in Messeguer Fernández, "Programa de gobierno," 35–51.

30. "Avisos," cap. I, § 1 and 4, in Messeguer Fernández, "Programa de gobierno," 37–38.

31. Messeguer Fernández, "Programa de gobierno," 7.

32. This family had produced Pedro de Luna (the antipope Benedict XIII, d. 1432), and Alvaro de Luna (d. 1453), who had ruled Castile under Juan II. Quiñones's kinship with Charles V came through his mother, Juana Enriquez, whose father was Enrique, Conde de Alba de Liste.

33. He had sought release from these duties for at least two years; Legg 1537, II, 90, gives the text of an unsuccessful petition in 1526 (from Wadding, ed., *Annales,* 16: 227).

34. To Quiñones's credit, it seems that he was actually promoted to the see of Coria twice, and each time resigned after a short period, alleging scruples about nonresidence. Legg, II, 102.

35. In the Breviary's preface Quiñones acknowledged having "called upon certain wise men in my household, skilled in the study of sacred literature and pontifical law and learned in Greek and Latin," (Legg 1535, xxi). He did not identify these assistants by name, but the Flemish humanist chronicler Joannes Vasaeus, in his *Chronici Rerum memorabilium Hispaniae* (1552), identified them as Neyla, Castro, and Sepúlveda; see Faustino Arévalo, "Breviarii Quignoniani fata" (appendix II), in *Hymnodia hispanica ad cantus, latinitatis, metrique leges revocata, et aucta* (Rome: e typographia Salomoniana, 1786) [Vatican rare book microfilms, list 46, no. 1], 406–9. Neyla was a doctor of canon law and later a canon of Salamanca. Less is known about Castro. Sepúlveda is better known than Quiñones himself.

36. Sepúlveda dedicated his 1531 work, *De ritu nuptiarum et dispensatione*, to Quiñones (Legg 1537, II, 103); and he referred to Quiñones in a letter to Neyla as "patronus noster" (Arévalo, *Hymnodia*, 407, note a).

37. The first (1535) version of the preface is reprinted in Legg 1535, and in Arévalo, *Hymnodia*, 413–20. I quote here from Legg. The second version, considerably revised and expanded, is reprinted (from a 1537 edition) in Legg 1537, I, xxiii–xxiv. Although Quiñones's collaborators may also have contributed to the preface, it is written in the first person under his name, and will be cited here accordingly. For the passage just quoted, see below, note 43.

38. Taft, *The Liturgy*, 300–301; Salmon, *The Breviary*, 13–20.

39. Legg 1535, xxvi.

40. Ibid.

41. "Accedit tam perplexus ordo, tamque difficilis precandi ratio, ut interdum paulo minor opera in inquirendo ponatur, quam cum inveneris, in legendo" (Legg 1535, xx). The English translation is that of Thomas Cranmer in the 1549 preface to *The Book of Common Prayer*, in which, as innumerable scholars have pointed out, Cranmer plagiarized extensively from Quiñones. *The Book of Common Prayer* (New York: Oxford University Press, 1979), 866.

42. Ditchfield, *Liturgy, Sanctity, and History*, 27.

43. Quiñones's summary of the Breviary's three main advantages reads: "Habet haec precandi ratio tres maximas commoditates. Primam, quod precantibus simul acquiritur utriusque testamenti peritia. Secundam, quod res est expeditissima propter summam ordinis simplicitatem, et nonnullam brevitatem. Tertiam, quod historiae sanctorum nihil habent, ut prius, quod graves, et doctas aures offendat" (Legg 1535, xxii).

44. Legg 1535, xix–xx.

45. Ibid., xx. The metaphor of "tasting" Scripture piecemeal ("degustamus magis quam legimus") is repeated ("una particula legitur carptim libros degustando") on xxiv.

46. The other exception was on Sunday, where the longest psalm, 118 (119), was broken down into eleven parts and spread out over four hours. See the table in Legg 1537, II, 42–43, for a clear overview.

47. The ordering of the Psalms seems to have been quite arbitrary. Quiñones did not suggest any guiding principle, nor has any of his modern commentators discerned any, other than that of equalizing the length of each hour.

48. J.D. Crichton, in Cheslyn Jones, Edward Yarnold, and Geoffrey Wainwright, eds., *The Study of Liturgy* (London: SPCK, 1978), 434. Cf. Ludwig Eisenhofer and Joseph Lechner, *The Liturgy of the Roman Rite* (Freiburg: Herder, 1961), 445, who charge that Quiñones "almost completely suppressed all non-Biblical elements."

49. Legg 1537, II, 33–34.

50. Legg 1535, xxii. For full text, see above, note 43.

51. Ditchfield, *Liturgy, Sanctity, and History*, 25–26.

52. Legg 1535, 141–42.

53. Ditchfield is the most generous to Quiñones, placing him at the beginning of a tradition of Catholic humanist historiography which he sees as the foundation for modern critical scholarship. But he also points out that (as Juan de Arze noted),

Quiñones's sources for his revised saints' lives were far from unimpeachable, and he did not always use them with the utmost care. In one instance he even reproduced some of Platina's misprints. See Arze's comments in Legg 1537, II, 203.

54. Legg 1537, I, xiii; II, 20.

55. See Paul III's letter of authorization specifying these conditions in Legg 1537, I, xxx. For numerous cases of individual clergy who obtained such licenses, see Legg 1537 II, 20–25.

56. Jungmann reports that "in 1546 St. Ignatius received from Paul III the general privilege for members of his order to use this Breviary," but both he and Legg also cite cases from the 1540s into the 1560s of individual Jesuits (including Francis Xavier) receiving papal licenses to use the Quiñones Breviary. Thus one wonders exactly what such a "general permission" meant. Josef A. Jungmann, *Pastoral Liturgy* (New York: Herder and Herder, 1962), 204–5; Legg 1537, II, 21–24.

57. *Constitutions of the Society of Jesus,* no. 586 (George E. Ganss, *The Constitutions of the Society of Jesus* [St. Louis: The Institute of Jesuit Sources, 1970], p. 261). Taft, *The Liturgy,* 301–6.

58. See, for example, Peter Canisius's report to Ignatius Loyola in 1560 on his experience with the new Breviary in Germany: "Many ecclesiastics never recited the canonical hours at all. We induced them to fulfil this task along with us, so that they might learn the method of saying them; and since they preferred to use the new Roman Breviary, we got leave for them from the papal legate to do so. And so they persevere in reciting daily the canonical hours" (Battifol, *History,* 243, n. 1).

59. This is reprinted in full in Legg 1537, II, 107–15.

60. Legg 1535, xxv.

61. Legg 1537, I, xxix. This is a very loose paraphrase of Paul's words in 1 Cor. 14:15, which actually refer to "praying in tongues" rather than "praying with the tongue." Quiñones seems unaware of this distinction, or is creatively ignoring it.

62. While the arrangement of the New Testament was unaltered between the two recensions, the ordering of the books of the Old Testament was altered somewhat; for two useful comparative tables, see Vincenzo Raffa, F. D. P, "Dal Breviario del Quignonez alla Liturgia delle Ore di Paolo IV," in *Liturgia delle Ore: Documenti ufficiali e studi* (*Quaderni di Rivista Liturgica,* 14) (Torino: Elle Di Ci, 1972), 302–5.

63. Whether they formally approved it or not is a matter of some ambiguity; Legg 1537, II, 18–20.

64. Domingo de Soto, *De Iustitia et Iure* (Antwerp, 1568), Lib. X, Q. V, Art. iv; reprinted in Legg 1537, II, 131–33; passage quoted, 131.

65. Ibid.

66. Legg 1537, II, 132.

67. This is edited (from MS Ottobon. Lat. 805 in the Vatican Library) in Legg 1537, II, 134–215. For a concise summary, see Jungmann, 205–7.

68. Legg 1537, II, 155–57.

69. Ibid., 196.

70. Ibid., 152.

71. Ibid., 148.

72. Ibid., 149.

73. ". . . non paucis vulgaris clericis, nudam lectionem et rudem sacrarum literarum." Ibid., 151.

74. Lactantius, *Diuinae Institutiones* c. 1 (PL vi, 119).

75. Azpilcueta, *Enchiridion seu Manuale de Oratione, Horis Canonicis, etc.* (vol. 3 of *Opera,* Lyons, 1597); reprinted in Legg 1537, II, 122–30. Passage quoted, 124–25. The first version of this was written in the 1540s or 1550s, but Azpilcueta revised it for subsequent editions. This version was clearly written after 1568.

76. Bäumer, *Histoire du Bréviaire,* 403; Jungmann, 207–8.

77. Legg 1537, II, 26.

78. Taft, *The Liturgy,* 301.

79. Legg 1535, xxiv; cf. Legg 1537, I, xxviii. In the later preface, the final phrase "in commodiorem, et cultiorem formam restitutionem" is replaced with the more modest "adhibito quodam temperamento restitutionem."

80. He grew somewhat more specific in the revised version. In the 1535 preface Quiñones had defended his central principles—reading the whole of Scripture each year and the whole Psalter weekly—as ideals of the "ancient fathers" (Legg 1535, xx). In 1536 he adduced Pope Gelasius (c. 496) and several early ecumenical councils (Legg 1537, I, xxv, xxviii). He also tried to place Clement VII more explicitly on his side by revising his account of the pope's instructions to him; in the original preface he had described Clement rather vaguely as instructing him to remove certain "difficulties" in the daily Office and make it more "enticing" to the clergy. In the second recension, Quiñones added the phrases: "and to restore the prayers as much as possible to that ancient form" and "so as not to deviate from that summit of reason which was once ordained by the ancient and holy fathers" (Legg 1535, xx; Legg 1537, I, xxv). But even these revised comments remain quite vague.

81. See, for example, Giles Constable, "Renewal and Reform in Religious Life: Concepts and Realities," in Robert Benson and Giles Constable, eds., *Renaissance and Renewal in the Twelfth Century* (Toronto: University of Toronto Press/Medieval Academy of America, 1991), 37–67.

82. On Cranmer's use of Quiñones, see Cuming, *The Godly Order;* Gasquet and Bishop, *Edward VI.*

Rites of Passage

eight

Water Surrounded by God's Word: The Diocese of Breslau as a Window into the Transformation of Baptism from the Medieval Period to the Reformation

KENT J. BURRESON

Editors' Introduction

In the Middle Ages, the entry point into the Christian Church was through baptism, a sacrament of the Church usually administered to infants, except in the relatively rare cases of adult conversions to Christianity. Baptism marked not only the child's reception into the Church, but also the washing away of original sin through the waters of the sacrament and the prayers and anointing done by the priest. As baptism was a rite that all Christians participated in, it is fitting to have a contribution focusing specifically on the ways in which the sacrament of baptism maintained similar characteristics or changed during the transitions from the medieval to the early modern world.

Kent Burreson's contribution examines the ways in which Lutheran baptismal rites retained but also transformed key aspects of the Catholic baptismal rites. At the same time, the Lutherans also had to counter the critiques of the Calvinists over what the latter perceived as the Lutherans' incomplete Reformation, especially regarding the sacraments.

Primary Sources Introduction

The following texts are three baptismal rituals (one Catholic and two Lutheran) used in the German lands from the fourteenth to the sixteenth century; they show how this central rite of the Christian faith was celebrated in the medieval and early modern periods. Notice how some parts of the liturgy are retained in all three rites, whereas other features are omitted or added in each case.

A. The Ritual of Bishop Henry I of Breslau (c. 1302–19)[1]

Order for the making of catechumens

First the priest, standing at the door of the church, places the boys to his right and the girls to his left. He blows in the face of the infant three times in the shape of a cross—for through this the driving out of the devil is demonstrated—and says: Withdraw, devil. Here begins the order of blessing the catechumens and of baptizing them in the name of the Lord.

1. Withdraw, devil, from this image of God, rebuked by him, and give place to the living and true God.
2. And make the sign of the cross on his forehead saying: The sign of the holy cross of our Lord Jesus Christ I place on your forehead.
3. Similarly to the breast: The sign of the salvation of our Lord Jesus Christ I place on your breast.
4. After placing the hand over his head the priest says: The Lord be with you. Let us pray . . . Almighty everlasting God, Father of our Lord Jesus Christ, look upon these your servants whom you have called to the elements of faith. Drive from them all blindness of heart: loose the bonds of Satan with which they were bound, open to them, O Lord, the door of your religion: that bearing the sign of your wisdom, they may turn from the squalor of fleshly lusts and delight in the sweet savor of your commandments and joyfully serve you in your church: that first taking the medicine they may increase in virtue day by day until by your favor they come to the grace of baptism. Through our Lord . . .
5. O Lord, we beseech you, of your goodness hear our prayers, and protect these your elect with the power of the Lord's cross, with which we sign them, that from this beginning of

the worship of your majesty, being ever set about by your commandments, they may attain to the glory of the second birth. Through . . .

6. God, you have created the human race that you might also restore it, look with mercy on your adopted people, set the offspring of your new race within your new covenant, that what they could not attain by nature, the children of promise may joyfully receive by grace. Through our Lord . . .
7. I exorcise you creature of salt in the Name of God the Father Almighty, and in the love of our Lord Jesus Christ, and in the power of the Holy Spirit. I exorcise you by the living God and by the true God, who has created you to be a safeguard of the human race, and has commanded you to be consecrated by his servants for those who come to faith. And therefore we ask you, O Lord our God, that in the Name of the Trinity this creature of salt may be a saving sacrament to drive away the enemy: O Lord, sanctify and bless it, that it may remain as a perfect medicine in the bowels of all who receive it, in the name of our Lord Jesus Christ, who will come again.
8. After this he asks the child's name and places the salt in the child's mouth and says: Receive the salt of wisdom which is a propitiation to the Lord for you to eternal life. After giving the salt he says: The Lord be with you. Let us pray.
9. O God of our Fathers, O God who establishes all truth, we humbly beseech you to look favorably upon this your servant, and grant that he who has taken this first morsel of salt may hunger only until he is filled with heavenly food. Until then, Lord, may he be fervent in spirit, rejoicing in hope, serving your name. Lead him to the bath of the second birth that with your faithful people he may be worthy to receive the eternal rewards of your promises. Through the Lord . . .
10. Say these prayers over all the males making the sign of the cross on their foreheads: Let us pray . . . God of Abraham, God of Isaac, God of Jacob, God who appeared to your servant Moses upon Mount Sinai and led the children of Israel out of the land of Egypt, sending to them the angel of your goodness to guard them by day and by night, we beseech you, O Lord, that you would send your holy angel, that likewise he may also guard these your servants and lead them to the grace of your baptism.
11. Over the males say this: Therefore accursed devil, remember your sentence and give honor to God, the living and true, give

honor to Jesus Christ his Son, and to the Holy Spirit, and depart from these servants of God. For Jesus Christ our Lord and God is pleased to call them to him and to give them his holy grace and blessing and the fount of baptism. This sign of the holy cross which we now make upon their brows, O accursed devil, dare never to violate.

12. Again over the males: O God, the unfailing support of all who seek your aid, the liberator of all who entreat you, the peace of all who implore you, life to believers, and resurrection to the dead! I invoke you on behalf of this your servant, N., who begs the gift of baptism, and longs to attain everlasting grace by being reborn spiritually. Take him to yourself, O Lord, and since you have mercifully promised: "Ask and you shall receive; seek and you shall find; knock and it shall be opened unto you," reach out the reward to him who asks, open wide the door to him who knocks. So may he gain the never failing blessing of the heavenly bath, and possess the kingdom which in your bounty you have promised. Through. . . Therefore, accursed . . .

13. Again over the males: Hearken accursed Satan, adjured by the Name of the eternal God, and of our Savior the Son of God: you and your envy are conquered, depart trembling and groaning. Let there be nothing between you and this servant of God, who even now ponders heavenly things, who is to renounce you and your kingdom and make his way to blessed immortality. Give honor therefore to the Holy Spirit as he approaches, descending from the highest place of heaven, who shall confound your deceits and at the divine fount shall cleanse and sanctify his breast unto a temple and dwelling place of God: so that, freed from all the inward hurts of past offenses, as the servant of God he may always praise the everlasting God, and bless his holy name throughout all ages. Through our Lord Jesus Christ who shall come to judge the living and the dead and this world by fire.

14. Exorcism over the males: I exorcise you, unclean spirit, in the name of the Father and the Son and the Holy Spirit, that you may go away and depart from this servant of God. For he himself commands you, accursed one, damned one, he who walked with his feet on the sea and stretched out his right hand to Peter as he sank. Therefore accursed . . .

15. These prayers are said over the females likewise making the sign of the cross on their foreheads as with the males: Let us

pray: God of heaven, God of earth, God of angels, God of archangels, God of the prophets, God of the apostles, God of the martyrs, God of the confessors, God of the virgins, God of all who live good lives, God whom every tongue confesses, of things in heaven and things in earth, and things under the earth, I call upon you, Lord, to watch over this your worthy servant N., and to lead her to the grace of baptism. Therefore, accursed . . .

16. Let us pray. God of Abraham, God of Isaac, God of Jacob, who liberated your people Israel from servitude in Egypt, through Moses your servant, who admonished those charged with watching over Israel in the desert and freed Susanna from false accusation, I humbly beseech you O Lord, to free also this your servant N., from the power of the devil and to lead her worthily to the grace of your baptism. Therefore accursed . . .

17. Exorcism over the females: I exorcise you, unclean spirit, in the name of the Father and the Son and the Holy Spirit, that you may go away and depart from this servant of God. For he himself commands you, accursed one, damned one, who opened the eyes of the man born blind, and on the fourth day raised Lazarus from the tomb. Therefore, accursed . . .

18. This is spoken over the males and females: Let us pray. O holy Lord, almighty Father, eternal God, the one who has established light and truth, I call upon your eternal and most just piety for this your servant N., so that you would lighten him with the light of your understanding, cleanse and sanctify him. Give him true knowledge that he may come worthily to the grace of your baptism. Let him hold a firm hope, right counsel, holy doctrine, so that he may be fitted to receive your grace.

19. Gospel according to Matthew 19:13–15. After this reading, laying his hand upon the head of the infant, he says the Lord's Prayer clearly—"Our Father"—and the creed—"I believe in . . . " Then he says what follows:

20. Be not deceived, Satan: punishment threatens you, torment threatens you, the day of judgment threatens you, the day which shall come as a burning furnace, when everlasting destruction shall come upon you and all your angels. And therefore, accursed one and condemned one, give honor to God, the living and the true, give honor to Jesus Christ his Son, and to the Holy Spirit, the Comforter, in whose Name and power I command you, whoever you are, unclean spirit.

Come out and depart from this servant of God, whom this day our Lord Jesus Christ has deigned to call to the gift of his holy grace and of his blessing and the fount of baptism: that he may become his temple, through the water of regeneration unto the remission of sins, in the Name of our Lord Jesus Christ, who shall come to judge the quick and the dead and this world by fire.

21. Then the priest touches the ears and nose with his spit and says while touching the right ear of the infant: "Effeta, that is be opened." And to the nose: "to the odor of sweetness." To the left ear: "But you, O devil, take flight, for the judgment of God has drawn near." Then being led into the church, the priest goes to the font. Meanwhile he makes sure the infant has not soiled itself. After this the male sponsor holds the infant while the priest asks him by name saying: Do you renounce Satan? I renounce; And all his works? I renounce; And all his pomps? I renounce.

22. Then he makes the sign of the cross with holy oil on the breast and between the shoulders on the back and says: I anoint you with the oil of salvation in Christ Jesus, our Lord, to eternal life. Amen.

23. Then calling the child by name he says: Do you believe in God the Father almighty, creator of heaven and earth? I believe; Do you believe in Jesus Christ his only Son our Lord, who was born and suffered? I believe; Do you believe in the Holy Spirit, the holy catholic church, the communion of saints, the forgiveness of sins, the resurrection of the body and eternal life after death? I believe.

24. N., do you desire to be baptized. Response: I so desire. Then he baptizes him as follows saying: N., I baptize you in the name of the Father—and immerse once—and the Son—and immerse a second time—and the Holy Spirit—and immerse a third time. And as soon as he has been lifted from the font, he makes the sign of the cross with chrism in the middle of his head saying:

25. We pray to you, almighty God, the Father of our Lord Jesus Christ, who has made your servants to be regenerated of water and the Holy Spirit, and has given them remission of all their sins, send O Lord, upon them the Holy Spirit, the Paraclete, and give them the spirit of wisdom and understanding, the spirit of counsel and might, the spirit of knowledge and godli-

ness, and fill them with the spirit of the fear of God, in the Name of our Lord Jesus Christ with whom you live and reign, ever God, with the Holy Spirit, throughout all ages of ages. Amen.

26. While the child receives the baptismal garment the priest says: Receive this holy, white, and immaculate garment and carry it unsullied before the judgment seat of our Lord Jesus Christ, that you may have eternal life.
27. Holding a candle in his right hand the priest says: Receive this burning light, safeguard your baptism by a blameless life, so that when our Lord comes for the wedding nuptials, you may meet him with all the saints in the court of heaven, and may have eternal life and live forever and ever. Amen. Peace be with you.

B. 1524 Translation of the Breslau Ritual[2]

The [pastor] blows three times under the child's eyes and says:

Depart you unclean spirit and make room for the Holy Spirit.

Then the [pastor] makes the sign of the cross on the child's forehead and breast and says:

Receive the sign of the holy cross both upon your forehead and upon your breast and receive the faith, through which you have fulfilled the divine command and may lead a [holy] life. Likewise, [through that faith] may you be the temple of God, walk within the church of God, and remember with joy that you have escaped the cords of death. Furthermore, may you flee from idols, despise graven images, and honor God the almighty Father and Jesus Christ his Son, who with the same Father and the Holy Spirit lives and reigns, one God, forever and ever. Amen.

Then the pastor says: Let us pray . . .

O Almighty eternal God, Father of our Lord Jesus Christ, look upon this N., your servant whom you have called to instruction in the faith, drive away from him all the blindness of his heart, break all the snares of the devil with which he is bound, open to him, Lord, the door of your grace: So that marked with the sign of your wisdom he may be free of the stench of all evil lusts and serve you joyfully according to the sweet savor of your commandments in your church and grow daily and be made meet to come to the grace of your baptism to receive the balm of life; through Christ our Lord. Amen.

Then the pastor takes salt and places it in the mouth of the child and says:

N., receive the salt of wisdom. May it aid you to eternal life. Amen.

Then the pastor says: Let us pray . . .

Almighty and eternal God, through the flood, according to your righteous judgment, you condemned the unfaithful world, and, according to your great mercy, you saved faithful Noah, even eight persons, and you drowned hardhearted Pharaoh with all his host in the Red Sea, and led your people Israel dry through it, thereby prefiguring this bath of your holy baptism, and through the baptism of your dear child, our Lord Jesus Christ, you sanctified and set apart the Jordan and all water for a saving flood, and an ample washing away of sins: we pray that through your same infinite mercy you will graciously look upon this N., and bless him [/her] with a right faith in the spirit, so that through this saving flood all that was born in him from Adam and all which he himself has added thereto may be drowned and submerged: and that he may be separated from the unfaithful, and preserved in the holy ark of Christendom dry and safe, and ever fervent in spirit and joyful in hope serve your name, so that he, with all the faithful, may be worthy to inherit your promise of eternal life, through Christ our Lord. Amen.

Then the pastor says over the male candidate(s): Let us pray . . .

God of Abraham, God of Isaac, God of Jacob, God who appeared to your servant Moses upon Mount Sinai and led the children of Israel out of the land of Egypt, sending to them the angel of your goodness to guard them by day and by night, we beseech you, O Lord, that you would send your holy angel that likewise he may also guard these your servants and lead them to the grace of your baptism; through Christ our Lord. Amen.

(It seems advisable to repeat this over each candidate.)

Therefore you miserable devil, acknowledge your judgment and give glory to the living and true God, give glory to his Son Jesus Christ, and to the Holy Spirit, and depart from this his servant N.; for God and our Lord Jesus Christ has of his goodness called him to his holy grace and blessing, and to the fountain of holy baptism so that you may never dare to disturb this sign of the holy cross which we make on his forehead; through him who comes again to judge the living and the dead. Amen.

Then the pastor says over the males:

So hearken now, you miserable devil, adjured by the name of the eternal God and of our Savior Jesus Christ, and depart trembling and groaning, conquered together with your hatred, so that you shall have nothing to do with the servant of God who now seeks that which is heavenly and renounces you and your world, and who shall live in blessed immortality. Give glory therefore now to the Holy Spirit who comes and descends from the loftiest castle of heaven in order to destroy your deceit and treachery, and having cleansed the heart with the divine fountain, to make it ready [to be] a holy temple and dwelling of God, so that this servant of God, freed from all the guilt of former sin, may always give thanks to the eternal God and praise his holy name forever and ever. Amen.

I adjure you, you unclean spirit, by the name of the Father and of the Son and of the Holy Spirit, that you come out of and depart from this servant of God, N., for he commands you, you miserable one, he who walked upon the sea and stretched forth his hand to sinking Peter.

(Then the above prayers are repeated over the female candidate[s].)

Then the pastor says over all the candidates: Let us pray . . .

Lord, holy Father, almighty eternal God from whom comes all the light of truth, we implore your eternal and most sweet goodness that you would shed your blessing upon this your servant N. and would enlighten him with the light of your knowledge, that he may hold to a sure hope, true counsel, and holy teaching and be made fit to receive the grace of your baptism; through Christ our Lord. Amen.

Then the pastor says: The Lord be with you.

The congregation responds: And with your spirit.

The pastor says: The Gospel according to St. Matthew, 19:13–15.

The congregation responds: Glory be to you, O Lord.

The Gospel is read.

(Or the Gospel according to St. Mark 10:13–16 may be read.)

Then the congregation says: Thanks be to God.

Then the pastor tells the godparents that they may speak the Our Father and Creed.

Then the pastor says:

Know this also, Satan, punishment threatens you, torment threatens you, the day of judgment threatens you, the day of eternal strife, the day which shall come as a burning furnace, when everlasting destruction shall come upon you and all your angels. Therefore, accursed and damned one, give honor to the living and true God, give honor to Jesus Christ his Son, and to the Holy Spirit. In whose name and power I command you, you who are the unclean spirit, come out and depart from this servant of God N., for God and our Lord Jesus Christ by his grace has deigned to call him to his holy grace and blessing and to the fount of holy baptism: that he may become a holy temple, through the water of regeneration for the forgiveness of all sin, in the Name of our Lord Jesus Christ, who shall come to judge the living and the dead and the world by fire.

Then the pastor says:

N. Ephphatha, that is, be opened to the odor of sweetness, but flee, o devil, for God's judgment comes speedily.

Then the pastor says:

The Lord preserve your coming in and your going out now and forevermore.

Do you renounce the devil?

Response: I renounce.

And all his works?

Response: I renounce.

And all his ways?

Response: I renounce.

Do you believe in God, the almighty Father, who created the heavens and the earth?

Response: I believe.

Do you believe in Jesus Christ his only Son, our Lord, who was born and suffered?

Response: I believe.

Do you believe in the Holy Spirit, one holy Christian church, the communion of saints, the forgiveness of sins, the resurrection of the body, and after death an eternal life?

Response: I believe.

Then the pastor says:

N. I anoint you with the oil of salvation in Christ Jesus our Lord. Amen.

Do you desire to be baptized?

Response: I so desire.

N. I baptize you in the name of the Father and of the Son and of the Holy Spirit. Amen.

Then the pastor touches the child and says: Let us pray . . .

The almighty God and Father of our Lord Jesus Christ who has regenerated you through water and the Holy Spirit and has forgiven you all your sin, anoint you with the chrism of salvation in Christ Jesus our Lord to eternal life. Amen.

N., receive the white, holy, and spotless robe and bring it before the judgment seat of Christ, so that you may receive eternal life. Amen.

N., receive this burning torch and preserve your baptism blameless, so that when the Lord comes to the wedding you may go to meet him to enter with all the saints into the heavenly mansion and receive eternal life. Amen.

The pastor says: The Lord be with you.

The congregation responds: And with your spirit.

The pastor says: The beginning of the Gospel according to St. John.

The congregation responds: Glory be to you, O Lord.

Reading of John 1:1–14.

The congregation responds: Thanks be to God.

The pastor says: The Word—Jesus Christ—protect you in this world and lead you to eternal life. Amen.

C. 1535 Sacramental Agreement for the Principalities of Liegnitz and Brieg[3]

Order and Form of Baptism

The pastor asks: Do you desire for this child to be baptized?

Response: Yes.

The pastor ascertains the child's name. Response: N.

An Admonition: Beloved in Christ, all of us have been born into such a difficult prison through the trespass of Adam, our first father. As a result, the evil spirit has great power over us and a great claim upon us, as upon children of wrath. If God our heavenly Father, out of his fatherly love and mercy in Christ his beloved Son, had not brought us forth through the washing of rebirth and renewal in the Holy Spirit, then there would have been no blessing for us. We would have remained completely damned for eternity. Therefore, since we are not able by our own power to attain wholeness, righteousness, or salvation and a renewed spiritual life, God has ordained his only begotten Son to be a mediator by whom eternal life comes to you. God has also appointed Christ as a reconciler between us and him and has sent him into the world to free us from our sins, by dying on the cross, suffering, and shedding his blood for us. O beloved Christ, we should note as closely as possible, what a burden and curse is upon us and all the children of Adam. We are laden from birth with the burdensome judgment [of God], until that time when we are received by God in grace. O beloved Christ we pray very fervently, that all Christian children may be released from this judgment, come to the recognition of our Savior, and also be reborn through water and the Holy Spirit. Therefore beloved Christians, out of true love and according to the will of God, let us pray that grace may be given to this child and that he/she may receive the sending of the Holy Spirit. By the Holy Spirit he/she is led out of the dominion of darkness into the light and is not considered one of the children of wrath, but one of the children of grace. As a result, he/she receives the unspeakable joy prepared for him/her from eternity. By that grace he/she is enlightened by the Holy Spirit in faith. Increase in this child the knowledge of Christ, through which he/she brings forth the fruits of faith. These fruits of faith are a result of the presence of God within the child's members, even though they are by nature inclined to serve sin and unrighteousness. As a result, this child is truly considered and called a member of the Christian church and a child [of God]. As we sacramentally incorporate and include this child among the faithful through baptism, at the same time he/she is received truly by our heavenly Father and his/her name is inscribed in the book of life.

Exorcism Prayer: Almighty and merciful Father, we pray for the sake of your beloved Son Jesus Christ, that you would drive out the unclean spirit from this little child. Destroy the evil spirit's kingdom within this child and give him/her your Holy Spirit.

Edited Flood Prayer: O Almighty eternal God, according to your severe judgment you condemned the unbelieving world through the flood and in your great mercy preserved believing Noah and his family. You drowned hardhearted Pharaoh with all his host in the Red Sea and led the people Israel through the sea with dry feet. So through your saving acts you prefigured this bath of rebirth. We pray on the basis of this same unconditional mercy of yours that you will graciously behold this your servant (male or female) and give him/her the light of faith in his/her heart so that he/she may be incorporated into your Son and with him rise to new life. By that unconditional mercy may he/she carry his/her cross daily, joyfully following Christ, and adhere to him with a true faith, strong hope and fervent love. We pray that he/she may live in this way and in no other until death. We pray that she/he may relinquish worldly things on account of you and that at the final day she/he may appear with undaunted confidence when faced with the universal judgment of your wrath; through the same our Lord Jesus Christ, your Son, who lives and reigns with you, one God, now and forever. Amen.

Another prayer: Almighty God, you have commanded us to pray with firm confidence in your promise, knowing that we are safeguarded with regard to all for which we pray when what we seek is to your honor and glory and out of love for our brothers and sisters in Christ. Since from birth onward this child does not live unencumbered by sin, it is our humble prayer, O beloved Father, that you would look upon this child in your mercy and according to your promise would bestow your good Spirit upon him/her. May he/she not be counted among the children of wrath, but always remain with you among the children of light and grace and a member of your undefiled church. May he/she confide in Jesus Christ through faith and in love; through the same our Lord Jesus Christ, who lives and reigns with you in the unity of the Holy Spirit, one God, now and forever. Amen.

Hear the Gospel: Mark 10.

Response: Praise and thanks be to God.

The pastor says: All speak together with trust and devotion the Our Father.

Our Father . . .

After this the pastor has them [the children] renounce the devil by asking: Do you renounce the devil? And all his works? And all his ways?

Response: I renounce.

The pastor asks: Do you believe in God, the almighty Father, creator? Response: I believe.

Do you believe in Jesus Christ? Response: I believe.

Do you believe in the Holy Spirit? Response: I believe.

Pastor: Do you desire to be baptized? Response: Yes, or I so desire.

Pastor: So I baptize you in the name of the Father and of the Son and of the Holy Spirit. Amen.

The pastor says: As a witness that you want to be faithful godparents, now touch the child.

The pastor says as the child is robed in a white garment: As you now have been clothed with this white garment, may God grant that you also appear at the last day with a pure conscience before Christ, the judge; through the same our Lord Jesus Christ. Amen.

Thanksgiving to God: Almighty eternal God, creator of heaven and earth, although we ought to thank you unceasingly for your manifold grace and benefits, in view of our complete need we especially thank you today for your fatherly grace by which you bestow on us your great benefits. We thank you that you not only created this child in the womb and gave it a rational soul, but also that you preserved and brought him/her into this poor life. We thank you that out of your special, eternal, fatherly love, as we had hoped, you have chosen [this child] in Christ and have allowed him/her to come to the grace of your baptism. Thus we also deliver, dedicate, and entrust [this child] to your goodness and faithfulness with our humble prayers. May you sustain, nourish, and guard him/her as your beloved child to eternal life through Jesus Christ our Lord. Amen.

Admonition to the Godparents: Beloved in Christ, the sacrament of baptism, as you have heard, is a washing of rebirth and renewal of the Holy Spirit and an attestation of a true Christian life. As our bodily impurity is washed away through the water, likewise through the grace of the Holy Spirit the forgiveness of sins is acquired and our unrighteousness is removed. Henceforth one does not love sin, but the death [of the old man]. In the Old Testament circumcision was both a seal of the faith of Abraham, making the circumcised submissive to the entire law, and also a witness to the covenant with God. Thus also this baptized child professes to lead a Christian life and to serve God freely with a hope [even more perfect than that of the old covenant] that God will not break the covenant with him/her, which God has made with him/her in baptism.

For this reason godparents are commanded, and you are obligated, to see that this child is instructed in the Christian faith, properly and completely, by you and its parents at the right time and is diligently exhorted in the Word of God. You are obligated to see that he/she is taught to place him/her trust in God, remain a loving, humble [child of God], bear the cross of Christ without shame, and live according to the will of the heavenly Father. Teach this child that he/she is not a child of the world, but of God, and [always] to remain so. Lead this child to all those things that are

honorable, so that Christ may dwell in him/her and the name of Christ may not be slandered by his/her evil life. To that end may God give you his grace in Christ. Amen.

Notes

1. Adolph Franz, ed., *Das Rituale des Bischofs Heinrich I. Von Breslau* (Freiburg im Breisgau: Herder, 1912). Translation by the author with portions of the translation taken from E. C. Whitaker, *Documents of the Baptismal Liturgy* (London: SPCK, 1970), 166–96.

2. Text translated by the author from Gustave Kawerau, "Liturgische Studien zu Luthers Taufbüchlein von 1523," *Zeitschrift für kirchliche Wissenschaft und kirchliches Leben* 10 (1889): 527–47. Portions of the translation taken from Martin Luther, "The Order of Baptism, 1523," in *Luther's Works,* edited by Helmut T. Lehmann, vol. 53, *Liturgy and Hymns,* edited by Ulrich S. Leupold (Philadelphia: Fortress Press, 1965), 96–103.

3. Emil Sehling, ed., *Die evangelischen Kirchenordnungen des XVI. Jahrhunderts,* vol. 3, *Die Mark Brandenburg, Die Markgrafentümer Oberlausitz und Niederlausitz, Schlesien* (Aalen: Scientia Verlag, 1970), 437–38. Translation by the author.

Although Christian Churches in the twentieth and twenty-first centuries increasingly agree on the theology and practice of baptism, nonetheless differences still exist. At the forefront of those differences is the manner of baptism itself. Numerous Churches, sometimes within the same tradition, baptize differently, whether by immersion, pouring, or sprinkling with various amounts of water. In contrast, the Churches of the medieval and Reformation eras demonstrated more commonality of practice, at least until the appearance of the Anabaptists and their advocacy of believer's baptism. Yet in spite of their move to adult baptism, the Anabaptists too followed the practice of their Roman Catholic and Reformation counterparts, in terms of the form of baptism, as they too baptized by pouring.

The high degree of convergence between the medieval tradition and the Reformation Churches when it came to baptism encouraged Luther to state in his seminal tract *The Babylonian Captivity of the Church,* "Blessed be God the Father of our Lord Jesus Christ, who according to the riches of his mercy has preserved in his church this sacrament at least, untouched and untainted by the ordinances of men, and has made it free to all nations and classes of mankind, and has not permitted it to be oppressed by the filthy and godless monsters of greed and superstition."[1] Unlike in the case of the Lord's Supper, baptism for Luther had not been turned into a human work. It was still performed according to the ordinance and command of God in Matthew 28:19: "Go therefore and make disciples of all nations, baptizing them in the name of the Father and of the Son and of the Holy Spirit." In fact, Luther's primary insistence that the practice and theology of baptism be consistent with its command and institution by Christ was a reflection of the medieval sacramental tradition. "In insisting on both institution by Christ and a visible sign," Luther, as James White notes, was adhering to the "thirteenth century qualification that only God can institute sacraments. And that means for him a New Testament proof text, the so-called dominical injunction."[2] Thus both the Reformers and many of the late medieval scholastic sacramental theologians rooted their understanding of the sacrament of baptism in the same theological starting point.

Likewise, when the Reformers altered baptismal praxis, they did so by reworking the medieval rites that they had inherited. The reform of baptismal practice did not happen in a vacuum, but based itself on particular rites of baptism within distinct areas in the Western Christian world. In order to assess the continuities and discontinuities in baptismal theology and praxis between the medieval and Reformation periods, the development of the baptismal rite within the medieval diocese of Breslau from the early fourteenth century to the mid-sixteenth century will be examined in light of the medieval and Reformation contexts. The seat of the diocese, the city of Breslau, was located within the duchy of Silesia, in the eastern part of the Holy Roman Empire, bordering on the kingdom of Poland. Three rites within the diocese will be compared: the rite from the fourteenth-century Breslau Ritual, from the 1524 translation of that ritual into German, and from the 1535 sacramental order for the principalities of Liegnitz and Brieg, situated within the Breslau diocese. The transitions in baptismal practice—especially the addition of evangelical texts highlighting the significance of baptism, either in addition to or in the place of medieval ceremonial actions, and the elimination of medieval ceremony—demonstrate the continuity and discontinuity in baptismal theology and practice. These substitutions and omissions were intended to accent the primary ceremony instituted by Christ—the pouring of water in the triune name—or, as Luther said in his postscript to his 1523 baptismal rite, "the glory of baptism."[3] The Lutheran territorial Reformers endeavored to follow Luther's advice that baptism be administered with "God's Word, true faith, and serious prayer."[4] Ceremonies and texts from the medieval rites were retained or omitted insofar as they expressed what took place in baptism. According to Luther that meant the ceremonies and texts could not contradict the reality that baptism—the application of the triune name of God with the water—brought regeneration to new life, liberation from sin, death, and hell, and incorporation into the Church as God's children.[5]

Ritually and liturgically baptism developed significantly from the seventh century to the sixteenth century.[6] This development began with the appearance of the *Old Gelasian Sacramentary*[7] and culminated in the diocesan rituals[8] of the thirteenth through fifteenth centuries. Starting with the *Old Gelasian Sacramentary* and stretching to the sixteenth century, people were initiated into the Church through a twofold process consisting of an adult catechumenate—a period of preparation for baptism essentially coterminous with the season of Lent—and an adult rite of baptism conducted primarily upon infants. No longer was the baptismal process perceived, as it had been in the fourth through sixth centuries, as a period of intense scriptural instruction, prayerful self-examination, renunciation of evil, and turning toward a life of holiness which culminated in the passover from death to life in the flowing waters of baptism at the Easter Vigil. Certainly, the rites that developed continued to view baptismal initiation into the Church as a process that began in the catechumenal experience and culminated in the ritual and ceremonial of the paschal vigils.[9] Yet this conversion experience, while still present in the texts of the rites, no longer paralleled the actual ritual experience of the catechumens.[10] In fact, the ritual experience of the infant candidates was primarily objective and passive in nature. Unlike adults who consciously participated in the baptismal event, infants received the actions of the rite. It was enacted upon them. They were passive "participants."[11] This necessitated a reorientation in the purpose of the catechumenate. Instruction toward conversion of life could no longer be the focus. Instead the catechumenate had to focus on preparing the infant child for baptism by purging the child of the substances of evil and sin.[12]

This change in the rite's theological purpose with regard to the infant candidates led also to the gradual condensing of the initiatory baptismal process into a rite conducted at one specific point in time.[13] In the early Church, baptism had constituted an initiatory process, spread out over the weeks of Lent, which had included catechumenal rites, baptismal rites, and postbaptismal rites. The concentration of this lengthy process of rites into one ritual moment generated two significant consequences. First, most of the rite now consisted of the prebaptismal ceremonies, much of which were exorcisms—the casting out of evil and Satan. For this reason, Hughes Old has said that the "whole service gave the impression of being a long series of exorcisms concluded by a baptism."[14] Second, the former process of initiatory rites now constituted three sacramental moments: baptism (including the prebaptismal, baptismal, and postbaptismal rites, excluding confirmation), confirmation or episcopal anointing/chrismation, and first Communion. Eventually these sacramental moments became distinct rites. Much of this concentration was the result of the desire for *quam primum* (immediate) celebration of infant baptism after birth. The concern for immediate baptism reflected the pervasive influence of the Augustinian doctrine of original sin. Given the high infant mortality rate during that time, all children born in the iniquity of original sin were to be brought to the font of regeneration, the grace of God, and the possibility of eternal life as quickly as possible. The desire for immediate baptism led to the disassociation of baptismal celebration from the Easter/Pentecost vigils. Baptism was now celebrated at any time deemed desirable following the child's birth. Thus the baptismal rite, by the time of the rituals, was often celebrated apart from the regular gathering of the Church for worship and "in private," most often still in the church, but with only the candidate, the sponsors (one of which may have been the midwife), relatives and friends of the couple, and perhaps the father of the child present.[15]

Originally, in the context of the Easter Vigil and the celebration of the Mass, baptism into the Body of Christ naturally led to participation in the meal that united that body as one—the Lord's Supper. This was not considered a separate rite (first Communion) but simply the natural result of one's baptism into Christ. Likewise, the anointing of the baptized by the priest or bishop following baptism signified the anointing of the Holy Spirit and the cleansing and life-giving power of baptism. However, as the Church came to insist that this chrismation (anointing with chrism oil) be conducted by the bishop as a demonstration of the Church's unity under his authority, it took on a ritual reality of its own. On account of the delay of the northern European bishops to anoint the newly baptized until much later—even years—the distinct sacrament of confirmation was born.[16]

In the meantime, Communion of the newly baptized infants began to wane. Initially, infants received Communion even when confirmation was delayed. By this time infants often received only the cup, given the difficulty of administering the bread to them. In the thirteenth and ensuing centuries, since the infants were not baptized most often during the Mass, in some ecclesiastical regions they received the ablution wine, the wine/water mixture used to cleanse the cup after the Mass. Two developments, however, removed the cup from the infants' lips permanently. First, medieval theologians expressed deep concern over the perceived sacrilege of spilling any of the contents of the cup, thus desecrating the blood of Christ. Second, this concern furthered the developing theory of concomitance—that both Christ's body and blood were completely present underneath the substance of either element—and allowed the Church justification for the administration of the bread only to the laity. The cup was removed from the laity and likewise from the infant neophytes.[17] As a result, the newly baptized did not receive the elements in any form.

Thus, baptism changed significantly from the wider use of the *Gelasian Sacramentary* in the seventh century to the appearance of the rituals in the eleventh and twelfth centuries. Originally infants were brought with their parents to receive the sacrament of holy baptism. Now they were the only candidates. Originally both the objective activity of God and the subjective appropriation of that activity were evident in the rites of baptism. Ultimately the objective elements apparent in the ceremonies of the rite came to the forefront, overshadowing the subjective appropriation of God's grace by faith. The infants were passive recipients of the ministry of the Church by which the substance of God's grace was made effective in their lives. These changes were manifested in the structure and the method of administering the rite of baptism in the medieval rituals.

Unquestionably the baptismal rites in the rituals afford a most fascinating glimpse into the baptismal praxis of the late Middle Ages.[18] More than other liturgical books, they reflect a wide diocesan diversity.[19] The Breslau Ritual (*Das Rituale des Bischofs Heinrich I. von Breslau*), the first published diocesan ritual for the bishopric of Breslau, concretely illustrates these developments. It was compiled and edited sometime between 1302 and 1319, during the time that Heinrich I was the bishop of the diocese.[20] The ritual itself does not reveal the compiler of the volume nor an exact date for the compilation. Issued for the use of the cathedral church in Breslau, the relevant sections, particularly those not related to episcopal functions, also applied to all the churches of the diocese. According to Adolph Franz, Bishop Wenceslaus (1382–1417) issued an edict in 1415 enforcing such application.[21] The oversight of the ritual was entrusted to the cathedral chapter, which took seriously its mandate to ensure that nothing was changed in the ritual without good reason and without an authoritative charge to do so.[22]

The Breslau Ritual exemplified the gradual melding of the baptismal practices reflected in the medieval pontificals (liturgical books for the use of the bishops) and those that emerged in the parish administration of baptism. The baptismal party gathered at the door of the church.[23] This gathering on the church steps echoed the character of the classical catechumenate, in which the catechumen stood on the threshold of membership in the Church. It expressed the fact that those to be baptized stood outside the Church and were brought into its fellowship through baptism. Gathering before the doors of the church also indicated that the immediate baptism of children after birth had become the predominant practice. If the baptisms had occurred as part of the Easter/Pentecost vigils they would have been conducted in the church at the font (or in the baptistery outside the church) while the scriptural readings of the vigil ensued. In other words, the infant candidates would already have been inside the church as part of the celebration of the vigil.

The prebaptismal rites stretched from this initial enrollment—division of the candidates by sex—to the final exorcism and opening of the nose and ears of the baptismal candidates. More than half of the baptismal rite consisted of the prebaptismal ceremonies. Likewise, the preponderance of exorcisms and exorcistic actions within the prebaptismal section was also apparent. The rite began with the priest's exsufflation or blowing upon the candidate, symbolizing the departure of the devil. The devil was then ordered to depart, and the sign of the cross was made on the child's forehead indicating that the child was claimed by the Triune God through the person and work of Jesus Christ. The prayers that followed, the old prayers over those elected to the catechumenate, called for God to protect the candidates from the influence of the devil and evil until the day of their baptism. The exorcistic aspect continued unabated in the exorcism and giving of salt to the candidate, accompanied by a prayer that God might drive away the enemy and protect those who came to faith. The importance of the salt lay not in its symbolic effect but in its actual power as a medicine against evil.

The heart of the prebaptismal rites was contained in the threefold set of exorcism prayers over both the males and the females. The sign of the cross was made repeatedly, and several times Satan was exorcised and cursed so that the candidates would arrive safely at the grace of holy baptism. As Hughes Old notes, commenting on these texts as originally found in the *Gelasian Sacramentary*,

> Most striking is the way these formulas of exorcism see Satan as an all-present and all-pervading power determined to delude, deceive, and dissuade every single human soul he can possibly entangle in his traps and snares. As the candidate approaches baptism, one can expect the devil to use all his wiles to prevent this event; and so the exorcisms are especially necessary, that the path to the baptismal font be cleared of Satanic interference. For Christians of the Middle Ages, this was evidently much more real and much more important than the catechetical teaching which in an earlier day had formed the core of the catechetical services.[24]

In fact, what follows in the ritual was the remnant of that catechetical instruction: the delivery of the Gospels, Lord's Prayer, and Creed to the catechumens. However, these were no longer entrusted to the infant candidates as they had been to adults. Rather, the delivery of the Gospels themselves was replaced by the recounting of Jesus' invitation to the little children to come to him in Matthew 19. The reading of this text underscored the ensuing ritual action of the entrance of the children into the church and thus, figuratively, into the kingdom of God. In addition, the Creed and Our Father were no longer considered elements entrusted to the neophytes, but prayers that were prayed by the Church, especially the priest and sponsors, for the sake of those who were to be baptized. These elements no longer constituted catechetical instruction, but expressed theologically what was happening to these children in baptism, that they were being received into the Church by God's grace.

The end of the prebaptismal rites in the Breslau Ritual returned to the theme of exorcism. The final, lengthy exorcism (*Nec te latet;* "Be not deceived") was spoken, which ordered Satan to depart for good because Christ had called this child "to the gift of his holy grace and of his blessing and the fount of baptism." This exorcism entailed the completion of the public catechization of the infant, ritually enacted.[25] Following the final exorcism, the *Effeta* was conducted—a ritualized opening of the ears and nose of the candidate for the devil to depart so that God's grace might enter. The casting out of Satan having been completed and the infant candidate having been entrusted to the activity of God, the baptismal party entered into the church and processed to the font.

The heart of the initiatory rites followed the entrance into the church—the baptismal rites themselves. Ironically these rites, which culminated in the baptismal immersion, began by addressing the power of Satan. Through the voice of the sponsor, the candidate was asked to renounce Satan, his works, and his ways. Having renounced Satan the candidate then could confess faith in God by responding to the creedal questions. These creedal questions reflected the substance of and shaped the development of the so-called Apostles' Creed.[26] Between the renunciation and the creedal questions the candidate was anointed with oil, which signified participation in the salvation of Jesus Christ. On the basis of the child's confession of faith the child was asked if he or she desired to receive baptism. Following this question of desire the pinnacle of the initiatory rites appeared: the triple submersion into the font in the name of the triune God. Everything preceding this action had pointed toward this moment as the consummation of the infant's reception of God's grace and his or her entrance into the kingdom of God.

The rite concluded quickly after the baptismal submersion with three ceremonial actions intended to enrich the theological significance of initiation. Immediately following the submersion the priest anointed the child on the crown of his or her head and prayed for the Holy Spirit's presence with the child. The child was from that point forward moved and motivated by the Spirit of God. The child was then clothed in a white garment signifying the purity possessed as a result of baptism, while the priest prayed for the child to be found morally pure at the second coming of Jesus Christ. Finally, the child was given a burning candle as a symbol that was intended to arouse the child to be prepared for Christ's return by leading a blameless life—that is, having one's lamp lighted. With the giving of the candle the baptismal rite came to an end. The infants did not receive the elements of Communion nor did the bishop anoint them. The Breslau Ritual clearly implies that these were separate ritual acts, if not separate sacramental actions: confirmation and first Communion. They had acquired their own ritual priority, time, and context.

In the end, the baptismal rite in the Breslau Ritual reflected a dramatic struggle taking place between God and the devil in the name of Jesus Christ. Clearly the enactment of the rite was considered a matter of eternal life and death for the infant candidates. Paraphrasing one of the prayers of exorcism, through the rite the devil gave honor to God and departed from the servants of God, whom God had called to his holy grace and blessing and the fount of baptism.

For their part, Luther and the territorial Reformers shaped their baptismal rites and theologies within the medieval heritage transmitted to them. Luther was able to praise God that the medieval Western Church had retained the practice of baptism according to the scriptural mandate, but deplored medieval baptismal theology that "deprived it (baptism) of all its strength and honor."[27] Thus, the various Reformers first translated the assorted diocesan Latin rites into the vernacular and taught their use in an evangelical manner. Eventually, however, these translation efforts proved unsatisfactory. For Luther, the translated rites were too encumbered with ceremonies and texts that concealed God's regenerative activity in baptism. Many of the Swiss and German Reformed theologians, such as Ulrich Zwingli, Martin Bucer, and John Calvin, desired a more thorough reform that would capture the intent of Jesus and the apostles with regard to the scriptural institution of baptism. In Hughes Old's words, they longed for a baptismal rite reformed purely according to God's Word, highlighting the baptismal washing, the invocation of the triune name, catechetical instruction, and the baptismal vows of the godparents on behalf of those baptized.[28] On the basis of these convictions they first developed reformed evangelical rites, shaped by the doctrine of justification by faith and the authority of Scripture.[29] As a result, they retained the medieval emphasis on the objectivity of God's grace conveyed in baptism. However, such objectivity did not apply to the entire rite, but only to that element of the rite commanded by Christ: the baptismal submersion in the triune name. The other ceremonies and texts were intended to explain the significance of baptism itself.[30] Second, modeling the prior translations and liturgical efforts of other Reformers, the Reformers attempted to maintain continuity with the unique practices of their individual dioceses and territories.

The effort to provide a catholic but evangelical practice was perhaps nowhere better demonstrated than in Martin Luther's 1523 *Das Taufbüchlein verdeutscht* (Little book on baptism in German).[31] Luther's *Taufbüchlein* reflected the baptismal heritage received through the Roman rituals. It was a respectful translation of the baptismal rite contained in whichever ritual(s) Luther had before him, probably that ritual at use in Wittenberg.[32] It represented one possible outcome of medieval baptismal liturgy within the Reformation.[33]

In the context of a Wittenberg reeling from the impact of radical ecclesiastical change, Luther believed the times demanded a very conservative liturgical revision. Luther's 1523 *Taufbüchlein* did not make substantive changes to the medieval rite. The sole exception was the Flood Prayer, apparently authored or edited by Luther since it did not appear in any existing ritual prior to his baptismal rite. This lengthy prayer, which followed the giving of salt and preceded the exorcisms, invoked scriptural images to pray for the regeneration of the one being baptized.[34] Luther retained the breadth of medieval ceremony and ritual, indicating that he believed it could be interpreted in an evangelical manner.[35]

With regard to the fundamental issues facing the rite of baptism during the medieval period, Luther's rite in many respects represented the culmination of the medieval trajectory. It reinforced the reality that infant baptism was the norm. The exorcisms, entrance into the church, Gospel reading, creedal interrogations, and question of desire all indicated for Luther that faith was born through the Word of God and God's promise in the breadth of the rite. For Luther, even an infant could only receive baptism and its benefits in faith. The structure and content of the baptismal rite reflected that reality.

Yet, the vitality of infant faith had no impact on the continued disintegration of what once was a unified initiation rite. The fact that there were ostensibly no Lutheran bishops, coupled with Luther's vehement rejection of confirmation as a sacrament, meant that confirmation in its original form as a sealing or anointing at baptism did not come to realization in Lutheran circles. Likewise, Luther did not directly address the possibility of infant Communion. The practice had already disappeared from the rituals he employed as models. Luther's rite, with the retention of two exorcisms and his thoroughgoing Augustinian understanding of original sin, reinforced the practice of *quam primum* (as soon as possible after birth) baptism. Yet an ecclesiastical context was not lost. Luther, along with later Lutheran orders, advocated that baptism be conducted within the context of the gathering of the Church, even if that did not mean necessarily the Mass. The one development against which Luther fought a losing battle was the alteration in the mode of baptism away from submersion toward affusion—the pouring of water. The trend toward affusion grew steadily throughout the fourteenth and fifteenth centuries. Admittedly this is an argument from silence since the sources do not tell us why submersion ceased to be used, but the most plausible explanation for the move to pouring resided in the difficulty of submersing a child. The child had to be undressed completely, submersed under the water while prevented from inhaling the water, and then re-dressed after the submersion. In addition, in many northern European lands the child was undressed in a cold church building. While the baptismal water could be warmed and no doubt often was, parents undoubtedly objected to the necessity of submersion. Luther and other Reformers attempted to restore submersion as the predominant practice. However, while Luther considered submersion desirable, he did not consider it essential to the rite. As a result, submersion, while a powerful symbol in Luther's baptismal theology, ceased to be the primary mode of baptism in many Lutheran territories.[36]

In the end, Luther's 1523 *Taufbüchlein* prepared the way for an evangelical appropriation of medieval baptismal heritage.[37] While the majority of Lutheran Church orders modeled their baptismal rites on Luther's 1526 *Taufbüchlein,* even the ceremony and ritual retained in that rite would not have been possible without the 1523 rite. The 1523 rite established the precedent that when traditional Church ceremony and ritual edified the Church's life and were not in conflict with the Gospel, they could be retained.

The 1524 baptismal rite for the city of Breslau (the *Taufbüchlein*) was truly an adaptation of the Breslau Ritual. Following Luther's lead with his 1523 translation, other Reformers attempted to adapt Luther's translation to their local German diocesan rite.[38] In these efforts, some Reformers followed Luther more closely, while others followed their diocesan tradition more directly. In either case, as Hughes Old notes, "Luther had made a breach in the wall of liturgical form through which" the other Reformers "also wanted to pass. They wanted to follow Luther and wanted to appear to follow Luther."[39] Johann Hess (1490–1547), the earliest Reformer of Breslau, was no exception. At the outbreak of the Reformation, Hess spent some time in Wittenberg in 1520 and became acquainted with both Luther and Philipp Melanchthon. In 1523, while he was preacher at the Dom in Breslau, he visited Nuremberg. It was at this point that he slowly began to initiate the Reformation in Breslau.[40]

The Breslau *Taufbüchlein,* which was introduced in 1524 as part of Hess's reforming endeavors, reflects the contents of the Breslau Ritual. But it translated that rite according to the pattern of Luther's 1523 *Taufbüchlein,* with some unique elements included from Andreas Osiander's baptismal rite for Nuremberg.[41] Nonetheless, the laypeople gathered for the baptisms of their children, godchildren, or relatives would not have noticed a substantive difference between the old rite and the new one, beyond the enactment of the rite in the vernacular as opposed to Latin (a rather significant change!). They would not have noticed significant changes because nearly all of the ceremonies from the old rite were retained in the new one, perhaps with the exception of the postbaptismal anointing. Although some of these ceremonies were rearranged by Hess and associated with texts differing from the Latin texts in the Breslau Ritual, without a knowledge of Latin these changes would not have been apparent to those bringing their children for baptism. As far as they were concerned, their children were being exorcised, anointed, submersed in water, and robed as they always had. Only now they could understand what the priest was saying!

The changes Hess made that paralleled the rites of Luther and Osiander reflected his desire to have a rite in conformity with evangelical reforms in other places where the Reformation was taking hold. Hess's rite altered the order of and omitted elements in the Breslau Ritual in only a few places.[42] The omissions included: the division of those being baptized into groups of males and females (the omission probably reflecting the fact that only one child was brought for baptism at a time); the laying on of hands during the catechumenal prayers; the second and third catechumenal prayers;[43] the exorcism of the salt;[44] the signs of the cross over the candidate during the exorcisms; and the laying on of hands during the reciting of the Lord's Prayer and Creed. In addition, the rite did not clearly indicate whether the anointing following the baptism, the so-called presbyteral anointing, was included or not. The prayer associated with the presbyteral anointing followed Luther's version, with the exception that it referred to the substance used in the anointing as "chrism" as opposed to Luther's "oil of salvation." The prayer was greatly shortened from the much longer prayer in the Breslau Ritual, and there was no rubric indicating that the child was to be anointed. However, the inclusion of the word *chrism* might have indicated Hess's desire to follow the Breslau rite since that was the term used in the rubrics in that rite. The inclusion of the phrase "anoint you with the oil of chrism" would seem to indicate that an actual anointing took place, even with the absence of a rubric. The rite generally tends to omit rubrics anyway.

In addition to these changes, Hess added some elements found in Luther's translation and Osiander's version of the rite. The most significant of these additions was the substitution of Luther's Flood Prayer, exactly as in Luther's rite, in place of the final catechumenal prayer following the bestowal of salt in the Breslau Ritual. The Flood Prayer was probably redacted and composed by Luther drawing upon a number of medieval sources, including the final catechumenal prayer, "O God of our Fathers."[45] The use of this prayer explicitly indicated the desire of territorial Reformers to follow the lead of Luther and to adapt their local practices to the evangelical message emanating from Wittenberg. A further example of this desire was Hess's inclusion of Mark 10:13–16 as an option for the Gospel reading, in addition to the parallel Gospel selection from Matthew 19 which appeared in the Breslau Ritual. The reading from Mark was the same as in Luther's rite and in the diocesan traditions for Magdeburg. Furthermore, a number of the texts followed the translations of Osiander as opposed to those of Luther or the Breslau Ritual, such as the rubric for making the sign of the cross following the exsufflation. Osiander's version was longer than that of Breslau or Luther and incorporated references to the commandments, including fleeing from idols and despising graven images. The final exorcism in the Breslau *Taufbüchlein* (the text that begins "Be not deceived"),[46] which was omitted by Luther, followed the translation in Osiander's rite.[47] This exorcism marked the final and most dramatic call for the devil to depart from the candidate so that he or she might become the holy temple of God through the fount of holy baptism. Hess also indicated that the godparents could pray the Lord's Prayer and Creed with the pastor after the reading of the Gospel. Osiander, who, with Luther, included only the Lord's Prayer, also indicated that the godparents could pray the Lord's Prayer. This effort to involve the godparents, which appeared in rituals dating after the Ritual of Breslau, was an attempt to ensure that they were properly qualified to assume their roles. The last and most significant departure in Hess's rite was the inclusion of a passage from John's Gospel, chapter 1, to be read at the rite's end after the child had received the burning candle. This element did not appear in the Breslau Ritual or in Luther's or Osiander's rites. It was added to later rituals as an expansion of the final blessing of the rite: the wish for the child to go in peace. Either this practice was an original addition to the rite in Breslau or Hess called upon another ritual tradition to conclude the rite with a specific reference to the protection of Christ into whom the newly baptized had just been incorporated.

In a very obvious manner the 1524 adaptation of the Breslau rite of baptism displayed continuity with the medieval baptismal heritage. Those present at baptisms would not have noticed that the rite had substantively changed from medieval practice. The same ceremonies and actions were included in the rite. Johann Hess had, however, subtly changed the orientation of the rite. By adapting the texts of the rite to bring them into conformity with texts prepared by Martin Luther and Andreas Osiander he made an explicit connection with the reforms taking place in Wittenberg and Nuremberg and prepared the way for a more thoroughgoing reform of the rite of baptism. Nonetheless, the rite as translated affirmed some fundamental theological convictions of the Reformers. The retention of the exorcisms indicated that baptism was God's action by which the child was freed from the clutches of sin and the devil.[48] The inclusion of medieval ceremonies, such as the postbaptismal anointing, the robing, and the giving of a burning candle, all signified that baptism, in the words of Luther, brought forgiveness of sins, redeemed from death and the devil, and gave eternal salvation to all who believed it, as the words and promises of God declared.[49] Most of the medieval texts and ceremonies could be applied and interpreted in such a way that the people understood that in baptism the promise of grace and the forgiveness of sins were offered and received, regenerating the one baptized to faith and new life.

However, while the translated/adapted rites prepared by the Reformers on the basis of the Latin rituals could be employed and interpreted in an evangelical way, in many ways these translations/adaptations were transitional. As Hughes Old writes with regard to the Reformers in Zurich, "Those German translations were merely stages in a transition. . . . It was a concession to the slow and weak of faith. The purpose was to help them make the adjustment, but the Reformers of Zurich hoped that it would soon be surpassed with the adoption of an order of baptism true to the institution of Christ."[50] While Luther and those closest to the reforms in Wittenberg more easily accepted the medieval baptismal traditions insofar as they were in conformity with the Gospel, they too desired a rite that would, in Luther's words, "sufficiently appreciate the glory of baptism."[51]

The 1535 Sacramental Agreement for the Principalities of Liegnitz and Brieg was an attempt to provide just such a truly reformed rite of baptism. The principalities of Liegnitz and Brieg were part of the diocese of Breslau and were located in Silesia, northwest and southeast of the city of Breslau respectively. Prince Friedrich II of Liegnitz inherited the principality of Brieg from his brother, Georg, an opponent of the Reformation, in 1521. Friedrich II issued a mandate for evangelical teaching for both territories in 1523. Friedrich II had conceived of the need for a new sacramental order in 1534 and submitted an outline for one to the spiritual leaders. This proposal resulted in a meeting held in Liegnitz in 1535 and led to the formation of a committee of pastors to formulate the teaching and use of the sacraments in the two territories. The results of this committee's work were published in late 1535, delineating the means of administering the sacraments. Essentially this was the first Church order, although the official version was published in 1542, including the rites as formulated in 1535. The transition in the practice of baptism from the Ritual of Breslau and the 1524 adaptation of Johann Hess to the Sacramental Order of Liegnitz and Brieg was thoroughgoing and complete. Indeed, there were some very significant changes in content and structure, particularly with regard to the role of ceremony and exhortation/instruction. Yet these documents demonstrated a structural and thematic commonality. As different as these baptismal rites were, they shared a common source: the praxis of baptism that predominated throughout the rituals of the thirteenth through the fifteenth centuries.[52]

While the points of continuity may have been more subtle, the areas of discontinuity between these baptismal rites became readily apparent when they were compared with one another. Unlike the adaptation of Hess, the amount of ceremony eliminated in the 1535 rite was patent. Nearly all of the ceremonies that were a consistent part of the medieval ritual tradition had been removed by 1535, especially from the prebaptismal rites. To those bringing their children for baptism after 1535, the change from the 1524 rite would have been striking.

The most significant omission in 1535 was the reduction in the number of exorcisms or ceremonial elements related to exorcism. The only elements related to the abrupt passage of the child from sin, evil, and the powers of darkness to the kingdom of God which were retained in the Sacramental Agreement were the renunciations of Satan and the creedal interrogations or confessions of belief in the triune God. The only other reference to exorcism in the 1535 rite was the short exorcistic prayer that followed the initial baptismal admonition and preceded the Flood Prayer. This prayer entreated that the Father would "drive out the unclean spirit from this child, destroy his kingdom within this child, and give him your Holy Spirit." There was no ritual action associated with this prayer—no sign of the cross, laying on of hands, or breathing upon the child. Clearly there was a desire to move away from any superstitious connotations of dislodging the power of evil from the child. Three puffs of breath, or repeated signs of the cross, or the application of spit or mud or ashes on the ears and nose did not magically retrieve the child from Satan's clutches. Following Martin Luther, the rite assumed that the devil did not flee from such things.[53]

On the other hand, even though the rite removed much of the ceremony attached to the transition from the kingdom of evil to the kingdom of God, the conceptual need for such a transition and even, in part, the way to accomplish it, had not changed. There was no doubt on the part of the Sacramental Agreement, as in the Ritual of Breslau, that the child was born sinful and under the power of evil. There was dire need for the child to be "converted" from a child of the devil to a child of God. So, as in Henry's Ritual, the 1535 rite prayed for the devil's kingdom to be destroyed in the child and the Holy Spirit to take up residence in its place. The prayers and exorcism formulas of the Breslau Ritual prayed for the very same thing, symbolizing it, however, with ritual action. The exsufflation itself corresponded well with the conceptual framework of the 1535 prayer: the blowing of the priest symbolized the casting out of the devil by the incoming and creative power of the breath of God, the presence of the Spirit. The 1535 rite took seriously the medieval stress on baptism's role in the transition from evil to good and invoked God for such a transition.

The omission of the bulk of exorcism texts and the ceremonial actions associated with them reflected the decreased amount of ceremony in the prebaptismal rites. The baptismal rites and the postbaptismal rites also witnessed the reduction of ceremonial elements. The prebaptismal anointing, which originally bore an exorcistic emphasis, was omitted from the 1535 rite. The speaking of the Our Father led directly into the renunciation of Satan, the creedal confession of God, and the baptism proper. The Lord's Prayer, the ultimate prayer for God to receive this child, was followed by the answer to that prayer, the reception of the child in baptism. No ceremonial elements intervened. Likewise, an anointing with chrism did not follow the baptism. Rather, the 1535 rite concluded quickly, reflecting the centrality and import of the baptismal washing. Ceremony was eliminated because it could become unduly superstitious and detract from the gift and action of God in the Trinitarian submersion/affusion itself. As a result, the giving of a candle to the newly baptized was also removed from the 1535 rite. The only ceremony that was retained was the robing of the child in a white garment. The retention of this element, while it followed Luther's 1526 baptismal rite, may have been due more to the manner in which the baptismal rite was conducted than to theological concerns or emphases. The child was baptized naked, due primarily to the original prevailing medieval practice of submersion or immersion, and therefore needed to be clothed following the washing. The text associated with the robing, while distinct from that in the Ritual of Breslau, retained the same basic emphasis, if with a Reformation twist: it prayed for the child to appear at the judgment of Christ in purity. A Lutheran emphasis was reflected in the concern for a pure "conscience" at the judgment which was also a primary concern in the Augsburg Confession. The Gospel was to be proclaimed rightly, so that consciences could be assured of God's mercy and grace.[54] In fact, the curtailment of postbaptismal ceremony, a trend in the rituals throughout the late medieval period and reflected in the Breslau Ritual, actually reached its culmination in the 1535 rite for Liegnitz and Brieg.

While the robing in the 1535 baptismal rite seemed to presume that the child was baptized naked and submersed or immersed, nevertheless the rubrics provided no indication for the mode of baptism. This also reflected an element of continuity with medieval tradition. While submersion/immersion dominated medieval practice, as reflected in the Breslau Ritual's specification that the child was to be immersed three times, medieval rites in various places allowed for baptism to be administered by affusion. By the end of the sixteenth century affusion had replaced submersion as the dominant mode throughout most German Lutheran territories. The 1535 rite represented a stage in that transition, providing no rubric indicating how the baptism ought to have been administered.

The divergence in content between Hess's translation of the Breslau Ritual and the 1535 Sacramental Agreement reflected the degree to which the Reformation had taken hold in Liegnitz and Brieg after 1523. Structurally the 1535 rite paralleled closely the 1526 *Taufbüchlein* of Martin Luther. The exhortations/admonitions and prayers that appeared in the Liegnitz/Brieg rite and which diverged from Luther's rite either originated in regional practice or were adapted from other Protestant rites. Nonetheless, the content of these prayers showed a relative amount of continuity with the ceremonial actions and texts of the Ritual of Breslau. For instance, the initial admonition and exorcism prayer essentially took the place of the exsufflation, catechumenal prayers, giving of salt, and the tripartite sets of exorcistic prayers and formulas. The admonition stressed many of the same thematic elements presented in the traditional prebaptismal rites, focusing on the overcoming of the evil spirit just as the exorcisms prayed for the departure of Satan. The admonition recognized and prayed for the grace of God in baptism and for rebirth through water and the Holy Spirit. Similarly, the Ritual of Breslau's second exorcism prayer over the males indicated that the baptismal candidate sought "to attain everlasting grace by being reborn spiritually." The admonition in the 1535 rite sought enlightenment for the baptismal candidate through the work of the Holy Spirit in baptism. This theme was reflected also in the final prayer after the exorcisms in the Ritual of Breslau, which entreated that God would enlighten the one being baptized "with the light of your understanding." Even the thanksgiving in the 1535 rite bore thematic resemblance to the texts associated with the robing and the candle ceremony in the Breslau Ritual, praying for the neophyte to be guarded to eternal life. Thus, while the ceremonies and texts were altered from their original shape and form in the ritual tradition, many of the basic concepts and themes remained the same.

Yet there were thematic differences. The Liegnitz/Brieg rite displayed characteristic Reformation emphases, many of them highlighted in additional texts added to the rite, such as the admonitions and thanksgivings. These texts indicated that for the Lutherans of Liegnitz and Brieg baptism was not focused on ceremonial action by which the substance of God's grace, mediated through the Church, was imparted to the believer. Rather, the focus was on the child born into the prison of original sin and subjected to damnation under the impact of that sin and delivered through baptism, a washing of rebirth and regeneration by the Holy Spirit. Salvation and righteousness were gained only through the merit and work of Jesus Christ in shedding his blood on the cross. The admonitions prayed that the child might receive the gracious activity of the Holy Spirit and the forgiveness of sins by faith. They likewise prayed that the child might be preserved in the grace conveyed in baptism. While this was clearly a rite rooted in the ritual tradition, it nonetheless theologically betrayed the marks of the impact of the Reformation within these two principalities.

The concern of the Reformers of Liegnitz and Brieg to establish a proper Lutheran theology within the baptismal rite itself was a consistent concern throughout the sixteenth century. This was true even to the point that certain medieval ceremonial actions retained in the rites became elements of contention between Lutherans and Calvinists in the German territories. The exorcisms were often at the center of these debates. As Bodo Nischan has demonstrated, the inclusion or omission of the exorcisms, which were thematically included in the rite for Liegnitz and Brieg, became a matter of theological debate amongst Lutherans in the 1550s in Thuringia and later in the 1580s–1590s in Saxony, Anhalt, and Brandenburg.[55] As already noted, prior to the 1550s, Lutheran rites could retain or omit the exorcisms (as with other ceremonial acts in the rite of baptism) depending upon whether they were considered by any particular Lutheran territory to be theologically helpful in demonstrating what took place in baptism. So, as Nischan notes, many of the southwestern German rites, such as those of Württemberg and Hesse, omitted the exorcisms.[56] However, it was in the territories of Anhalt and Brandenburg in the 1580s and 1590s that the theological ramifications of omitting the exorcisms became pronounced. In these territories, the princes, influenced by Reformed theology, ordered the omission of the exorcisms from the baptismal rites in their territories. As Nischan indicates, the divergent theologies of baptism between Calvin and Luther, as understood by their theological heirs, formed the substance of the struggle over the exorcisms. For the Calvinists, baptism served as a sign of the reception of the children of believers into the kingdom of God through the covenant of God's grace. They insisted that the exorcisms violated the reality of this covenant established through God's election of believers in Christ.[57] Many Lutherans, on the other hand, while recognizing the freedom to omit or retain the exorcisms, nonetheless believed the ceremonies had to be retained to counter Calvinist teaching about baptism.[58] Through the exorcisms, the doctrine of original sin and the salvific power of baptism—that it imparted forgiveness of sins and delivered from sin, death, and the devil—were demonstrated. Their omission confirmed a denial of the doctrine of original sin and the sacramental nature and efficaciousness of baptism.[59] As Nischan concludes, "Because of different sacramental theologies, whose origins can be traced back to the early sixteenth century Wittenberg and Geneva, the two had arrived at diametrically opposed views of exorcism and so had turned a minor rite into a major confessional issue."[60] By the end of the eighteenth century, the course of development of Lutheran baptismal theology and practice, under the influence of Pietism and Rationalism, led to the elimination of the exorcisms and the conflict surrounding them, in addition to much of the remainder of ceremony in the Lutheran baptismal rites. Only at that point were the connections to medieval baptismal practice and theology effectively severed.

In the end, Lutheran baptismal rites of the sixteenth century often did not look very different from medieval rites. Even if ceremonies were omitted or changed, the texts continued to emphasize many of the same realities found in the medieval texts: the realities of sin, Satan, and hell, and the need for rebirth and deliverance from those realities. Like their medieval forebears, even if the particular expressions were different, Luther and his followers believed that this deliverance and renewal took place in the water surrounded by God's Word. The more things changed, the more, in some ways, they stayed the same.

Appendix

The Baptismal Rites of Breslau and of Martin Luther

Ritual of Breslau	1523 Luther Translation	1524 Breslau	Liegnitz/Brieg Agreement
At door of the church			
Division of males/ females			Questions of desire
			Naming of child
Exsufflation	Exsufflation (3x)	Exsufflation	
Sign of cross on forehead and breast	Sign of cross on forehead and breast	Sign of cross on forehead and breast	
Laying on of hands			
Salutation			
Catechumenal prayers (3)	Catechumenal prayers (2)	Catechumenal prayer (1)	Admonition— pray for baptism
			Exorcism prayer
Exorcism of salt			
Asking of name			
Giving of salt	Giving of salt	Giving of salt	
Salutation		Invitation: "Let us pray"	
Prayer: "O God of Fathers"	Flood Prayer	Flood Prayer (Luther)	Version of Martin Luther's Flood Prayer
Sign of cross— males	Sign of cross		
Prayers of exorcism over males	Exorcisms (3)	Prayers of exorcism over males	Prayer for spirit/ faith for the candidate
Sign of cross— females	[Sign of cross (3x)]		
Prayers of exorcism over females		Prayers of exorcism over females	
Final exorcism prayer over males/females	Final exorcism prayer over males/females	Final exorcism prayer over males/females	
	Salutation	Salutation	
		Gospel response	
Gospel: Mt. 19:13–15	Gospel: Mk. 10: 13–16	Gospel: Mt. 19:13–15 or Mk. 10: 13–16	Gospel: Mk. 10: 13–16
Laying on of hands	Laying on of hands		

Appendix

The Baptismal Rites of Breslau and of Martin Luther (*cont.*)

Ritual of Breslau	1523 Luther Translation	1524 Breslau	Liegnitz/Brieg Agreement
Delivery of: Lord'sPrayer/Creed	Delivery of: Lord'sPrayer	Delivery of: Lord'sPrayer/Creed	Recitation of: Lord'sPrayer
Final exorcism		Final exorcism	
Effeta with spit on the ears and nose	Effeta with spit on the ears and nose	Effeta with spit on the ears and nose	
Entrance into church	Entrance into church	Entrance into church	
Renunciation of Satan	Renunciation of Satan	Renunciation of Satan	Renunciation of Satan
	Creedal interrogations	Creedal interrogations	Creedal interrogations
Anoint with oil of catechumens on breast/shoulders	Anoint with oil of catechumens on breast/shoulders	Anoint with oil of catechumens on breast/shoulders	
Naming			
Creedal interrogations			
Question of desire	Question of desire	Question of desire	Question of desire
Triune immersion with Triune Name	Triune immersion with Triune Name	Triune immersion with Triune Name	Baptism with Triune Name (mode unspecified)
		Touching of Child	
Presbyteral anointing	Presbyteral anointing	Presbyteral anointing	
		Prayer	
	The Peace		
Robing	Robing	Robing	Robing
	The Peace		
Giving of candle	Giving of candle		
			Thanksgiving–Baptism
			Admonition: godparents

Notes

1. Martin Luther, "The Babylonian Captivity of the Church," in *Luther's Works,* vol. 36, *Word and Sacrament II,* (Philadelphia: Fortress Press, 1959), 57.

2. James F. White, *The Sacraments in Protestant Faith and Practice* (Nashville: Abingdon Press, 1999), 24–25.

3. *Luther's Works,* vol. 53, 103.

4. Ibid.

5. See Luther's *Small Catechism,* IV, 5–6, in Robert Kolb and Timothy J. Wengert, eds., *The Book of Concord: The Confessions of the Evangelical Lutheran Church* (Minneapolis: Fortress Press, 2000), 359.

6. Susan C. Karant-Nunn provides a helpful overview of the changes and developments in baptism during the late medieval period, demonstrating how ritual change affected the theology and social impact of baptism, in her book *The Reformation of Ritual: An Interpretation of Early Modern Germany* (London: Routledge, 1997), chap. 2, "To Beat the Devil: Baptism and the Conquest of Sin," 43–50.

7. A sacramentary was a book containing all of the texts (not the rubrics) necessary for the presider to celebrate the sacraments and liturgical rites. The *Old Gelasian Sacramentary* appeared at the end of the seventh century and provides the first actual liturgical evidence for baptismal practice in Rome after the fourth century. For more information on the development of medieval liturgical books see Eric Palazzo, *A History of Liturgical Books from the Beginning to the Thirteenth Century* (Collegeville, Minn.: Liturgical Press, 1998).

8. Rituals developed in the twelfth century as independent books that contained both the ceremonial actions and rubrics and the pastoral commentary necessary for priests to conduct pastoral, liturgical acts. They contained all the liturgical rites necessary for a priest in a particular diocese, with the exception of the rites for the daily prayer offices and for the Mass.

9. Baptism was also conducted at the vigil before the feast of Pentecost.

10. This is not to deny the reality that infants had been baptized at least from the third century. However, during earlier centuries infants were baptized with adults as the conversion of the non-Christian world ensued. By the seventh century infants became the primary baptismal candidates, and adults were the rare exception.

11. The passive nature of the prebaptismal rites is described effectively by Karant-Nunn, *The Reformation of Ritual,* 43–45.

12. This purging called exorcism was no longer a daily turning from evil in association with catechesis. It was now a ritual and ceremony repeated at least three times and was itself the substance of the catechumenate. The purging that had to occur was the purging of original sin. The exorcisms and baptism accomplished that purging. This emphasis on the purging of original sin might have contributed to the compartmentalization of baptism and penance, baptism addressing original sin and penance addressing postbaptismal sin. This division was at the heart of Luther's reaction to the medieval view of baptism. This division, likewise, might have contributed to the development of purgatory, which accomplished the final purging of postbaptismal sin after death and prior to the judgment. For further information on the development

of purgatory, see Jacques Le Goff, *The Birth of Purgatory*, trans. Arthur Goldhammer (Chicago: University of Chicago Press, 1984), especially 220–25.

13. For further details on the development of baptismal praxis see Maxwell Johnson, *The Rites of Christian Initiation: Their Evolution and Interpretation* (Collegeville, Minn.: Liturgical Press, 1999), 201–21; and Hughes Oliphant Old, *The Shaping of the Reformed Baptismal Rite in the Sixteenth Century* (Grand Rapids, Mich.: Eerdmans, 1992), 1–31.

14. Old, *Reformed Baptismal Rite*, 10. Karant-Nunn (*The Reformation of Ritual*, 45–46) notes the moral dualism and the liminal nature of baptism inherent in the emphasis upon exorcisms.

15. The mother would still have been at home recovering from the child's birth. As Susan Karant-Nunn notes (*The Reformation of Ritual*, 64), fathers too were often absent from their children's baptisms.

16. This failure was primarily due to the large size of the dioceses.

17. For instance, the twelfth-century pontificals provided for communication of the infants with the wine, while no reference was made to the bread. Yet the distribution formula referred to the Body and Blood preserving the neophyte.

18. The appendix provides a chart comparing the ceremonial structure of all the baptismal rites under consideration in this chapter.

19. The beginnings of the ritual can be traced to the development in the ninth and tenth centuries of *libelli*, little booklets, which contained one or more particular rites from medieval *ordines*, or books of rubrics and outlines of services. See Palazzo, *History of Liturgical Books*, 189. Throughout his description Palazzo is heavily dependent upon P. M. Gy's work, "Collectaire, rituel, processional," *Revue des Sciences philosophiques et théologiques* 44 (1960): 441–69. These *libelli* were intended for the use of the presbyter in his "mobile practice of the liturgy." Palazzo, *History of Liturgical Books*, 190. Originally the rite of baptism was exempted from such *libelli* since it was included in the sacramentary within the course of the Easter and/or Pentecost Vigil Mass. However, during the Renaissance the *manuale* or *pastorale*, collections of counsels or guides for pastors, particularly those for the administration of the sacraments, began to merge with the ritual. In the twelfth century the ritual truly became an independent book, no longer a booklet, including all the rites—ritual and ceremonial—and pastoral commentary necessary for priestly liturgical conduct. These pure rituals included both the complete prayers, not simply prayer *incipits* (that is the beginning texts of prayers, but not the full text), and the *ordines* or rubrics for administering the rites. Although not yet called rituals, a term that did not appear until official editions were printed in the sixteenth century, they were referred to as *baptisteria, orationale, agenda, sacerdotale,* and *obsequiale,* terms that usually denoted the liturgical act that appeared first in the book. The predominant titles for the fourteenth and fifteenth centuries included *agenda* or *obsequiale* in Germany; *manuale* in England, France, and Spain; and *rituale* in Italy.

20. This agenda was edited and reissued, substantially in the same form, in the 1499 Breslau Agenda, edited by Vicar and Vice-deacon Martin Paulsdorf under the oversight of Bishop Johannes IV Roth.

21. Adolph Franz, ed., *Das Rituale des Bischofs Heinrich I. Von Breslau* (Freiburg im Breisgau: Herder, 1912), 54.

22. Ibid., 53.

23. This already reflects the fact that the old catechumenal rites had been subsumed within the one ritual rite of baptism and were clearly to be celebrated as a unit immediately prior to and as a part of baptism.

24. Old, *Reformed Baptismal Rite,* 12.

25. Gustav Kawerau, "Liturgische Studien zu Luthers Taufbüchlein von 1523," *Zeitschrift für kirchliche Wissenschaft und kirchliches Leben* 10 (1889): 413.

26. The Ritual indicates that the confession of faith was considered to be the child's confession by addressing the questions to the child by name.

27. Martin Luther, "The Private Mass and the Consecration of Priests," in *Luther's Works,* vol. 38, *Word and Sacrament 4,* ed. Martin E. Lehmann (St. Louis: Concordia; Philadelphia: Fortress Press, 1971), 183.

28. See Old, *Reformed Baptismal Rite,* 51, 73–76, for the theological principles that guided the baptismal reforms among the German and Swiss Reformers.

29. The Lutheran territorial Churches adopted a critical but reverential attitude toward church tradition. This reverence is perhaps best expressed by Philipp Melanchthon in the *Apology to the Augsburg Confession:* "We gladly keep the old traditions set up in the churches because they are useful and promote tranquility, and we interpret them in an evangelical way, excluding the false opinion which holds that they justify." *Apology to the Augsburg Confession* XV, 38; Theodore G. Tappert, ed., *The Book of Concord* (Philadelphia: Fortress Press, 1959), 230; *Die Bekenntnisschriften der Evangelisch-Lutherischen Kirche* (Göttingen: Vandenhoeck and Ruprecht, 1986), 304.

30. The classic enunciation of the role of Church tradition amongst sixteenth-century Lutherans can be found in the section "Concerning Tradition" in Martin Chemnitz's *Examination of the Council of Trent,* trans. Fred Kramer, vol. 1 (St. Louis: Concordia, 1971), 267–71.

31. The text for Luther's 1523 *Taufbüchlein* may be found in *D. Martin Luthers Werke, Kritische Gesamtausgabe* (Weimarer Ausgabe), vol. 12 (Weimar: Hermann Böhlaus, 1891), 42–48.

32. Wittenberg was positioned within the bishopric of Brandenburg and within the archbishopric of Magdeburg. Unfortunately there is no extant ritual for the diocese of Brandenburg. Thus, the historian must rely upon the only source from Magdeburg, the *Magdeburg Agenda of 1497,* and a source from the neighboring bishopric of Ermland in Prussia, the *Agenda communis, die älteste Agende in der Diözese Ermland und den Deutschordenstaate Preußen nach dem ersten Druckausgaben von 1512 und 1520.* The latter is available in Fr. K. Nümann, "Zur Entstehung des lutherschen Taufbüchleins von Jahre 1523," *Monatsschrift für Gottesdienst und kirchliches Kunst* 33 (1928): 214–19. For the former, see Kawerau, "Liturgische Studien zu Luthers Taufbüchlein von 1523," 420–23.

33. Karant-Nunn (*The Reformation of Ritual,* 50–53) effectively summarizes Luther's theological perspectives and goals in the preparation of his two baptismal rites.

34. The other changes involved the elimination of some of the exorcisms and the elimination of the delivery of the Creed to the candidate.

35. As Martin Ferel, *Gepredigte Taufe; eine homiletische Untersuchung zur Taufpredigt bei Luther* (Tübingen: Mohr, 1969), 48, notes, the absence of a critique on Luther's part of the liturgical and practical working out of baptism in the medieval period indicates that Luther did not find any real theological problems here.

36. Karant-Nunn, *The Reformation of Ritual,* 57–58.

37. See Hughes Old's discussion of the first evangelical translations, *Reformed Baptismal Rite,* 33–49.

38. Ibid., 41.

39. Ibid., 43.

40. Much of the information provided here regarding the Reformation in Breslau and the unique aspects of the rite of baptism developed by Hess comes from Bruno Jordahn, "Der Taufgottesdienst im Mittelalter bis zur Gegenwart," in *Leiturgia: Handbuch des evangelischen Gottesdienstes* (Kassel: Johannes Stauda, 1970), 5:438.

41. This reflects the fact that the practical task of ecclesiastical reform was carried out by a network of Reformers connected by a variety of factors including personal background, family background, community of origin, common educational experiences, and common social and religious stature and position. Thus, at certain points, as seems to be the case with Hess, Reformers followed the lead of their closest associates and colleagues in reform, rather than the medieval traditions that they had inherited. This network of Reformers was very influential and collaborative. See Jeffrey Jaynes, "'Ordo et Libertas': Church Discipline and the Makers of Church Order in Sixteenth Century North Germany" (Ph.D. diss., Ohio State University, Columbus, Ohio, 1993).

42. See the appendix.

43. Luther and Osiander omitted only the third catechumenal prayer.

44. This follows Luther and Osiander. This omission guarded against a potentially magical interpretation of the substances of baptism—i.e., that exorcized salt was holy salt and effective when used for whatever purpose.

45. See the text in the Breslau Ritual—a source document provided with this contribution.

46. Ibid.

47. The text for the robing also follows Osiander's text, altering the last phrase so that it does not imply that the white robe is actually what brings a person eternal life. The phrase now indicates that one is to bring the white robe before the judgment seat of Christ at which one will receive eternal life.

48. Karant-Nunn (*The Reformation of Ritual,* 70–71) enunciates well the shift in perspective from the medieval Church to the Reformation with regard to the understanding of evil and Satan. While her characterization (70) that in the Reformation "the Devil was no longer the objectified, exterior force" would not be accurate with regard to Luther and the Lutheran Reformers, she is correct in noting a shift in their understanding of the responsibility for evil from the Devil to human beings. The Lutheran Reformers can continue to use the language of the medieval rites regarding the Devil, evil, and sin while understanding their connotations in a different way.

49. These are the words of Martin Luther in his Small Catechism to explain what gifts or benefits baptism grants. *Small Catechism,* IV, 5–6, in Kolb and Wengert, *The Book of Concord,* 359.

50. Old, *Reformed Baptismal Rite,* 51.

51. *Luther's Works,* vol. 53, 103. The contrasting approaches within the Swiss and south German reformations are successfully summarized in Karant-Nunn, *The Reformation of Ritual,* 54–58.

52. The historical developments leading to the promulgation of the Sacramental Agreement may be found in Emil Sehling, ed., *Die Evangelischen Kirchenordnungen des XVI. Jahrhunderts* (Leipzig: O. R. Riesland, 1919; Aalen: Scientia Verlag, 1970), 3: 418–19.

53. *Luther's Works,* vol. 53, 102.

54. Augsburg Confession XX, 15, in Kolb and Wengert, *The Book of Concord,* 54.

55. Bodo Nischan, "The Exorcism Controversy and Baptism in the Late Reformation," *The Sixteenth Century Journal* 18:1 (Spring 1987): 31–52.

56. Ibid., 33.

57. Ibid., 48.

58. See also Karant-Nunn, *The Reformation of Ritual,* 59–61.

59. Nischan, "Exorcism Controversy," 49.

60. Ibid., 50.

nine

Conservation and Innovation in Sixteenth-Century Marriage Rites

BRYAN D. SPINKS

Editors' Introduction

Our assessment of change and continuity must take into account differences among types of liturgical celebrations. Indeed, forms of worship fall into quite different categories: daily prayer for monastic communities, weekly gatherings of local congregations, private or family observances, occasional gatherings for national or political purposes. Another distinct category includes the rites that mark important milestones in life, including marriage and funeral rites.

In this essay, Bryan Spinks analyzes sixteenth-century marriage rites in four traditions: Lutheran (one German and one Swedish rite), Reformed, Anglican, and French Catholic. As he does so, he notes a social or cultural conservatism that held sway across the confessional spectrum, whether Catholic or Protestant, Reformed or Anglican. Social customs appear to be especially tenacious in the case of rites of passage. Even when great changes are imposed by new Church authorities, social customs may still persist, and weave a thread of continuity through a pattern of change from medieval marriage liturgies.

Primary Sources Introduction

The following texts are taken from five marriage liturgies used in Lutheran, Reformed, Anglican, and Catholic churches in the sixteenth and seventeenth centuries. These sources show that the marriage rite in all traditions followed a sequence of steps, some of which were altered or omitted altogether in the later rituals.

A. Martin Luther: The Order of Marriage for Common Pastors (1529)[1]

1.
First, publishing the banns from the pulpit with such words as these:
Hans N. and Greta N. purpose to enter into the holy estate of matrimony according to God's ordinance. They desire that common Christian prayer be made on their behalf so that they may begin it in God's name and prosper therein.

And should anyone have anything to say against it, let him speak in time or afterward hold his peace. God grant them his blessing. Amen.

2.
Marrying them at the entrance to the church with words such as these:
Hans, dost thou desire Greta to thy wedded wife?
He shall say:
Yes.
Greta, dost thou desire Hans to thy wedded husband?
She shall say:
Yes.

3.
Then let them give each other the wedding rings and join their right hands together, and say to them:

4.
What God hath joined together, let no man put asunder.
Then shall he say:
Since Hans N. and Greta N. desire each other in marriage and acknowledge the same here publicly before God and the world,

in testimony of which they have given each other their hands and wedding rings, I pronounce them joined in marriage, in the name of the Father, and of the Son, and of the Holy Ghost. Amen.

5.
Before the altar he shall read God's word over the bridegroom and bride, Genesis, the second chapter.

6.
Thereupon, he shall turn to both of them and speak to them thus: Since both of you have entered the married estate in God's name, hear first of all God's commandment concerning this estate. Thus speaketh St. Paul: Husbands, love your wives, even as Christ also loved the Church and gave himself for it; that he might sanctify and cleanse it with the washing of water by the word, that he might present it to himself a glorious Church, not having spot, or wrinkle or any such thing, but that it should be holy and without blemish. So ought men to love their wives as their own bodies. He that loveth his wife loveth himself. For no man ever yet hated his own flesh; but nourisheth and cherisheth it, even as the Lord the Church.

Wives, submit yourselves unto your husbands, as unto the Lord. For the husband is head of the wife, even as Christ is the head of the Church; and he is the savior of the body. Therefore, as the Church is subject unto Christ, so let wives be to their own husbands in everything. Second, hear also the cross which God has placed upon this estate. God spake thus to the woman: I will greatly multiply thy sorrow and thy conception; in sorrow thou shalt bring forth children; and thy desire shall be to thy husband, and he shall rule over thee. And God spake to the man: Because thou hast hearkened unto the voice of thy wife, and hast eaten of the tree of which I commanded thee, saying, Thou shalt not eat of it: cursed is the ground for thy sake; in sorrow shalt thou eat of it all the days of thy life; thorns and thistles shall it bring forth to thee; and thou shalt eat the herb of the field; in the sweat of thy face shalt thou eat bread, till thou return to the ground; for out of it wast thou taken, for dust thou art, and unto dust shalt thou return. Third, this is your comfort, that you may know and believe that your estate is pleasing to God and blessed by him. For it is written: God created man in his own image, in the image of God created he him; male and female created he them. And God blessed them, and God said unto them, Be fruitful, and multiply, and replenish the earth and subdue it; and have dominion over the fish of the sea, and over the fowl of the air and over every living thing that moveth upon the earth. And God saw everything that he had made, and, behold, it was very good. Therefore, Solomon also says: Whoso findeth a wife findeth a good thing, and obtaineth favor of the Lord.

7.
And he shall spread forth his hands over them and pray:
O God, who hast created man and woman and hast ordained them for the married state, hast blessed them also with fruits of the womb, and hast typified therein the sacramental union of thy dear Son, the Lord Jesus Christ, and the Church, his bride: we beseech thy boundless goodness and mercy that thou wouldst not permit this thy creation, ordinance and blessing to be disturbed or destroyed, but graciously preserve the same, through Jesus Christ our Lord. Amen.

B. From the *Manual* of Olavus Petri: Swedish Lutheran Marriage Liturgy, 1529[2]

A Form for Dealing with Them That Wish to Be Married
First and foremost it were very convenient that the priest should duly exhort them that intend to contract a marriage, that they should on both their parts consider and ponder well the covenant that they are to make together; that they do not wed each other after a light evening flirtation and in so hasty a fashion, that they repent of it so long as they live. From this it followeth that instead of living together in all the greatest harmony to the glory and praise of God, they will live together in enmity and strife to the great wrath of God. Likewise it were very convenient that, before they are united, the priest should give them on both their parts some goodly instruction how they shall behave themselves the one toward the other, on this fashion:

Dear friends, ye shall here be mindful that God hath made man the head of the woman, that he may be her guardian to govern and direct her in the fear of God for her good, and hold her dear, as Christ loved his Christian church, for which he gave himself up to death. The man shall remember carefully that albeit he is made the guardian of the woman, he is not thereby given the power to treat her ill according to his own temper, as (alas) is oftentimes seen. But he shall often spare her frailness and bear with it; and (as saith St Peter) give honour unto the womanly kind, seeing that she is the weaker vessel. And forasmuch as the man is endowed with greater intelligence and a stronger nature than the woman, he shall use such gifts of God for the confirmation of his wife, and not for her subjection. He shall so behave himself toward her as toward one who shall be heir together with him of the kingdom of God. And forasmuch as Christ hath purchased the woman as dearly as the man, and she is a member of Christ as well as he, therefore shall he so deal with her as he would that Christ should deal with him. For as the man is the head of the woman, so is Christ also the head of the man. The man shall cloke the defects and frailness of the woman with his intelligence and strength. He shall be her shield and defence, and love her as his own flesh and blood, for she was created for his good; forasmuch as God himself said that it was not good for man to be alone, therefore created he a woman to be a help for him; and since the woman was created as a help for him, so shall he give thanks to God for such help, love her and keep her in chastity and sobriety for God's sake who hath given her to him, and hath so commanded. Likewise also shall the woman be obedient and attentive to the man, love him as her head and guardian, considering that she was created to be a help for the man. She shall not try to have the rule over him, since woman was created for the sake of man, and not man for the sake of woman. She shall follow the example and pattern of the holy women who were in the Old Testament, such as Sarah who called her husband Abraham Lord; and many other holy women who were obedient and attentive to their husbands. She shall surely so behave herself that she may please her husband, to whom she hath been given as a help. And as she hath been given to him as a help, so shall she at all times behave herself that she may be to him a help. The woman is the glory of the man, as Paul saith; she shall behave herself accordingly, and consider that she is set by God under the authority of the man. And, most chiefly, the man and the woman shall on both their parts so love each other, that they hold none dearer than themselves mutually. For the scripture saith that the man shall leave his father and mother and cleave unto his wife, so that the love that he hath to his wife shall pass the love that he hath to his father and mother. So likewise shall it be with the woman. They shall be mindful indeed that they are giving themselves to that estate in which God hath so joined together the man and the woman, that no man shall put them asunder. The man shall not doubt but that as God did give Eve to Adam for his wife, so he giveth to every man his particular wife, and to every woman her particular husband. Therefore it is very necessary on both their parts that they pray God for such a spouse, that they may live in harmony and love and the fear of God, and that their marriage may be begun in God according to the mind of God, and not according to any wantonness or desire of man. Thus shall happiness and blessedness attend their marriage on both their parts.

When as such an instruction hath been given and it hath been published from the pulpit thrice, according to the ancient custom, that such persons intend to contract a marriage, and they are come to the doors of the church, then shall the priest inquire of both their intent, saying to the man:

I DEMAND of thee N. the first time, the second time and the third time, whether thou wilt take this person to thy wife and love her for better for worse.

The man answereth: Yea.

Then the priest inquireth of her likewise whether she will take him to her wedded husband, etc. When this hath been done, they incline their heads together, and the priest saith:

O GOD, almighty Father, eternal God, thou who hast created man and woman that they shall be one flesh and blood together, increase according to thy blessing, multiply and replenish the earth, give now to these thy servants grace that they may so come together according to thy holy will and ordinance, that it may be to thy praise and honour (O heavenly Father), and to their benefit, advantage, and eternal salvation, through thy beloved Son Jesus Christ our Lord. Amen.

Then the priest taketh the ring and saith:
Let us pray.

O God, almighty Father, who of thine incomprehensible goodness hast created all things, that they should serve for the good of mankind, we pray thee that thou wilt send thy blessing upon this thy servant who shall wear this ring as a token of her marriage, that she may live blamelessly in that holy estate to which thou hast called her, through thy Son Jesus Christ our Lord. Amen.

Thereafter the bridegroom taketh the ring and saith to the bride:

I N. take thee N. to my wedded wife, to love thee for better for worse, and in token thereof I give thee this ring.

The bride answereth:

I N. take thee N. to my wedded husband, to love thee for better for worse, and in token thereof I take from thee this ring.

Then the bridegroom putteth the ring upon her hand, first on the thumb, then on the longest finger, and then on that which is next, and there the ring remaineth; and as he putteth on the ring he saith:

In the name of the Father, and the Son and the Holy Ghost.

Then the priest saith:

Good Christian people, all ye who are here present, I call upon you to witness what hath here been done, exhorting you to remember the same.

Furthermore the priest saith:
Let us hear the holy Gospel as it is written by St. Matthew:
The Pharisees also came unto Jesus, tempting him, and saying unto him, Is it lawful for a man to put away his wife for every cause? And he answered and said unto them, Have ye not read, that he which made them at the beginning made them male and female, and said, For this cause shall a man leave father and mother, and shall cleave to his wife: and they twain shall be one flesh? Wherefore they are no more twain, but one flesh. What therefore God hath joined together, let not man put asunder.
Praise be to God.

And then the priest saith to them:
Think upon these words of God, and remember them carefully, and put your whole trust in them.

Thereafter the priest saith:
The Lord be with you.
Answer: And with thy spirit.
Let us pray.

O Almighty eternal God, who didst say concerning man when thou didst first create him, that it was not good for him to be alone, for thou didst create woman to be a help for him, and so joined them together that they should be one flesh: we pray thee, almighty Father, that thou wilt fill with thy Holy Spirit these thy servants, whom thou hast joined together in the estate of matrimony, that they may preserve it rightly and blamelessly, and grant them thy blessing, that their marriage may be adorned with the fruit whereunto thou hast instituted it, as thou didst with Abraham, Isaac, and Jacob. Preserve them, O merciful Father, from the enticement of the devil, as thou didst preserve thy servant Tobias by thine angel, that they be not beguiled with unclean lust and unchastity; but that they may live together in true faith and loving concord unto a good old age, to thy praise and honour, through thine only-begotten Son Jesus Christ our Lord, who liveth and reigneth with thee and the Holy Ghost for evermore. Amen.

When they are come before the altar, the priest saith:
Let us pray.
O God of Abraham, God of Isaac, and God of Jacob, pour thy Holy Spirit into the hearts of these thy servants, and fill them with all spiritual blessing, that they may so live in their marriage which they have undertaken, that they do not with any uncleanness offend thee, who hast instituted marriage; but rather, seeing that marriage is honourable and good among all men, that they may live therein honourably and well, to thy honour and praise, and their own eternal salvation, through Jesus Christ our Lord. Amen.

Then beginneth the Mass.
When they stand beneath the canopy, the priest saith:
Let us pray.
O Lord God, mercifully consider our prayers, and assist this marriage; and, forasmuch as thou hast instituted it for the increase of mankind, so now preserve that which thou hast joined together, through our Lord Jesus Christ, who liveth and reigneth with thee and the Holy Ghost for evermore. Amen.

Thereafter the priest singeth the preface, saying:
The Lord be with you. And with thy spirit.
Lift up your hearts to God. We lift up our hearts.
Let us give thanks unto our Lord God. It is right and meet.

It is very meet, right and blessed that we should at all times and in all places give thanks unto thee, O Lord, holy Father, almighty, eternal God, who of thy power hast created all things out of nothing: thou who, when all things were created, didst create man that he should be lord thereof, and didst say that it was not good for man to be alone: for as a help for him thou didst make woman from a rib, which thou didst take from his side; and didst declare therewith that, as woman had her beginning from man, so should they at all times be together: O God who willest to signify in marriage the great mystery, that, as man and woman become one flesh, so also is Christ one with his holy church: O God who hast joined man and woman together, and given unto them such a blessing, that neither the sin of Adam nor the flood of Noah could take it away: so now look in clemency upon this thy servant, who is given into the power of the man, and seeketh thy protection. Give her grace (O God) that she may be filled with love and tranquillity: and be faithful and chaste: and give herself in marriage according to the mind of Christ: and that she may in her life follow after holy women, and be welcome as Rachel was to her husband, wise as Rebecca, live long and be faithful as Sarah. Let not the devil have any dealing with her: but rather let her remain firmly established in thy holy commandments.

Give her grace that she may be in peace with her own husband: and flee from all unlawful and carnal lust: and that she may cloke her frailness with chastity and sobriety. Let her flourish and be fruitful in children: and may she come to a desirable old age, and see her children's children unto the third and fourth generation: and then after this life attain eternal joy.

The priest readeth these words hereafter written:
Through our Lord Jesus Christ thy Son, who liveth and reigneth with thee and the Holy Ghost for evermore. Amen.

Then he turneth toward the altar, and the Mass continueth.

Blessing of the Bridal House
O Almighty eternal God, give thy blessing to this bridal house, that all they who dwell herein may remain in peace, follow after thy will, and live in thy love to a good old age, through Jesus Christ our Lord. Amen.

And he pronounceth this upon them:
Almighty God bless you in body and soul, and suffer his blessing to come upon you, even as he blessed Abraham, Isaac and Jacob. May the hand of God protect you, and may he send his holy angel to preserve you all the days of your life. May God, Father, and Son, and the Holy Ghost, suffer his blessing to come upon you. Amen.

C. The Manner of Celebrating Holy Matrimony (John Calvin, Geneva, 1542)[3]

It must be noted, that before the one on which the marriage is to be celebrated, it must be published in the Church for three Sundays: in order that, anyone who knows an impediment may declare it in good time; or if someone else has an interest, they have time to oppose it.

Our help is in the Name of God, who made heaven and earth. Amen.

God our Father, after creating the heaven and the earth, and everything which is in them, he created and formed man after his image and likeness, who had dominion and lordship over the beasts of the earth, the fish of the sea, the birds of heaven: he said after having created man: it is not good that the man should be alone: let us make for him a helper similar to himself. And our Lord made a great slumber fall upon Adam: and as Adam slept, God took one of his ribs from him, and formed Eve, giving us to understand that man and wife are one body, one flesh and one blood. For which cause the man leaves father and mother, and is joined to his wife: whom he should also love, as Jesus loves his Church, that is to say the true faithful and Christians, for whom he died *[and his blood which he had shed to wash, purge and cleanse them to render them without spot, wrinkle or blemish]*. And also the wife should serve and obey her husband, in all holiness and honesty. For she is subject, and in the governance of her husband as long as she lives with him. And this holy marriage, honourable, instituted by God, is of such virtue, that the husband has no power over his own body, but the wife: also the wife has no power over her body, but the husband. For this reason the ones joined by God cannot be separated, unless for a time by mutual agreement, to devote to fasting or prayer, guarding well that they are not tempted by Satan through incontinence. And for that reason, they should return together again. Because for avoiding fornication, each needs to have his wife, and each woman her husband: so that all those who cannot be continent, and who do not have the gift of continence, are obliged, by the commandment of God, to marry: so that the holy temple of God—that is to say our bodies—may not be violated and corrupted, because since our bodies are members of Jesus Christ, it would be a great outrage to make them members of the harlot. Wherefore everyone must preserve themselves in all holiness, for whoever violates the Temple of God, God will destroy him *[and peculiar to the holy estate of matrimony, as our Lord well demonstrated, commands that the wife who breaks her marriage, is put to death, her and the adulterer]*.

You, then, N and N, having knowledge that God has thus ordained it, do you wish to live in this holy estate of Marriage which God has so greatly honoured? Have you such a purpose as you testify here before his Holy Assembly, requesting that it approves?

They reply: Yes.

The Minister:

I take you all, who are present here in witness, requesting you to have recollection: moreover, if anyone who knows some impediment *[according as God has prohibited]* or if one of the parties has promised marriage to another, let them in Christian *[good]* charity declare it and make it public.

If no person contests it, the Minister says this:

Since no one has contested, and no one has pointed out an impediment, our Lord God confirms your holy intention which he has given you. And that same one who created and made the heaven and the earth wishes to give increase to your commencements and render them with happiness. And your commencement is in the Name of God, who made heaven and earth. Amen.

The Minister speaking to the groom says this:

Do You, N, confess here before God and his holy congregation, that you have taken and do take N here present to be your wife and spouse, whom you promise to protect, in loving her and holding together faithfully, at the same time having the duty of a true and faithful husband to his wife: living in holiness with her, keeping faith and loyalty in all things, according to the Holy Word of God and his Holy Gospel?

Answer: Yes.

Then speaking to the bride, he says:

Do you, N, confess here before God, and his Holy assembly, that you have taken and do take N for your lawful husband, to whom you promise to obey, serving him and being subject to him, living in holiness with him, keeping faith and loyalty in all things, as one whose duty as a faithful and loyal spouse to her husband, according to the word of God and the Holy Gospel?

Reply: Yes.

Then the Minister says:

The Father of all mercy, who by his grace has called you to this holy estate of marriage, for the love of Jesus Christ his son, that by his holy presence has sanctified marriage making it the first sign before the apostles, give you his Holy Spirit, to serve him and honour him in this noble estate. Amen.

Hear the Gospel how our Lord wishes to have marriage regarded: and how it is firm and indissoluble, as it is written in St. Matthew in the 19th Chapter: (Gospel reading) Believe these holy words, that our Lord Jesus pronounced, as the Evangelist recites them: and be certain that our Lord God has joined you in this holy estate of marriage: wherefore live together holily, in good love, peace and unity, keeping true charity, faith and loyalty, one to the other, according to the Word of God *[for which reason our Lord provides you the grace (De quoy nostre seigneur vous en doint la grace)].*

Let us all now pray with one heart to our Father:

Almighty God, all good and all knowing, who has foreseen from the beginning, that it is not good for man to be alone; and for this reason you created for him a help similar to himself, and has ordained that the two should be one. We pray you, and humbly request, since it has pleased you to call these here to the holy estate of marriage, that by your grace and goodness you would give them and send your Holy Spirit: in order that, through a true and firm faith, as willing to accept your good, they may live holily, surmounting all naughty affections: and living in purity, building up one another in all honesty and chastity, giving them your benediction, as you did to your faithful servants Abraham, Isaac and Jacob: that having a holy lineage, they may praise you and serve you, and nurturing them in your praise and glory, and by service to the neighbour *(l'utilité du prochain)* in the advancement and exaltation of your Holy Gospel. Grant us, merciful father, through our Lord Jesus Christ your most dear Son, Amen.

Our Lord replenish you with all graces, and in all good things, giving you a long and holy life together.

Go in peace. God be with you always. Amen.

D. The Forme of Solemnizacion of Matrimonie, from the 1549 *Book of Common Prayer.*[4]

First the bannes must be asked three several Soondaies or holye dayes, in the service tyme, the people beeyng presente, after the accustomed maner.

And if the persones that woulde bee maried dwel in divers parishes, the bannes muste bee asked in bothe parishes, and the Curate of thone parish shall not solemnize matrimonie betwixt them, withoute a certificate of the bannes beeyng thrise asked from the Curate of thother parishe.

At the daye appointed for Solemnizacion of Matrimonie, the persones to be maried shal come into the bodie of ye churche, with theyr frendes and neighbours. And there the priest shal thus saye.

Deerely beloved frendes, we are gathered together here in the syght of God, and in the face of his congregacion, to joyne together this man and this woman in holy matrimonie, which is an honorable estate instituted of God in paradise, in the time of mannes innocencie, signifying unto us the misticall union that is betwixte Christe and his Churche: whiche holy estate, Christe adorned a nd beutified with his presence, and first miracle that he wrought in Cana of Galile, and is commended of Sainct Paule to be honourable emong all men; and therefore is not to bee enterprised, nor taken in hande unadvisedlye, lightelye, or wantonly, to satisfie mens carnal lustes and appetites, like brute beastes that have no understanding: but reverentely, discretely, advisedly, soberly, and in the feare of God. Duely considering the causes for the whiche matrimonie was ordained. One cause was the procreacion of children, to be brought up in the feare and nurture of the Lord, and prayse of God. Secondly it was ordeined for a remedie agaynst sinne, and to avoide fornicacion, that suche persones as bee maried, might live chastlie in matrimonie, and kepe themselves undefiled membres of Christes bodye. Thirdelye for the mutuall societie, helpe, and coumfort, that the one oughte to have of thother, both in prosperitie and in adversitie. Into the whiche holy estate these two persones present: come nowe to be joyned. Therefore if any man can shewe any juste cause why they maie not lawfully be joyned so together: Leat him now speake, or els hereafter for ever hold his peace.

And also speakyng to the persones that shalbe maried, he shall saie.

I require and charge you (as you will aunswere at the dreadefull daye of judgemente, when the secretes of all hartes shalbee disclosed) that if either of you doe knowe any impedimente, why ye maie not bee lawfully joyned together in matrimonie, that ye confesse it. For be ye wel assured, that so manye as bee coupled together otherwaies then Goddes woord doeth allowe: are not joyned of God, neither is their matrimonie lawful.

At which daye of mariage yf any man doe allege any impediment why they maye not be coupled together in matrimonie: And will be bound, and sureties with hym, to the parties, or els put in a caution to the full value of suche charges as the persones to bee maried dooe susteyne to prove his allegacion: then the Solemnizacion muste bee differred, unto suche tyme as the trueth bee tried. Yf no impedimente bee alleged, then shall the Curate saye unto the man.

N. Wilte thou have this woman to thy wedded wife, to live together after Goddes ordeinaunce in the holy estate of matrimonie? Wilt thou love her, coumforte her, honor, and kepe her in sickenesse and in health? And forsaking all other kepe thee only to her, so long as you both shall live?

The man shall aunswere,

I will.

Then shall the priest saye to the woman.

N. Wilt thou have this man to thy wedded houseband, to live together after Goddes ordeinaunce, in the holy estate of matrimonie? Wilt thou obey him, and serve him, love, honor, and kepe him in sickenes and in health? And forsaking al other kepe thee onely to him, so long as you bothe shall live?

The woman shall aunswere,

I will.

Then shall the Minister say,

Who geveth this woman to be maried to this man?

And the minister receiving the woman at her father or frendes handes: shall cause the man to take the woman by the right hande, and so either to geve their trouth to other: the man first saying.

I N. take thee N. to my wedded wife, to have and to holde from this day forwarde, for better, for wurse, for richer, for poorer, in sickenes, and in health, to love and to cherishe, til death us departe: according to Goddes holy ordeinaunce: and therto I plight thee my trouth.

Then shall they looce theyr handes, and the woman taking again the man by the right hande shall say,

I N. take thee N. to my wedded husbande, to have and to holde from this day forwarde, for better, for woorse, for richer, for poorer, in sickenes, and in health, to love, cherishe, and to obey, till death us departe: accordyng to Goddes holy ordeinaunce: And thereto I geve thee my trouth.

Then shall they agayne looce theyr handes, and the manne shall geve unto the womanne a ring, and other tokens of spousage, as golde or silver, laying the same upon the boke: And the Priest taking the ring shall deliver it unto the man: to put it upon the fowerth finger of the womans left hande. And the man taught by the priest, shall say.

With thys ring I thee wed: Thys golde and silver I thee geve: with my body I thee wurship: and withal my worldly Goodes I thee endowe. In the name of the father, and of the sonne, and of the holy goste. Amen.

Then the man leavyng the ring upon the fowerth finger of the womans lef hande, the minister shal say,

Let us pray.

O Eternal God creator and preserver of al mankinde, gever of al spiritual grace, the author of everlasting life: sende they blessing upon these thy servauntes, thys manne, and this woman, whome we blesse in thy name, that as Isaac and Rebecca (after bracellets and Jewels of golde geven of thone to thother for tokes of their matrimonie) lived faithfully together; so these persos may surely perfourme and kepe the vowe and covenaunt betwixt them made, wherof this ring geven, and received, is a token and pledge. And may ever remayne in perfite love and peace together; And lyve according to thy lawes; through Jesus Christe our lorde. Amen.

Then shal the prieste joyne theyr ryght handes together, and say.

Those whome god hath joyned together: let no man put a sundre.

Then shall the minister speake unto the people.

Forasmuche as N. and N. have consented together in holye wedlocke, and have witnessed the same here before god and this company; And therto have geven and pledged theyr trouth eyther to other, and have declared the same by gevyng and receyvyng golde and sylver, and by joyning of handes: I pronounce that they bee man and wyfe together. In the name of the father, of the sonne, and of the holy gost. Amen.

And the minister shall adde this blessing.

God the father blesse you. God the sonne kepe you: god the holye gost lighte your understanding: the Lorde mercifully with his favour loke upon you, and so fil you with al spiritual benediction, and grace, that you may have remission of your sinnes in this life, and in the worlde to come lyfe everlastyng. Amen.

Then shal they goe into the quier, and the ministers or clerkes shal saye or syng, this psalme folowyng. Beati omnes. Cxxviii

Blessed are al they that feare the lord, and walke in his wayes.
For thou shalte eate the laboure of thy handes. O wel is thee, and happie shalt thou bee.
Thy wife shalbee as the fruitful vine, upon the walles of thy house.
Thy children like the olife braunches rounde about thy table.
Loe, thus shal the man be blessed, that feareth the lord.
The lord from out of Sion, shall so blesse thee: that thou shalt see Hierusalem in prosperitie, al thy life long.
Yea that thou shalt see they childers children: and peace upon Israel.

Glory to the father, &c.
As it was in the beginning, &c.

Or els this psalme folowyng. Deus misereatur nostri. Psalm lxvii

God be merciful unto us, and blesse us, and shew us the lighte of his countenaunce: and bee mercifull unto us.
That thy waye maye bee knowen upon yearth, thy saving health among all nacions.
Leate the people praise thee (o god) yea leate all people prayse thee.
O leate the nacions rejoice and bee glad, for thou shalte judge the folke righteously, and governe the nacions upon yearth.
Leat the people prayse thee (o god) leat al people prayse thee.
Then shal the yearth bring foorth her increase: and god, even our owne God, shal geve us his blessyng.
God shal blesse us, and all the endes of the worlde shall feare hym.

Glory to the father, &c.
As it was in the beginning, &c.

The psalme ended, and the manne and woman knelyng afore the aulter: the prieste standyng at the aulter, and turnyng his face towarde them, shall saye.

Lorde have mercie upon us.
Answere. Christe have mercie upon us.

Minister. Lorde have mercie upon us.
Our father whiche art in heaven, &c.
And leade us not into temptacion.
Answere. But deliver us from evill. Amen.
Minister. O lorde save thy servaunte, and thy hand-maide.
Answere. Whiche put theyr truste in the.
Minister. O lorde sende them helpe from thy holy place.
Answere. And evermore defende them.
Minister. Bee unto them a tower of strength.
Answere. From the face of their enemie.
Minister. O lorde heare my prayer.
Answere. And leate my crie come unto the.
The Minister. Leat us praye.
O God of Abraham, God of Isaac, God of Jacob, blesse these thy servaunts, and sowe the seede of eternall life in their mindes, that whatsoever in they holy woorde they shall profitablye learne: they may in dede fulfill the same. Looke, O Lord, mercifully upon them from heaven, and blesse them; And as thou diddest sende thy Aungell Raphaell to Thobie, and Sara, the daughter of Raguel, to their great comfort; so vouchsafe to send thy blessyng upon these thy servaunts, that thei obeyng thy wil, and alwaye beyng in safetie under thy proteccion: may abyde in thy love unto theyr lyves ende: throughe Jesu Christe our Lorde. Amen.

This prayer folowing shalbe omitted where the woman is past childe byrth

O merciful Lord, and heavely father, by whose graciouse gifte makind is increased: We beseche thee assiste with thy blessing these two persones, that they may both be fruictful in procreacion of children; and also live together so long in godlye love and honestie, that they may see their childers children, unto the thirde and fourth generacion, unto thy prayse and honour: through Jesus Christe our Lorde. Amen.

O God, whiche by thy myghtye power haste made all thinges of naughte, whiche alos after other thinges set in order diddeste appoint that out of man (created after thine own image and similitude) woma should take her beginning: and, knitting them together, diddest teache, that it should never be lawful to put a sondre those, whome thou by matrimonie haddeste made one: O god, whiche hast consecrated the state of matrimonie to such an excellent misterie, that in it is signified and represeted the spirituall mariage and unitie betwixte Christe and his churche: Loke mercifully upo these thy servaunts, that both this manne may love his wyfe, accordyng to thy word (as Christ did love his spouse the churche, who gave himself for it, loving and cherishing it even as his own flesh); And also that this woma may be loving and amiable to her houseband as Rachel, wise as Rebecca, faithful and obediet as Sara; and in al quietnes, sobrietie, and peace, bee a folower of holy and godlye matrones. O lorde, blesse them bothe, and graunte them to inherite thy everlasting kyngdome, throughe Jesu Christe our Lorde. Amen.

Then shall the prieste blesse the man and the woman, saiyng

Almighty god, which at the beginnyng did create oure firste parentes Adam and Eve, and dyd sanctifie and joyne the together in mariage: Powre upon you the rychesse of his grace, sanctifie and blisse you, that ye may please him bothe in bodye and soule; and live together in holy love unto your lives ende. Amen.

Then shalbee sayed after the gospell a sermon, wherein ordinarily (so oft as there is any marriage) thoffice of man and wife shall bee declared according to holy scripture. Or if there be no sermon, the minister shall reade this that foloweth.

Al ye whiche bee maried, or whiche entende to take the holye estate of matrimonie upon you: heare what holye scripture dooeth saye, as touchyng the duetye of housbandes towarde their wives, and wives towarde their housbandes.
Saincte Paule (in his epistle to the Ephesians, the fyfth chapter) doeth geve this commaundement to al maried men.
Ye housebandes love your wives, even as Christ loved the churche, and hathe geven hymselfe for it, to sanctifie it, purgeyng it in the fountayne of water, throughe the word, that he might make it unto himself, a glorious congregacion, not having spot or wrincle, or any such thing; but that it should be holy and blameles. So me are bounde to love their owne wives as their owne bodies: he that loveth his owne wife, loveth himself. For never did any man hate his owne flesh, but nourisheth and cherisheth it, even as the lorde doeth the congregacion, for wee are membres of his bodie, of his fleshe, and of his bones. For this cause shal a man leave father and mother, and shalbe joyned unto his wife, and they two shalbe one fleshe. This mistery is great, but I speake of Christ and of the congregacion. Neverthelesse let every one of you so love his owne wife, even as himselfe.
Likewise the same Saint Paule (writing to the Colossians) speaketh thus to al menne that be maried: ye men, love your wives and be not bitter unto them. Coloss. iii.

Heare also what saint Peter thapostle of Christ, (which was himselfe a maried man,) sayeth unto al menne that are maried. Ye husbandes, dwel with your wives according to knowledge: Gevyng honor unto the wife, as unto the weaker vessel, and as heyres together of the grace of lyfe, so that your prayers be not hindred. I Pet. iii.

Hitherto ye have heard the duetie of the husbande towarde the wife. Nowe likewise, ye wives, heare and lerne your duetie toward your husbandes, even as it is playnely set furth in holy scripture. Saint Paul (in the forenamed epistle to the Ephesians) teacheth you thus: Ye weomen submit yourselves unto your own husbandes as unto the lord: for the husbad is the wives head, even as Christ is the head of the church: and he also is the saviour of the whole bodye. Therefore as the Churche, or congregacyon is subiecte unto Christe: So likewise let the wives also be in subieccyon unto theyr owne husbandes in all thynges. Ephes. V. And agayn he sayeth: Let the wife reverence her husbande. And (in his epistle to the Colossians) Saincte Paule geveth you this short lesson. Ye wives, submit yourselves unto your owne husbandes, as it is conveniente in the Lorde. Coloss. iii.

Saincte Peter also doeth instructe you very godly, thus saying, Let wives be subject to theyr owne husbandes, so that if any obey not the woorde, they may bee wonne without the woorde, by the conversacyon of the wives. Whyle they beholde your chaste conversacyon, coupled with feare, whose apparell let it not bee outwarde, with broyded heare, and trymmyng about with golde, either in putting on of gorgeous apparell: But leat the hyd man whiche is in the hearte, be without all corrupcion, so that the spirite be milde and quiete, which is a precious thing in the sight of god. For after this maner (in the olde tyme) did the holy women, which trusted in God, apparell themselves, beeing subjecte to theyr own husbandes: as Sara obeied Abraham calling him lorde, whose daughters ye are made, doing wel, and being not dismaied with any feare. I Pet. iii.

E. Rite for the Celebration of the Sacrament of Matrimony, from the *Rituale Romanum,* 1614.[5]

1.

After publishing the banns on three feast days, as aforesaid, and if no lawful impediment stands in the way, the parish priest who is to celebrate the marriage, being vested in surplice and white stole and attended by at least one cleric likewise vested in a surplice and carrying the book and the vessel of holy water with its sprinkler, shall, in the presence of two or three witnesses, in the church, ask the man and the woman separately, preferably in the presence of their parents or relatives, the question about their consent to the marriage, using the vernacular tongue and the following form:

N., will you take N., here present, to be your lawful wife, according to the rite of holy mother Church?
The bridegroom answers:
I will.
Then the priest asks the bride:
N., will you take N., here present, to be your lawful husband, according to the rite of holy mother Church?
The bride answers:
I will.
The consent of one does not suffice; it must be of both. And it must be expressed in some sensible sign, either by the parties themselves or through an intermediary.

2.
Having understood the mutual consent of the parties, the priest orders them to join their right hands, saying:
I join you in matrimony, in the name of the Father and of the Son and of the Holy Spirit.
Or other words may be used according to the received rite of each province. Afterwards, he sprinkles them with holy water.

3.
Then he blesses the ring.

Blessing of the Ring
V. Our help is in the name of the Lord.
R. Who made heaven and earth.
V. Lord, hear my prayer.
R. And let my cry come to you.
V. The Lord be with you.
R. And also with you.
Let us pray:
Bless, O Lord, this ring which we bless in your name, so that she who shall wear it, remaining totally faithful to her husband, may

remain in peace and in your will, and live always in mutual charity. Through Christ, etc.
Then the priest sprinkles the ring with holy water in the form of a cross.

4.
Receiving the ring from the priest's hand, the bridegroom places it on the ring finger of his bride's left hand, while the priest says:
In the name of the Father, and of the Son, and of the Holy Spirit. Amen.

5.
Then he adds:
V. Confirm, O God, what you have wrought among us.
R. From your holy temple, which is in Jerusalem.
Kyrie eleison.
Christe eleison.
Our Father. *silently*
V. And lead us not into temptation.
R. But deliver us from evil.
V. Save your servants.
R. Who put their trust in you, my God.
V. Lord, send them help from your holy place.
R. And defend them out of Sion.
V. Be a tower of strength to them, O Lord.
R. In the face of the enemy.
V. Lord, hear my prayer.
R. And let my cry come to you.
V. The Lord be with you.
R. And also with you.
Let us pray:
Look down, we beseech you, O Lord, upon these your servants, and graciously assist this ordinance of yours, which you have provided for the propagation of the human race; that those who are joined together by your authority may be preserved by your help. Through Christ our Lord. Amen.

6.
When all this is done, and if the marriage is to be blessed, the parish priest celebrates the Mass for Bride and Groom, as found in the Roman Missal, observing everything prescribed there.

7.
Moreover, if, besides the above, some provinces are accustomed to using other laudable customs and ceremonies in the celebration of the sacrament of matrimony, the holy Council of Trent desires that they should be retained.

8.
When everything has been completed, the parish priest enters in the register of marriages, in his own hand, the names of the couple, of the witnesses and the other things required; and that he, or some other priest delegated either by him or by the ordinary, has celebrated the marriage.

Notes

1. Martin Luther, "The Order of Marriage for Common Pastors," in *Luther's Works,* edited by Ulrich Leupold, vol. 53, 111–15.
2. Text taken from Eric Yelverton, ed., *The Manual of Olavus Petri* (London: SPCK, 1953), 69–75.
3. P. Barth and W. Niesel, eds., *Joannis Calvini: Opera Selecta* (Munich: Kaiser, 1952), II: 50–56. Bracketed italics give the text of Farel which Calvin omitted. He dispensed entirely with the declaration with which Farel had prefaced his 1533 rite.
4. "The Forme of Solemnizacion of Matrimonie," in *The First and Second Prayer Books of Edward VI* (London: Dent, 1968), 252–58.
5. Mark Searle and Kenneth Stevenson, eds., *Documents of the Marriage Liturgy* (Collegeville, Minn.: Liturgical Press, 1992), 185–88.

In his formulation of "liturgical laws," Anton Baumstark noted that "primitive conditions are maintained with greater tenacity in the more sacred seasons of the liturgical year."[1] One classic example of this was the solemn prayers of the Roman rite for Good Friday, which, because a solemn occasion and only once a year, had withstood the erosions that affected the intercessions in the Ordinary of the Mass.[2] But Baumstark might well also have glanced at another type of rite—namely, rites of passage. These, too, frequently attest a tenacity, even though of a different type. The rites of passage—baptism, marriage, and funerals—all have an embedded social dimension, sometimes caused by, and sometimes quite unrelated to, the ecclesial rites themselves. Social custom gives a society its roots and continuity, and the repetition of rites and ceremonies from generation to generation provides a stability and shared identity that is fundamental in most human societies. Recent studies, for example, have shown how with funerary rites, the great changes in liturgical rites in the Reformation Churches failed to supplant certain customs, such as praying at the graveside, which were associated with Catholicism.[3] No doubt some folk secretly held Catholic views; many others simply refused to give up performing customs and gestures which in common belief, stretched back to time immemorial and to which their deceased kinsmen, regardless of religion, were justly entitled. This is equally applicable to marriage rites and customs.

Marriage, like funerals, was not a Christian invention. The early history of the marriage rite suggests that for some long while there were no peculiarly Christian rites, only the normal domestic rites applied to Christians.[4] No doubt the ceremonies associated with specific pagan religious ideals were jettisoned, or played down, but many customs and rituals in the wider sense of the word, secular, domestic, social, and often bordering on the bawdy, were simply taken over and practiced within a Christian piety, and eventually, within the marriage liturgies that evolved. Obvious examples of this social and cultural continuity are evidenced by the use of the veil in the Roman rites, and the crowning with garlands in the Eastern rites, both of which antedate Christianity. The concern of this essay is not so much with the social customs that surrounded weddings in different places, though certainly some reference to these will be made; neither is it primarily concerned with the legalities that surrounded marriage. Rather, the concern is to look more closely at selected early modern marriage rituals, marking out both innovation and conservation. Even a study of the liturgical texts of the change (seemingly the sources least affected by cultural dynamics) reveals a persistent shaping of practice by cultural norms and customs.

In the introduction to his *Traubüchlein* Luther began with a German proverb, "many lands, many customs," to underline the fact that marriage rites and customs varied greatly from one district to another, as well as from one country to another. This chapter will therefore concentrate on five particular rites and places: The *Traubüchlein* of Luther, 1529; the Swedish Lutheran Marriage Liturgy of 1529; Calvin's rite for Geneva, 1542; the rite formulated by Thomas Cranmer in the Church of England's *Book of Common Prayer,* 1549 and 1552; and the Roman rite in France before and after the Tridentine Ritual of 1614. The selectivity is partly dictated by availability of texts, but also because of the apparent differences in perspective the four Churches took with regard to marriage. This has been conveniently described by John Witte as marriage as "sacrament" in Roman Catholicism, marriage as "social estate" in Lutheranism, marriage as "covenant" in Calvinism, and marriage as "commonwealth" in the Anglican tradition.[5] Although these categories are not as clear-cut as Witte would have us believe—for example, for all the protests of the pioneer English Reformers, the conservative nature of the English canon law helped preserve a strong concept of marriage as sacrament in Anglicanism—nevertheless they draw attention to significant differences in understanding and approach.

Whereas it is possible to speak of a fairly standard late medieval Ordinary of the Mass (though even this is an oversimplification),[6] marriage rites show considerable diversity among dioceses and countries. Thus the Meaux rite from the Paris area is very different from that of Saint Maurdes Fosses, though both are French from the thirteenth century.[7] In general, the medieval Western Catholic rites witness to a fusion of three different and once separate elements. One element was the distinct Roman and Italian Nuptial Mass in church with its blessing of the bride, originally connected with a canopy or veil—a church-based rite. Another was the Visigothic-Gallican blessings of tokens of espousal, rings, and the bedchamber—having originally a domestic setting. Third was the late inclusion of what had been private and domestic vows of betrothal and marriage. When added together, these made for a rich and complex series of rites, which, in some traditions, could also be supplemented with a form for Vespers and Lauds.[8] However, here it is necessary to distinguish between *ecclesiastical liturgical provision as an ideal* and *actual usage*. As Lyndal Roper has pointed out, popular wedding ritual was based around three themes: property and honor, sexual identity, and kinship, celebrated with popular rituals, and quite independent of ecclesiastical ideals and concerns.[9] The celebration of all the possible rites was probably rare, and many made do with *only the minimum*—blessing and exchange of rings and vows, with some prayers. A good many marriage celebrations dispensed with a Mass. Though canon law required marriage to be public—before the door of the church—there was considerable reluctance to hand over private domestic arrangements completely to the Church, and there was often a blurring between private betrothal, after which the couple lived as husband and wife, and then later, weeks or months, made the "church-walk" that made it public and official in the eyes of the Church. In some places the couple was married first, and then on a separate occasion "blessed" in church—sometimes the bride on her own. In some rites we find a common love cup drunk at the end of the rite. Furthermore, there was frequently a gulf between the ecclesiastical ideal, in terms of sequence and rites, and actual practice. Thus in tracing any continuity and change in Reformation marriage rites, each locality has to be treated separately.

With his usual vehemence Luther launched a three-pronged attack on the received medieval Catholic view of marriage. First, Luther denied that marriage was a sacrament. In the *Babylonian Captivity* (1520) he asserted, "Not only is marriage regarded as a sacrament without the least warrant of Scripture, but the very ordinances which extol it as a sacrament have turned it into a farce."[10] Luther argued that *sacramentum* used in connection with marriage meant simply "mystery," being an allegory of Christ and the Church, and not a sacrament in the technical sense. Sacraments were mandated by Christ and belonged to the heavenly realm. Marriage was not a sacrament, and so belonged to the earthly realm. It was thus a natural and social estate.

Since marriage belonged to the natural and social realm, then it was a gift of God for all. Thus Luther attacked clerical celibacy. As a natural estate, it also belonged to the realm of civil law, and not canon law, and so Luther also attacked the complex canon law in respect of marriage. The canon lawyers were sellers of "vulvas and genitals—merchandise indeed most worthy of such merchants, grown altogether filthy and obscene through greed and godlessness."[11] He especially singled out the problem of the insistence of the exchange of vows in the present tense. Valid marriages were based on consent in the present tense (Do you take/I take), or a future promise (Will you take/I will take) followed by consummation, though this second option was frowned upon. Canon law insisted on the terms "Accepio te in uxorem," or "Ich nehme Dich zu meinen Weibe" (I take you to be my wife), though neither formula was the popular Germanic custom. Luther defended the future tense—"Ich will Dich zum Weibe haben" (I will have you as a wife) or "Ich will Dich nehmen" (I will take you); "Ich will Dich haben" (I will have you); "Du sollst mein sein" (You shall be mine)—pointing out that in the German language the future tense was used to mean and express the present.[12] But Luther was also clear that many things relating to marriage were no business of the Church.

> Since marriage and the married estate are worldly matters, it behooves us pastors or ministers of the church not to attempt to order or govern anything connected with it, but to permit every city and land to continue its own use and custom in this connection. Some lead the bride to the church twice, both morning and evening, some only once. Some announce it formally and publish the banns from the pulpit two or three weeks in advance. All such things and the like I leave to the lords and the council to order and arrange as they see fit. It does not concern me.[13]

The liturgical rite that Luther provided appears at first sight to be quite spare. It consisted of three sections:

1. The publication of banns.
2. The marriage proper, which took place at the entrance to the church. It consisted of a declaration of consent, giving of rings, the joining of right hands, and the pronouncement of Matthew 19:6.
3. The church blessing. This took place before the altar. It consisted of a reading from Genesis, an exhortation, and a blessing by the pastor.

We should note a number of things here. First, although concise, this merely reflected the meager material found in many of the German agendas (instructions and texts for the services), including Luther's diocesan Agenda of Magdeburg.[14] Second, it seems to provide for what was the most common usage—the legal vows, and the *einleitung* or *kirchgang* (church-walk) for a blessing, which could be used at separate times, or the one could follow immediately after the other. Here there is obvious continuity. No Mass was provided, since that would constitute a private Mass, and these had been abolished as contrary to the Gospel. To make no provision for the Mass was a textual liturgical innovation, but since many couples did not make use of it, this can also be seen as a practicality. Luther included vows that were ambiguous regarding present/future, though the Lutheran canon lawyers such as Melchior Kling (1504–71) and Joachim von Beust (1522–94) continued to interpret betrothal and marriage with the same criteria as their Catholic predecessors.[15] No blessing of the bed or Saint John's cup were provided. Indeed, the former was thought to encourage bawdy behavior, and so was suppressed by providing no liturgical provisions for the custom. However, the reality of the situation meant that many customs continued regardless of whether there was official liturgical provision. First, Luther envisaged this, and from the various Lutheran Church Orders, it becomes apparent that additions were made to Luther's suggested rite. Thus in Calenberg-Gottingen, 1542, and Mark-Brandenburg, 1561, very different interrogative vows were used, and the former incorporated a blessing from the diocese of Breslau.[16] However, evidence from many cities throughout Germany suggests that the new "evangelical" provisions were supplemented by custom and tradition. The betrothal was still very much a domestic matter, and the financial arrangements were sealed by the *lovelbier* or *Lovede-Beker,* which seems to have been an established social custom that the Saint John's cup attempted to sacralize with a liturgical rite. Despite the repeated call of pastors, and the edicts of princes, that couples should remain chaste until the church ceremony, it is clear that custom considered betrothal as a private marriage, and sexual activity before the public marriage at the church door was not unexpected. Dancing and drinking before and after the church ceremonies drew forth the scorn of pastors, but to little avail. And even if the Lutheran Church deemed the blessing of the bed superstitious and too closely linked with lewd songs and obscene jokes, the *Ansingwein* continued to survive as a popular and expected secular custom.[17]

In the Swedish Lutheran rite in the Manual of Olavus Petri, we find a triple consent and then a prayer in which the bride and groom incline their heads together, preserving a peculiarly Swedish custom. The sign of the cross was retained during a blessing of the ring, and the use of a canopy, the provision for a Nuptial Mass, and the blessing of the home (rather than bed) all continued to occur. Clearly Petri felt that provision for these did not contradict Lutheran theology, and he provided a rite that was in direct continuity with its Catholic predecessor.[18]

In sum, what we find in the Lutheran liturgical revision and discussion of marriage celebration is first and foremost a concern with contracting a valid marriage. Luther's attempt to make this a little wider in terms of the tense of the vow was repudiated by the Lutheran lawyers who were at one with their Catholic counterparts. No Church wanted the embarrassing situation of presiding over marriages that later could be found to be invalid on account of the liturgical formulae. Second, we find in Lutheranism the concept of adiaphora, allowing considerable variations between localities, and a certain regional or national freedom in retaining or abandoning certain ceremonies of a liturgical nature. In Sweden the force of tradition and the judgment of Olavus Petri meant that the Lutheran rite looked very much like its Catholic liturgical antecedent. Third, we see the efforts of pastors to curb the more "profane" and flippant customs ignored. If customs like that of the Saint John's cup were discontinued liturgically, they were simply entirely secularized and retained in a far less pious form.

With Calvin's marriage rite of 1542, we come to a rite that in many respects represents a conservation of a complete innovation, at least as far as Geneva was concerned. The rites of marriage contained in the *Manuale ad usum Gebennensem* of 1500 contained fairly common material for marriage: blessings of the ring and the nuptial blessing, together with vernacular vows at the church door.[19] But by the time Calvin arrived in Geneva, these forms had already been replaced by the liturgical forms introduced by Farel. Thus Calvin found that the blessing of the ring, and Nuptial Mass and blessing of the bed had already been abolished.

Farel's rite for marriage has a complex origin, deriving from his own experience in Strasbourg, Zurich, and Berne. In 1529 he had been given the task of preparing a French liturgy for Aigle which conformed to the German rites of Berne. This in turn seems to have been the basis of his *La Maniere et fasson,* which was published at Neuchâtel in 1533, and which he then introduced in Geneva. The marriage formulary was mainly based on the *Form und gestalt Eeelüten ynfurung und kilchgang* in the 1529 Berne *Ordnung unnd satzung.*[20] That in turn was a combination of material from the Reformed rites of Strasbourg and Zurich. Calvin's rite was only a modification of Farel's rite. It is thus an interesting example of conserving (or maintaining) an innovation. Given the Reformed antecedents of the rite, it can be regarded as a Reformed synthesis, but it has little relation at all to the Catholic antecedent of Geneva.

The celebration took place on a Sunday, unless it was one of the four Sundays when there was a service of the Lord's Supper. Here we find the very opposite to the Catholic ideal of a Nuptial Mass, as the context was the assembled congregation, and the marriage took place within the liturgy of the Word. The vows were thus contracted before God and the congregation. The vows were in the passive form—as in Strasbourg since 1530, but also in the Constance ritual and Zurich, and in the Berne 1529 Reformed rite. The vow "Do you, N, confess here before God and his holy congregation, that you have taken and do take N here present for your wife and spouse" reflects that this is an ecclesial and public ratification of the betrothal, which in Switzerland was still a domestic arrangement. The Gospel reading, which was the old Nuptial Mass Gospel, is almost a ratification and blessing of the marriage.

However, along with this ecclesial setting of marriage there went a complete renovation of the laws of marriage. Jeffrey Watt has pointed out that Calvin had more formal training in law than in theology, and probably had the best legal background of all magisterial reformers, and this was brought to bear on the Marriage Ordinance of 1545.[21] He made a reform and synthesis of the previous canon and civil law relating to marriage, which was administered in part through the consistory, and in part by the civil magistrate. Betrothals were to be registered with the civil magistrate, who would issue a license for marriage. The church ceremony should follow between three and six weeks following the betrothal. Cohabitation before the church ceremony was condemned in Geneva, and pregnant brides were supposed to be married veiled as a sign of shame. And as John Witte has demonstrated, Calvin set out a theology of marriage in the context of its being a mutual and solemn covenant, reflecting the covenant between God and the church.[22]

With a city of some thirteen thousand inhabitants, more public social celebrations could be and were suppressed, and even during Calvin's first stay in Geneva, adornment of the bride's hair was banned. Dancing and lewd songs were punishable. However, human nature being what it is, no doubt some of the prohibited customs were celebrated behind closed and locked doors.[23]

In Calvin's Geneva we therefore find that the Reformed rite entirely replaced the old Catholic forms. There seems to have been an attempt to regulate and harness the domestic betrothal, making sure that it led fairly quickly to a public wedding, thus avoiding problems of validity, and also, one assumes, minimizing the opportunity for sexual activity between the parties.

The Reformation in England was sparked by the marital problems of Henry VIII, and in the initial years of the conservative Henrician reform, some changes were made to the canon law. During the Edwardian period, wide sweeping reforms were proposed in the *Reformatio legum,* which would have brought Church of England marriage laws and practice broadly into line with the Continental Reformed Churches. The Catholic reversion under Mary meant that this legislation was stillborn. Under Elizabeth, the traditional canon law remained virtually intact. Witte aptly comments: "England in the later sixteenth century circles back to much of the marriage law of the medieval Catholic tradition. It largely spurned both the bold common law reforms proffered by the Protestants and the milder canon law refinements promulgated by the Council of Trent."[24] Along with this conservatism, the marriage rites contained in the two Books of Common Prayer, mainly compiled by Thomas Cranmer, also show a marked conservatism in source and structure.

The prevailing rites in use in England on the eve of the Reformation were those of the dioceses of Sarum, York, and Hereford. Of these, Sarum was by far the most widely used and was the basis of Cranmer's reforms. In contrast to the German Agendas, the English provision—or more accurately, the Anglo-Norman provision—was far more elaborate. After banns a final request for knowledge of impediment was made at the door of the church, followed by the consent in the interrogative or passive form (the old betrothal), and vows in the active form. Gold and silver—the tokens of espousal—and the ring were placed on a dish or book, and the ring blessed. It was placed on the bride's thumb, and with the recitation of the Trinitarian formula, moved to the second and third fingers, before finally being placed on the fourth finger of the left hand. The bride and groom were blessed. They then processed inside the church with Psalm 127, and prayers of intercession and blessing. For the Nuptial Mass, the priest was to use the propers for the Mass of the Holy Trinity, and during the nuptial blessing a veil or pall was held over the couple. Finally, provision was made for the blessing of bread and wine, and for the blessing of the bed.

Cranmer's 1549 rite transferred the whole ceremony inside the church building. An exhortation (vernacular exhortations were provided for in the Sarum and York rites) outlined the biblical origins and reasons for marriage, which was now referred to as a holy ordinance rather than a sacrament. The question of impediment, the passive consent, and active vows (with only minor alteration to the medieval wording) were retained, as were also tokens of espousal and the ring. However, the blessing of the ring was transposed to a blessing of the couple, assembled from phraseology from a number of the prayers in the Sarum rite. The priest then joined their right hands and pronounced Matthew 19:6, appropriated from Lutheran rites. Kenneth Stevenson has commented:

> Cranmer follows Luther in using Scripture, but like Calvin (who does not use the short Matthean formula but instead has a reading of the whole passage) he places a prayer for the couple immediately after their consent. In other words, Cranmer is anxious to put the scripture formula from Matt. 19.6 in its proper place, *after* a prayer, not before it, in order to express a Reformed theology of the marriage rite: the couple make their vows, on which the Church prays for divine blessing. And as if to hammer the point home, the priest now declares the couple married, in a formula taken straight from Hermann's *Consultation:* "Forasmuche as N. and N. have consented together. . . . ," but inserting "golde and silver" after the giving of the ring; he ends by "declaring" ("*So spreche ich*" in the German original) that "they be man and

> wyfe together." Only now does the priest actually bless the couple, in a prayer based heavily on a medieval blessing: "God the father blesse you. God the sone kepe you: god the holy gost lighten your understanding . . ."[25]

Stevenson's observations give in a nutshell the conservation and innovation that were blended in this rite.

The second part of the rite begins with Psalm 127, as with Sarum, but with Psalm 67 as an alternative. The prayers that then followed were again crafted from a variety of prayers from the Roman rite. A rubric provided for a Communion service, though no propers were provided. Perhaps the assumption was that clergy would use the propers of Trinity Sunday.

Although in many respects the rites of 1552 represent a radical revision, the marriage rite was little altered. The main alteration was the exclusion of reference to the gold and silver, the tokens of espousal.

The theology of the rite shows Protestant symptoms, and there are dashes of Lutheran liturgical sources; however, the structure and phraseology link the rite with its Roman Catholic antecedent, giving it a conservative character. But alongside the rite was a conservative canon law, a tendency to regard the ordinance as sacramental, and this conservatism was buttressed by social custom. The domestic betrothal, or handfasting, was still popular, and frequently performed in front of a priest. Richard Greenham, vicar of Dry Drayton, Cambridgeshire, provided a formula for this: "I, R., do promise to thee, F., that I will be thine husband, which I will confirm by public manner, in pledge whereof I give thee mine hand. In like manner doth the woman to the man. Then after prayer the parties are dismissed."[26] William Gouge provided a slightly different form: "first the man taking the woman by the hand to say: I A take thee B to my espoused wife, and do faithfully promise to marry thee in time meet and convenient. And then the woman again taking the man by the hand to say: I B take thee A to be my espoused husband and do faithfully promise to yield to be married to thee in time meet and convenient."[27]

At Romford in 1607 the betrothal or handfasting between Richard Harrison and Anne Bayle was witnessed by William Jefferson, who recalled that Harrison said: "Anne, I, before this man, do take thee to my wedded wife, forsaking all other, keeping myself to thee, as long as we both shall live." Anne responded with similar words, and as confirmation or pledge, Harrison gave her a gold coin.[28] Gouge recorded that many made the handfasting "a very marriage, and thereupon have a greater solemnity at their contract than at their marriage."[29] Indeed, as elsewhere in early modern Europe, a powerful cultural current permitted sexual intimacy after betrothal, with the result that pregnant brides were quite common at late-sixteenth-century altars, accounting for between 20 and 30 percent of all brides.[30] In spite of the fact that from 1552 the reference to tokens of espousal was dropped, as late as 1590 in some parts of Lancashire some clergy continued the practice of laying down sums of money in the service as an endowment, and also the practice of transposing the ring from finger to finger at the several names of the Father, the Son, and the Holy Spirit.[31] And although no provision was made for blessing the bread and wine, and the bed, the bride cup, bride cakes and sops in wine were customary, and wedding parties still escorted bride and groom to bed. Cressy notes, "Notoriously the air was filled with sexual jokes and commendations. The bed itself might be flower-strewn, 'decked with ribbons and scented with violets and essence of jasmine,' if anyone had taken the trouble."[32] The new husband and wife were given a drink of fortified wine, and stockings were thrown at them. Protestant reform may have deprived them of a sacral bed blessing, but the liturgical vacuum was more than filled by social custom.

The diversity found in French diocesan rituals has already been noted in discussing medieval rites. Molin and Mutembe grouped them around two models: the Norman model, found not only in Normandy but also in northwestern and western France, where the juridical aspect is predominant; and the southern model, found not only in the south but also in northeast France from Champagne to Alsace, where the sacramental predominates.[33] In the Norman model the vows were pledged at the door of the church, and free consent was given before the joining of hands. In the southern model the whole took place inside the church, and the joining of hands preceded consent. In some books provision was given for the blessing of two rings, and sometimes included Matthew 19:6, exorcisms to ensure fertility, and the drinking of a common cup. Some standardization was attempted in the *Liber Sacerdotalis* of Castello in 1523, and this book was quite popular in Italy and France. In theory the various rituals and customs were brought into some sort of conformity with the Tridentine declaration on marriage, *Tametsi*. The decree was concerned to ensure the public celebration of marriage and a certain reverence. A valid Catholic marriage must be made with an exchange of vows before a priest who sealed it with the words "I join you together in matrimony . . ." or some equivalent. The Tridentine missal provided a Nuptial Mass of the Roman type, thus replacing votive Masses of the Trinity formerly found in the Sarum and Scandinavian rites. Cardinal Santori was charged with the task of producing a new *Rituale,* and a draft version appeared in 1583 in a *Sacerdotale Romanum.* The marriage rite was an interesting and lengthy combination of various usages. However, in 1614 the *Rituale Romanum* was issued, giving an extremely brief normative minimum. It consisted of passive vows, similar to those in the 1523 *Liber Sacerdotalis,* the declaration by the priest, the blessing of the ring, and brief preces. Catholic clergy, no less than Protestant ministers, found the lewdness that accompanied the blessing of the bed reason to suppress the rite. However, a rubric lifted from the *Tametsi* decree noted: "Moreover, if, besides the above, some provinces are accustomed to using other laudable customs and ceremonies in the celebration of the sacrament of matrimony, the holy Council of Trent desires that they should be retained."

In France at least this was taken at face value, and diocesan rituals with local customs continued. Some provided for the popular betrothal ceremony with the drinking of the cup, the use of the pall or veil, and the blessing of the bedchamber. The Ritual of Coutances, for example, provided a rite of betrothal, the marriage vows, blessing of the ring, and coins, blessing of the couple, Mass blessing, use of the pall or veil, blessing of the bridal chamber, as well as prayers for undoing witchcraft.[34] The betrothal, as in England, was often regarded as more important than the church ceremony, which was merely ratification. Andre Burguière notes that an exchange of some goods, sealed with a drink, was often deemed sufficient.[35] Judging from the prohibitions, the custom of sexual intimacy after betrothal seems to have been common.[36] The *Rituale* of Chartres, 1689, instructed the priest to bless the marriage bed only in the presence of the parents of the newlyweds and two or three persons of venerable age. It added: "He will admonish the spouses and all those present that they must not engage in laughter or unseemly banter, nor by any illicit and profane behavior . . . appear to pollute the sanctity of holy matrimony in any manner whatsoever."[37] In 1657 the ecclesiastical judge of the diocese of Paris sent out a letter condemning several superstitions, insults, and acts of violence committed by the young bachelors of the village of Montrouge when marriages were celebrated in the church, stating that "they continue these insults at the time of the blessing of the marriage bed and that, on the day after the celebration of the marriage, they capture the newlyweds and to that effect lead them . . . to a shallow pond at the edge of the village, force her to genuflect and even make her drink the water of the said pond, to dip into it and then to kiss the doors and entryways of nearby houses and [to engage in] other actions marked by paganism."[38] The 1677 *Rituale de la province de Reim* noted: "Parish priests are exhorted to display a great deal of seriousness in all ceremonies connected with marriage, to keep those present within the bounds of modesty, and, above all, to prevent anything secular and contrary to the holiness of the place and the sacrament of marriage from being done in the church; for example, presents and gifts are not to be given to the newlyweds there, nor are traveling entertainers, fiddlers, and other such folk to be brought in on the excuse of providing joyous music."[39]

Clerical prohibitions witness to what popularly took place, and most laity have always, wisely, ignored such prohibitions. Thus, although in many places the austere rite of the *Rituale Romanum* replaced more exuberant medieval rites, in France at least, we find considerable conservation of the traditional rites, and the secular customs that accompanied them. Of the rites in four different traditions that have been surveyed, it emerges that in the English, Swedish and French rites we find the most continuity in terms of the medieval liturgical antecedents. Even though Cranmer jettisoned the blessing of the bed and propers for a Nuptial Mass, the rite he provided conserved much of what was familiar to English parishioners. Luther marks a break with the tradition, though his evangelical provisions mirror that part of the German rites which were most frequently used. Calvin was lazy in liturgy, and simply reimposed or ratified Farel's 1533 rite. Thus he conserved what he found in use almost in its entirety. However, Farel's rite itself drew on various earlier Reformed rites from elsewhere, and thus was a complete innovation in Geneva.

All the rites show the concern of the medieval canon lawyers regarding what constitutes a valid marriage. This was a major preoccupation, not only from a concern for Christian morality, but also a social one, affecting questions of legitimacy and inheritance. Hence we find an emphasis on the public exchange of vows. Yet the custom of domestic betrothal was deep, and it continued regardless of the concern for public marriage vows. In popular secular minds, the betrothal was as good as marriage. Thus we find Luther's discussion about the tense of the verb in the German language, a religious form provided by Richard Greenham and the rite of Coutances, and the vow in the Genevan rite looking back to the betrothal. The diversity between active and passive vows of the pre-Reformation period continued in the post-Reformation traditions. In England both forms were incorporated—passive for consent, active for the vow. In the latter Cranmer brought a polish to the inherited English form, a liturgical masterpiece given to the English-speaking world.[40] But the continued popular understanding that betrothal and handfasting were as good as ecclesiastical marriage was a reminder that the Church was in fact a guest at something that is as old as human society.

Alongside ecclesiastical reforms, Catholic and Protestant, the force of social custom insisted on retaining rituals and customs beyond the official liturgical provisions. The sixteenth and seventeenth centuries witness to a puritanical moral streak amongst clergy, Catholic and Protestant, which regarded raw sexuality as alien to the more serious and more spiritual concerns of a marriage liturgy. Activities associated with blessing the bed were regarded as beyond the pale, and they were either condemned or, in most Reformation rites, the liturgical ceremony was suppressed. If the clergy and authorities thought that would end the matter, they were wrong. The bed ceremony with lewd songs and bawdy behavior simply took on a secular life of its own. The risqué jokes about the "wedding night," so common at wedding receptions, remind us that perhaps raw sexuality is, after all, part of what marriage is about.

Notes

1. A. Baumstark, *Comparative Liturgy* (London: A. R. Mowbray, 1958), 27ff.

2. See G. G. Willis, *Essays in Early Roman Liturgy* (London: SPCK, 1964), 1–48; and P. De Clerck, *La prière universelle dans les liturgies Latines anciennes: Témoignages Patristiques et textes liturgiques* (Munster: Aschendorff, 1977).

3. Susan Karant-Nunn, *The Reformation of Ritual: An Interpretation of Early Modern Germany* (London: Routledge, 1997), for Germany; and David Cressy, *Birth, Marriage and Death: Ritual, Religion, and the Life Cycle in Tudor and Stuart England* (Oxford: Oxford University Press, 1997), for England.

4. For an overall survey, Kenneth Stevenson, *Nuptial Blessing* (London: Alcuin Club/SPCK, 1982).

5. John Witte, *From Sacrament to Contract* (Louisville, Ky.: Westminster/John Knox Press, 1997).

6. The failure to recognize this, as well as other cavalier generalizations about the premodern and early modern periods, is one of the glaring flaws in methodology in Catherine Pickstock, *After Writing: On the Liturgical Consummation of Philosophy* (Oxford: Blackwell, 1998). The arbitrary reading of history is emerging as a major Achilles' heel in that movement that styles itself "Radical Orthodoxy," but which perhaps is more appropriately called Postmodern Romanticism.

7. Jean-Baptiste Molin and Protais Mutembe, *Le rituel du mariage en France du XII au XVI siecle* (Paris: Beauchesne, 1973).

8. See John K. Leonard, "Rites of Marriage in the Western Middle Ages," in Lizette Larson-Miller, ed., *Medieval Liturgy: A Book of Essays* (New York: Garland, 1997), 165–202, for a good summary.

9. Lyndal Roper, "Going to Church and Street: Weddings in Reformation Augsburg," *Past and Present* 106 (1985): 62–101, esp. 71.

10. *LW* 36: 92.

11. *LW* 36: 97.

12. "On Marriage Matters," 1530. *LW* 46: 274.

13. *LW* 53: 111.

14. See Stevenson, *Nuptial Blessing,* 88–91; also Bryan D. Spinks, "Luther's Other Major Liturgical Reforms: 3. The Traubüchlein," *Liturgical Review* 10 (1980): 33–38.

15. Pamela Biel, "Let the Fiancées Beware: Luther, the Lawyers and Betrothal in Sixteenth Century Saxony," in Bruce Gordon, ed., *Protestant History and Identity in Sixteenth Century Europe* (Aldershot: Scolar Press, 1996), 121–58.

16. Karant-Nunn, *Reformation of Ritual,* 20–21.

17. See Karant-Nunn, *Reformation of Ritual,* and Roper, "Going to Church and Street."

18. E. E. Yelverton, *The Manual of Olavus Petri 1529* (London: SPCK, 1953). Also Bryan D. Spinks, "Adiaphora: Marriage and Funeral Liturgies," *Concordia Theological Quarterly* 62 (1998): 7–23.

19. François Huot, *Les manuscrits liturgiques du canon de Genève* (Fribourg: Editions Universitaires, 1990), 331.

20. Bryan D. Spinks, "The Liturgical Origins and Theology of Calvin's Genevan Marriage Rite," *Ecclesia Orans* 3 (1986): 195–210.

21. Jeffrey Watt, "The Marriage Laws Calvin Drafted for Geneva," in Wilhelm H. Neuser ed., *Calvinus Sacrae Scripturae Professor* (Grand Rapids, Mich.: Eerdmans, 1994), 245–55.

22. Witte, *From Sacrament to Contract.*

23. See E. William Monter, "Women in Calvinist Geneva (1550–1800)," "The Consistory of Geneva 1559–1569," and "Crime and Punishment in Calvin's Geneva, 1562," in *Enforcing Morality in Early Modern Europe* (London: Variorum Reprints, 1987).

24. Witte, *From Sacrament to Contract,* 131.

25. Stevenson, *Nuptial Blessing,* 137.

26. Cressy, *Birth, Marriage and Death,* 269.

27. Quoted in Mary Abbott, *Life Cycles in England 1560–1720* (London and New York: Routledge, 1996), 107.

28. Cited in ibid., 106.

29. Cressy, *Birth, Marriage and Death,* 271. Handfasting was still common in England until it was (in theory) suppressed by Hardwicke's Act in 1753. For Scotland see James Scott Marshall, "Irregular Marriage in Scotland as Reflected in Kirk Session Records," *Records of the Scottish Church History Society* 18 (1974): 10–25.

30. Eric Carlson, *Marriage and the English Reformation* (Oxford: Blackwell, 1994), 131.

31. Cressy, *Birth, Marriage and Death,* 344.

32. Ibid., 374.

33. Molin and Mutembe, *Le Rituel du mariage.*

34. Text in Searle and Stevenson, *Documents of the Marriage Liturgy* (Collegeville, Minn.: Liturgical Press, 1992).

35. "The Marriage Ritual in France: Ecclesiastical Practices and Popular Practices (Sixteenth to Eighteenth Centuries)," in R. Forster and O. Ranum, eds., *Ritual, Religion, and the Sacred,* vol.7 (Baltimore: Johns Hopkins University Press, 1982), 8–23, esp. 16.

36. Ibid., 19.

37. Ibid.

38. Ibid., 20.

39. Cited in A. G. Martimort, *The Church at Prayer* (Collegeville, Minn.: Liturgical Press, 1988), 3: 201.

40. K. W. Stevenson, "Cranmer's Marriage Vow: Its Place in the Tradition," in P. Ayris and D. Selwyn, eds., *Thomas Cranmer: Churchman and Scholar* (Woodbridge: Boydell Press, 1993), 189–98, 196.

Visual and Musical Dimensions

The Art of Devotion in Haarlem Before and After the Introduction of Calvinism

HENRY LUTTIKHUIZEN

Editors' Introduction

Iconoclasm is one of the most famous aspects of discontinuity in Calvinist liturgical reforms. Yet what is often presented as a simple story of smashing images and removing relics was at times the result of a complex interplay of social, political, and religious dynamics. In this essay, Henry Luttikhuizen chronicles the process of image removal in Haarlem, one of the leading cities in the Calvinist Netherlands. In doing so, he teaches us that the seemingly simple discontinuity between churches full of images prior to the Reformation and bare and empty churches afterward is not the whole story. Instead, some images were retained, both in the churches of Haarlem and in civic buildings, though the official purpose of the images changed from being a source of veneration to being mainly decorative or illustrating the city's glorious past.

Luttikhuizen's contribution reminds us that a range of factors determined the use of visual art in worship in the medieval and early modern periods, including religious motivations but also issues of prestige and appropriateness of location. Thus some of the images that were retained in Haarlem's main churches were kept not for purposes of veneration but rather to highlight significant moments in Haarlem's civic history. In the end the pattern of retention versus removal of art in Haarlem reflects continuing dynamics of social relations among the city's elite as much as it does confessional change.

Note: There is no primary sources introduction for this contribution, as the primary sources in this case are images that are integrated into the text.

During the late sixteenth century, Catholic churches in the Netherlands were confiscated by Calvinists and transformed into places appropriate for Reformed worship. Interiors were often whitewashed and stripped bare of images. Sanctified and cleansed, altered churches could now serve as ideal settings for the presentation of God's Word. Not surprisingly, these places of worship were often lauded for their purity. For example, in 1628 the Calvinist preacher and civic chronicler Samuel Ampzing praised the Grote Kerk or Great Church, for its pristine harmony. Also known as Saint Bavokerk, the Grote Kerk once served as the cathedral of Haarlem and was the largest church in Holland. Ampzing, however, does not call attention to the building's heroic scale. Rather he lauds it as a beautiful place for preaching. Consider his remarks about the church's interior:

> Here you are led into the inside of our church,
> As elegant a creation as your eyes have ever seen,
> Yes, if they can see, give your gaze its fill,
> Revel, delight your heart in looking at this building.
>
> Aye, see how the parts grow out of each other!
> Aye, see how the parts fit each other!
> The piers, the vault, the arches, all the rest,
> The wood, the stone, the brass work, they are all the best!
>
> Indeed, this is quite considerable and not to be despised:
> But because we practice there God's holy service,
> And also His word is taught there sound and pure,
> For that this church is rightly and mostly honored.[1]

Upon reading these stanzas, it is tempting to assume that Calvinism effectively erased the late medieval art of devotion. But as we shall see, this was not the case. Ampzing may have praised the interior decoration of Saint Bavokerk in terms of its design and the quality of its materials, but he failed to mention that visual images remained in the church long after its conversion for Reformed worship. The relationship between art and devotion in Haarlem, before and after the introduction of Calvinism, was more complicated and nuanced than the words of Ampzing suggest. Calvinist iconoclasts may have advocated a radical break from the late medieval use of devotional images, but in many ways, visual images continued to play a positive role in Calvinist worship.

Interpreting the role of visual images in late medieval devotion, however, is not an easy task. For instance, many of the altarpieces that were once displayed in Dutch church interiors are now exhibited in museums and galleries. Although relocation has helped preserve these paintings, it also has unfortunately removed them from their locus of meaning. Presented primarily as objects for aesthetic delight, these altarpieces are seldom recognized as tools made for religious purposes. If we are to understand the power of altarpieces beyond their initial aesthetic appeal, then we need to be willing to confront them in a manner that acknowledges the importance of their original setting. Not only must we consider such paintings within their respective ecclesiastical sites, but we also need to discover how people received them within those architectural settings. Understanding liturgical art, regardless of whether it is a lectern, stained glass window, organ shutters, or an altarpiece, demands a thoughtful consideration of the audience for whom such art was made. In this essay we will examine works of art from two of the most important ecclesiastical sites in Haarlem, the Grote Kerk and the Commandery of Sint Jan, a religious house of the Hospitallers, in hopes of better understanding the function of art in late medieval and Calvinist devotion.

Constructed during the fifteenth century, the Grote Kerk was furnished with numerous altarpieces. Unfortunately, none of the fifteenth-century altarpieces produced for Saint Bavokerk remains. Not every panel painting, however, was destroyed. An anonymous painting of the church's exterior, once attributed to Geertgen tot Sint Jans, still hangs above the entrance of the Chapel of the Holy Ghost.[2] In addition, organ shutters painted by Vrederic Hoon in 1465 survived until the eighteenth century.[3] It is somewhat surprising that the organ shutters remained in the church after the Calvinist alteration, for they depict the Resurrection of Christ. Perhaps it was believed that the image was removed far enough away from the altar to keep worshipers from practicing idolatry.

Even though sculpted figures were removed from the church's columns and grillwork, a brass lectern representing a pelican, produced by Jan Fierens in 1498–99, survived.[4] The iconography of this lectern is unusual. Typically, lecterns are cast in the shape of an open-winged eagle, symbolizing Saint John the Evangelist, whose Gospel appropriately enough starts with the phrase, "In the beginning was the Word." The pelican, however, can also serve as a fitting symbol for the presentation of Christ, for like Christ, the bird offers its own blood so that its children may live. The iconography of the decorated lectern likely seemed too symbolic and abstract to entice false worship. Besides, the risk of treating a lectern as an object of veneration may have been too small to raise concerns.

Early Netherlandish devotional images commonly blurred the distinction between the visual and visionary, between eyesight and insight.[5] This posed great problems for Calvinists, who did not believe that visual images could help localize the divine, and may have encouraged them to destroy late medieval altarpieces, devotional sculptures, and even stained glass windows. For instance, in the westwork windows of Saint Bavokerk, the donor of the stained glass, Joris van Egmond, the bishop of Utrecht, was depicted with the Holy Trinity.[6] Consider this example. The windows, based on designs by the Flemish artist Bernard van Orley, revealed not only the patron's wealth, prestige, and presumed piety, they also revealed his desire to imitate, reenact, and participate in mystical visions. By extension, the windows also provided a model for pious observers to imitate as they sought for God. Not surprisingly, these windows were replaced after the conversion of Saint Bavokerk for Reformed worship.

Around 1485, the knightly monks at the nearby Commandery of Sint Jan asked Geertgen tot Sint Jans, a lay member of their order, to paint a large altarpiece for the high altar of the commandery's chapel. This painting was one of the largest triptychs of its day, measuring approximately six by twenty feet when opened (see figures 10.1 and 10.2). Its impressive scale, complex iconography, and vivid naturalism reinforced late medieval devotion. On the inner panels Geertgen depicted scenes from Christ's Passion, and on the exterior panels he painted the two martyrdoms of Saint John the Baptist: his beheading and the burning of his bones in the fourth century.[7] Geertgen's altarpiece served many interrelated religious functions. It helped reinforce late medieval devotional beliefs and practices, including monasticism, mystical experience, the affirmation of Christ's "real presence" in the Eucharist, and the veneration of relics.[8]

Geertgen's altarpiece was not a liturgical necessity, as the altar could function without it. After all, the ritual on the altar is directed not at the image but at the Host. Altarpieces do not consecrate their settings, for they

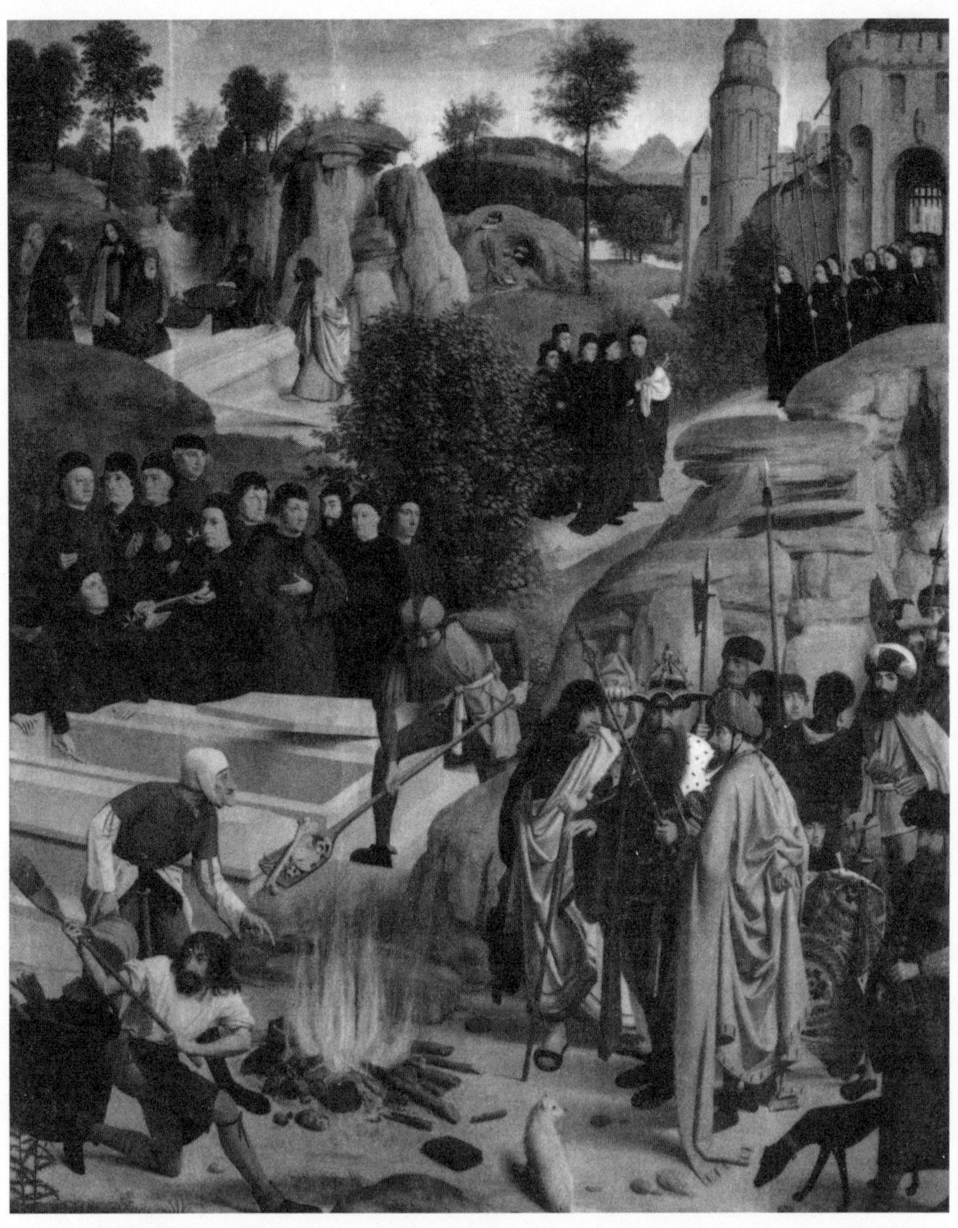

10.1. Geertgen tot Sint Jans, *The Burning of the Bones of St. John the Baptist*. Exterior of the right wing of the *Altarpiece for the Haarlem Jansheren*. Circa 1485. Oil on panel. Courtesy of the Kunsthistorisches Museum, Vienna.

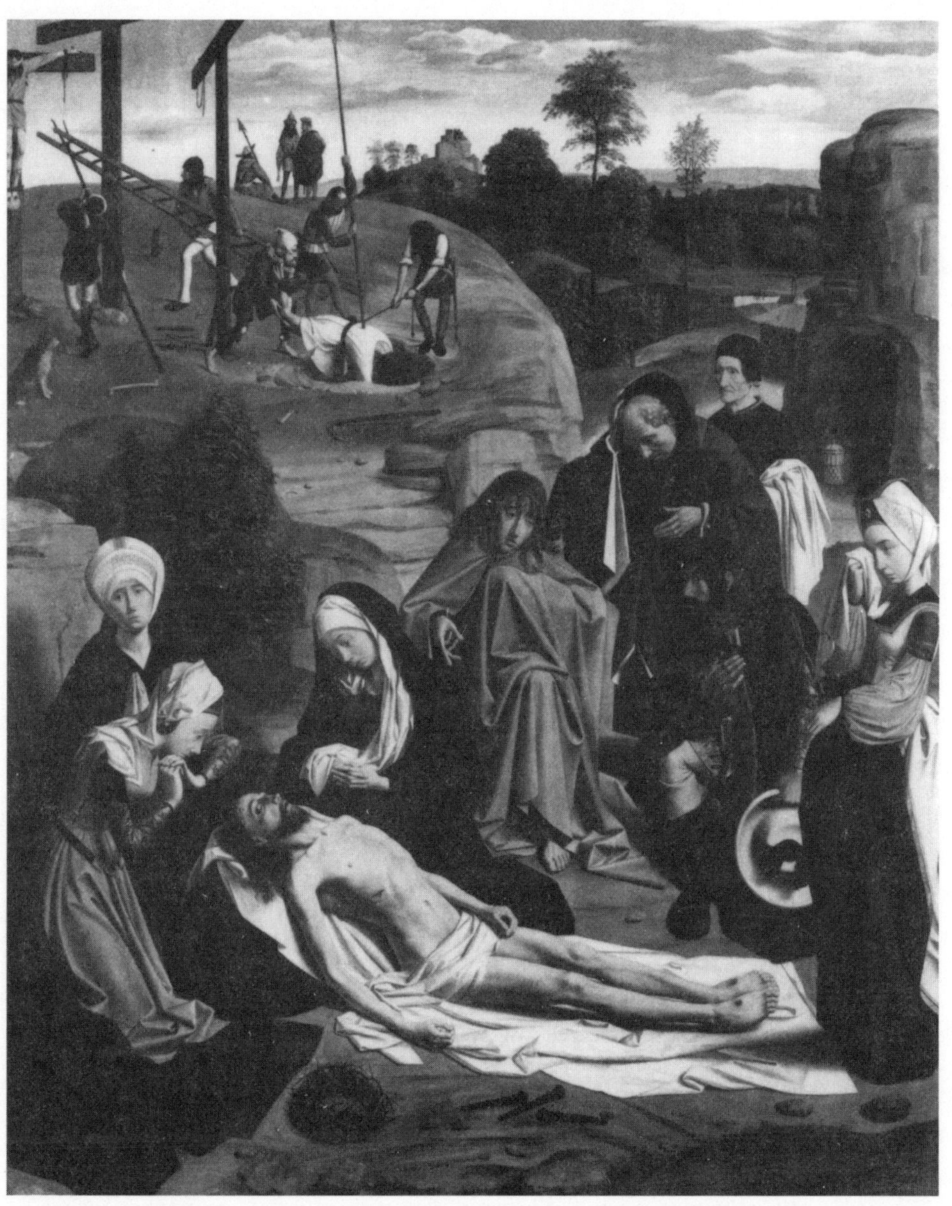

10.2. Geertgen tot Sint Jans, *The Lamentation*. Interior of the right wing of the *Altarpiece for the Haarlem Jansheren*. Circa 1485. Oil on panel. Courtesy of the Kunsthistorisches Museum, Vienna.

are located in areas that are already holy sites, sacred places where the miracle of transubstantiation can occur. In other words, altarpieces do not sanctify churches. On the contrary, they become potentially sacred by entering into a liturgical context.[9] Although altarpieces are supplementary to the altar, they provided ample opportunities for revealing what happens on and above the table, namely, the presentation of Christ's Body and Blood. Disclosing the realm of grace and the means of salvation, images such as Geertgen's triptych helped persuade beholders of the presence of Christ as it called them to partake in the Eucharist.[10]

The intense naturalism of this painting serves a rhetorical function, helping to persuade viewers of the presence of the divine in the here and now. It makes the transcendent appear immanent and accessible to human experience. By unveiling sacred events in a believable commonplace, spectators and saints can meet one another and encounter God. The vivid naturalism in Geertgen's painting is analogous to the detailed descriptions found in contemporary devotional literature. It did not simply record Christian sentiments; it gave structure and direction to religious experience. The altarpiece promoted piety by fostering meditative empathy. Observers are drawn to tears as they witness saints lamenting the death of Christ.[11]

The exterior panel representing the burning of Saint John the Baptist's saintly remains shows the fifteenth-century patrons mystically salvaging his bones before the fourth-century henchmen of Julian the Apostate got a chance to burn them. Geertgen's painting likely commemorates the translation of these relics to Rhodes. Nonetheless, the panel also provided devout viewers opportunities to become intimate with the bones of the Baptist through mystical contemplation. In a sense, the power of Geertgen's altarpiece is analogous to the Stations of the Cross, which allow participants to retrace the steps of Christ's Passion without setting foot in the Holy Land. It offered viewers in Haarlem a vehicle for taking meditational pilgrimages to Palestine and Rhodes.[12]

This is not to say that the altarpiece was ever considered to be a miraculous image. Judging from existing records, Geertgen's triptych never bled or shed tears. No one was ever reported to have been healed or protected simply by gazing at it. In fact, there is no evidence that one could receive an indulgence by venerating the altarpiece. Nonetheless, like most religious images, Geertgen's painting potentially makes present what it shows; it apparently localizes the divine.[13]

The knightly monks in Haarlem also housed devotional paintings by Geertgen, including a picture of their patron saint Saint John the Baptist and a depiction of the Holy Kinship. Like Geertgen's altarpiece, these smaller paintings also encouraged viewers to become intimate with the sacred figures and events depicted by evoking an empathetic response.[14]

During the sixteenth century the Commandery of Sint Jan continued to collect devotional paintings. Around 1530 it commissioned Jan van Scorel to paint two paintings, one of the Baptism of Christ and another of Mary Magdalene (see figures 10.3 and 10.4). In addition, it owned at least five devotional paintings by van Scorel's pupil, Maarten van Heemskerck. The Italianate character of these works reveals how much the aesthetic taste of the knightly monks had changed since the time of Geertgen tot Sint Jans. Jan van Scorel was a very prestigious artist in the northern Netherlands, for earlier in his career, the painter had worked for the Dutch pope Adrian VI in Rome. Despite their Italianate appearance, his paintings and those of van Heemskerck continued to reinforce late medieval devotional beliefs and practices at the Haarlem commandery.[15]

At Saint Bavokerk, Maarten van Heemskerck produced an altarpiece for the chapel of the Drapers' Guild in 1546. When the wings of the triptych were closed, the Annunciation could be seen, and when opened, the Adoration of the Shepherds was revealed.[16] As moments within Christ's infancy cycle, both narratives call attention to the Incarnation and were frequently depicted in altarpieces to affirm the real presence of Christ in the sacrament of the Mass.

In 1561 the Grote Kerk of Haarlem became a cathedral. Five years later, however, iconoclasm broke out across the northern Netherlands. In the late summer and autumn of 1566, Calvinists destroyed numerous works of art in churches and monasteries throughout the Netherlands in a war against idolatry.[17] Paintings and sculptures that promoted the localization of the divine were at odds with Reformed notions regarding the transcendence of God and consequently were attacked. After all, Calvinists stressed that attempts to pinpoint God's place on earth detracted from God's divinity by imprisoning God in the works of human hands. Furthermore, works of art commissioned by monks would have been particularly suspect, for Calvin and his followers rejected not only the use of liturgical art but also the practice of monasticism as a calling. Not only was the vow of celibacy deemed impossible to carry out, it seemed to contradict God's cultural mandate to be fruitful and multiply. Paintings housed in the commandery, however, were spared. They may have violated the religious sensibilities of Dutch Calvinists, but they remained intact.

Compared with other cities in the region, Haarlem's churches and monasteries suffered little damage. The Catholic majority in Haarlem vastly outnumbered the Calvinist minority and may have encouraged Reformed Christians to be more tolerant toward Catholic practices. In addition, civic magistrates exercised their authority to prevent destruction. The threat posed by iconoclasm was minimal. In fact, less than a decade after the *beeldenstorm,* the Bakers' Guild of Haarlem commissioned Pieter Pietersz. to paint

10.3 . Jan van Scorel, *The Baptism of Christ*. Circa 1528. Oil on panel. Courtesy of the Frans Halsmuseum, Haarlem.

an altarpiece, *Three Men in the Fiery Furnace,* for its chapel in Saint Bavokerk (see figure 10.5).[18] According to the Book of Daniel, Shadrach, Meshach, and Abednego were condemned to the furnace for their refusal to worship the monumental golden image of King Nebuchadnezzar, but God miraculously intervened, saving the three men from certain death. Although some may find it tempting to interpret Pietersz.'s painting as a sympathetic response to iconoclasm, this is highly unlikely. Instead, the altarpiece probably reinforced the traditional distinction between Christian images and pagan idols as it revealed to pious observers the means of their redemption. Besides, the story of the fiery furnace is easily associated with the vocation of baking and could readily direct attention to the guild that commissioned the work. There are no records indicating any objections to the use of Pietersz.'s altarpiece as a liturgical aid.

10.4. Jan van Scorel, *Mary Magdalene*. Circa 1530. Oil on panel. By permission of the Rijksmuseum, Amsterdam.

Although most devotional images in Haarlem were defended from the iconoclastic attacks of Calvinists, they were not protected from Spanish soldiers, who besieged the city from December 1572 to July 1573. Many liturgical items in Saint Bavokerk were stolen; others, such as the central panel of van Heemkerck's altarpiece for the Drapers' Guild, were destroyed. On April 2, 1573, troops stormed the Commandery of Sint Jan, destroying many works of art. Only the right wing, front and reverse, of Geertgen's altarpiece survived the attack. The Siege of Haarlem was directed at the city, which supported the Dutch rebels and the authority of the House of Orange. Nonetheless, the commandery was not spared, despite its loyalty to the Grand

10.5. Pieter Pietersz., *Three Men in the Fiery Furnace*. 1575. Oil on panel. Courtesy of the Frans Halsmuseum, Haarlem.

Master of their religious order and the ardent Catholicism of the king of Spain Philip II, and of his military leader, Don Fernando de Alvarez de Toledo, otherwise known as the Duke of Alva. The remains of Geertgen's altarpiece and other works were transported to the Utrecht Commandery of Sint Jan for safekeeping.

Haarlem was one of the last towns in Holland where Catholic worship was permitted. At the end of the Spanish occupation of the city in January 1577, the Prince of Orange signed a document with the deputies of Haarlem, their bishop Godfried van Mierlo, and the States of Holland agreeing to protect religious communities and granting Catholics the freedom to worship publicly. Less than six months later, however, the States-General gave civic magistrates the right to confiscate the properties of all churches and monasteries within their jurisdiction to help compensate the city for its losses during the Dutch Revolt. A year later, on May 29, 1578, Protestants sacked the Grote Kerk, killed a priest, and demolished the high altar and numerous images within the church. Civic magistrates chose not to intervene, and Catholic masses at Saint Bavokerk were discontinued. In 1581 Haarlem became officially Protestant and Catholic worship was officially banned. The alteration of the Grote Kerk to Reformed worship began. However, two of the church's altarpieces were spared. The remaining panels of Maarten van Heemskerck's altarpiece for the Drapers' Guild were removed and stored at the Prinsenhof in Haarlem as booty. In addition, Pieter Pietersz.'s painting for the Bakers' Guild was relocated to the Commandery of Sint Jan. The cleansing of the temple had begun.

The high altar was replaced by an altar plaque. A text now stood alone where visual images had been venerated. The words of the Lord's Supper were inscribed on the front of the plaque in Dutch, as a reference to the sacrament of Communion. The reverse of the plaque was also printed with words. The text, however, was extrabiblical. In fact, it described a civic legend concerning how Haarlem had acquired its coat of arms.[19] According to the tale, a Haarlem warship heroically defeated the Egyptian city of Damiate on the Nile River during the Second Crusade. As a reward for this act of bravery, Emperor Frederick II offered the city four stars and a silver sword, and the Patriarch of Jerusalem gave Haarlem a cross. The four stars, silver sword, and cross all appear on the city's coat of arms.[20]

During the alteration the westwork windows were also replaced. The representation of the Holy Trinity violated the Calvinist prohibition against depicting God, for the infinite could not be contained in the finite. In addition, the donor portrait of Joris van Egmond, a Catholic bishop, was not acceptable for a Reformed church. Consequently, around 1585 it was removed in exchange for a scene representing the acquisition of the Haarlem escutcheon.[21]

Patriotic images promoting civic pride were introduced into Saint Bavokerk, soon after devotional images for Catholic veneration were eliminated.

When civic magistrates confiscated the monasteries of Haarlem, one confraternity refused to comply. Citing allegiance to the Grand Master of its order, the Haarlem commander of the knightly brotherhood of Sint Jan claimed that city officials had no authority to take its property. Civic leaders appealed to the States-General to intervene, but the leaders of the new republic, concerned with diplomatic ramifications, refused. Interpreting the power of the Grand Master to be analogous to that of a secular prince, the States-General sided with the monks of Sint Jan. In 1582, however, the magistrates were able to negotiate an agreement with the confraternity's commander. Under this contract, the knightly brotherhood was not allowed to induct new members but was permitted to remain open until the death of its last surviving member.[22] The commander probably agreed to these terms for two reasons. Most likely, he believed that the political climate could change for the better prior to the last brother's death; and second, he wanted to rebuild the commandery, which suffered extensive damage in the Spanish siege, as soon as possible. In 1595 the commandery was able to reopen even though the city of Haarlem remained under Protestant control. Works of art preserved in Utrecht, including the right wing of Geertgen's triptych and paintings by Jan van Scorel, were probably returned to the commandery in that same year, shortly after the agreement was signed.

Although the commandery's chapel was rebuilt around the turn of the century, it no longer housed Geertgen's altarpiece. The surviving panels were relocated to the commandery's *grote zaal,* its great hall.[23] This new placement may have reminded viewers of the commandery's glorious past as it suggested the knightly brotherhood's right to govern itself, free from the tyranny of either the Spanish monarch or the civic magistrates. Members of the confraternity may have also continued to venerate the image, as a substitute for their patron saint's relics, in hopes of divine intervention, to protect the commandery from further damage and restore its previously held authority.

During the late sixteenth century, thousands of Flemish Calvinists immigrated to Holland, and many of them settled in Haarlem. Nonetheless, Haarlem continued to maintain a Catholic majority throughout the seventeenth century. Haarlem Catholics may not have been able to worship publicly or function as civil servants. However, they were able to maintain positions of authority within the city's charitable houses and guilds. Magistrates may have been Calvinists, but many of them had Catholic relatives and friends. Although civic life in Haarlem was not always harmonious, its citizens were able to negotiate enough religious tolerance to ensure economic growth and political stability. Catholic artists even received municipal commissions.[24]

In the early 1590s, Cornelis Cornelisz. van Haarlem completed four paintings for one of the buildings in the Stadhuis or town hall complex, namely the Prinsenhof, where members of the House of Orange would reside while in Haarlem. One of these works, a large triptych, included restored panels from Maarten van Heemskerck's altarpiece for the Drapers' Guild. The central panel of this painting, produced by Cornelisz. van Haarlem's hand, was quite heroic in scale, nearly five-foot square, and represented the Massacre of the Innocents. Although a depiction of the Nativity would have been more appropriate for an altarpiece, this altered triptych was no longer a liturgical image for Catholic veneration. There was no need to promote Marian piety or advocate the real presence of Christ in the Sacrament. In fact, a representation of the Nativity would have been problematic and would have likely clashed with Calvinist doctrine.[25] The triptych, after all, was located in a secular context, a temporary residence for royalty with loyalties to the Reformed Church. A painting of the Massacre of the Innocents, however, was quite fitting for the Prinsenhof. Interpreted allegorically, the image could easily point to injustices of a Herod-like king during the Spanish siege against the innocent Dutch.

Although the triptych may have had strong political connotations, this is not to say, however, that the work was simply an object of veneration in some kind of civil religion. Dutch Calvinists did not pray or light candles in front of the painting. Nonetheless, it may have reminded observers, Catholic and Protestant viewers with access to the *Prinsenhof,* of those who died in the war for Dutch independence.[26] Furthermore, because the painting had religious connotations often associated with Catholic devotion, one can easily imagine both Catholics and Calvinists, in opposition to Reformed principles, silently venerating the image by meditating on the life of Christ as they viewed the Massacre.

When the last member of the Haarlem Commandery of Sint Jan died in 1625, all properties, including the art collection, were turned over to the city. The magistrates kept late medieval devotional images, such as Jan van Scorel's *Mary Magdalene* and Pieter Pietersz.'s *Three Men in a Fiery Furnace,* which did not offend Calvinist religious beliefs and placed them in the Prinsenhof, apparently to celebrate the long tradition of painting in Haarlem. Some images, such as the surviving panels from Geertgen's altarpiece, however, violated Reformed convictions, for they represented extrabiblical events as sacred scenes and falsely promoted the localization of the divine. No longer enchanted by the altarpiece's presentation of Christian piety, the Haarlem magistrates labeled the image idolatrous. Like the iconoclasts of 1566, the civic authorities of 1625 wanted to eradicate the presence of Geertgen's false image. However, unlike their predecessors, the magistrates recognized the economic value of such imagery. Consequently, they sold Geertgen's panels, but this also posed an ethical problem. To cleanse their hands of the "dirty money" made from the sale of Geertgen's idol, the magistrates likely used the income *ad pios usos,* for pious uses, such as paying the salaries of Reformed ministers.[27]

During the 1620s, some Calvinists in Haarlem continued the call to purify the city of false worship, complaining about the "public idols" still found in area churches.[28] Although objects of veneration were often placed under attack, this did not stop Catholics from wearing crucifixes or rosary beads. Nor did it keep them from believing in the power of images. During the last days of December 1627, miraculous images were said to have been found in the cross-section of an apple tree branch cut down in the countryside just outside of Haarlem. The miraculous images included two violins, four nuns, a priest, and a monk. The following year an anonymous etching was circulated to promote the sacred discovery.

Needless to say, Calvinists had their doubts about the miraculous nature of this occurrence, and in response they published an illustrated broadsheet entitled "Out of Love for the Truth," challenging the validity of the event. The broadsheet does not deny the appearance of these figures within the cross-section of the branch. On the contrary, it argues that this is common phenomenon. Pieter Saenredam's illustrations of cross-sections affirm the apparent regularity with which these images occur. For Calvinists, the miracle of the apple tree was bogus: it was just another act of superstition threatening to mislead the spiritually weak. Simply put, the figures seen in the tree were nothing special. They could be easily recognized in numerous apple tree branches.[29]

Calvinists frequently described Catholic worship in terms of idolatry and viewed it as a contamination of the pure and true religion of the early Church, which incidentally was believed to be imageless. They did not consider Reformed worship something new. On the contrary, Calvinists saw it as a return to the beginnings of Christianity. As we have seen, sometimes this apparent restoration of orthodox worship was intertwined with patriotic zeal. For example, in his description of Haarlem, Dominee Ampzing even suggested that true Christianity was preached in the Netherlands during or shortly after the age of the apostles and therefore, was older than the papacy.[30]

The actions of Reformed iconoclasts and Spanish soldiers may have made it difficult to reconstruct the history of liturgical art in the northern Netherlands. The city of Haarlem, however, was one of the most tolerant cities in Holland in regard to Catholic practices. And yet one of the main reasons why more late medieval images survived in Haarlem than elsewhere in the northern Netherlands is that knightly monks from the Commandery of Sint Jan worked hard to preserve them.

During the late sixteenth century, the interior of Saint Bavo may have been cleansed of its Catholic altars and altarpieces. But it was never as pristine as Samuel Ampzing suggested. Some late medieval images, such as organ shutters and a choir lectern remained. In addition, works introduced by Calvinists, including the altar plaque and redesigned windows, may not have served as objects of veneration. Nonetheless, they promoted closer intimacy between the Reformed Church, the city government, and God.[31] Although Calvinists in Haarlem challenged the use of liturgical images to communicate the presence of the divine, they seem to have continued to advocate the localization of the divine through the use of sacred inscriptions and civic iconography.

Notes

1. Hier word u onse Kerk van binnen voorgedragen,
So zierelyk een werk, als oyt uw ogen sagen,
Ja alsze konnen sien! Versadigt uw gesicht,
Vernoegt verlust uw hert door 't sien van dit gesticht.

Ey siet de werken toch eens uyt malkund'ren wassen!
Ey siet de werken toch eens op malkund'ren passen!
De stylen, het verwerf, de bogen, al de rest,
'Thout, steen, en koper-werk is al te mael om best!

Gewis! Dit is vry veel, en niet gering te achten:
Maer dat wy daer voor God syn heyl'gen dienst betrachten,
En datmen dart syn woord gesond en suyver leerd,
Daer door word dese Kerk eerst recht en meest geerd.

From Samuel Ampzing, *Beschryvinge ende lof der stad Haerlem* (Haarlem, 1628), trans. Gary Schwartz and Maarten Jan Bok in *Pieter Saenredam: The Painter and His Time* (New York: Abbeville Press, 1989), 258.

2. E.H. ter Kuile has suggested that the painting served as a "model" of the church and that it was completed by Pieter Gerritsz. in 1518. For more on the work, see E.H. ter Kuile, "Nogs een: De Maquette van de St. Bavo te Haarlem," *Oud Holland* 50 (1933): 132.

3. Josua Bruyn, "Vrederick Hoon anno 1465—Een Haarlemse primitief in effigie in het Rijksmuseum," *Bulletin van het Rijksmuseum* 11 (1963): 31–38.

4. Jeremy Dupertuis Bangs, *Church Art and Architecture in the Low Countries Before 1566* (Kirksville, Mo.: Sixteenth Century Journal Publishers, 1997), 80.

5. For more on early Netherlandish painting and mysticism, see Jeffrey Hamburger, "Visions and the Visionary: The Image in Late Medieval Monastic Devotions," *Viator* 20 (1990): 161–82; Craig Harbison, "Visions and Meditations in Early Flemish

Painting," *Simiolus* 15 (1985): 87–118; and Sixten Ringbom, "Devotional Images and Imaginative Devotions: Notes on the Place of Art in Late Medieval Private Piety," *Gazette des Beaux-Arts* ser. 6, 73 (1969): 159–70.

6. Wouder Th. Kloek, "Northern Netherlandish Art 1580–1620: A Survey," in *Dawn of the Golden Age: Northern Netherlandish Art 1580–1620* (exhibition catalogue, Amsterdam, 1993), 36.

7. Cf. Jacobus de Voragine, *Legenda aurea,* trans. William Granger Ryan as *The Golden Legend* (Princeton: Princeton University Press, 1993), 1: 132–40.

8. For an extensive analysis of this painting, see Henry M. Luttikhuizen, "Late Medieval Piety and Geertgen tot Sint Jans' Altarpiece for the Haarlem Jansheren" (Ph.D. diss., University of Virginia, 1997).

9. Hans Belting, *Kult und Bild. Eine Geschischte des Bildes vor dem Zeitalter der Kunst* [1990], trans. E. Jephcott as *Likeness and Presence: A History of the Image Before the Era of Art* (Chicago: University of Chicago Press, 1994), 452, and David Summers, "Real Metaphor: Towards a Redefinition of the 'Conceptual' Image," in N. Bryson, M.A. Holly, and K. Moxey, eds., *Visual Theory: Painting and Interpretation* (Cambridge: Blackwell, Polity Press, 1991), 246.

10. Alfred Acres, "The Columbia Altarpiece and the Time of the World," *Art Bulletin* 80 (1998): 422–51, and Barbara G. Lane, *The Altar and the Altarpiece: Sacramental Themes in Early Netherlandish Painting* (New York: Harper & Row, 1984).

11. Lloyd Benjamin, "The Empathic Relation of Observer to Image in Fifteenth-Century Northern Art" (Ph.D. diss., University of North Carolina, 1973); F.O. Büttner, *Imitatio Pietatis: Motive der christlichen Ikonographie als Modelle zur Verähnlichung* (Berlin: Mann, 1983); James H. Marrow, *Passion Iconography in Northern European Art of the Late Middle Ages and Early Renaissance: A Study of the Transformation from Sacred Metaphor to Descriptive Narrative* (Kortrijk: Van Ghemmert, 1979); and idem, "Symbol and Meaning in Northern European Art of the Late Middle Ages and Early Renaissance," *Simiolus* 16 (1986): 151–67.

12. Matthew Botvinick, "The Painting as Pilgrimage: Traces of a Subtext in the Work of Campin and His Contemporaries," *Art History* 15 (1992): 1–18.

13. For more on religious efforts to localize the divine, see Peter Brown, *The Cult of Saints: Its Rise and Function in Latin Christianity* (Chicago: University of Chicago Press, 1981); William A. Christian, Jr., *Local Religion in Sixteenth-Century Spain* (Princeton: Princeton University Press, 1981); Carlos M.N. Eire, *War Against the Idols: The Reformation of Worship from Erasmus to Calvin* (Cambridge: Cambridge University Press, 1986), 8–27; and Summers, "Real Metaphor."

14. For more on devotional paintings by Geertgen, see James Snyder, "The Early Haarlem School of Painting. II. Geertgen tot Sint Jans," *Art Bulletin* 42 (1960): 113–32.

15. For more information on works by Jan van Scorel at the Haarlem Commandery, see *Kunst voor de beeldenstorm* (exhibition catalogue, Amsterdam, 1986), 183–85. For more on van Heemskerck, see Ilja M. Veldman, *Maarten van Heemskerck and Dutch Humanism in the Sixteenth Century* (Amsterdam: Meulenhoff, 1977).

16. From Carel van Mander, *Het Schilderboeck* (Haarlem, 1604), trans. Wolfgang Stechow in *Northern Renaissance Art 1400–1600. Sources and Documents* (Englewood Cliffs: Prentice Hall, 1966), 50.

17. For more on iconoclasm in the Netherlands, see Bob Scribner, ed., *Bilder und Bildersturm im Spätmittelalter und in der frühen Neuzeit* (Wiesbaden: Harrassowitz, 1990), Phyllis Mack Crew, *Calvinist Preaching and Iconoclasm in the Netherlands, 1544–1569* (Cambridge: Cambridge University Press, 1978); Eire, *War Against the Idols;* David Freedberg, *Iconoclasm and Painting in the Revolt of the Netherlands, 1566–1609* (New York: Garland, 1998); and idem, "Art and Iconoclasm, 1525–1580—The Case of the Northern Netherlands," in *Kunst voor de beeldenstorm,* 39–84.

18. *Kunst voor de beeldenstorm,* 408–10.

19. C.A. van Swigchem, "Kerkborden en kolomschilderingen in de St.-Bavo te Haarlem 1580–1585," *Bulletin van het Rijksmuseum* 35 (1987): 211–23.

20. Julie L. McGee, *Cornelis Corneliszoon van Haarlem (1562–1638): Patrons, Friends, and Dutch Humanists* (Nieuwkoop: De Graaf, 1991), 98–99. For more on the history of this legend, see Henri van de Waal, *Drie eeuwen vaderlandsche geschied-uitbeelding 1500–1800: Een iconologische studie* (The Hague: Nijhoff, 1952), 1: 30–33, 143–45, 243–45.

21. Kloek, "Northern Netherlandish Art," 36. In the eighteenth century, the westwork windows were bricked to accommodate a new organ.

22. Truus van Bueren, *Macht en onderhorigheid binnen Ridderlijke Orde van Sint Jan* (Haarlem: Schuyt, 1991).

23. Truus van Bueren, *Tot lof van Haarlem: Het belied van de stad Haarlem ten aanzien van de kunstwerken uit geconfisqueerde geestlijke instellingen* (Hilversum: Verloren, 1993), 172–83.

24. Joke Spaans, *Haarlem na de reformatie: Stedelijke cultuur en kerkelijk leven, 1577–1620* (The Hague: Stichting Hollandse Historische Reeks, 1989), and Jonathan I. Israel, *The Dutch Republic: Its Rise, Greatness, and Fall, 1477–1806* (Oxford: Oxford University Press, 1995), 361–98.

25. Pieter Biesboer, *Schilderijnen voor het stadhuis Haarlem. 16e en 17e eeuw kunstopdrachten ter verfraaiing* (Haarlem: De Vrieseborch, 1983), 23–27, and McGee, *Cornelis Corneliszoon van Haarlem,* 92.

26. Many American Protestants have advocated the use of visual images to promote memory as an alternative to veneration. Cf. David Morgan, *Visual Piety: A History and Theory of Popular Images* (Berkeley: University of California Press, 1998), esp. 181–202.

27. Van Bueren, *Tot lof van Haarlem,* 156–59, 660–65.

28. Arie Theodorus van Deursen, *Het kopergeld van de Gouden Eeuw,* trans. Maarten Utlee as *Plain Lives in a Golden Age: Popular Culture, Religion, and Society in Seventeenth-Century Holland* (Cambridge: Cambridge University Press, 1994), 244.

29. Schwartz and Bok, in *Pieter Saenredam,* 6–7.

30. From Ampzing, *Beschryvinge ende lof der stad Haerlem,* 418, trans. Schwartz and Bok, *Pieter Saenredam,* 39.

31. For more on the relationship between Dutch Calvinism and nationalism in the seventeenth century, see Simon Schama, *The Embarrassment of Riches: An Interpretation of Dutch Culture in the Golden Age* (Berkeley: University of California Press, 1988), esp. 51–125.

eleven

Sequences and Responsories: Continuity of Forms in Luther's Liturgical Provisions

ROBIN A. LEAVER

Editors' Introduction

An honest account of change and continuity requires not only examining the large patterns and habits of worship, but also the minor adaptations. Here we focus on what may appear initially to be inconsequential details of Luther's reforms. Robin Leaver examines two specific elements of the eucharistic liturgy: the Sequence and the Responsory—both of which were sung as responses to liturgical Scripture readings. The interesting story of continuity here is found in the details.

While eliminating the medieval Latin sequence, Luther retained its liturgical function and form in the evangelical church services. He was especially interested in retaining the music used in many of the Catholic Responsories and Sequences but changed the texts to ones taken from Scripture. In doing so, Luther and his followers preserved significant aspects of Catholic liturgical practice, while at the same time adapting these forms to suit the changed theological emphases.

Primary Sources Introduction

These documents are taken from liturgical manuals, and provide the texts of medieval and Lutheran Sequences and Responsories.

A. *The Liber Usualis with Introduction and Rubrics in English* (Tournai: Desclée, 1934) (hereafter cited as LU), 780. Translation: *The Antiphoner and Grail* (1880), as altered in the Episcopal *Hymnal 1982,* no.183.

1. Victimae paschali laudes immolent Christiani.	Christians, to the Paschal victim offer your thankful praises!
2. Agnus redemit oves: Christus innocens Patri reconciliavit peccatores.	A Lamb the sheep redeemeth: Christ, who only is sinless, reconcileth sinners to the Father.
3. Mors et vita duello conflixere mirando: dux vitae mortuus, regnat vivus.	Death and life have contended in that combat stupendous: the Prince of life, who died, reigns immortal.
4. Dic nobis Maria, quid vidisti in via?	Speak, Mary, declaring what thou sawest, wayfaring?
5. Sepulcrum Christi viventis, et gloriam vidi resurgentis:	"The tomb of Christ, who is living, the glory of Jesus' resurrection:
6. Angelis testes, sudarium et vestes.	Bright angels attesting, the shroud and napkin resting.
7. Surrexit Christus, spes mea: praecedet suos in Galiaeam.	Yes, Christ my hope is arisen: to Galilee he will go before you."
8. Scimus Christum surexisse ex mortuis vere: tu nobis, victor Rex, miserere.	Christ indeed from death is arisen, our new life obtaining: have mercy, victor King, ever reigning!

B. Martin Luther, *Die deutschen geistlichen Lieder,* ed. Gerhard Hahn (Tübingen: Niemeyer, 1967), 14–16, spelling modernized. Translation partially based on that of Richard Massie (1854).

1. Christ lag in Todesbanden,
für unsre Sünd' gegeben.
Der ist wieder erstanden
und hat uns bracht das Leben.
Des wir sollen fröhlich sein,
Gott loben und dankbar sein
und singen Alleluia.
Alleluia.

Christ Jesus lay in death's strong bands,
for our offenses given;
but now at God's right hand He stands
and brings us life from heaven.
Therefore let us joyful be
And sing to God right thankfully
Loud songs of Alleluia!
Alleluia.

2. Den Tod niemand zwingen konnt
bei allen Menschen-Kindern.
Das macht alles unsre Sünd,
kein Unschuld war zu finden.
Davon kam der Tod so bald
und nahm über uns Gewalt,
hielt uns in seim Reich gefangen.
Alleluia.

No man from death could victory win—
all sons of men were helpless.
This was the strength of all our sin,
for no one yet was guiltless.
Therefore death in triumph came,
and over us a right did claim,
to hold us in his kingdom.
Alleluia.

3. Jesus Christus, Gottes Sohn,
an unser Statt ist kommen
und hat die Sünd abgetan,
damit dem Tod genommen all sein Recht und sein Gewalt.
Da bleibt nichts denn Tods Gestalt.
Den Stachel hat er verloren.
Alleluia.

Christ Jesus, God's own Son, came down,
that he might us deliver,
and sin destroying, on his own,
has dealt with death forever:
stripped of power, no more death reigns,
an empty shape alone remains,
his sting is lost for ever.
Alleluia.

4. Es war ein wunderlich Krieg,
da Tod und Leben rungen.
Das Leben behielt den Sieg,
es hat den Tod verschlungen.
Die Schrift hat verkündet das,

It was a strange and dreadful strife
when Life and Death contended;
the victory remained with life,
the reign of death was ended;

wie ein Tod den andern fraß.
Ein Spott aus dem Tod ist worden.
Alleluia.

Scripture now is clear to state
how one great death the other ate
and made it a derision.
Alleluia.

5. Hier ist das recht Osterlamm,
davon Gott hat geboten.
Das ist an des Kreuzes Stamm
in heißer Lieb gebraten.
Das Blut zeichnet unsere Tür.
Das hällt der Glaub dem Tod für.
Der Würger kann uns nicht mehr rühren.
Alleluia.

Here the true Paschal Lamb we see,
whom God so freely gave us.
he died on the accursed tree,
roasted in love to save us.
See, his blood now marks our door;
faith points to it, death passes o'er,
the murderer cannot harm us.
Alleluia.

6. So feieren wir das hohe Fest
mit Herzens-Freud und Wonne,
das uns der Herre scheinen lässt.
Er ist selber die Sonne,
der durch seiner Gnade Glanz
erleucht' unser Herzen ganz.
Der Sünden Nacht ist vergangen.
Alleluia.

So let us keep the festival,
to which the Lord invites us;
Christ is himself the joy of all,
the sun that warms and lights us.
Now his grace to us imparts
Eternal sunshine to the heart;
the night of sin is ended.
Alleluia.

7. Wir essen und leben wohl
in rechten Oster-Fladen.
Der alte Sauerteig nicht soll
sein bei dem Wort der Gnaden,
Christus will die Koste sein
und speisen die Seel allein.
Der Glaub will keins andern leben
Alleluia.

Then let us feast this Easter Day
on Christ, the bread of heaven;
the Word of grace hath purged
away
the old and evil leaven.
Christ alone our souls will feed,
he is our meat and drink indeed;
faith lives upon no other.
Alleluia.

C. *LU,* 880–81. Translation by Charles P. Price, in Raymond F. Glover, ed., *The Hymnal 1982 Companion* (New York: Church Hymnal Corporation, 1990–94), 3: 226.

1. Veni, sancte Spiritus, et emitte caelitus lucis tuae radium.	Come, thou Holy Spirit bright; come with thy celestial light; pour on us thy love divine.
2. Veni, pater pauperum, veni, dator munerum, veni, lumen cordium.	Come, protector of the poor; come, thou source of blessings sure; come within our hearts to shine.
3. Consolator optime, dulcis hospes animae, dulce refrigerium.	Thou, of comforters the best, thou, the soul's most welcome guest of our peace thou art the sign.
4. In labore requies, in aestu temperies, in fletu solatium.	In our labor, be our aid; in our summer, cooling shade. Every bitter tear refine.
5. O lux beatissima, reple cordis intima tuorum fidelium . . .	Brighter than the noon-day sun, fill our lives which Christ has won; fill our hearts and make them thine . . .

D. Martin Luther, *Die deutschen geistlichen Lieder,* ed. Gerhard Hahn (Tübingen: Niemeyer, 1967), 1, spelling modernized. Composite translation.

1. Nun bitten wir den Heiligen Geist um den rechten Glauben, allermeist, daß er uns behüte an unserm Ende, bis wir heim fahren aus diesem Elende. Kyrioleis.	To God the Holy Ghost let us pray, most of all for faith upon our way, that he may defend us when life is ending, and through these sorrows to home are wending. Kyrioleis.
2. Du werdes Licht, gib uns deinen Schein,	Shine in our hearts, revealing light,

Lern uns Jesum Christ kennen allein,	teach us Jesus Christ to know aright,
Daß wir an ihm bleiben den treuen Heiland	that we may abide in the Lord who bought us,
der uns bracht hat zum rechten Vaterland.	who to our true Fatherland has brought us.
Kyrioleis.	Kyrioleis.
3. Du süße Lieb, schenk uns deine Gunst,	O sweetest love, kindness bestow;
Laß uns empfinden der Liebe Brunst,	set our hearts with sacred fire aglow,
daß wir uns von Herzen ein ander lieben	that with hearts united we love each other,
und im Friede, auf einem Sinn bleiben.	and in peace and joy live with our brother.
Kyrioleis.	Kyrioleis.
4. Du höchster Tröster in all Not,	Transcendent comfort in all need,
hilf daß wir nicht fürchten, Schand noch Tod,	help us neither shame or death to heed,
daß in uns die Sinnen nicht versagen,	that we may not falter, nor courage fail us
wenn der Feind wird das Leben verklagen.	when the foe with his taunts shall assail us.
Kyrioleis.	Kyrioleis.

E. Martin Luther, *Die deutschen geistlichen Lieder,* ed. Gerhard Hahn (Tübingen: Niemeyer, 1967), 39, spelling modernized. Translation in Jaroslav Pelikan and Helmut Lehmann, eds., *Luther's Works: American Edition* (Philadelphia: Fortress, 1965) (hereafter cited as *LW*), 53: 82–83.

Jesaja, dem Propheten, das geschah,	Isaiah 'twas the prophet who did see
daß er im Geist den Herren sitzen sach	seated above the Lord in majesty
auf einem hohen Thron in hellem Glanz.	high on a lofty throne in splendor bright;
Seines Kleides Saum den Chor füllet ganz.	the train of his robe filled the temple quite.

Es stunden zween Seraph bei ihn daran.	Standing beside him were two seraphim;
Sechs Flügel sach er einen jedern han.	six wings, six wings he saw on each of them.
Mit zween verbargen sie ihr Antlitz klar.	With twain they hid in awe their faces clear;
Mit zween bedeckten sie die Füße gar.	with twain they hid their feet in rev'rent fear.
Und mit den andern zween sie flogen frei.	And with the other two they flew about;
Gen ander rufen sie mit großem Schrei:	one to the other loudly raised the shout:
Heilig ist Gott, der Herre Zebaoth!	Holy is God, the Lord of Sabaoth,
Heilig ist Gott, der Herre Zebaoth!	Holy is God, the Lord of Sabaoth,
Heilig ist Gott, der Herre Zebaoth!	Holy is God, the Lord of Sabaoth.
Sein Ehr die ganze Welt erfüllet hat!	Behold his glory filleth all the earth.
Von dem Schrei zittert Schwell und Balken gar.	The angels' cry made beams and lintels shake;
Das Haus auch ganz voll Rauchs und Nebel war.	the house also was filled with clouds of smoke.

F. Martin Luther, *Die deutschen geistlichen Lieder,* ed. Gerhard Hahn (Tübingen: Niemeyer, 1967), 54–55, spelling modernized. The translation is my own, an approximation of the octosyllabic couplets of the original. For an alternative translation, see *LW* 53: 187–88.

All Ehr und Lob soll Gottes sein,	All glory, praise to God be giv'n,
Er ist und heißt der Höchst allein.	Who reigns supreme in highest heav'n.
Sein Zorn auff Erden hab ein End,	His wrath on earth comes to an end;
Sein Fried und Gnad sich zu uns wend.	His peace and grace to us extend.

Den Menschen das gefalle wohl,	Good will among humanity,
Dafür man herzlich danken soll.	Who thus should give thanks heartily.
Ach lieber Gott, Dich loben wir,	O dearest God, we honor thee
Und preisen dich mit gantzen [Be]gier.	And praise thee whole-heartedly.
Auch knieend wir anbeten dich,	Upon our knees we pray to thee,
Dein Ehr wir rühmen stetiglich.	And honor thee continually.
Wir danken dir zu aller Zeit,	At all times we give thanks to thee
Um deine große Herrlichkeit.	For the greatness of thy glory.
Herr Gott, im Himmel Kön'g du bist,	Lord God, heav'ns King in majesty,
Ein Vater der allmächtig ist.	Who is the Father Almighty.
Du Gottes Sohn vom Vater bist,	From the Father, made manifest,
Einig geborn Herr Jesu Christ.	Only begotten Jesus Christ.
Herr Gott, du zartes Gotteslamm,	Lord God, tender Lamb, and holy,
Ein Sohn aus Gott des Vaters stamm.	Son of God the Father truly;
Der du der Welt Sünd trägst allein,	Who alone the world's sin carries
Wollst uns gnädig, barmhertzig sein.	Wills to us his grace and mercies.
Der du der Welt Sünd trägst allein	Who alone the world's sin carries
Laß dir unser Bitt g'fällig sein.	Be pleased to hear our prayers and cries.
Der du gleich sitzst dem Vater dein	Thou, who thy Father's nature carries
Wollst uns gnädig, barmhertzig sein.	Will to us his grace and mercies.
Du bist und bleibst heilig allein,	Thou only art the Holy One,
Über alles der Herr allein.	Over all things, the Lord alone.
Der Allerhöchst allein du bist,	Thou the Highest, thou art solely,
Du lieber Heiland, Jesu Christ.	Dear Lord Jesus, Savior only,

Samt dem Vater und Heilgen Geist.	With Father and Spirit truly
In göttlicher Majestät gleich.	Divinity in majesty.
Amen, das ist gewißlich wahr,[1]	Amen, most certain it is true,
Das bekennt aller Engel Schar,	Confess'd by all the angels, too,
Und alle Welt, so weit und breit,	And all the world, in unity,
Von Anfang bis in Ewigkeit.	Till now and in eternity.

G. Cited in Markus Jenny, "Sieben biblische Begräbnisgesänge: Ein unerkanntes unediertes Werk Martin Luthers," in Gerhard Hammer and Karl-Heinz zur Mühen, eds., *Lutherana zum 500. Geburtstag Martin Luthers von den Mitarbeitern der Weimarer Ausgabe* (Cologne: Böhlau, 1984), 458. The translation is my own.

[Respond:] Rogamus te, Domine Deus	We implore thee, O Lord our God,
noster, ut suscipias animas nostrorum	to receive the soul of our departed,
defunctorum, quaesumus, pro quibus	for whom thy blood was shed;
sanguinem tuum fudisti; recordare	remember that we are dust,
quia pulvis sumus, et homo sicut	and that man is as grass and a
foenum et flos agri.	flower of the field.
[Versus:] Misericors et miserator et clemens Domine.	Merciful and pitying and forbearing art thou, O Lord.
[Respond:] Recordare quia pulvis	Remember that we are dust, and that
sumus, et homo sicut foenum et flos agri.	man is as grass and a flower of the field.

Notes

1. The words in italics are cited from Luther's *Small Catechism,* where they appear at the end of each of the answers that expound the meaning of the

three paragraphs of the Creed; see *Die Bekenntnisschriften der Evangelisch-Lutherischen Kirche,* 5th ed., (Göttingen: Vandenhoeck & Ruprecht, 1963), 510–12; Robert Kolb and Timothy J. Wengert, eds., *The Book of Concord: The Confessions of the Evangelical Lutheran Church* (Minneapolis: Fortress, 2000), 355–56. This would suggest that *All Ehr und Lob soll Gottes sein* was written after 1529, when the *Small Catechism* was first published. These last four lines may well have served as the prototype for the final stanza of Luther's Lord's Prayer hymn, *Vater unser im Himmelreich,* which first appeared in 1539; see *Luther's Works* 53: 298.

11.1a. Easter Sequence “Victimae paschali laudes.”

11.1b. Luther’s “Christ lag in Todesbanden” (1524).

11.2a. Pentecost sequence "Veni Sancte Spiritus."

11.2b. Luther's "Nun bitten wir den Heiligen Geist" (1524).

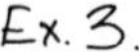

11.3. Comparison of melodies derived from "Gloria paschali": A = "Gloria paschali" chant; B = "All Ehr und Lob" (1537); C = "Allein Gott in der Höh sei Ehr," with texts by Decius (a) and Luther (b).

Jaroslav Pelikan has characterized Luther's Reformation in Wittenberg as an amalgam of "Catholic substance and Protestant principle," continuity integrated with the discontinuity of reform.[1] In an earlier essay I explored the themes of continuity and discontinuity with regard to the music of worship in the Reformation era, in which Luther's liturgical provisions were discussed.[2] In this essay, the concern is with two specific liturgical-musical forms in which Luther combined Catholic principle with Protestant substance: the Sequence and the Responsory.[3]

Although the exact origin of the Sequence is disputed, it appears that from the late eighth century it was sung by cantor and choir after the Alleluia at Mass on feast days. It developed as an expansion of the Alleluia[4] and was therefore sung in between the Epistle and Gospel readings, following the Gradual and Alleluia. The Sequence functioned as a musical hermeneutic, a homiletic exposition of the primary teaching of the day or celebration.[5] Early Sequences were prose texts, but from the eleventh century they were written in meter and rhyme (somewhat irregularly), one of the earliest being "Victimae paschali laudes" for Easter Day (see fig. 11.1a and primary source A).[6] From the first half of the twelfth century Sequences tended to be composed with a regular meter and rhyming scheme. Thus the Marian Sequence "Hodierne lux diei" is composed of five six-line stanzas (each sung to its own repeated melody), with an aabccb rhyming scheme.[7]

Hodierne lux diei
celebris in matris Dei
agitur memoria,
Decantemus in hac die
semper virginus Marie
laudis et preconia . . .

The Sequence for Pentecost, "Veni sancte Spiritus," is composed of ten three-line stanzas, with a simple aab rhyming scheme—effectively a rhymed couplet followed by a third line that always concludes with a word ending in "-ium."[8]

By the beginning of the sixteenth century there was a proliferation of sequences, with one assigned to every minor saint's day, as well as every Sunday, major feast and other celebrations of the Church year. At the Council of Trent (1545–63) sequences, together with other liturgical tropes (expansions of the basic liturgical texts), were almost entirely eliminated, with only four remaining (the "Stabat mater" was reintroduced later for the feast of the Seven Sorrows of the Blessed Virgin Mary): "Victimae paschali laudes" (Easter), "Veni sancte Spiritus" (Pentecost), "Lauda Sion" (Corpus Christi), and "Dies irae" (All Souls). For Luther the traditional Latin Sequence provided both a model and a form for different kinds of congregational song.

Like the later Council of Trent, Luther was critical of most sequences. In his evangelical Latin Mass, the *Formula missae* published in Wittenberg in 1523, he wrote: "We allow no Sequences or Proses unless the bishop[9] wishes to use a short one for the Nativity of Christ, 'Grates nunc omnes.' There are hardly any which smack of the Spirit, save those of the Holy Spirit [at Pentecost]: 'Sancti Spiritus' and 'Veni sancti Spiritus.'"[10] Thus a few Latin Sequences continued to be sung in Wittenberg, principally those of the primary feasts of the Church year. Later in the *Formula missae* Luther expressed his concern for congregational hymnody:

> I also wish that we had as many songs as possible in the vernacular which the people could sing during Mass, immediately after the Gradual [that is, in place of the traditional Latin Sequence] and also after the Sanctus and Agnus Dei . . . The bishops [pastors] may have these hymns sung either after these Latin chants, or use the Latin on one day and the vernacular on the next, until the time comes that the whole Mass is sung in the vernacular. But poets are wanting among us, or not yet known, who could compose evangelical and spiritual songs.[11]

Here it is clear that Luther wanted vernacular hymnody effectively to replace the Latin Sequence on most Sundays of the Church year, but at this stage (1523), apart from a few vernacular folk-hymns, such as "Nun bitten wir den Heiligen Geist," no such repertoire of hymns was available. Over the winter of 1523–24 Luther and his Wittenberg colleagues began writing vernacular hymns for congregational use. They were published in a number of collections in 1524, and in the *Deutsche Messe,* written toward the end of 1525, Luther again underscored the use of congregational songs as "Sequence" hymns—though the term that eventually came into use was *Graduallieder* (Gradual hymns): "After the Epistle a German hymn, either 'Nun bitten wir den Heiligen Geist' or any other, is sung with the whole choir."[12] The hymn as the congregational counterpart of the Sequence is underscored by the practice revealed during visitations in Wittenberg in 1528 and 1533. "At Easter and until the Sunday after Ascension one shall sing after the Alleluia 'Victimae paschali' together with 'Christ lag in Todesbanden,' verse by verse, until both alike are completed; at Pentecost the sequence 'Veni sancte Spiritus' with the hymn 'Nun bitten wir den Heiligen Geist' [are sung], as arranged above" (see figs. 11.1a, 11.1b, 11.2a, 11.2b, and 11.3, and primary sources A, B, C, and D).[13] The verses of the respective Latin chant were sung in alternation with the stanzas of its vernacular partner, the former being sung by the choir, the latter by the congregation. But even here Luther was building on an earlier practice, since in some areas vernacular hymns had been sung in Germany during the Mass on special feast days, some in connection with the respective Sequence.[14] Luther, however, went much further than such occasional use and introduced seasonal "Sequence" hymns as a regular feature of his evangelical Mass. The first section of the Wittenberg congregational hymnal, issued in 1529, presents a Church-year series of ten such hymns, translated, written or rewritten by Martin Luther:[15]

"Nun komm der Heiden Heiland"	Advent
"Christum wir sollen loben schon"	Christmas
"Gelobet seist du, Jesu Christ"	Christmas
"Mit Fried und Freud ich fahr dahin"	Purification
"Christ lag in Todesbanden"	Easter
"Jesus Christus, unser Heiland der den Tod"	Easter
"Komm, Gott Schöpfer, Heiliger Geist"	Pentecost
"Komm, Heiliger Geist, Herre Gott"	Pentecost
"Nun bitten wir den Heiligen Geist"	Pentecost
"Gott der Vater wohn uns bei"	Trinity

Of these, one is based on a specific Latin Sequence ("Christ lag in Todesbanden" = "Victimae paschali laudes"); one is based on an antiphon that has the same incipit as the Pentecost Sequence ("Komm, Heiliger Geist, Herre Gott" = "Veni sancte Spiritus"); three are reworkings of earlier *Leisen* (vernacular folk-hymns), a genre closely related to Latin Sequences ("Gelobet seist du, Jesu Christ," "Nun bitten wir den Heiligen Geist," and "Gott der Vater wohn uns bei"). To these should be added one more that, although no medieval model has been discovered, is clearly written in a *Leisen* style ("Jesus Christus, unser Heiland der den Tod"); and three are translations of

Latin office hymns ("Nun komm der Heiden Heiland" = "Veni redemptor gentium" [Christmas], "Christum wir sollen loben schon" = "A solis ortus cardine" [Christmas], and "Komm, Gott Schöpfer, Heiliger Geist" = "Veni creator Spiritus" [Pentecost]). Only one can be said to be newly written, "Mit Fried und Freud ich fahr dahin," but even that is a versification of the Song of Simeon (Luke 2:29–32), the liturgical canticle known as the "Nunc dimittis." The "new" "Sequence" hymns for the congregation to sing were therefore in every case effectively new forms of older liturgical material.

In addition to using the traditional Sequence as a model for hymns that were to be sung in the traditional position of the Sequence in the Mass, that is in between the Epistle and Gospel, Luther also adapted the traditional form of the Latin Sequence to create new congregational versions of parts of the Ordinary of the Mass. The Ordinary comprised the unchanging elements of the Roman Mass which were customarily sung: Kyrie, Gloria, Credo, Sanctus, and Agnus Dei. In the *Deutsche Messe* of 1526 Luther introduced the concept of singing metrical, strophic forms of these parts of the Ordinary: "After the Gospel the whole congregation sings the Creed in German, 'Wir glauben all an einen Gott' . . . Meanwhile [during the distribution of Communion], the German Sanctus or [Eucharistic hymns] . . . could be sung . . . or the German Agnus Dei."[16] Neither the text of "Wir glauben all an einen Gott" nor the German Agnus Dei, "Christe, du Lamm Gottes," was included in the *Deutsche Messe,* but the German Sanctus was given, complete with text and melody: "Jesaiah, dem Propheten, das geschah."[17]

In the *Deutsche Messe,* from which Luther had eliminated the traditional Eucharistic Canon (Thanksgiving Prayer) in favor of the Words of Institution alone, there was also no place for a vernacular Sursum corda with a Preface leading to the Sanctus. Thus both the German Agnus Dei and the German Sanctus were to be sung as *musica sub communionem,* that is, during the distribution of Communion. The melodic form of Luther's chant for "Jesaiah, dem Propheten, das geschah" is an adaptation of the plainchant Sanctus for Sundays in Advent and Lent,[18] a reflection of the period when Luther was working on the *Deutsche Messe,* that is, during Advent 1525. Although it was called the "German Sanctus," and based on a traditional Sanctus chant melody, it is a versification of the broader biblical passage, Isaiah 6:1–4, rather than the narrower liturgical Sanctus, Isaiah 6:3. In its form it is in effect a vernacular Sequence. The traditional Sequence was an exposition of the primary teaching of the day or celebration, usually the Gospel. Here, following the form of a Latin Sequence, Luther gives the context of the origin of the Seraphic hymn rather than just the liturgical Sanctus. Further, it is written in rhymed couplets of ten syllables and thus in its form follows the traditional Sequence, even though it was to be sung during Communion rather than in between the Epistle and Gospel.

A further example of Luther's use of the Sequence form for another part of the Ordinary is the versification of the Gloria in excelsis Deo found in the manuscript liturgical provisions in the Church Order drawn up for use in Naumburg in 1537, and thereafter in a variety of hymnals. Some Luther scholars have been skeptical about its provenance, but recently the tendency has been to accept it as being the work of the Wittenberg Reformer. There are a number of features—such as the use of octosyllabic lines, the quotation from Luther's *Small Catechism,* the general relationship between text and melody, and the similarity to "Jesaiah, dem Propheten, das geschah"—which suggest that Luther was its author.[19]

Like the German Sanctus, the melody for this German Gloria is an adaptation of a traditional Ordinary chant, the "Gloria tempore paschali," the Gloria for the Easter season.[20] Similarly, it is also written in rhymed couplets and thus is another example of Luther's using the form of the Latin Sequence as a model for creating new liturgical music for the evangelical Mass. In sum, while Luther almost entirely eliminated sequences in his liturgies, he did retain their liturgical function and form.

In general the Responsory was sung in "response" to the reading of Scripture, such as the Gradual in the Roman Mass. Some, such as those at Matins, could be quite lengthy and melismatic chants (*responsoria prolixa*). Others, such as those following the short lesson of the Little Hours of Prime, Terce, Sext, None, and Compline, were somewhat shorter and more syllabic (*responsoria brevia*).[21] At the Office of the Dead there were specific responsories following each of the biblical lessons.[22] In the medieval Church there were more funerary responsories than were included in the Tridentine Office of the Dead. The form of a funerary Responsory comprises a "respond" followed by a verse (but without the Gloria Patri as with other responsories), with the respond (or its concluding section) repeated after the verse.[23] The second part of the respond in primary source G (repeated after the Versus) is closely based on Psalm 102 (Vulgate Psalm 103):14–15, and the Versus is reminiscent of verse 8 of the same psalm. It is this Responsory form that Luther adapted for evangelical use during the last few years of his life.

In 1542 the Wittenberg printer Joseph Klug published a small songbook: *Christliche Geseng Lateinsich und Deudsch zum Begrebnis. D. Martinus Luther* (Latin and German Christian songs for Burials. Dr. Martin Luther). It contained one Latin hymn, "Iam moesta quiesce querela," by Prudentius, and six German hymns, all except one the work of Luther: "Aus tiefer Not" (Psalm 130), "Mitten wir im Leben sind," "Wir glauben all an einen Gott," "Mit Fried und Freud ich fahr dahin," "Nun laßt uns den leib begraben" (by Michael Weiss),[24] and "Nun bitten wir den Heiligen Geist." But these items are preceded by seven Latin biblical responsories, complete with notated chants. Although reprinted in numerous Lutheran hymnals and anthologies of chant in the sixteenth and seventeenth centuries, they were neglected by later Luther scholarship: none was included in the various collected editions of Luther's works and the seven responsories first appeared in a critical edition as late as 1984.[25] The Latin incipits are as follows:

I. "Credo quod redemptor meus vivit"
II. "Ecce quomodo moritur iustus"
III. "Cum venisset Jesus"
IV. "Ecce mysterium magnum dico vobis"
V. "Stella enim differt a stella in daritate"
VI. "Nolumus autem vos fratres"
VII. "Si credimus quod Jesus Christus"

A further Responsory appears later in the volume[26]—together with three Antiphons: "Corpora Sanctorum," "Media vita in morte sua" (which Luther translated as "Mitten wir im Leben sind"), and "In pace simil dormiam et requiescam"—a text that is similar to that of VII, but with an entirely different chant melody:

[VIII.] "Si enim credimus"

Of the associated melodies four (and probably a fifth) are of responsories of the medieval Office of the Dead:

III. In tono "Rogamus te"
IV. In tono "Absolve"
V. In tono "Deus aeterne"
VI. In tono "Ne tradas Domine"
[VIII.] [In tono ??]

Two are texts that appear with their associated melodies:

I. "Credo quod redemptor," a variant form of the Responsory that follows the first lesson at Matins of the Office for the Dead[27]
II. "Ecce quomodo moritur," a variant of the Reponsory that follows the sixth lesson at Matins on Holy Saturday,[28] but used on Good Friday in the later medieval period

One melody is based on a nonfunerary Responsory:

VII. In tono "Surge virgo," which employs the beginning of the medieval Responsory for the Ascension of Mary

Luther's funerary responsories therefore generally employ traditional chant melodies with different texts; in every case the texts are entirely biblical:

Responsory	Respond	Verse
I.	Job 19:25	Psalm 146 [145]:1–2
II.	Isaiah 57:1–2	Psalm 17 [16]:15
III.	Matthew 9:23–24	Mark 5:41–42
IV.	I Corinthians 15:51–52	I Corinthians 15:54
V.	I Corinthians 15:41–44	I Corinthians 15:45
VI.	I Thessalonians 4:13	I Thessalonians 4:14
VII.	I Thessalonians 4:13, 14	I Corinthians 15:22
[VIII.]	I Thessalonians 4:14	I Corinthians 15:22

In contrast to the "doom and gloom" of many of the medieval funerary responsories, Luther's biblical responsories were created from the primary passages of the New Testament which stress resurrection. But in every case these "new" responsories used the traditional Responsory form, together with pre-existing chant melodies. The preservation of these earlier melodic forms was a deliberate policy on Luther's part. He explained his purpose in the preface to the booklet:

> We have collected the fine music and songs which under the papacy were used at vigils, masses for the dead, and burials. Some fine examples of these we have printed in this booklet and we, or whoever is more gifted than we, will select more of them in the future. But we have adapted other texts to the music so that they may adorn our article of resurrection, instead of purgatory with its torment and satisfaction which lets their dead neither sleep nor rest. The melodies and notes are precious. It would be a pity to let them perish. But the texts and words are non-Christian and absurd. They deserve to perish . . . [The papists] also possess a lot of splendid songs and music, especially in the cathedral and parish churches. But these are used to adorn all sorts of impure and idolatrous texts. Therefore, we have unclothed these idolatrous, lifeless, and foolish texts, and divested them of their beautiful music. We have put this music on the living and holy word of God in order to sing, praise, and honor it. . . . We are concerned with changing the text, not the music.[29]

Thus, in a revised form, the Responsory had a continuing significance for Luther.

Although congregational hymnody was employed at various junctures within the Lutheran forms of worship of later generations, it remained customary for an appropriate hymn to be sung in between the Epistle and Gospel. Most of the time the hymn sung in this liturgical position effectively replaced the traditional Sequence. As more congregational hymnals were produced during the sixteenth century, the basic corpus of ten seasonal "Sequence" hymns of the 1529 Wittenberg hymnal were expanded so that there was at least one hymn for such use on every Sunday, feast, and celebration of the Church year, a "Sequence" hymn that was closely related to the particular Gospel reading. By the eighteenth century these "hymns of the day" had grown into a rich corpus that included many different hymns appropriate for the days and celebrations throughout the Church year.[30] Although there were many options, in practice generally only one of the hymns for a given occasion—established by widespread usage—was sung as the specific "Sequence" hymn. Thus by the eighteenth century around seventy to eighty hymns became the primary hymns that were sung as Lutheran "Sequences," chorales that were memorized by Lutheran congregations and sung on the respective Sundays and celebrations. The same chorales figure again and again over the next few centuries in the organ and vocal compositions of most of the composers of Lutheran Germany, notably in the music of Johann Sebastian Bach.

The Sequence principle (that is, a homiletic commentary, in musical form, on the primary teaching of the day or celebration) not only influenced the development of an important aspect of the Lutheran congregational chorale, it also contributed to the evolution of two specifically Lutheran genres: the *Spruchmotette* and cantata. The *Spruchmotette* ([biblical] verse motet), or *Evangelienmotette* (Gospel motet), was a choral setting of the primary verse(s) of the Gospel of the day which was customarily sung in between the reading/chanting of the Gospel and the sermon, which was an exposition of the same passage. Many annual cycles of such motets were published between the middle of the sixteenth century and the end of the seventeenth century, by such composers as Raselius, Calvisius, Demantius, Vulpius, and Franck, among others, with settings that ranged from two to eight or more voices.[31] The cantata form that evolved during the seventeenth century and reached its zenith in the cantatas of Bach, while in musical terms was far from the chant forms of the traditional Sequence, was nevertheless an extension of the Sequence principle. Like the medieval Sequence, the cantata was an exposition of the biblical lessons (primarily the Gospel) of the day or celebration, but in a succession of different movements (choruses, arias, recitatives, and chorales) with orchestral accompaniment. The musical form was more complex but the liturgical function was the same as that of the traditional Sequence.

The Latin Sequence was not entirely displaced but continued to be sung at major festivals in Lutheran worship when both a Latin Sequence and a vernacular hymn were sung in close proximity, such as "Grates nunc omnes" with "Gelobet seist du, Jesu Christ" at Christmas; "Victimae paschali laudes" with the old folk-hymn "Christ ist erstanden," or Luther's reworking of its primary themes in "Christ lag in Todesbanden," at Easter; and "Veni sancte Spiritus" with either "Komm, Heiliger Geist, erfüll die Herzen" or "Komm, Heiliger Geist, Herre Gott" at Pentecost. In the sixteenth century the two forms were generally sung in an integrated pattern of alternation, each verse or stanza following its equivalent in the other language. During the seventeenth century the usual practice was for the congregation to sing the German hymn after the choir had sung the Latin Sequence. Latin sequences thus survived well into the eighteenth century. For example, the *Neu Leipziger Gesangbuch* (Leipzig, 1682), edited by Gottfried Vopelius—still in use during Bach's time as the Thomaskantor in the city—includes seasonal Latin sequences with notation, two of which are given with German translations so that either, or both, could be sung:

Advent:	"Mittit ad virginem" ("Als der gütige Gott")
Christmas:	"Grates nunc omnes" ("Danksagen wir alle")
Easter:	"Victimae paschali laudes"
Pentecost:	"Veni sancte Spiritus"
Trinity:	"Benedicta semper sancta sit Trinitas"[32]

Luther's Sequence-like Gloria "All Ehr und Lob soll Gottes sein" did not enter in general use. It had been preceded by Nicolaus Decius's strophic form "Allein Gott in der Höh sei Ehr" (1522), with a melody also based on the same chant that Luther used, the "Gloria tempore paschali." "Allein Gott in der Höh sei Ehr" quickly became the Gloria hymn commonly sung by Lutheran congregations. "All Ehr und Lob soll Gottes sein" did appear in a number of mid-sixteenth-century hymnals and was also adapted into a strophic form to be sung with the "Allein Gott in der Höh sei Ehr" melody in the *Bapst Gesangbuch* of 1545.[33] But it soon disappeared from mainstream hymnals, though it was resurrected in some nineteenth-century hymnals.[34] In contrast Luther's German Sanctus "Jesaiah, dem Propheten, das geschah," in the Sequence form of rhymed couplets, has never been displaced from Lutheran hymnals.

Luther's Latin funerary responsories had fairly widespread currency in hymnals and anthologies of chant published in the second half of the sixteenth century. But by the early seventeenth century the only Latin element from Luther's 1542 booklet generally found in hymnals was the Latin hymn by Prudentius, "Iam moesta quiesce querela." This hymn is found in Johann Herman Schein's *Cantional Oder Gesangbuch Augspurgischer Confession* (Leipzig, 1627) as well as in Vopelius's *Neu Leipzig Gesangbuch* (1682).[35] But the influence of one of the responsories in Luther's 1542 collection was significant and widespread. While the second Responsory "Ecce quomodo moritur iustus" was not much used after the sixteenth century, its basic text, in a through-composed setting by Jacob Handl (Gallus) composed toward the end of the sixteenth century, was widely sung in Lutheran Germany during Holy Week. Handl's motet was included in cantionals, such as Vopelius's *Neu Leipziger Gesangbuch* (1682).[36] For example, the motet was sung three times in Holy Week in the Leipzig churches during Bach's kantorate, always after the singing of passion settings: on Palm Sunday it was heard after Johann Walter's *Saint Matthew Passion,* sung as the Gospel of the day; on Good Friday morning it was similarly heard after Walter's *Saint John Passion,* sung as the Gospel for that day; and on Good Friday afternoon it was sung again, at the close of a concerted setting of the passion, such as Bach's *Saint John* or *Saint Matthew Passion.*[37] Clearly the chant form "Ecce quomodo moritur iustus" found in Luther's funerary collection must have exerted some influence on the later use of the Handl motet on the same text.

Luther's funerary responsories, however, were significantly influential in ensuring the continuity of chant forms being sung within the worship of the Lutheran churches. The responsories themselves provided models to be followed by others, and in his preface to the 1542 collection Luther effectively set the agenda for the continued use of such chant forms:

> But we do not hold that the notes need to be sung the same in all the churches. Let every church follow the music according to their own book and custom. For I do not like to hear the notes in a Responsory or other song changed from what I was accustomed to in my youth.[38]

The passage was quoted by Michael Praetorius in his appendix to the first volume of his *Syntagma musicum* (1614/15).[39] In this appendix Praetorius quotes, from a manuscript source, Johann Walter's words about Luther's ability in adapting Latin chant forms to the German language. Though Walter's words about Luther have been often cited the context is frequently glossed over. Walter's broader purpose was to underscore the continued use of Gregorian chant forms, with both Latin and German texts, and as part of this he cites Luther's particular ability in adapting Latin chant forms for German texts. Praetorius's purpose in including Walter's words was to endorse the continued use of chant forms in Lutheran worship. Luther's policy expressed in his 1542 preface, and cited by Praetorius—"But we do not hold that the notes need to be sung the same in all the churches. Let every church follow the music according to their own book and custom"—was put into effect in the second half of the sixteenth century. Various anthologies of chant for the Church year were published for Lutheran use which reflected the pre-Reformation usage of those areas: in Nordhausen Johann Spangenberg produced *Cantiones ecclesiatica latinae . . . Kirchen Gesenge Deutsch* (Magdeburg, 1545, and later editions); in Lüneberg Lucas Lossius created *Psalmodia, hoc est, cantica sacra veteris ecclesiae selecta* (Nuremberg, 1553, and later editions); in St. Andreasberg Johannes Keuchenthal edited *Kirchen Gesenge lateinisch und deudsch* (Wittenberg, 1573); and in Hamburg Franz Eler produced *Cantica sacra* (Hamburg, 1588). These publications, together with various hymnals that reprinted various items from them, ensured that pre-Reformation chant forms continued to be sung in Lutheran churches at least until the eighteenth century.[40] In those towns and cities where there were Latin schools, Matins and Vespers continued to be sung in Latin by the pupils. Thus in Leipzig during Bach's time, though Luther's funerary responsories were apparently no longer sung, seasonal responsories were, since they were available in Vopelius's *Neu Leipziger Gesangbuch* (1682):

"Rex noster adveniet"	Advent
"Verbum caro factum est"	Christmas Day and Purification
"Illuminare, illuminare Jesusalem"	Epiphany
"Discubuit Jesus"	Maundy Thursday
"Tenebrae factae sunt"	Good Friday
"Dum transisset Sabbathum"	Easter Day
"Ite in orbem universum"	Ascension
"Apparuerunt apostolis"	Pentecost
"Summae Trinitatis"	Trinity
"Inter natus mulierum"	St. John the Baptist
"Magnificat anima mea"	Visitation
"Te sanctum Dominum"	St. Michael
"Fuerunt sine querela"	Apostle Days[41]

These two pre-Reformation liturgical-musical forms, the Sequence and Responsory, which Luther adapted for use in Reformation worship are examples of the way he combined Catholic principle with Protestant substance, the marriage of *cantica sacra veteris ecclesiae* (sacred songs of the old church) with *sola scriptura* (Scripture alone). The Sequence supplied him with a model for expounding the primary message of the Gospel of the day in congregational hymnody, as well as providing a paradigm for the versification of two parts of the Ordinary that were scripturally based: the German Gloria and the German Sanctus. The Responsory presented him the opportunity to invest such melodies with consistent Scriptural texts, and Luther's important models contributed significantly to the preservation of the older chant forms within Lutheran worship. Continuity and change lie at the root of Luther's liturgical reforms. As he wrote near the beginning of his *Formula missae:* "We therefore first assert: It is not now or ever has been our intention to abolish the liturgical service of God completely, but rather to purify the one that is now in use from the wretched accretions which corrupt it and to point out an evangelical use."[42]

Luther's use of both the Sequence and Responsory are examples of how his liturgical reform was a creative amalgam of existing practice with newly espoused Reformation ideals. In some areas, continuity was more prominent than change, such as Luther's acceptance of the traditional structure of the Mass in both his *Formula missae* (1523) and *Deutsche Messe* (1526), his conservative translations of the Latin collects,[43] and the retention of Latin in towns and cities that had Latin grammar schools and/or universities. On the other hand, in some of his other liturgical provisions change displaced continuity, such as his rejection of the Canon of the Mass, replacing it with the Words of Institution alone,[44] and his creation of the so-called Flood-Prayer for the *Order of Baptism* (1523).[45] But much of his liturgical reforms are ingenious syntheses of continuity and change, as shown in his "sequences" and responsories. The following are among the most important examples.

First, there is Luther's creative use of the traditional Passion tones heard only during Holy Week when the Passion narratives were sung as the Gospel on various days. The different *personae* in the narratives were depicted by the use of different pitches: the voice of the evangelist in the tenor range, the voices of individuals and groups in the descant range, and the voice of Jesus being the lowest in the bass range. In the *Deutsche Messe* Luther applied the principles of this annual practice, heard in only one week each year, to the chanting of the Gospel on every Sunday and celebration throughout the Church year. Second, there is Luther's understanding that the Canon of the Mass was effectively framed by the same melodic forms employed for both the preface near its beginning and the Lord's Prayer at its end.[46] This gave him the principle for framing the Creed, the central confession of faith, with the proclamation of the Gospel during the ministry of the Word, and the Words of Institution during the ministry of the Sacrament: in the *Deutsche Messe* both the Gospel of the Day and the Words of Institution were to be sung to the same melodic formulae that Luther created for them.[47]

But Luther was not alone in combining continuity with change in liturgical provisions. Some time before Luther's *Deutsche Messe* Thomas Müntzer, a proto-Anabaptist, produced a vernacular, evangelical Mass, *Deutsch Evangelische Messze* (Alstedt, 1524), a conservative, vernacular revision of the Roman Mass—which was given in five forms, one for each of the seasons of Advent, Christmas, Holy Week, Easter, and Pentecost—but with all the associated traditional chants.[48] Similarly, in Zurich Ulrich Zwingli, the radical Reformer who rejected all music in public worship, nevertheless made use of traditional forms in his liturgical provisions. Most striking is his willingness to continue using a vernacular form of the Gloria in excelsis Deo—in dialogical corporate speech—in his *Aktion oder Brauch des Nachtmals* (Zurich, 1525). In this liturgical form Zwingli directed that his German Gloria should be placed in between the Epistle and Gospel, effectively changing it from Ordinary to Proper, by making it function as the Gradual.[49] The Gloria was retained in continuity with the past, but its context involved a significant change. Another example is Thomas Cranmer's unwillingness to omit both the Kyrie and Gloria from the revised Communion Service in the 1552 *Book of Common Prayer.* Following Strasbourg liturgical practice, the Ten Commandments were incorporated into the beginning of this liturgy, displacing the traditional Kyrie and Gloria. Cranmer therefore moved the Gloria to the end of the Communion Service, but in a sense kept the Kyrie in its traditional place, and even retained its ninefold form. It was expanded by troping to become a response to each of the first nine commandments: "Lord have mercy upon us, and incline our hearts to keep this law." After the tenth commandment there was a different troped Kyrie: "Lord have mercy upon us, and write all these thy laws in our hearts we beseech thee."[50] Continuity was in the retention of the Kyrie, though in a translated and modified form; change in its use as a responsive prayer. Thus, patterns of Reformation worship, rather than being a radical new departure from the old, were frequently creative fusions of Catholic principle with Protestant substance.

Notes

1. Jaroslav Pelikan, *Obedient Rebels: Catholic Substance and Protestant Principle in Luther's Reformation* (New York: Harper, 1964); see also Jaroslav Pelikan, *Spirit versus Structure: Luther and the Institutions of the Church* (New York: Harper, 1968).

2. Robin A. Leaver, "Christian Liturgical Music in the Wake of the Protestant Reformation," in Lawrence A. Hoffman and Janet R. Walton, eds., *Sacred Sound and Social Change: Liturgical Music in Jewish and Christian Experience* (Notre Dame, Ind.: University of Notre Dame Press, 1992), 124–44.

3. There are, of course, other instances of Luther's adaptations and use of traditional liturgical-musical forms, some of which will be referred to in the following discussion, but these are chosen because they have not received the attention they deserve.

4. For the background, see David Hiley, *Western Plainchant: A Handbook* (Oxford: Clarendon, 1993), 172–95.

5. For the background, see William T. Flynn, *Medieval Music as Medieval Exegesis* (Lanham, Md.: Scarecrow, 1999).

6. *The Liber Usualis with Introduction and Rubrics in English* (Tournai: Desclée, 1934) (hereafter cited as *LU*), 780. See figure 11.1a and primary source A accompanying this contribution.

7. See Hiley, *Western Plainchant*, 192 (Ex. II.22.11).

8. See primary source C accompanying this contribution.

9. Luther means the senior pastor rather than the diocesan bishop.

10. Jaroslav Pelikan and Helmut Lehmann, eds., *Luther's Works: American Edition*, 55 vols. (St. Louis and Philadelphia: Concordia and Fortress, 1955–86) (hereafter cited as *LW*), 53: 24–25.

11. *LW* 53: 36.

12. *LW* 53: 74. There is an ambiguity here: does "with the whole choir" mean "only the choir," or "the congregation with the choir"? Received opinion favors the latter, though some recent scholars suggest the former.

13. Cited in Adolf Boës, "Die Reformatorischen Gottesdienst in der Wittenberger Pfarrkirche von 1523 an und die 'Ordenung der gesenge der Wittenbergischen Kirchen' von 1543/44," *Jahrbuch für Liturgik und Hymnologie* 4 (1958/59): 7. See figures 11.1a, 11.1b, 11.2a, 11.2b and 11.3, and primary sources A, B, C, and D accompanying this contribution.

14. See the examples cited by Anthony Ruff, "A Millennium of Congregational Song," *Pastoral Music* 21 (1997): 11–15.

15. See Robin A. Leaver, *"Goostly Psalmes and Spirituall Songes": English and Dutch Metrical Psalms from Coverdale to Utenhove 1535–1566* (Oxford: Clarendon, 1991), 282–83.

16. *LW* 53: 78, 81–82.

17. See primary source E accompanying this contribution.

18. *LU*, 61.

19. For example, Markus Jenny (see Markus Jenny, ed., *Luthers geistliche Lieder und Kirchengesänge: Vollständige Neuedition in Ergänzung zu Band 35 der Weimarer Ausgabe* [Cologne: Böhlau, 1985], 132–34) is of the opinion that it has been falsely ascribed to Luther, whereas Konrad Ameln thinks it authentic (see Konrad Ameln, "*All Ehr und Lob soll Gottes sein*: Ein deutsches Gloria—von Martin Luther?" in Heinrich Riehm, ed., *Festschrift für Frieder Schulz: Freude am Gottesdienst* [Heidelberg: Riehm, 1988], 255–71; also in *Jahrbuch für Liturgik und Hymnologie* 31 [1987/88]: 38–52). See also the brief summary (in favor of Luther's authorship) by Ulrich Leopold in *LW* 53: 184–86. For the text of the Gloria in excelsis Deo, including the quotation from Luther's *Small Catechism*, see primary source F accompanying this contribution.

20. *LU,* 16–18. See figure 11.3.

21. See Hiley, *Western Plainchant,* 69–76, 85–88.

22. See *LU,* 1772–1806.

23. The medieval performance practice was: respond (solo), respond repeated (choir), verse (solo), respond, or a truncated version of the respond (choir). For an example of a Responsory see primary source G accompanying this contribution.

24. Luther added a stanza; see Markus Jenny, "Sieben biblische Begräbnisgesänge: Ein unerkanntes unediertes Werk Martin Luthers," in Gerhard Hammer and Karl-Heintz zur Mühen, eds., *Lutherana zum 500. Geburtstag Martin Luthers von den Mitarbeitern der Weimarer Ausgabe* (Cologne: Böhlau, 1984),120–22.

25. Ibid., 455–74.

26. Noted, but not included in Jenny, "Sieben biblische Begräbnisgesänge."

27. *LU,* 1785–86.

28. *LU,* 728.

29. *LW* 53: 327–28.

30. See Rochus Freiherr von Liliencron, *Liturgisch-musikalische Geschichte der evangelischen Gottesdienste von 1523– bis 1700* (Schleswig: Bergas, 1893), 61–77; Detlef Gojowy, "Kirchenlieder im Umkreis von J. S. Bach," *Jahrbuch für Liturgik und Hymnologie* 22 (1978): 79–123.

31. In the twentieth century some composers returned to composing such liturgical motets, such as those by Ernst Pepping found in his *Spandauer Chorbuch* (1934–38).

32. See Jürgen Grimm, *Das Neu Leipziger Gesangbuch des Gottfried Vopelius (Leipzig 1682): Untersuchung zur Klärung seiner geschichtlichen Stellung* (Berlin: Merseburger, 1969), 54, 60, 63, and 66.

33. Valentin Babst, *Das Babstsche Gesangbuch von 1545,* facsimile ed., Konrad Ameln, ed. (Kassel: Bärenreiter, 1966), no. 61. See figure 11.3.

34. For example, it appeared as no. 142 in the Missouri Synod's *Kirchen-Gesangbuch für Evangelisch-Lutherische Gemeinden ungeänderter Augsburgischer Confession* (St. Louis: Concordia, 1847).

35. See Walter Reckziegel, *Das Cantional von Johann Herman Schein: Seine geschichtlichen Grundlagen* (Berlin: Merseburger, 1963), 216; Grimm, *Das Neu Leipziger Gesangbuch,* 90.

36. Grimm, *Das Neu Leipziger Gesangbuch,* 59.

37. See Charles Sanford Terry, *Joh. Seb. Bach Cantata Texts Sacred and Secular, with a Reconstruction of the Leipzig Liturgy of His Period* (1929; reprint, London: Holland, 1964), 201, 207, 209. Both Passions were to be found in Vopelius; see Grimm, *Das Neu Leipziger Gesangbuch,* 59.

38. *LW* 53: 327–28.

39. Michael Praetorius, *Syntagma musicum I: Musicae artis Analecta. Wittenberg 1614/15,* facsimile ed., Wilibald Gurlitt, ed. (Kassel: Bärenreiter, 1959), 447–53, here 448.

40. The chants began to be recovered for Lutheran use in the later nineteenth and early twentieth centuries. For a study of these German forms of traditional chant, see Otto Brodde, "Evangelische Choralkunde: Der gregoriansische Choral im evangelischen Gottesdienst," in Karl Ferdinand Müller and Walter Blakenburg, eds.,

Leiturgia: Handbuch des evangelischen Gottesdienstes, vol. 4, *Die Musik des evangelischen Gottesdienstes* (Kassel: Stauda, 1961), 343–557.

41. Grimm, *Das Neu Leipziger Gesangbuch,* 50–68.

42. *LW* 53: 20.

43. See ibid., 131–46.

44. Ibid., 27–28, 80–81.

45. Ibid., 97–98.

46. See ibid., 27–28; see also Robin A. Leaver, "Liturgical Music as Homily and Hermeneutic," in Robin A. Leaver and Joyce Ann Zimmerman, eds., *Liturgy & Music: Lifetime Learning* (Collegeville, Minn.: Liturgical Press, 1998), 340–59, esp. 350–51.

47. For the background, see Robin A. Leaver, "Theological Consistency, Liturgical Integrity, and Musical Hermeneutic in Luther's Liturgical Reforms," *Lutheran Quarterly* 9 (1995): 117–38; and Robin A. Leaver, "Thematic Building Blocks: Liturgical, Pedagogical and Political Concerns in Early Lutheran Church Music," *Cross Accent: Journal of the Association of Lutheran Church Musicians* 8/2 (2000): 24–36.

48. See Thomas Müntzer, *Schriften und Briefe: Kritische Gesamtausgabe,* Paul Kirn and Günther Franz, eds., (Gütersloh: Mohn, 1968), 161–206.

49. Bard Thompson, *Liturgies of the Western Church* (Philadelphia: Fortress, 1980), 152. In the event the magistrates forbade the dialogical speech of the men and women and instead directed that the Gloria should be a monologue spoken by the minister.

50. Ibid., 270–71.

Conclusion

Conclusion: Assessing Continuity and Change in Late Medieval and Early Modern Christian Worship

JOHN D. WITVLIET

Any assessment of continuity and change in the medieval and early modern period should start with the obvious. First, among Protestants, liturgical discontinuity was pervasive and significant. The early modern period resulted in the demise—to a greater or lesser degree depending on the particular Protestant tradition and geographic location—of the cult of the saints, Marian piety, memorial Masses, images and sculptures, liturgical drama and processions, and the complex medieval calendar of feast days. It resulted in the transformation of liturgical language, preaching, vestments, liturgical space, and the nature of participation in the Eucharist. Little was left unchanged.

Nevertheless, even among the most radical Protestants, there were also obvious continuities in practice. Public worship remained an important part of Christian experience. Disciplined piety was important. Religious instruction continued to be a means for encouraging participation in worship. Central rituals, such as baptism and the Lord's Supper, were still practiced, as were elements common to worship in all Christian traditions, such as prayer, Scripture reading, and preaching. In all traditions, the laity embraced worship with varying degrees of enthusiasm, and the clergy led various rituals with varying degrees of competence.

Meanwhile, Roman Catholic worship was hardly static. Various liturgical books continued to be compiled and revised. Artistic and musical forms continued to evolve, some in response to Protestant pressures. Preaching practices evolved in response to the historical development of rhetorical forms and conventions. Within the broad context of overarching continuity of Catholic practice, there remained a steady stream of new liturgical and artistic contributions.

These basic assertions are the typical starting point for describing worship in the period. If historical textbooks include anything about worship, it is likely to be assertions like these. Yet, as this collection of essays has demonstrated, there is significant historical data available to refine these working assumptions about continuity and change, as well as to help us better sense how these changes were experienced by typical worshipers of the period.

Continuity

On the one hand, these essays help us perceive important continuities that are otherwise easy to overlook. The following six assertions are the kinds of statements that do not appear either in most historical textbooks or even in more extensive liturgical histories. Yet they helpfully correct assumptions that modern students may bring to study of this period either from their experience of worship today or from their study of other periods in Church history.

First, in both the pre- and post-Reformation Church, there was considerable concern for disciplined piety. Margot Fassler notes that the existence of relatively unstudied late medieval prayer books points to a concern for private prayer rarely acknowledged in standard histories. Susan Felch demonstrates that private prayer books had a venerable history in both pre- and post-Reformation England. Karin Maag observes that the schools in Geneva mandated students' participation in worship both before and after the Reformation. Historians well may argue about the relative vitality and contrasting dynamics of personal piety in various locations before and after the Reformation, but they cannot assume that efforts to inform, enhance, and discipline that piety were somehow an innovation.

Second, in both the pre- and post-Reformation Church, prayer practices relied on the use of set prayers. Susan Felch notes that though content of specific prayers in English prayer books changed, the importance of printed, set prayers did not. Frank Senn notes that the conservative reforms of Lutheran Sweden retained both the form and content of many texts. Meanwhile, in Calvin's Geneva the town council insisted that worshipers memorize the Lord's Prayer in the vernacular, while pastors used one of the set liturgies for Sunday worship. (Both Catholic and Protestant worship gave significant attention to the Lord's Prayer—Catholics through its use in devotional prayer books, Protestants through exposition in catechisms.) By and large, the Reformation traditions studied in this volume did not yet move to the kind of spontaneous or extemporaneous prayers that are widely associated with free church Protestantism.

Third, both before and after the Reformation, the biblical Psalter was a primary liturgical resource across traditions. In Catholic practice Psalms were recited in disciplined ways in monasteries and excerpted for literate laity in medieval prayer books. In Reformed practice, the Psalms were sung to metrical settings by entire congregations and served as the text for countless sermons. Interestingly, both before and after the Reformation, there was great flexibility in how the Psalms were used. Medieval prayer books often featured a kind of cut-and-paste use of favorite verses. Protestant Psalters featured Psalm texts that were reworked in metrical form so that they could be sung more easily. In both Catholic and Protestant worship, the Psalms were the primary and paradigmatic prayer book.

Fourth, both before and after the Reformation, church worship was practiced in dramatic visual spaces that made significant theological assertions through visual means. As Henry Luttikhuizen has explained, if you received the sacrament of the Lord's Supper in Haarlem in 1580 you would have been looking at a painted altarpiece. In 1590 you would have been looking at an inscription of the Words of Institution. In both cases, your eyesight would be engaged. The iconoclasts changed the decorations, but they did not quit seeing!

Fifth, in both Catholic and Protestant locations, liturgical norms were enforced by political institutions. Nearly universally, the political powers in a given region associated with one Church. Nowhere were there churches of five denominations within a single downtown block. The widespread religious pluralism with which we are so familiar came much later. In this context, one remarkable feature of the period, especially in contrast to twenty-first-century North America, is the frequency with which civic institutions dealt with liturgical issues. As Frank Senn explains, the history of Swedish liturgy is inextricably intertwined with political history. The history of Swedish reforms is essentially a history of the shifting objectives of the ruling monarch. Meanwhile, the town council of Geneva, as Robert Kingdon explains, was remarkable not only for enforcing clerical practice, but also for its rather intimate and sustained dealings with individual worshipers.

Sixth, there were instructive similarities between Catholic and Protestant practice as both traditions moved into the early modern era. Some of the obvious similarities are the common centrality of baptism, prayer, preaching, and the Lord's Supper in both wide streams of Western Christianity, as well as the use of a common stock of images and themes to explain the meaning of each, such as the common baptismal images described by Kent Burreson in his explication of baptismal rites.[1] These basic formal similarities are not surprising. The Reformation was, after all, a reformation of Christianity. It was a set of changes *within* a religion, not the founding of a new one.

In addition, there were many other common developments across the Catholic/Protestant divide which go unacknowledged in popular understanding. The reform of the Daily Office was not only a Protestant but also a Catholic project, as Katherine Elliot van Liere describes. Both Catholic and Protestant developments involved the interplay of public ritual and personal piety. Both Catholic and Protestant leaders promoted a more knowledgeable participation in worship.[2]

Other similarities, while more mundane, further help us sense the nature of religious experience in the period. As Bryan Spinks notes, both Protestants and Catholics who found themselves in unwanted marriages looked for loopholes to get out of them. As Robert Kingdon describes, both Protestants and Catholics sometimes arrived at worship only for the main event—Protestants for the sermon, Catholics for the elevation of the Host. As Susan Felch notes, prayers in all traditions featured prominent references to death, a reminder of how fragile life was in an era before modern medicine. The foibles and limitations of human experience are, of course, common across traditions.

Discontinuity

These essays also teach us to comprehend better the significance of discontinuity for many typical worshipers in the period.

First, these essays reinforce the fact that specific changes in practice were rooted in broad patterns of cultural change. One of the most pervasive shifts was from visual to auditory participation in some traditions, as Robert Kingdon explains. The rise of print culture led individual prayer book users to read, not memorize their prayers, as Susan Felch describes. These observations point us to deep patterns of change that affect nearly every area of life, not just worship.

Second, the essays point out several significant discontinuities that nearly always go unnoticed in liturgical histories of the period. As Margot Fassler notes, the use of the Bible as a liturgical book changed significantly—moving from a book that was prayed to a book that was taught. Meanwhile, in some communities, liturgical participation became a more (not less) significant part of life. Lay participation in the Eucharist likely increased, as did schoolboys' prayer during the day and attendance at services, as Karin Maag explains.

Third, the essays highlight other changes that, while more mundane, still help us better imagine life in the period:

- If you were married in Geneva in 1500 it would have been on a weekday in a private ceremony; if you were married in Geneva in 1550, it would have been on Sunday in a public worship service (Spinks).
- In 1520, if you were a weak-voiced Genevan man, you could become a priest. In 1550, if you were a weak-voiced Genevan man, you could not become a minister (Kingdon).
- If you went to church in Strasbourg or Geneva in 1515, you would have heard men in a choir singing and the woman next to you speaking a private prayer. If you went in 1550, you might have heard the woman next to you singing with everyone else (introduction), though the older woman in front of you might still have been whispering a private prayer (Kingdon).
- If you went to church as a Protestant in 1550, you probably took Communion more often than did your Catholic grandparents (something today's practicing Christian might not expect was the case!).

These are the kinds of details that make the teaching of liturgical history so much easier, helping students to sense the concrete ways in which daily life would be forever changed for worshipers of the period.

Methods for Assessing Continuity and Change

In addition to their contributions about the content of continuity and change in the period, these essays also help us explore the complementary methods that are useful for studying the period. As well as serving as an explication of a given source, each essay has pointed to at least one fundamental issue that must be taken into consideration when assessing liturgical continuity and change.

- Margot Fassler provides a sympathetic and nuanced reading of a medieval source, exhibiting the importance of careful and honest assessment of medieval piety not always present, especially in Protestant treatments of the period.
- By studying consistory minutes, Robert Kingdon shows the value of nontraditional sources for illuminating our understanding of liturgical experience.
- Frank Senn demonstrates the tenacious conservatism of parts of the Protestant world and reminds us that every geographic region should be treated on its own terms.
- Bodo Nischan reminds us of both the significantly different degrees of discontinuity among Protestant traditions, and the importance of distinguishing developments in the early and late sixteenth century.

- Karin Maag expands our view of the scope of liturgical action to include not just worship in church but also worship practices in schools, a reminder that worship is not an airtight category limited to official sanctuaries.
- Susan Felch demonstrates the importance of private and domestic worship as a barometer of theological and cultural change.
- Katherine Elliot van Liere illustrates that change was occurring throughout this period not only between Catholic and Protestant traditions but also within Catholic practice.
- Henry Luttikhuizen spares us from an exclusive focus on texts, reminding us of the significance of visual culture for worship, and demonstrating that theological ideals were often complicated by political and social dynamics.
- Bryan Spinks reminds us that not all liturgical actions are alike. In particular, life cycle rituals such as weddings (and funerals) give evidence of tenacious social mores. They complicate our otherwise simplistic understanding of the relationship of worship and culture.
- Robin Leaver and Kent Burreson teach us the significance of microanalysis of liturgical texts. They remind us that the detailed adaptations of texts reveal significant concerns for the adaptor as well as testify to the staying power of the larger form in question.

Thus, these essays are instructive not only for their content but also for their varying methods, for the kinds of questions they ask and the scholarly tools they use. A comprehensive survey of change and continuity for even one locale would ideally address each of the methodological issues raised here. Illustrating these complementary methodological strategies has been one of the primary goals of this volume.

Part of the contribution of this volume lies in simply highlighting these dimensions of change and continuity, and the methods for studying them. But we hope to accomplish one additional task. On the basis of these observations, and other recently published work, we can work toward developing a broader interpretive framework and set of strategies for describing continuity and change. These are the kinds of strategies that historians work with instinctively, but which students and more casual observers might not consider.

Multiple Levels for Assessing Change and Continuity

One fairly straightforward but necessary strategy is simply taking into account the different, independent levels on which change can be observed. The following six levels are illustrative of the different kinds of analysis needed for a full assessment of continuity and change.

First, continuity and change can be studied at the level of the *broad category* of a given liturgical action or artifact (e.g., funeral, baptism, altar/table, prayer book, etc.). So while the Reformations—both Catholic and Protestant—reordered the formal structure, the relative importance, and the details of many liturgical actions and artifacts, many broad categories of actions or artifacts remained the same. What is significant about the period is not necessarily that either Catholics or Protestants produced so many new types of rites, liturgical books, or artifacts, but rather the changes made to the form or content of existing ones.

Second, continuity and change can be studied at the level of the *formal structure* of a liturgical action or artifact. Thus, some Reformers retained the practices of baptism, preaching, the Lord's Supper, and prayer, while radically altering their form. Zwingli, for example, abolished the traditional structure of the eucharistic prayer. Others retained both the larger practice and the basic formal structure. German Lutheran reforms of medieval baptism rites retained their basic structure (as Kent Burreson points out), while Swedish Lutheran reforms of the Mass did the same (as Frank Senn describes). This formal continuity is also seen in the structure of devotional prayer books, which remain relatively constant (as Susan Felch explains).

Third, continuity and change can be studied at the level of textual, musical, or artistic *detail*. Even when the form of a rite or artifact remains the same, radical changes can be introduced by editing the details of a given text or practice. Thus, while Luther was much indebted to medieval musical forms, the results are unmistakably Protestant (as Robin Leaver explains).

Fourth, continuity and change can be studied at the level of the *intent or use*. Sometimes, while the form or details of a practice changed, the intent remained the same, as Karin Maag notes regarding worship practices in the schools. Conversely, sometimes the very same practice can be used with remarkably different intentions. For example, in Protestant contexts, artworks changed from devotional objects to instructional aids (Luttikhuizen). Likewise, with some prayer books, a "liturgical genre is turned to private use" (Felch).

Fifth, continuity and change can be studied at the level of the *underlying experience or piety of the participants*. It has been customary (especially among Protestant sources) quickly to dismiss late medieval eucharistic theology, not acknowledging the sincere piety that Margot Fassler describes in her analysis of Beinecke 757. As for the Reformation itself, while the form of the Lord's Supper dramatically changed in most Protestant practice, these new rites may well have been experienced by many worshipers in terms of the same underlying penitential piety associated with medieval practice.[3] Conversely, the very same liturgical practice or text might become associated with vastly different experiences or piety over time. So, for example, the

Lord's Prayer might have been experienced by one community as prayer and in another as a source for doctrinal reflection.

Sixth, liturgical change and continuity can be studied at the level of *deep, societal structure.* Some continuities were perhaps imperceptible or at least not self-conscious, but are significant from the perspective of five hundred years later. Some continuity happened without apparent self-conscious awareness (e.g., how many Calvinists thought of their disciplined singing of metrical Psalms as a matter of continuity with monastic piety?). Some features of life of the period are only noticeable from a perspective of a radically different time or place (e.g., would we even notice, as Susan Felch does, the sacralization of daily life that was common before and after the Reformation, were it not for the secularized culture of our own time and place?).

Distinguishing these levels of analysis is very helpful for achieving an accurate and nuanced understanding of this (or any) period. Some discontinuity that seems extremely impressive from one perspective almost disappears when viewed from another. For example, the deletion of the canon from the Lutheran Mass is significant from the perspective of the presider, but not from that of the worshiper, who never would have heard it spoken in the first place (as Frank Senn and Robert Kingdon observe). Indeed, one problem with a good deal of traditional liturgical history is that it has examined only two of these levels (form and text detail) apart from the broader considerations of context, intentionality, and underlying piety.

Multiple Forces That Shape Change and Continuity

A second necessary strategy is to take into account the many different forces that contribute to continuity and change. In this period, as in any other, the dynamics that led to relative degrees of continuity and change depended on a complex web of social, theological, political, and symbolic variables. Any simplistic account of only one of these variables is bound to misunderstand the nature of the change.

Many practices involved deep sensibilities that were irreducibly theological. Note Bodo Nischan's exploration of different views regarding the relation of spiritual and material issues and their implications for liturgical furniture designs. The alterations in prayer texts described by Kent Burreson reflect sophisticated theological judgments.

Nevertheless, most reforms were not simply a matter of theological judgment but were also shaped by political, social, and other pragmatic considerations. Calvin wanted weekly Communion (a radical discontinuity), but was kept from that by the more conservative, political judgment of the Genevan council (Kingdon). Similarly, some continuity in experience was the result of the tenacity of popular piety and a reluctance to learn new patterns of prayer which had little regard for official theological pronouncements (Kingdon).[4]

And always, the specific nature of change and continuity is local. Local factors often mitigate the broad patterns of change for a given region or tradition. Henry Luttikhuizen notes that the significant Catholic presence in Haarlem significantly altered the context and outcomes of Protestant iconoclasm. As Frank Senn notes, capital cities, such as Stockholm, are often unique because of the close proximity of civic and ecclesiastical authorities. Katherine Elliot van Liere's description of the Quiñones Breviary demonstrates that some efforts at reform stayed local because political dynamics within the Church prevented further reception.

Handling Ambiguity

A third necessary strategy for assessing continuity and change is to find rhetorical devices to convey the ambiguity or untidiness of a given change. In describing historical change, we are describing something much more like a living organism than a tidy syllogism. Almost always, there is another side to the story that can help nuance our descriptions. Here are five sample statements illustrated in the essays of this volume.

Some continuity remained not because of intention but expediency, where the reform efforts simply did not expend the energy to be exhaustive. Thus, the iconic organ shutters remained in Haarlem even after iconoclasm (Luttikhuizen). Note here how social, political factors (i.e., the Catholic majority) mitigated Protestant theological ideals.[5] Not all reform efforts were equally complete or exhaustive.

Some continuity was the result of a tolerance of medieval practice rather than advocacy for it, such as Luther's tolerance of the altar (Nischan) and many common marriage customs (Spinks).

Some continuity re-emerged after initial radical change. For example, death rituals, once abandoned in Geneva, returned in the second generation of the Reformation—people could not live (or die) without them. As Frank Senn has described, Swedish liturgical reforms featured an ebb and flow of more conservative and progressive impulses, such that the mid-sixteenth century actually brought about a reclaiming of Latin language and forms.

Some radical changes happened overnight, while some subtle changes took decades. In other words, the *degree* of lasting discontinuity and the *speed* of the change are two independent variables. Some drastic changes happened fast, such as iconoclasm or use of vernacular language in Zurich, while others took several years, such as the use of vernacular language in rural Sweden. Likewise, some more subtle changes could happen quickly, such as the practice of the prayer of confession in Calvin's two published liturgies, while others took decades, such as the revision of textual details in any number of Roman liturgical books.

Sometimes, a given discontinuity might have resulted in an unintended continuity with medieval practice. For example, the pruning of the medieval liturgical calendar to focus on Christological feasts may have made room for a whole constellation of national and secular observances in English culture.[6] Likewise, the iconoclasm in Haarlem made room for civic images in windows. In the end the result was a full calendar and image-full worship space.

These are the kinds of statements that help us avoid simplistic historical judgments and help us sense the messiness or organic quality of a given historical period. Another set of essays on liturgical topics in the period would, no doubt, provide many more examples under each category.

Informing Present Practice

In addition to illuminating both the content and method of assessing liturgical change and continuity, these essays can helpfully inform present practice. At a very basic level, like all good history, they give us a greater sense of our own historical situatedness in a period of significant cultural upheaval. They remind us that liturgical change has always involved a mixture of theological ideals, practical expediency, and a cultural milieu far beyond the control of any given innovator. A century from now, our own practice of worship will no doubt feature the same kinds of foibles described here, as will the histories of the period in which we now live.

Further, these essays call us to avoid the use of history as propaganda in current disputes. Liturgical history, especially of the Reformation period, is often used as a warrant for present practice—and for both conservative and progressive causes. "Luther retained the altar, and so should we." Or, "the Reformers were free to implement radical change, and so should we." Often people see in history what they want to see. Often the use of historical examples in discussions about worship does not feature the kind of humility that asks, "What can we learn from models and ways of understanding very different from our own?" May these essays make a small contribution to cultivating this kind of humility.

Finally, these essays also give us a sense of the remarkable depth and diversity within the body of Christ. Many current students may think of the range of topics included here as remarkably narrow, in light of opportunities for daily exposure to information about global practice. And even within the period in question, the topics chosen here do not explore the full range of Christian practices (we are very aware that there are no essays on monastic liturgy on the one hand, and on radical Protestant practice, on the other). Yet even within a narrow range of topics in a relatively narrow window of time, we encounter a remarkable diversity of ideals and practices. The central concerns of many of the Christians described in this volume are only of passing interest to others. Entire areas of visceral debate in one group of Christians may not even be recognized topics of discussion for another. For the student of Christian worship, analyzing this or any period, the task of approaching a complete understanding of all these varying interests remains remarkably elusive. For the practicing Christian, perhaps these chapters help to suggest, in small part, what the apostle Paul might have meant when he described one purpose of his own missionary efforts: that "through the church the wisdom of God in its rich variety might now be made known . . ." (Eph. 3:10).

Notes

1. For similar analysis, see H. O. Old, *The Shaping of the Reformed Baptismal Rite in the Sixteenth Century* (Grand Rapids, Mich.: Eerdmans, 1992), 30–31, 283–86.

2. According to Andrew Barnes, "On the devout fringe of lay Catholicism there was an effort, similar to that in lay Protestantism, to claim a level of daily devotion previously reserved for clerics." In "Religious Anxiety and Devotional Change in Sixteenth Century French Penitential Confraternities," *Sixteenth Century Journal* 19 (1988): 405. See also John Bossy, *Christianity in the West, 1400–1700* (Oxford: Oxford University Press, 1985), 97–104. On public worship (the Mass in particular), see Virginia Reinburg, "Liturgy and Laity in Late Medieval and Reformation France," *Sixteenth Century Journal* 33 (1992): 526–46, esp. 545. Reinburg argues that while "late medieval French expositions of the mass suggest that the clergy expected lay people to participate in the liturgy in a distinctive way—a way distinguishable from the clergy's more doctrinally instructed participation" (529), both Calvin and the Catholic reformers insisted on "more doctrinally informed lay participation" (545). On private worship, see Virginia Reinburg, "Hearing Lay People's Prayer," in B. Diefendorf and C. Hesse, eds., *Culture and Identity in Early Modern Europe (1500–1800): Essays in Honor of Natalie Zemon Davis* (Ann Arbor: University of Michigan Press, 1993).

3. As discussed in James F. White, *A Brief History of Christian Worship* (Nashville: Abingdon Press, 1993), 125–27; Thomas Tentler, *Sin and Confession on the Eve of the Reformation* (Princeton: Princeton University Press, 1977), Lawrence Duggan, "Fear and Confession on the Eve of the Reformation," *Archiv für Reformationsgeschichte* 75 (1984): 153–75; and Jean Delumeau, *Sin and Fear: The Emergence of a Western Guilt Culture 13th–18th Centuries,* trans. Eric Nicholson (New York: St. Martin's Press, 1990).

4. See also Lorna Jane Abray on Strasbourg, in R. Po-Chia Hsia, ed., *The German People and the Reformation* (Ithaca: Cornell University Press, 1988), 221; R. W. Scribner,

"Ritual and Popular Religion in Catholic Germany at the Time of the Reformation," *Journal of Ecclesiastical History* 35 (1984): 47–77; Bruce Gordon, *Clerical Discipline and the Rural Reformation: The Synod in Zurich, 1532–1580* (Bern: Peter Lang, 1992), C. Scott Dixon, *The Reformation and Rural Society: The Parishes of Brandenburg-Ansbach-Kulmbach, 1528–1603* (Cambridge: Cambridge University Press, 1996).

5. For other examples, such as the persistence of Palm Sunday processions, see Scribner, "Ritual and Popular Religion," 76.

6. See David Cressy, *Bonfires and Bells: National Memory and the Protestant Calendar in Elizabethan and Stuart England* (Berkeley: University of California Press, 1989).

index

Page numbers printed in italics refer to illustrations.